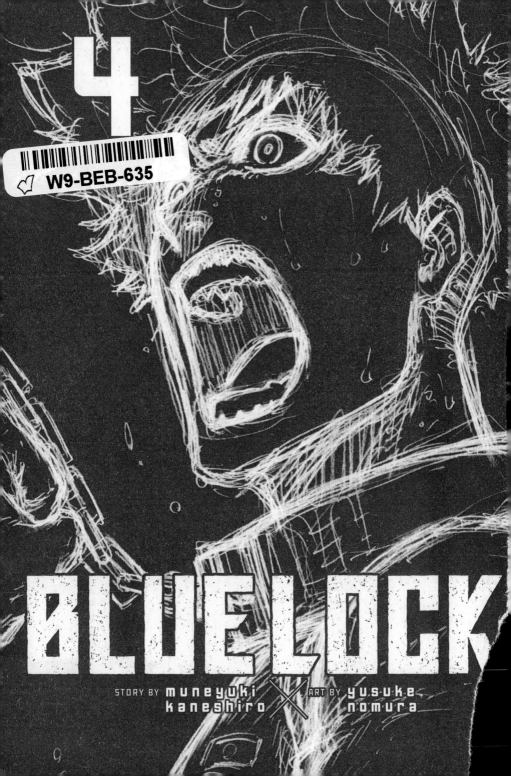

4

BLUE LOCK

STORY BY muneyuki kaneshiro ╳ ART BY yusuke nomura

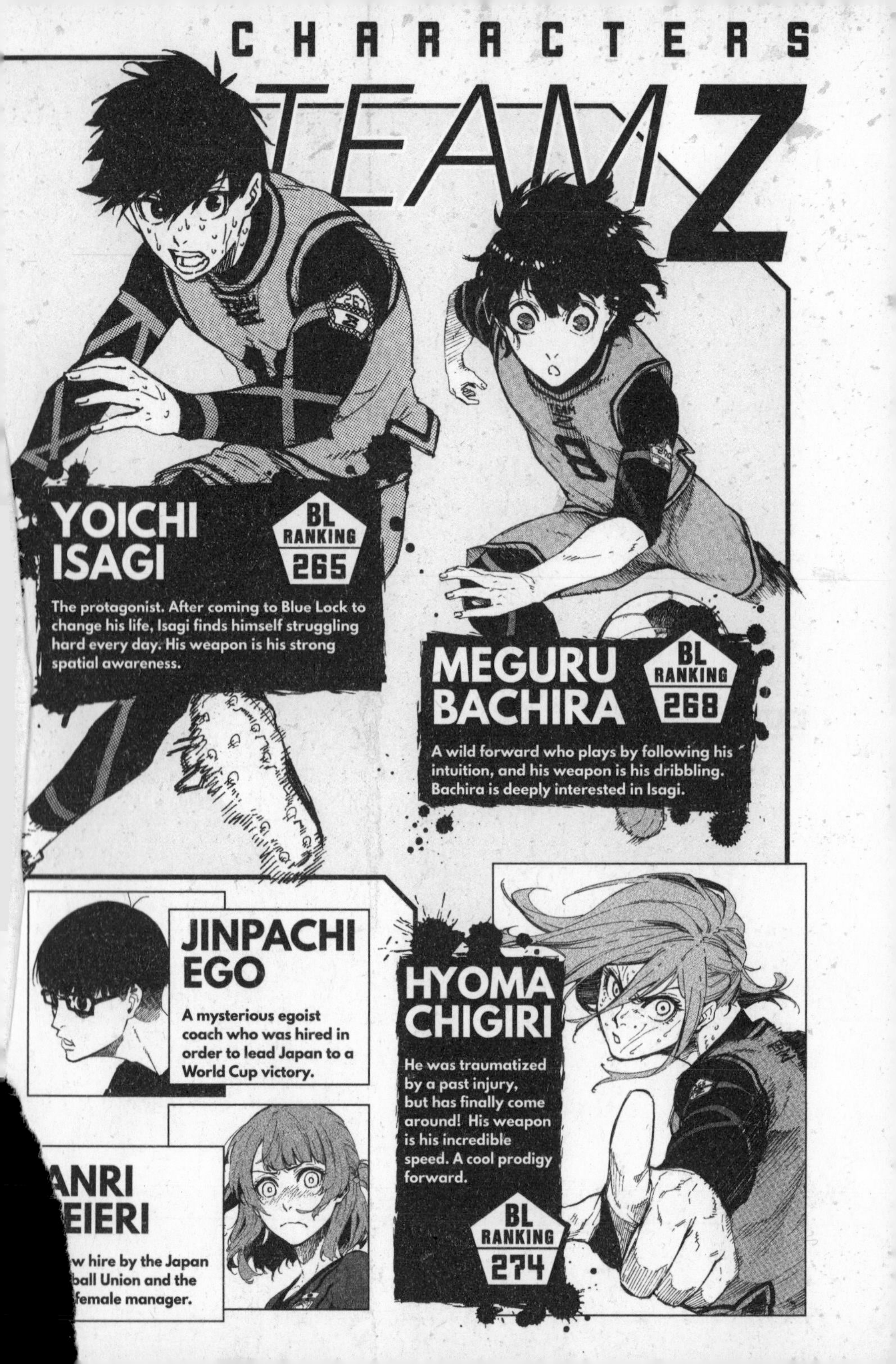

CHARACTERS
TEAM Z
YOICHI ISAGI
BL RANKING 265
The protagonist. After coming to Blue Lock to change his life, Isagi finds himself struggling hard every day. His weapon is his strong spatial awareness.
MEGURU BACHIRA
BL RANKING 268
A wild forward who plays by following his intuition, and his weapon is his dribbling. Bachira is deeply interested in Isagi.
JINPACHI EGO
A mysterious egoist coach who was hired in order to lead Japan to a World Cup victory.
HYOMA CHIGIRI
He was traumatized by a past injury, but has finally come around! His weapon is his incredible speed. A cool prodigy forward.
BL RANKING 274
ANRI
EIERI
w hire by the Japan
ball Union and the
female manager.

A Kodansha Trade Paperback Original

Published in the United States by
Kodansha USA Publishing, LLC, New York.

Publication rights for this English edition arranged through
Kodansha Ltd., Tokyo.

First published in Japan in 2019 by Kodansha Ltd., Tokyo
as *Buruu rokku*, volume 4.

ISBN 978-1-64651-657-5

Printed in the United States of America.

9 8 7 6 5 4 3 2 1

Original Digital Edition Translation: Nate Derr
Original Digital Edition Lettering: Chris Burgener
Original Digital Edition Editing: Thalia Sutton
Print Edition Lettering: Scott O. Brown
Print Edition Editing: Maggie Le
YKS Services LLC/SKY JAPAN, Inc.
Kodansha USA Publishing edition cover design by Matthew Akuginow

Publisher: Kiichiro Sugawara

Director of Publishing Services: Ben Applegate
Director of Publishing Operations: Dave Barrett
Associate Director of Publishing Operations: Stephen Pakula
Publishing Services Managing Editors: Alanna Ruse, Madison Salters,
with Grace Chen
Production Manager: Jocelyn O'Dowd

KODANSHA.US

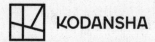 KODANSHA

One of CLAMP's biggest hits returns in this definitive, premium, hardcover 20th anniversary collector's edition!

Chobits © CLAMP·ShigatsuTsuitachi CO.,LTD./Kodansha Ltd.

"A wonderfully entertaining story that would be a great installment in anybody's manga collection."
— Anime News Network

"CLAMP is an all-female manga-creating team whose feminine touch shows in this entertaining, sci-fi soap opera."
— Publishers Weekly

Poor college student Hideki is down on his luck. All he wants is a good job, a girlfriend, and his very own "persocom"—the latest and greatest in humanoid computer technology. Hideki's luck changes one night when he finds Chi—a persocom thrown out in a pile of trash. But Hideki soon discovers that there's much more to his cute new persocom than meets the eye.

KC
KODANSHA COMICS

The art-deco cyberpunk classic from the creators of *xxxHOLiC* and *Cardcaptor Sakura*!

"Starred Review.
This experimental
sci-fi work from
CLAMP reads like a
romantic version of
AKIRA."
—Publishers Weekly

CLAMP

CLOVER

—— COLLECTOR'S EDITION ——

CLOVER © CLAMP·ShigatsuTsuitachi CO.,LTD./Kodansha Ltd.

Su was born into a bleak future, where the government keeps
tight control over children with magical powers—codenamed
"Clovers." With Su being the only "four-leaf" Clover in the
world, she has been kept isolated nearly her whole life. Can
ex-military agent Kazuhiko deliver her to the happiness she
seeks? Experience the complete series in this hardcover
edition, which also includes over twenty pages of ravishing
color art!

KC
KODANSHA
COMICS

"Clever, sassy, and original....*xxxHOLiC* has the inherent hallmarks of a runaway hit."
—NewType magazine

Beautifully seductive artwork and uniquely Japanese depictions of the supernatural will hypnotize CLAMP fans!

Kimihiro Watanuki is haunted by visions of ghosts and spirits. He seeks help from a mysterious woman named Yuko, who claims she can help. However, Watanuki must work for Yuko in order to pay for her aid. Soon Watanuki finds himself employed in Yuko's shop, where he sees things and meets customers that are stranger than anything he could have ever imagined.

KC
KODANSHA
COMICS

The beloved characters from *Cardcaptor Sakura* return in a brand new, reimagined fantasy adventure!

"[*Tsubasa*] takes readers on a fantastic ride that only gets more exhilarating with each successive chapter." —Anime News Network

In the Kingdom of Clow, an archaeological dig unleashes an incredible power, causing Princess Sakura to lose her memories. To save her, her childhood friend Syaoran must follow the orders of the Dimension Witch and travel alongside Kurogane, an unrivaled warrior; Fai, a powerful magician; and Mokona, a curiously strange creature, to retrieve Sakura's dispersed memories!

◀ KAMOME ▶
SHIRAHAMA

Witch Hat Atelier

A magical manga
adventure for
fans of Disney
and Studio
Ghibli!

Witch Hat Atelier © Kamome Shirahama/Kodansha Ltd.

The magical adventure that took Japan by storm is finally here, from acclaimed DC and Marvel cover artist Kamome Shirahama!

In a world where everyone takes wonders like magic spells
and dragons for granted, Coco is a girl with a simple dream:
She wants to be a witch. But everybody knows magicians
are born, not made, and Coco was not born with a gift for
magic. Resigned to her un-magical life, Coco is about to
give up on her dream to become a witch...until the day
she meets Qifrey, a mysterious, traveling magician. After
secretly seeing Qifrey perform magic in a way she's never
seen before, Coco soon learns what everybody "knows"
might not be the truth, and discovers that her magical
dream may not be as far away as it may seem...

KC
KODANSHA
COMICS

The adorable new odd-couple cat comedy manga from the creator of the beloved *Chi's Sweet Home*, in full color!

Sue & Tai-chan

Konami Kanata

Sue is an aging housecat who's looking forward to living out her life in peace... but her plans change when the mischievous black tomcat Tai-chan enters the picture! Hey! Sue never signed up to be a catsitter! *Sue & Tai-chan* is the latest from the reigning meow-narch of cute kitty comics, Konami Kanata.

THE SWEET SCENT OF LOVE IS IN THE AIR! FOR FANS OF OFFBEAT ROMANCES LIKE *WOTAKOI*

Sweat and Soap © Kintetsu Yamada / Kodansha Ltd.

In an office romance, there's a fine line between sexy and awkward... and that line is where Asako — a woman who sweats copiously — meets Koutarou — a perfume developer who can't get enough of Asako's, er, scent. Don't miss a romcom manga like no other!

SAINT ☆ YOUNG MEN

A LONG AWAITED ARRIVAL IN PREMIUM 2-IN-1 HARDCOVER

After centuries of hard work, Jesus and Buddha take a break from their heavenly duties to relax among the people of Japan, and their adventures in this lighthearted buddy comedy are sure to bring mirth and merriment to all!

"Brilliant…the physical comedy and facial expressions will make you literally LOL."

—Sam Humphries (host of *DC Daily*; writer, *Green Lanterns*, *Legendary Star-Lord*)

Saint Young Men © Hikaru Nakamura/Kodansha Ltd.

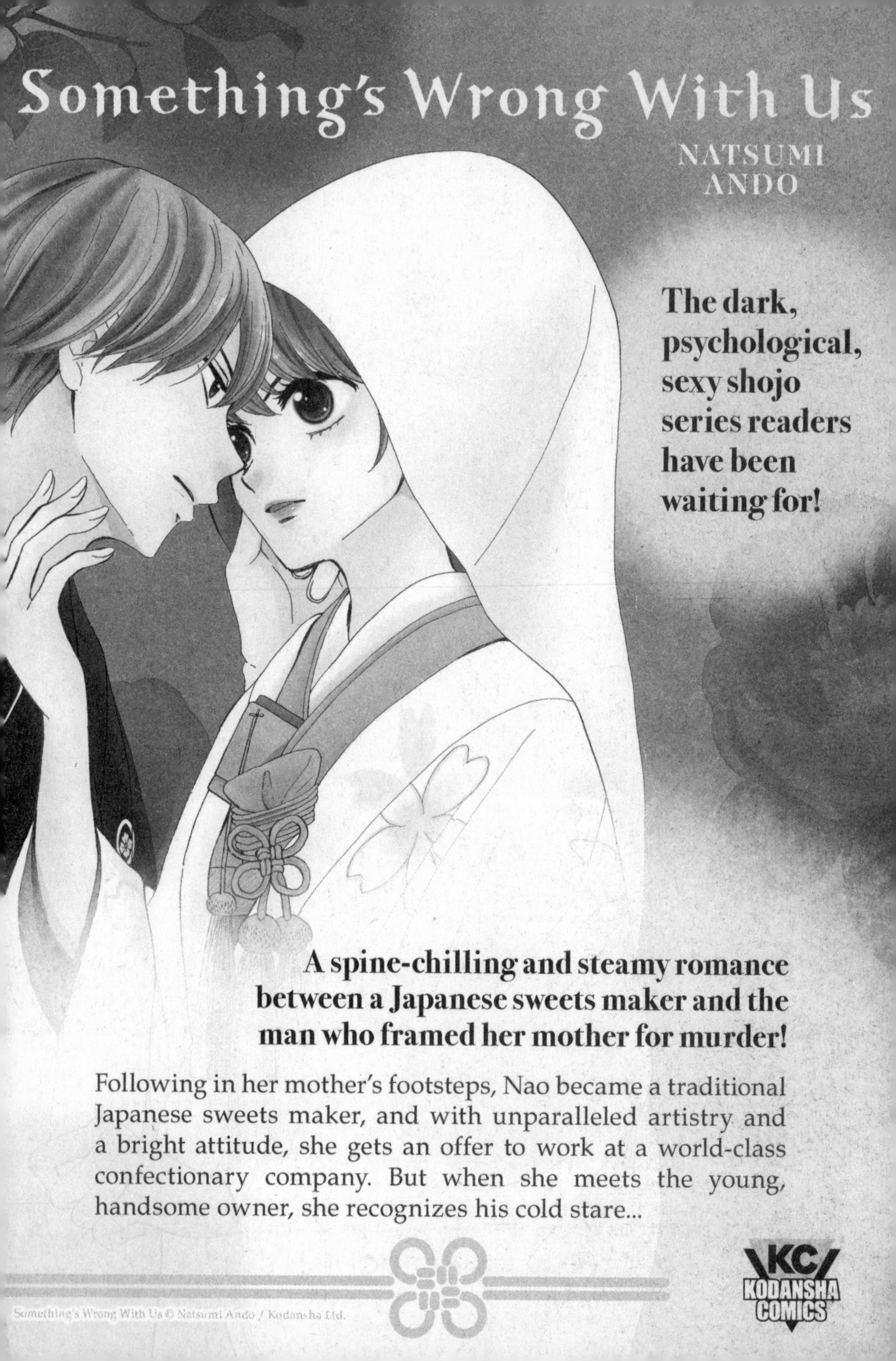
Something's Wrong With Us
NATSUMI ANDO
The dark, psychological, sexy shojo series readers have been waiting for!
A spine-chilling and steamy romance between a Japanese sweets maker and the man who framed her mother for murder!
Following in her mother's footsteps, Nao became a traditional Japanese sweets maker, and with unparalleled artistry and a bright attitude, she gets an offer to work at a world-class confectionary company. But when she meets the young, handsome owner, she recognizes his cold stare...
Something's Wrong With Us © Natsumi Ando / Kodansha Ltd.
KC KODANSHA COMICS

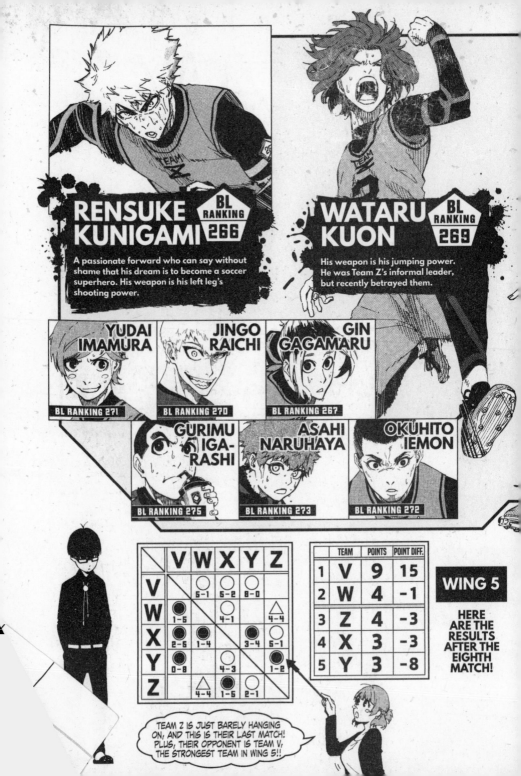

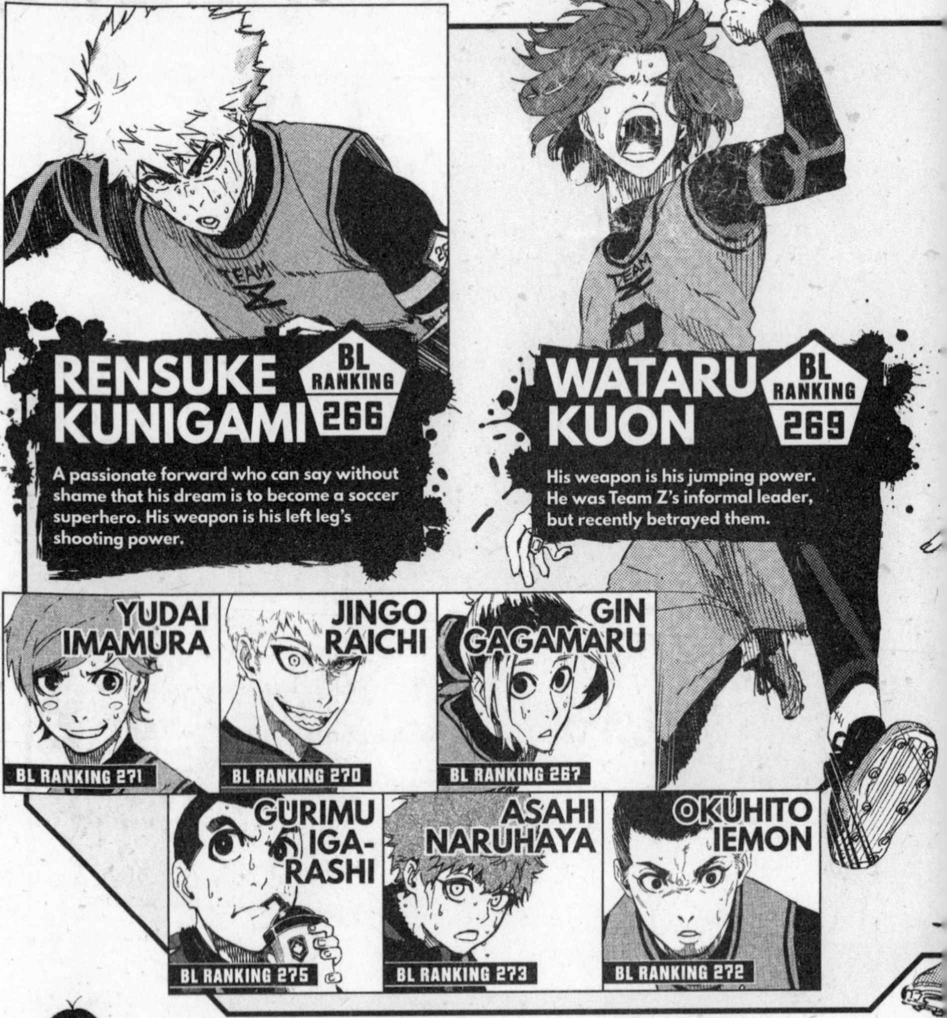
RENSUKE KUNIGAMI
BL RANKING 266
A passionate forward who can say without shame that his dream is to become a soccer superhero. His weapon is his left leg's shooting power.
WATARU KUON
BL RANKING 269
His weapon is his jumping power. He was Team Z's informal leader, but recently betrayed them.
YUDAI IMAMURA
BL RANKING 271
JINGO RAICHI
BL RANKING 270
GIN GAGAMARU
BL RANKING 267
GURIMU IGA-RASHI
BL RANKING 275
ASAHI NARUHAYA
BL RANKING 273
OKUHITO IEMON
BL RANKING 272

WING 5

HERE ARE THE RESULTS AFTER THE EIGHTH MATCH!

	V	W	X	Y	Z
V		○ 5-1	○ 5-2	○ 8-0	
W	● 1-5		○ 4-1		△ 4-4
X	● 2-5	● 1-4		● 3-4	○ 5-1
Y	● 0-8		○ 4-3		● 1-2
Z		△ 4-4	● 1-5	○ 2-1	

	TEAM	POINTS	POINT DIFF.
1	V	9	15
2	W	4	-1
3	Z	4	-3
4	X	3	-3
5	Y	3	-8

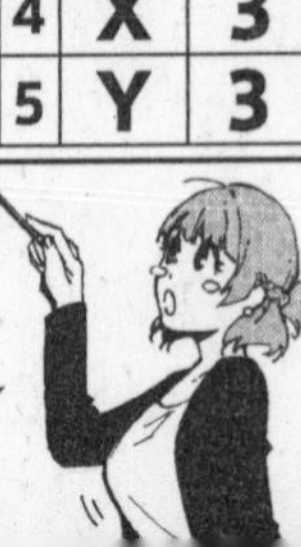
TEAM Z IS JUST BARELY HANGING ON, AND THIS IS THEIR LAST MATCH! PLUS, THEIR OPPONENT IS TEAM V, THE STRONGEST TEAM IN WING 5!!

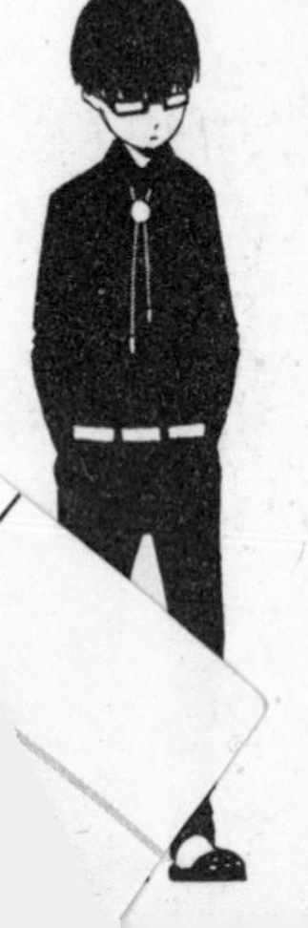

CONTENTS

CHAPTER 23 UNTIL HE MET — 005

CHAPTER 24 GOAL FORMULA — 025

CHAPTER 25 TRICK — 045

CHAPTER 26 LAST GAME — 065

CHAPTER 27 ONLY ONE — 085

CHAPTER 28 SUPER SPECIAL — 105

CHAPTER 29 FLASH OF EVOLUTION — 125

CHAPTER 30 EXTREME FRENZY — 145

CHAPTER 31 AWAKENING — 165

CHAPTER 23: UNTIL HE MET

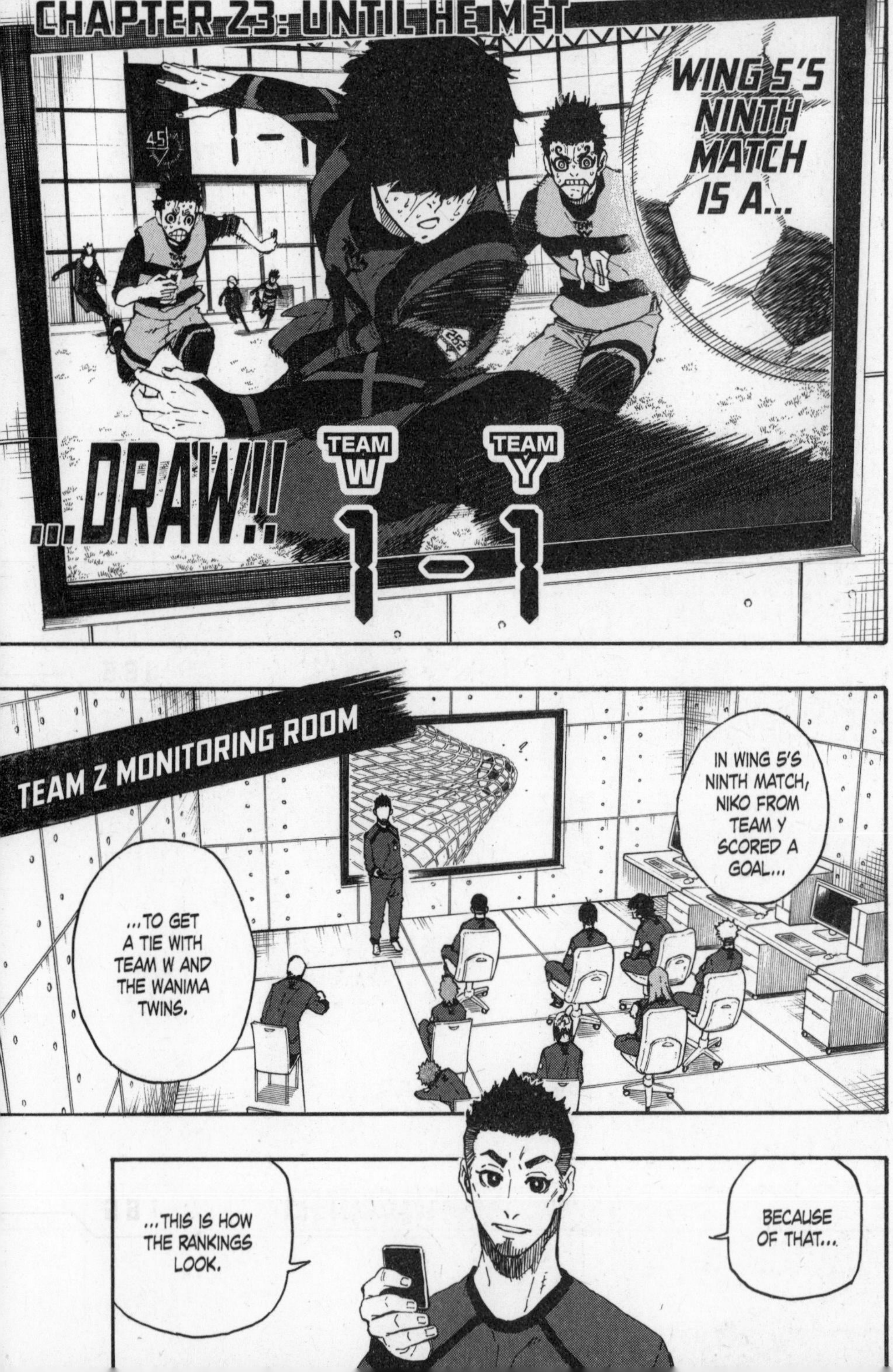
WING 5'S NINTH MATCH IS A...
...DRAW!!
TEAM W
TEAM Y
1 - 1
TEAM Z MONITORING ROOM
IN WING 5'S NINTH MATCH, NIKO FROM TEAM Y SCORED A GOAL...
...TO GET A TIE WITH TEAM W AND THE WANIMA TWINS.
BECAUSE OF THAT...
...THIS IS HOW THE RANKINGS LOOK.

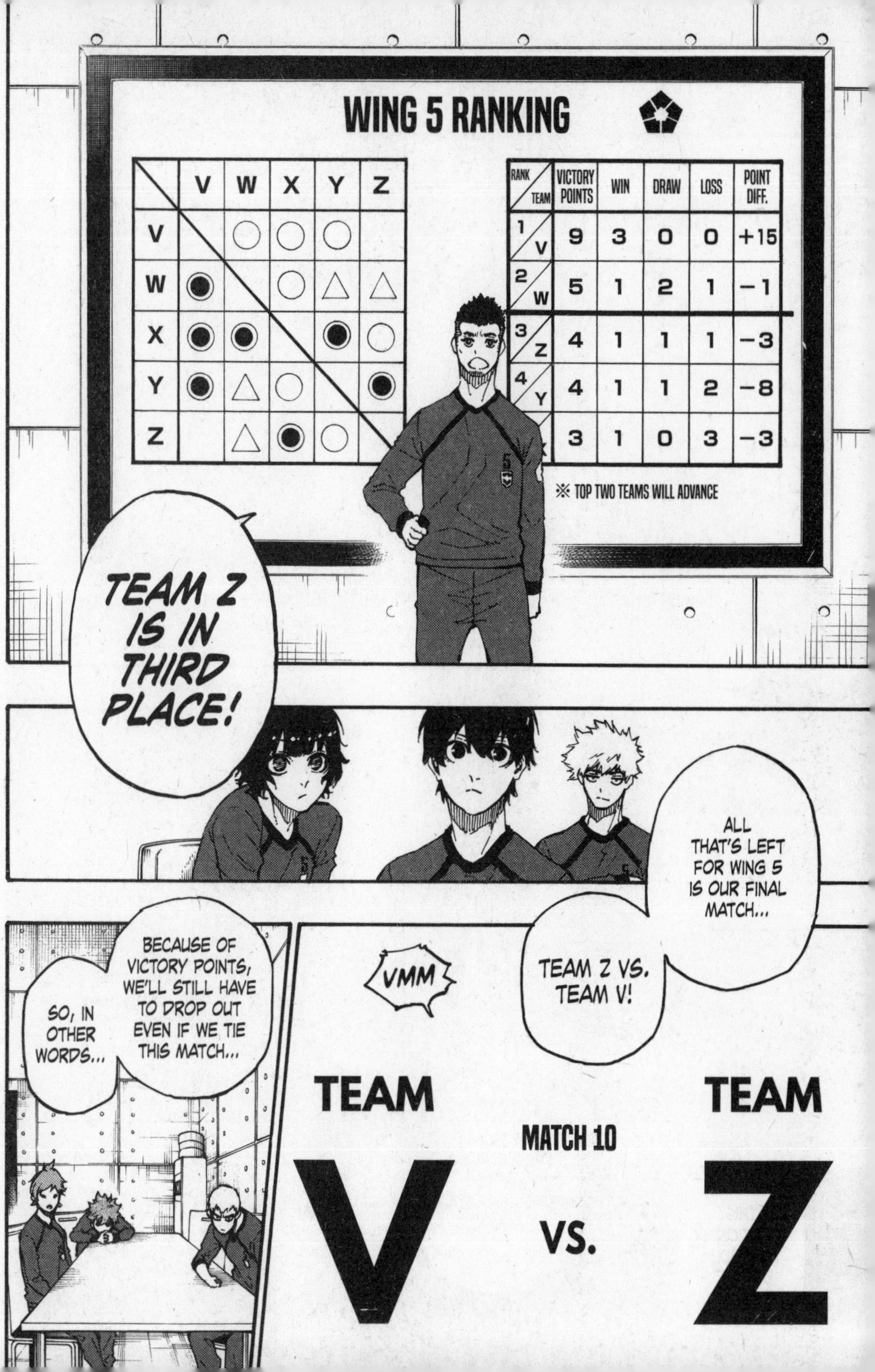
WING 5 RANKING
V W X Y Z
RANK TEAM | VICTORY POINTS | WIN | DRAW | LOSS | POINT DIFF.
1 V 9 3 0 0 +15
2 W 5 1 2 1 −1
3 Z 4 1 1 1 −3
4 Y 4 1 1 2 −8
3 1 0 3 −3
※ TOP TWO TEAMS WILL ADVANCE
TEAM Z IS IN THIRD PLACE!
ALL THAT'S LEFT FOR WING 5 IS OUR FINAL MATCH...
TEAM Z VS. TEAM V!
VMM
TEAM V
MATCH 10
VS.
TEAM Z
BECAUSE OF VICTORY POINTS, WE'LL STILL HAVE TO DROP OUT EVEN IF WE TIE THIS MATCH...
SO, IN OTHER WORDS...

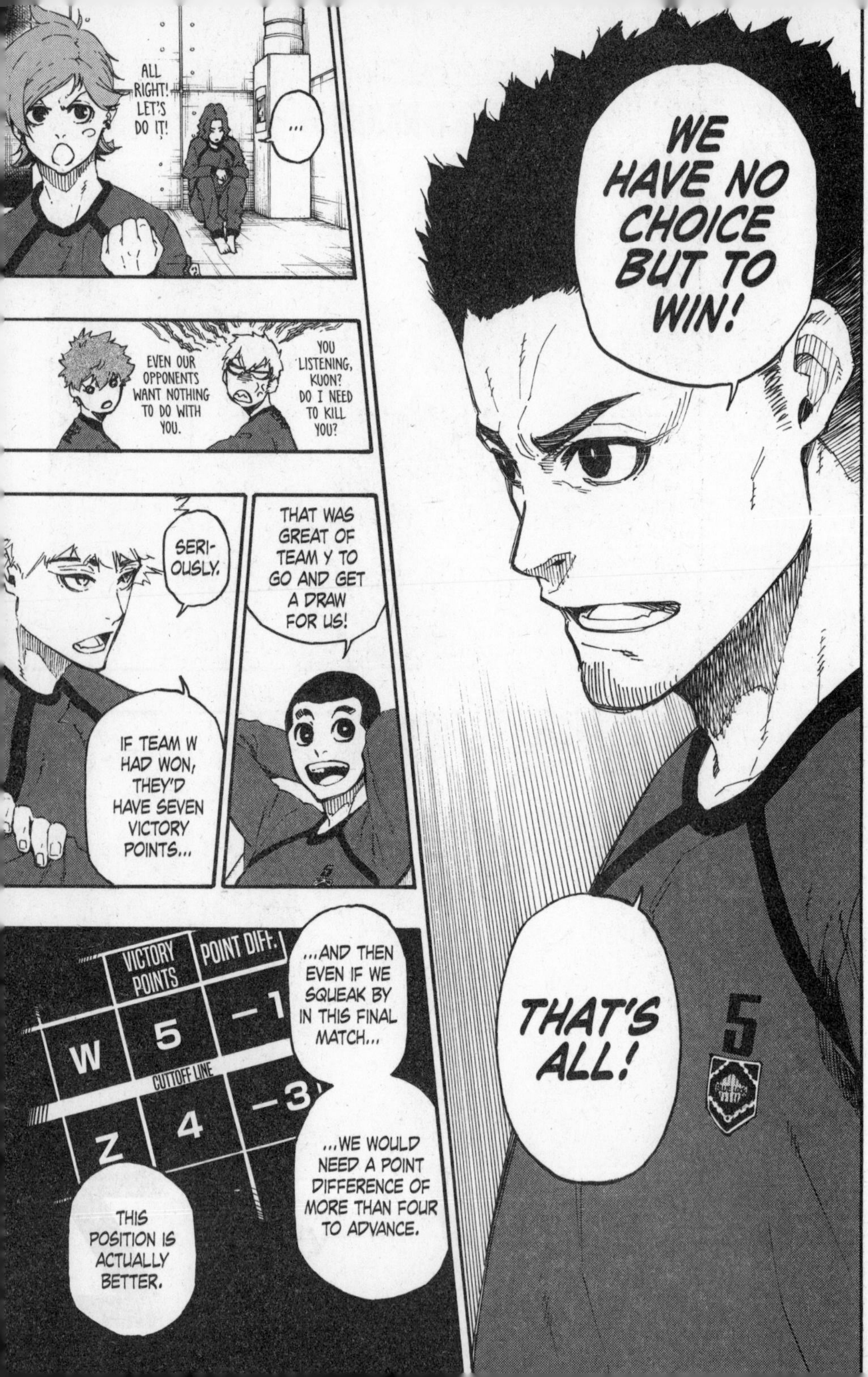
WE HAVE NO CHOICE BUT TO WIN!
THAT'S ALL!
5
...
ALL RIGHT! LET'S DO IT!
YOU LISTENING, KUON? DO I NEED TO KILL YOU?
EVEN OUR OPPONENTS WANT NOTHING TO DO WITH YOU.
THAT WAS GREAT OF TEAM Y TO GO AND GET A DRAW FOR US!
SERI-OUSLY.
IF TEAM W HAD WON, THEY'D HAVE SEVEN VICTORY POINTS...
...AND THEN EVEN IF WE SQUEAK BY IN THIS FINAL MATCH...
...WE WOULD NEED A POINT DIFFERENCE OF MORE THAN FOUR TO ADVANCE.
THIS POSITION IS ACTUALLY BETTER.
VICTORY POINTS
POINT DIFF.
W
5
—1
CUTOFF LINE
Z
4
—3

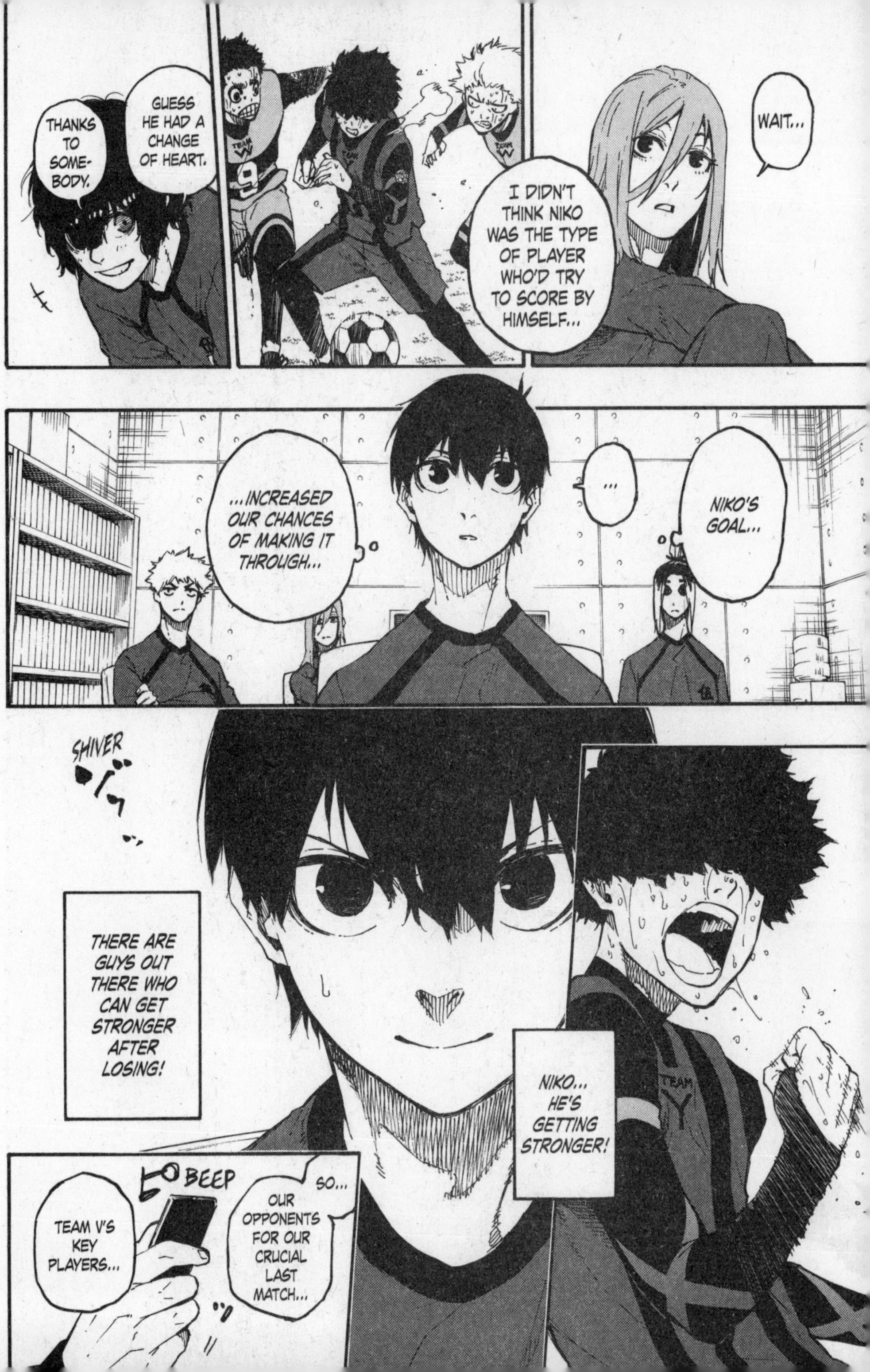
WAIT...
I DIDN'T THINK NIKO WAS THE TYPE OF PLAYER WHO'D TRY TO SCORE BY HIMSELF...
GUESS HE HAD A CHANGE OF HEART.
THANKS TO SOME-BODY.
NIKO'S GOAL...
...
...INCREASED OUR CHANCES OF MAKING IT THROUGH...
NIKO... HE'S GETTING STRONGER!
SHIVER
THERE ARE GUYS OUT THERE WHO CAN GET STRONGER AFTER LOSING!
BEEP
SO...
OUR OPPONENTS FOR OUR CRUCIAL LAST MATCH...
TEAM V'S KEY PLAYERS...

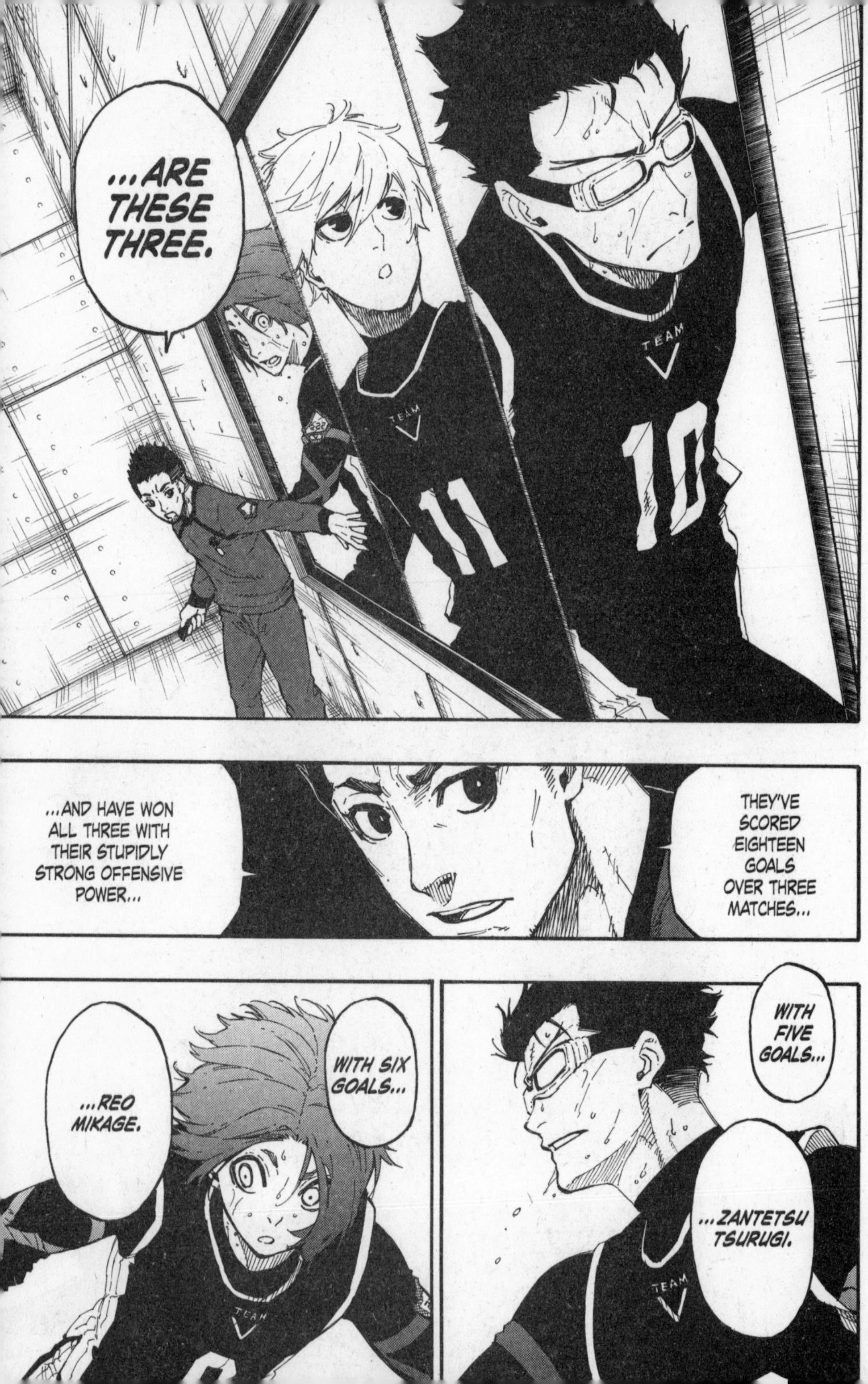
...ARE THESE THREE.
THEY'VE SCORED EIGHTEEN GOALS OVER THREE MATCHES...
...AND HAVE WON ALL THREE WITH THEIR STUPIDLY STRONG OFFENSIVE POWER...
WITH FIVE GOALS...
...ZANTETSU TSURUGI.
WITH SIX GOALS...
...REO MIKAGE.

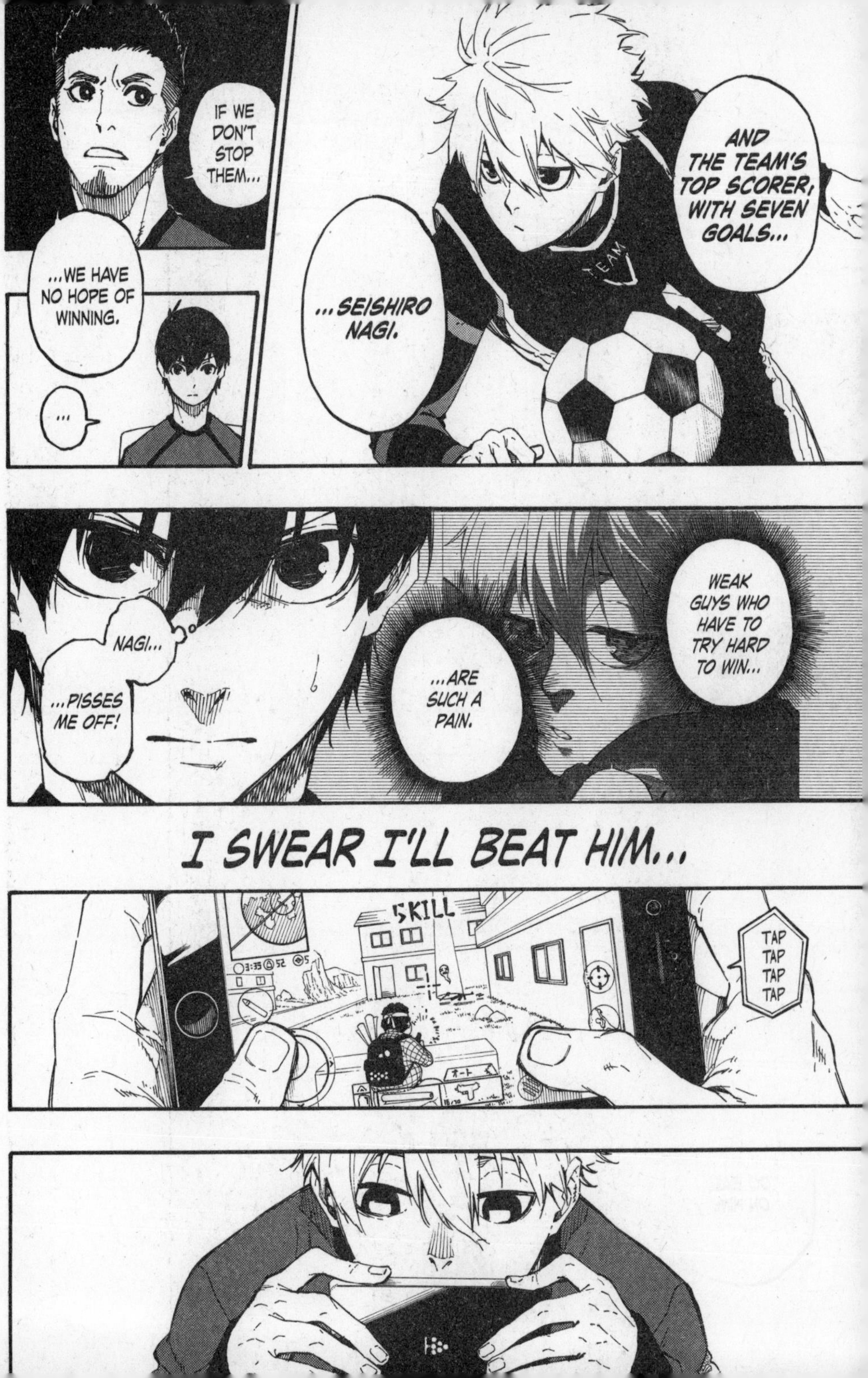
AND THE TEAM'S TOP SCORER, WITH SEVEN GOALS...
...SEISHIRO NAGI.
IF WE DON'T STOP THEM...
...WE HAVE NO HOPE OF WINNING.
...
WEAK GUYS WHO HAVE TO TRY HARD TO WIN...
...ARE SUCH A PAIN.
NAGI...
...PISSES ME OFF!
I SWEAR I'LL BEAT HIM...
TAP TAP TAP TAP
5KILL

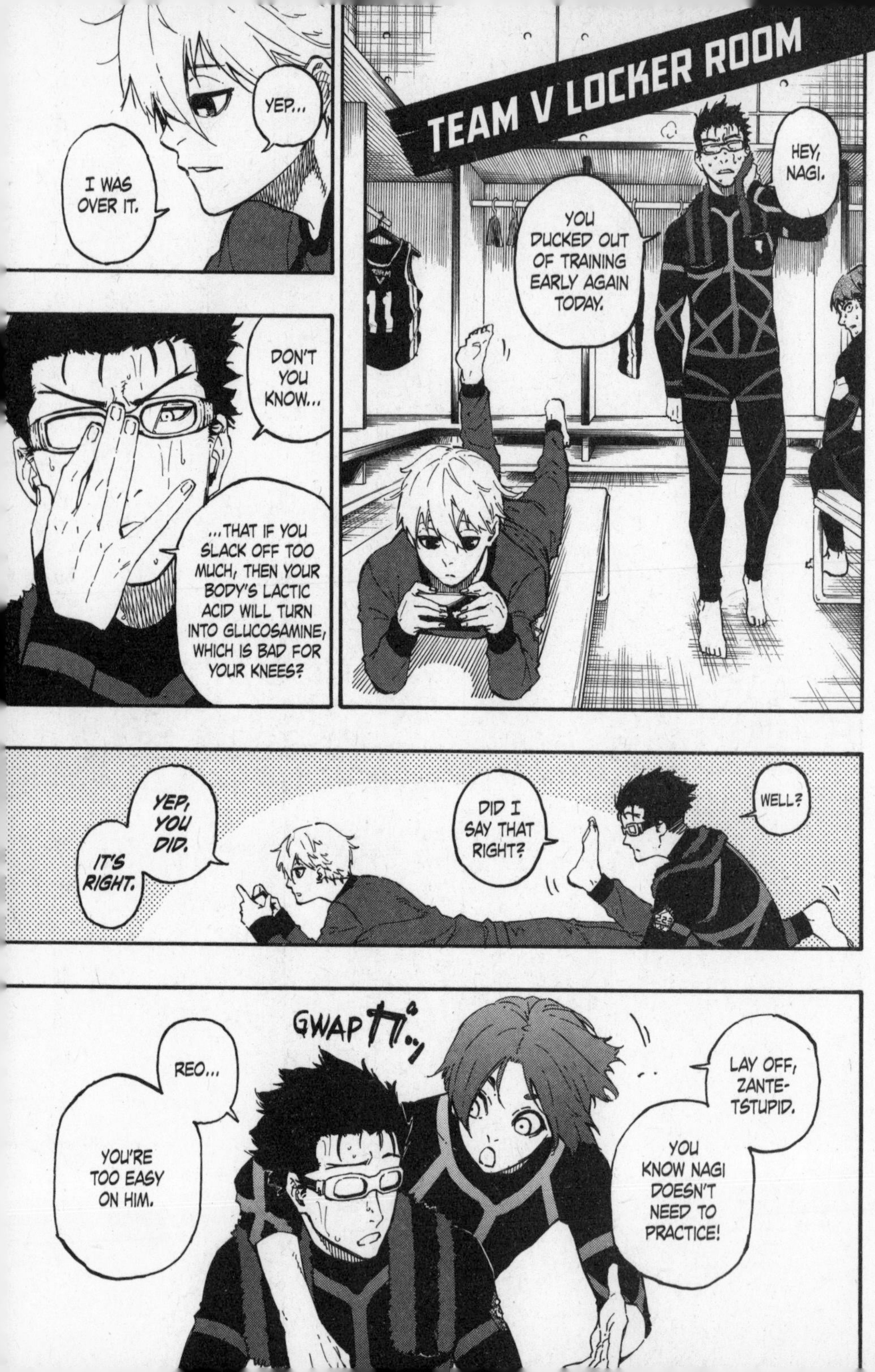
TEAM V LOCKER ROOM
HEY, NAGI.
YOU DUCKED OUT OF TRAINING EARLY AGAIN TODAY.
YEP...
I WAS OVER IT.
DON'T YOU KNOW...
...THAT IF YOU SLACK OFF TOO MUCH, THEN YOUR BODY'S LACTIC ACID WILL TURN INTO GLUCOSAMINE, WHICH IS BAD FOR YOUR KNEES?
WELL?
DID I SAY THAT RIGHT?
YEP, YOU DID.
IT'S RIGHT.
GWAP
LAY OFF, ZANTE-TSTUPID.
YOU KNOW NAGI DOESN'T NEED TO PRACTICE!
REO...
YOU'RE TOO EASY ON HIM.

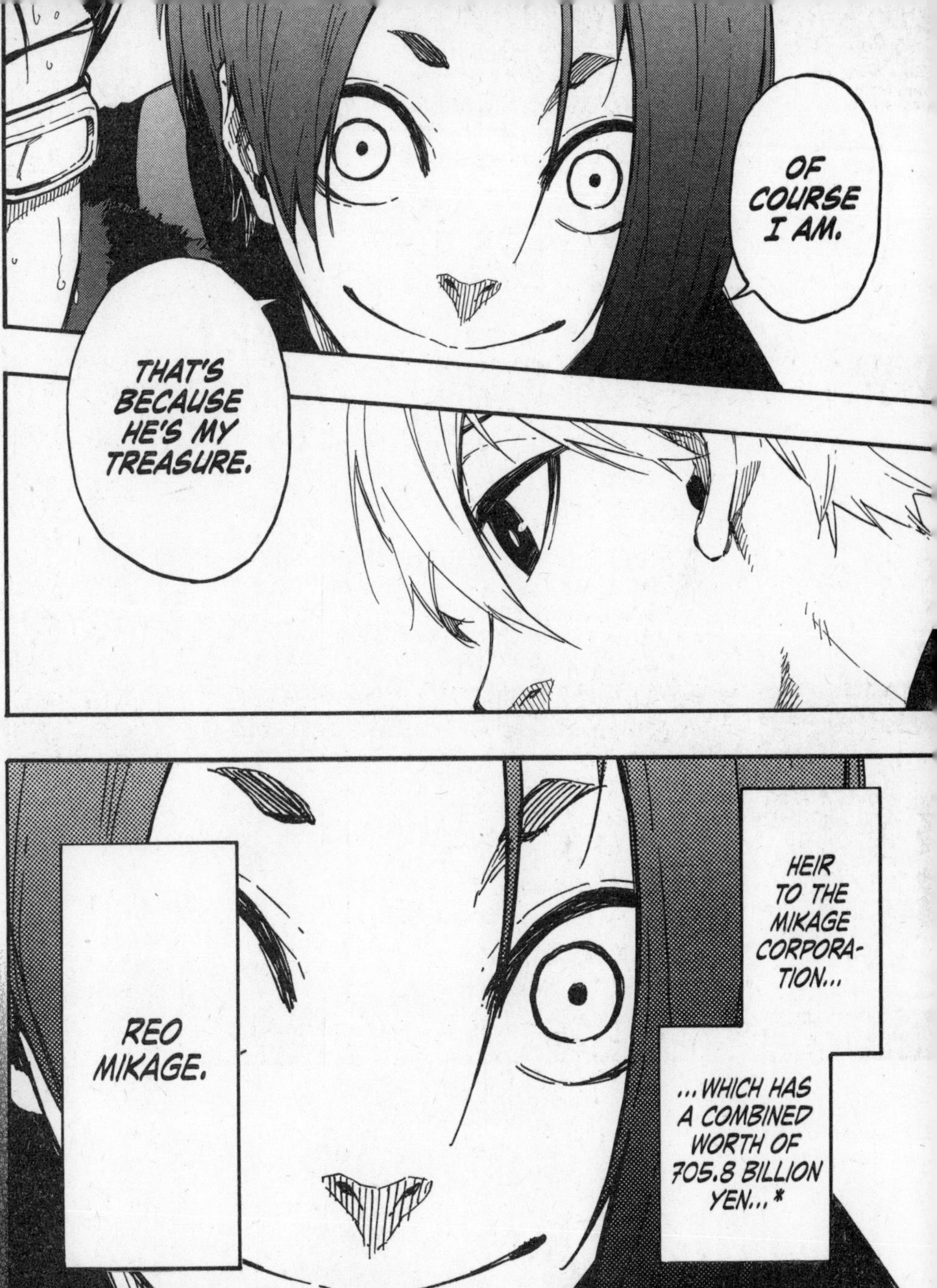
OF COURSE I AM.
THAT'S BECAUSE HE'S MY TREASURE.
HEIR TO THE MIKAGE CORPORA-TION...
...WHICH HAS A COMBINED WORTH OF 705.8 BILLION YEN...*
REO MIKAGE.

*ABOUT $7 BILLION

THIS BOY'S LIFE...

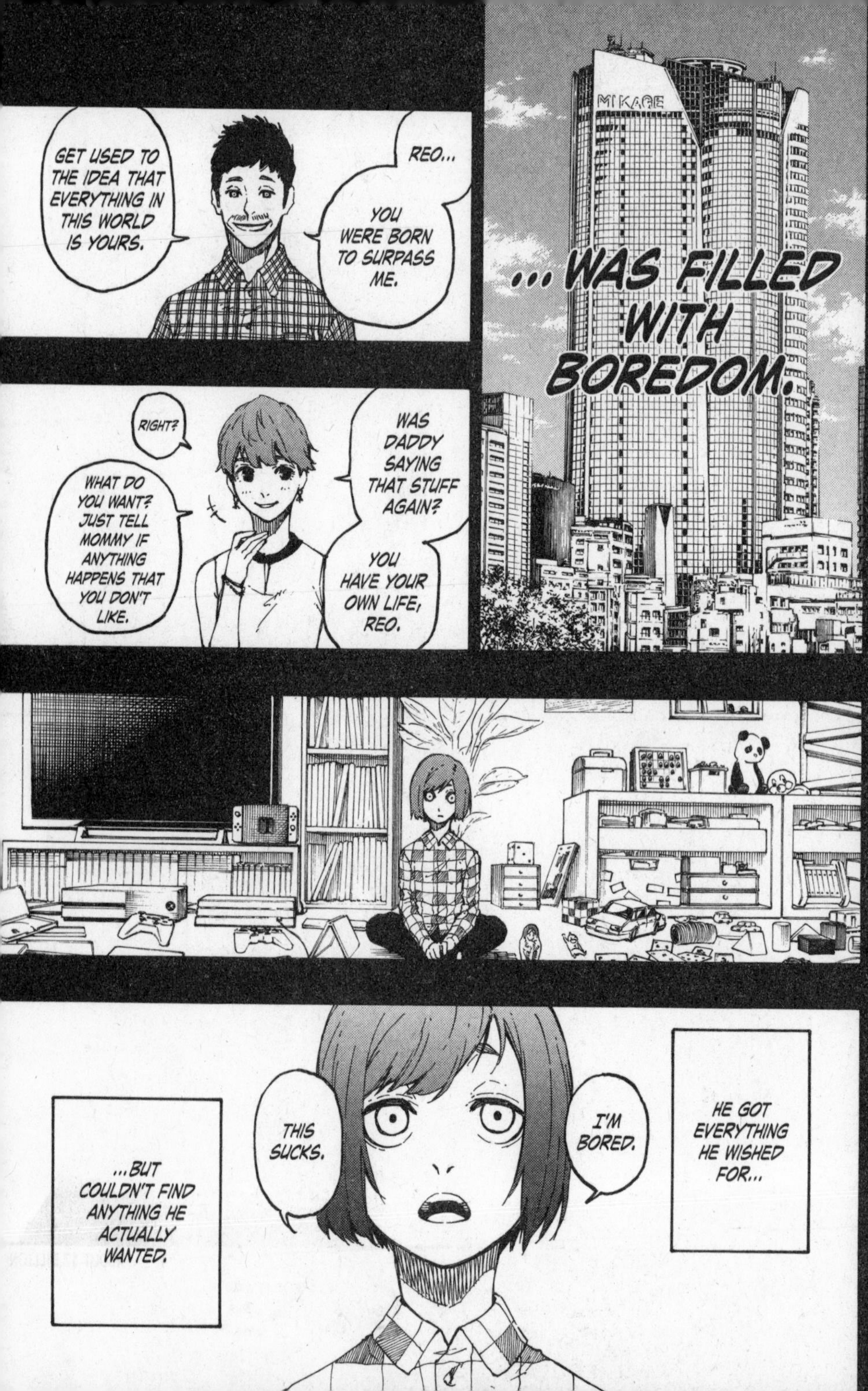

...WAS FILLED WITH BOREDOM.
MIKAGE
REO...
YOU WERE BORN TO SURPASS ME.
GET USED TO THE IDEA THAT EVERYTHING IN THIS WORLD IS YOURS.
WAS DADDY SAYING THAT STUFF AGAIN?
YOU HAVE YOUR OWN LIFE, REO.
RIGHT?
WHAT DO YOU WANT? JUST TELL MOMMY IF ANYTHING HAPPENS THAT YOU DON'T LIKE.
HE GOT EVERYTHING HE WISHED FOR...
I'M BORED.
THIS SUCKS.
...BUT COULDN'T FIND ANYTHING HE ACTUALLY WANTED.

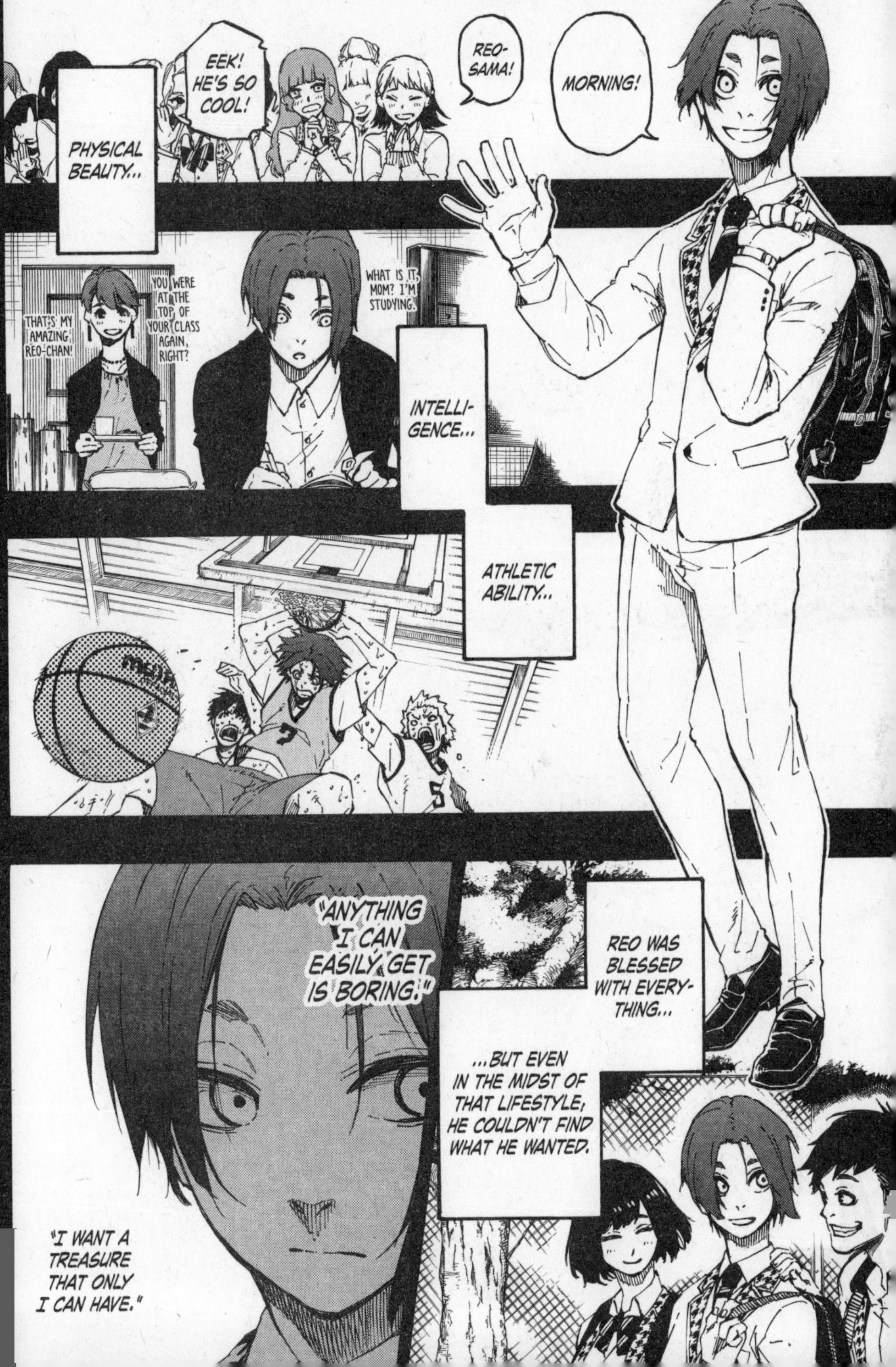
MORNING!
REO-SAMA!
EEK! HE'S SO COOL!
PHYSICAL BEAUTY...
WHAT IS IT, MOM? I'M STUDYING.
YOU WERE AT THE TOP OF YOUR CLASS AGAIN, RIGHT?
THAT'S MY AMAZING REO-CHAN!
INTELLIGENCE...
ATHLETIC ABILITY...
REO WAS BLESSED WITH EVERYTHING...
...BUT EVEN IN THE MIDST OF THAT LIFESTYLE, HE COULDN'T FIND WHAT HE WANTED.
"ANYTHING I CAN EASILY GET IS BORING."
"I WANT A TREASURE THAT ONLY I CAN HAVE."

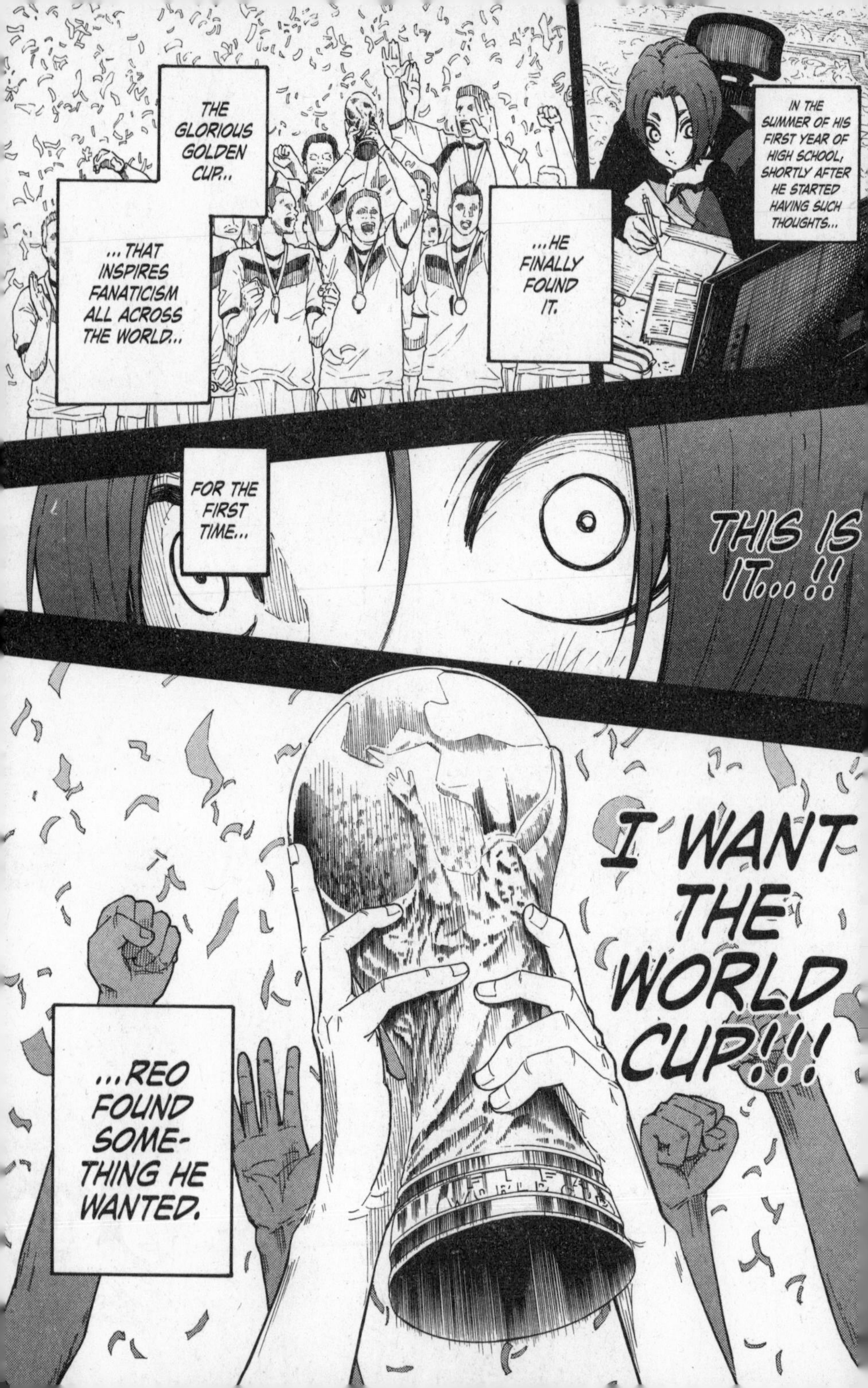
IN THE SUMMER OF HIS FIRST YEAR OF HIGH SCHOOL, SHORTLY AFTER HE STARTED HAVING SUCH THOUGHTS...
...HE FINALLY FOUND IT.
THE GLORIOUS GOLDEN CUP...
...THAT INSPIRES FANATICISM ALL ACROSS THE WORLD...
THIS IS IT...!!
FOR THE FIRST TIME...
I WANT THE WORLD CUP!!!
...REO FOUND SOME-THING HE WANTED.

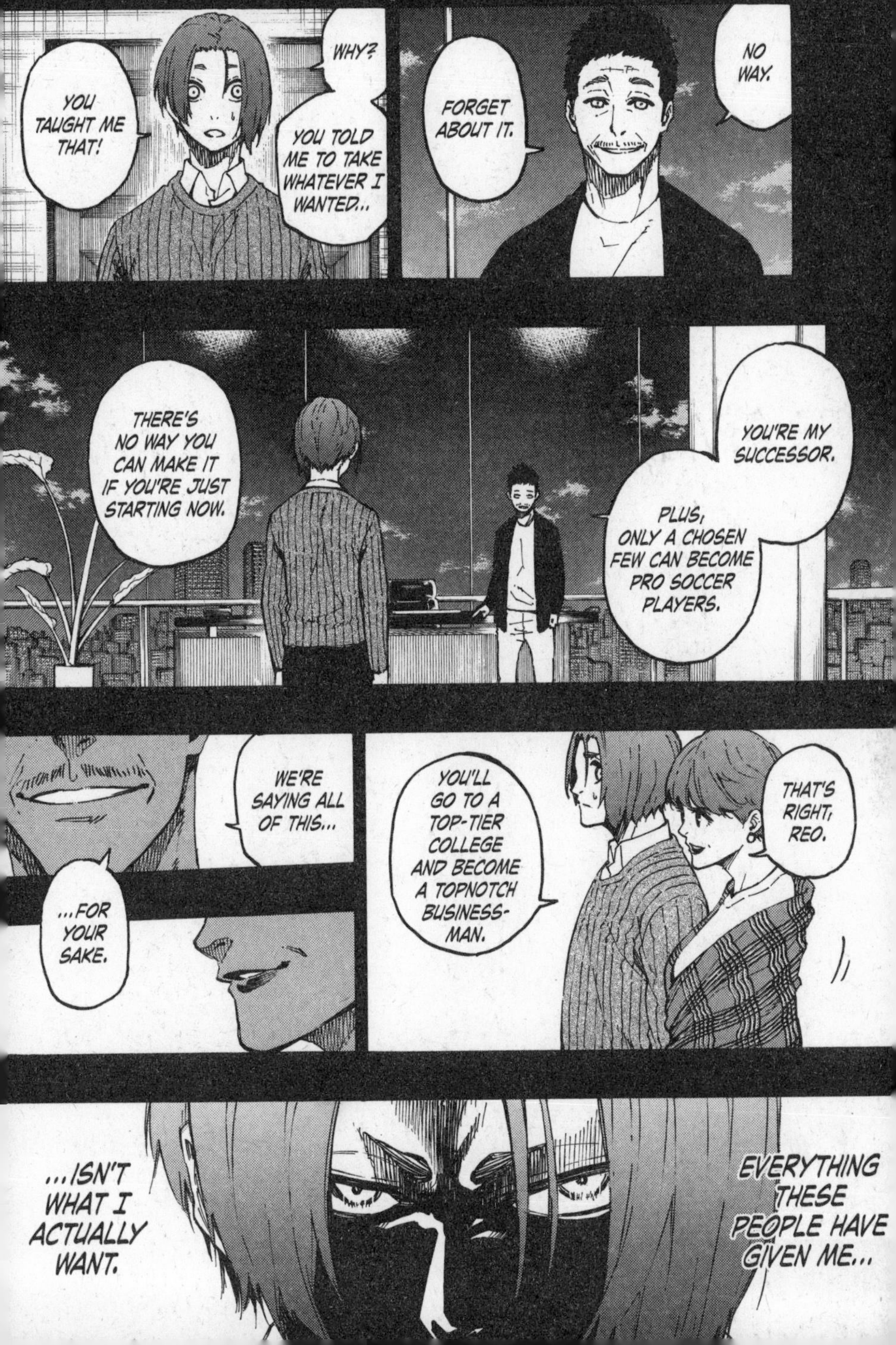
NO WAY.
FORGET ABOUT IT.
WHY?
YOU TOLD ME TO TAKE WHATEVER I WANTED...
YOU TAUGHT ME THAT!
YOU'RE MY SUCCESSOR.
PLUS, ONLY A CHOSEN FEW CAN BECOME PRO SOCCER PLAYERS.
THERE'S NO WAY YOU CAN MAKE IT IF YOU'RE JUST STARTING NOW.
THAT'S RIGHT, REO.
YOU'LL GO TO A TOP-TIER COLLEGE AND BECOME A TOPNOTCH BUSINESS-MAN.
WE'RE SAYING ALL OF THIS...
...FOR YOUR SAKE.
EVERYTHING THESE PEOPLE HAVE GIVEN ME...
...ISN'T WHAT I ACTUALLY WANT.

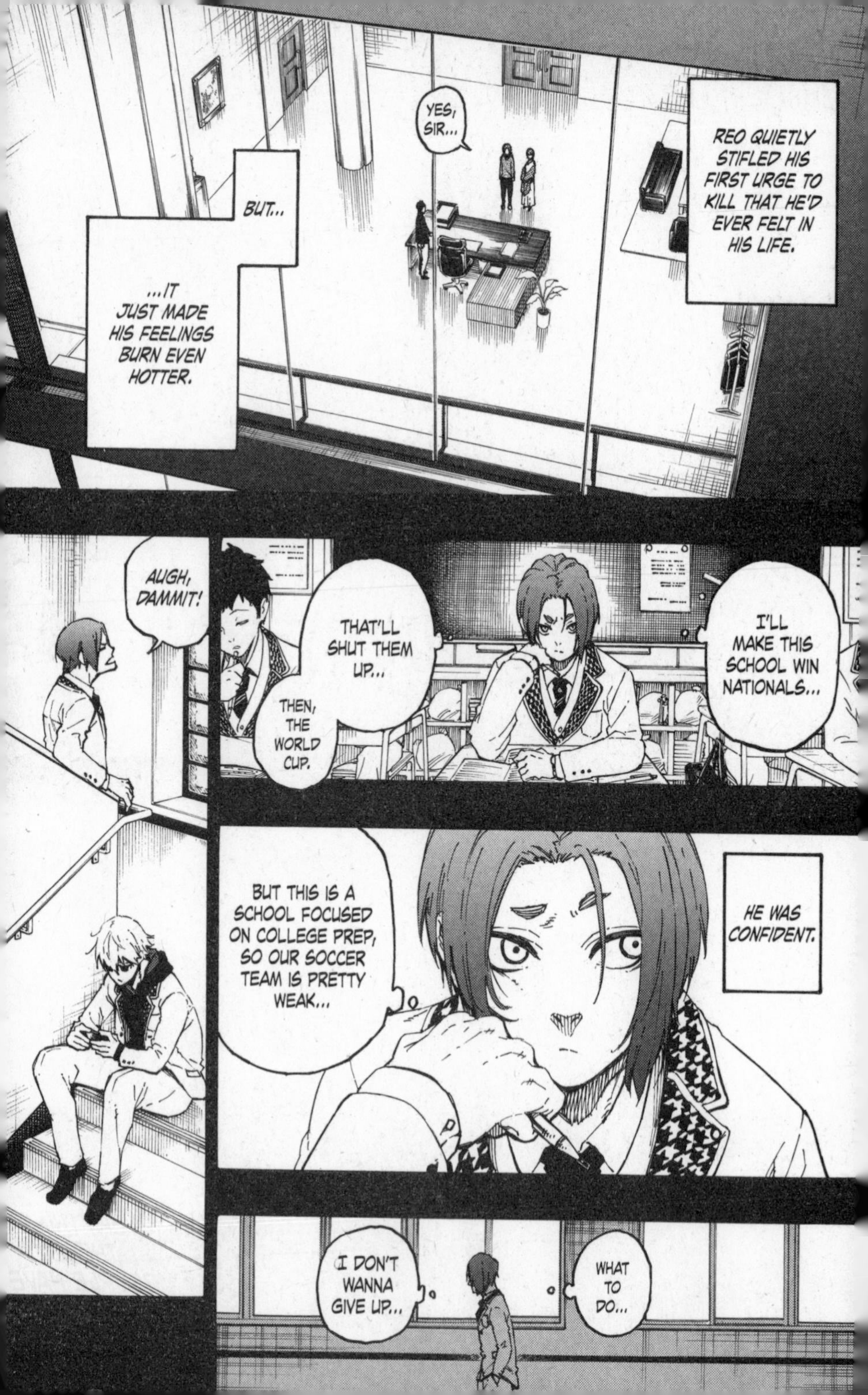
REO QUIETLY STIFLED HIS FIRST URGE TO KILL THAT HE'D EVER FELT IN HIS LIFE.
YES, SIR...
BUT...
...IT JUST MADE HIS FEELINGS BURN EVEN HOTTER.
I'LL MAKE THIS SCHOOL WIN NATIONALS...
THAT'LL SHUT THEM UP...
THEN, THE WORLD CUP.
HE WAS CONFIDENT.
BUT THIS IS A SCHOOL FOCUSED ON COLLEGE PREP, SO OUR SOCCER TEAM IS PRETTY WEAK...
WHAT TO DO...
I DON'T WANNA GIVE UP...
AUGH, DAMMIT!

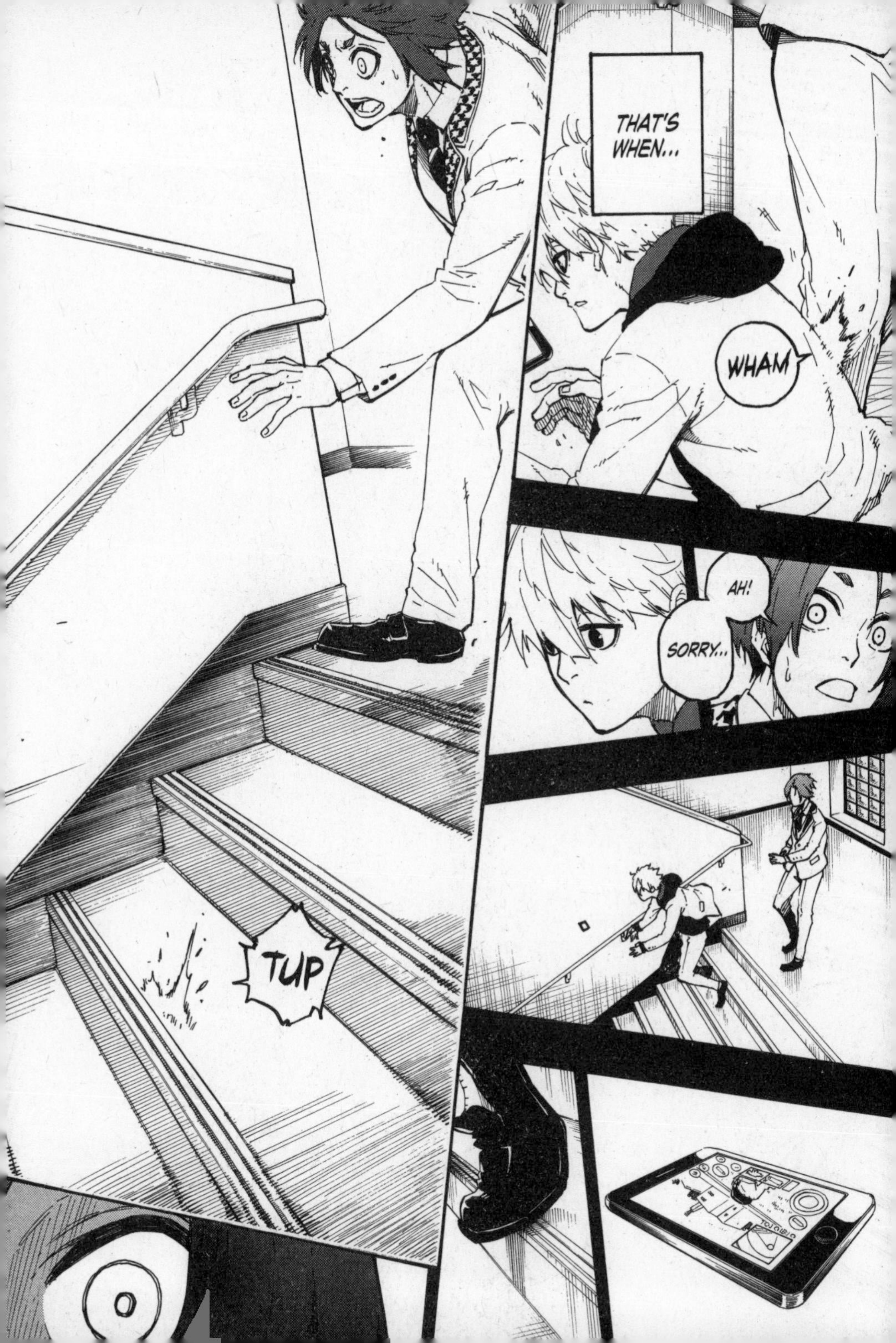
THAT'S WHEN...
WHAM
AH!
SORRY...
TUP

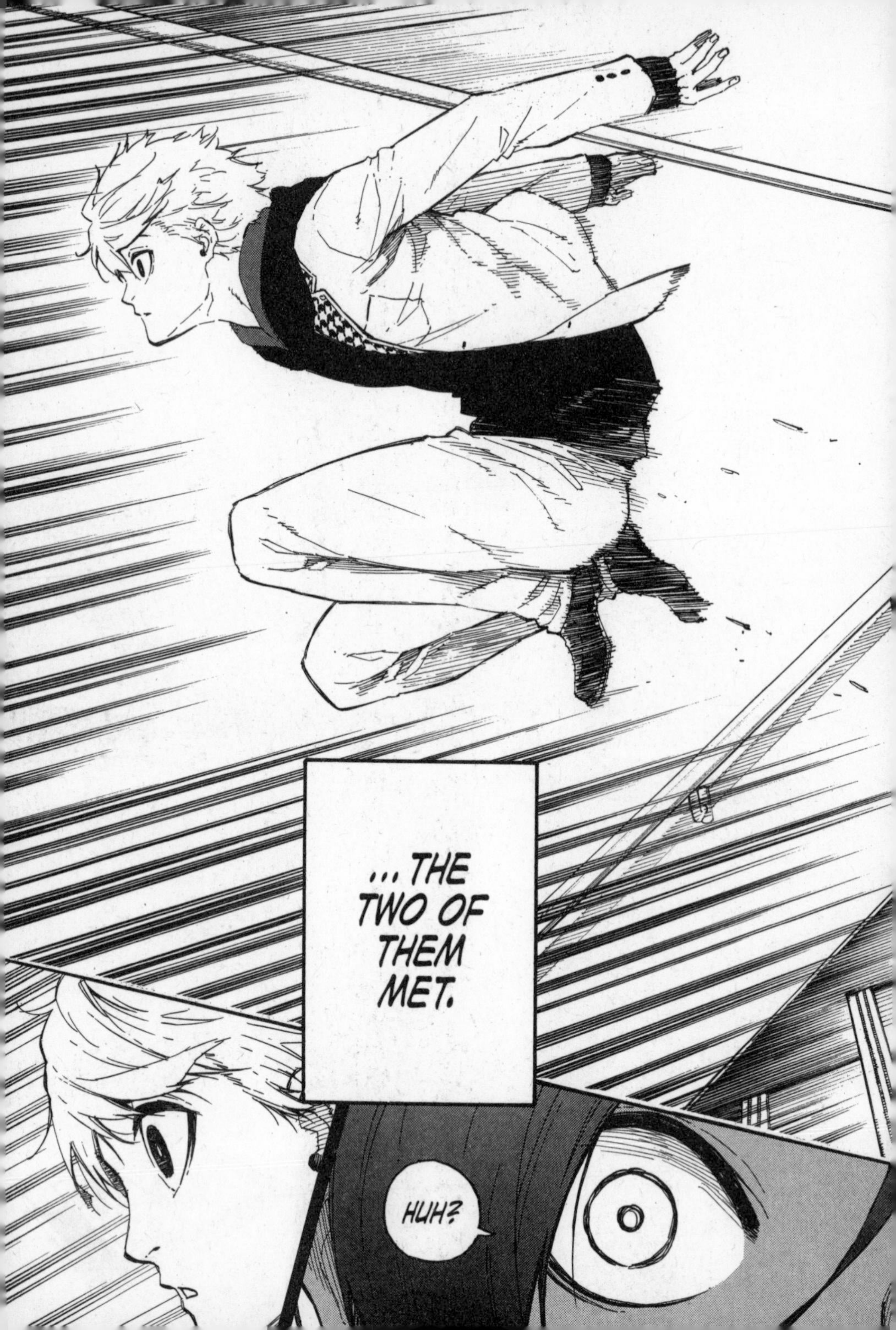
...THE TWO OF THEM MET.
HUH?

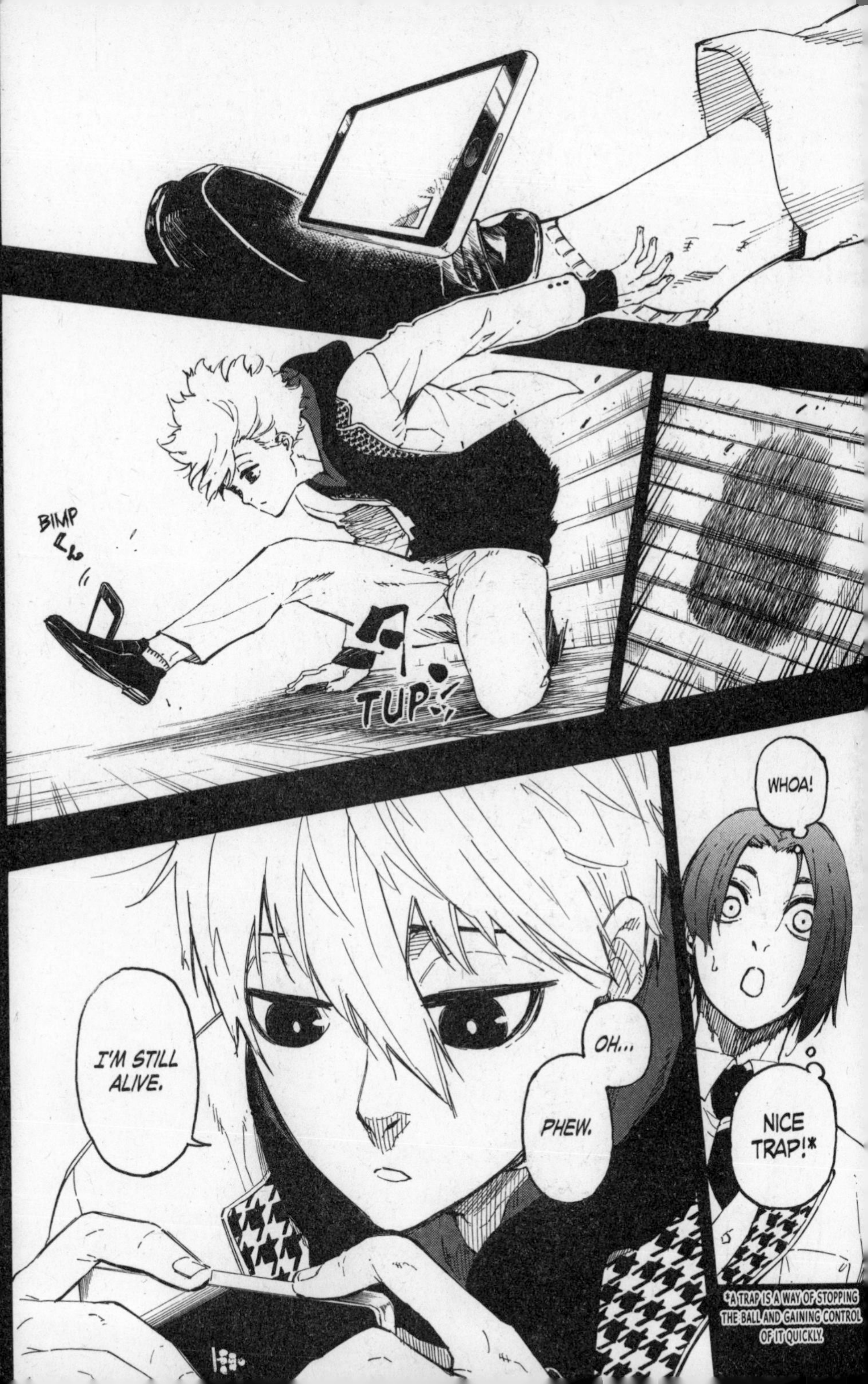
BIMP
TUP
WHOA!
NICE TRAP!*
OH...
PHEW.
I'M STILL ALIVE.
*A TRAP IS A WAY OF STOPPING THE BALL AND GAINING CONTROL OF IT QUICKLY.

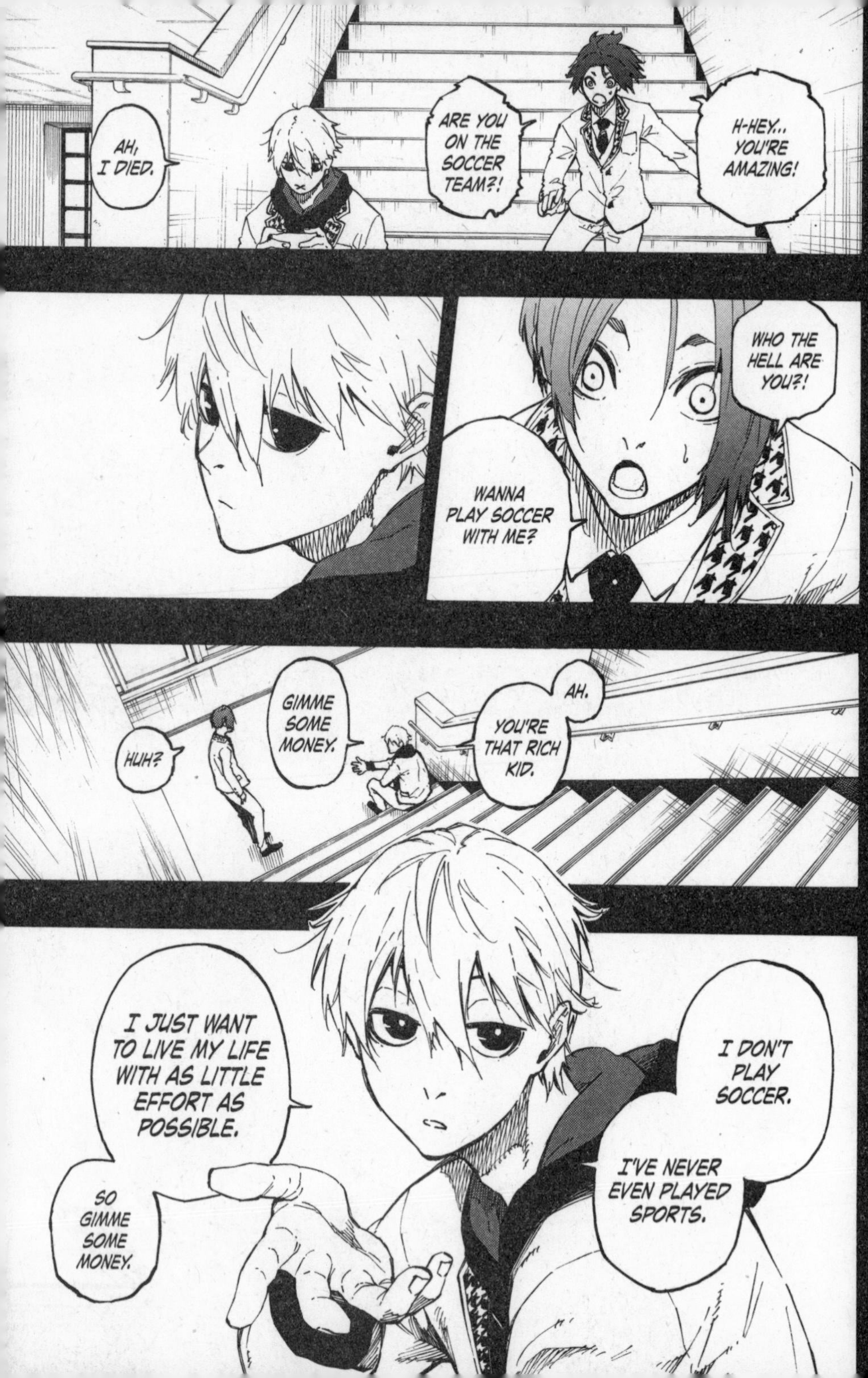
H-HEY... YOU'RE AMAZING!
ARE YOU ON THE SOCCER TEAM?!
AH, I DIED.
WHO THE HELL ARE YOU?!
WANNA PLAY SOCCER WITH ME?
AH. YOU'RE THAT RICH KID.
GIMME SOME MONEY.
HUH?
I DON'T PLAY SOCCER.
I'VE NEVER EVEN PLAYED SPORTS.
I JUST WANT TO LIVE MY LIFE WITH AS LITTLE EFFORT AS POSSIBLE.
SO GIMME SOME MONEY.

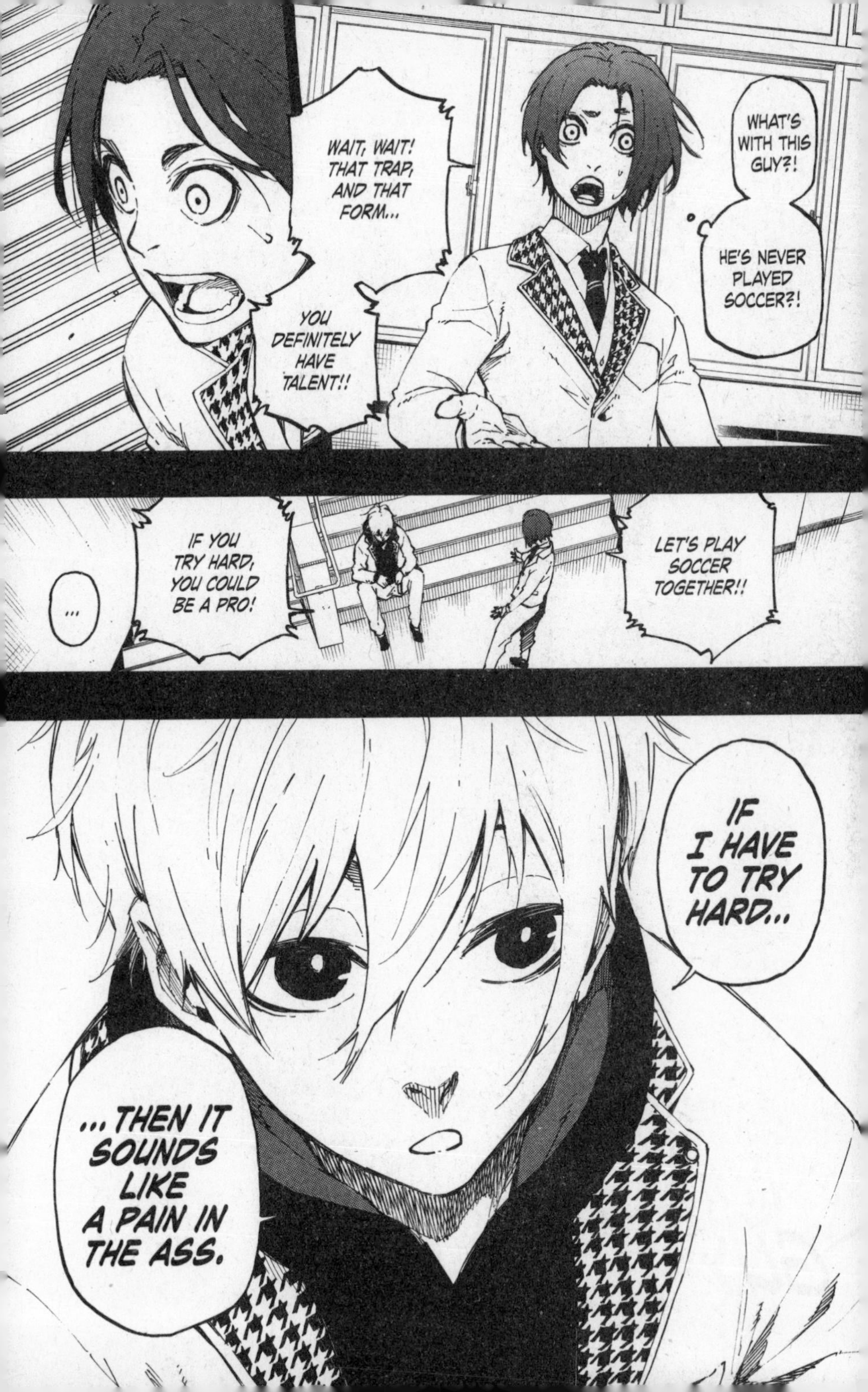
WHAT'S WITH THIS GUY?!
HE'S NEVER PLAYED SOCCER?!
WAIT, WAIT! THAT TRAP, AND THAT FORM...
YOU DEFINITELY HAVE TALENT!!
LET'S PLAY SOCCER TOGETHER!!
IF YOU TRY HARD, YOU COULD BE A PRO!
...
IF I HAVE TO TRY HARD...
...THEN IT SOUNDS LIKE A PAIN IN THE ASS.

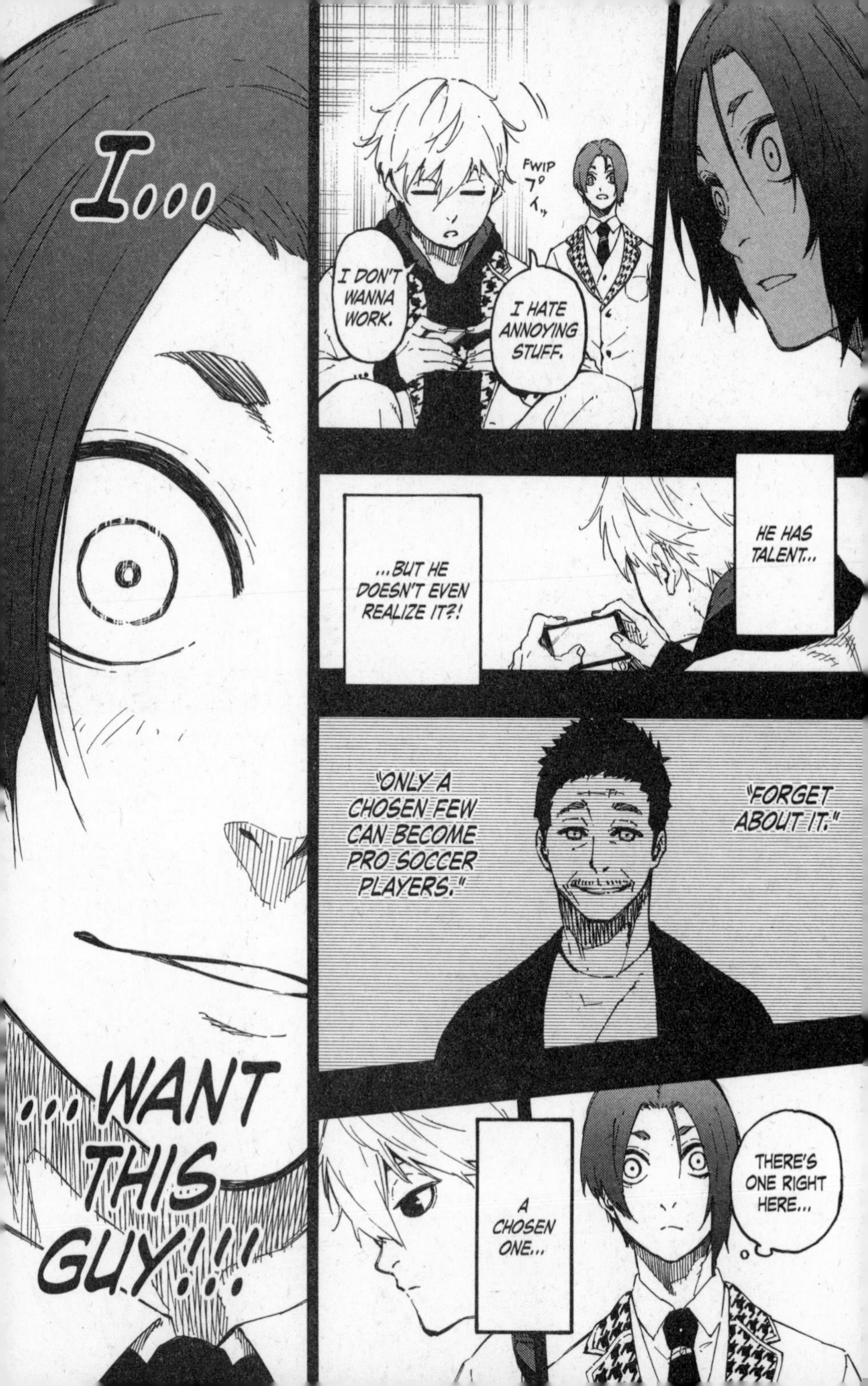
FWIP
プイッ
I HATE ANNOYING STUFF.
I DON'T WANNA WORK.
HE HAS TALENT...
...BUT HE DOESN'T EVEN REALIZE IT?!
"FORGET ABOUT IT."
"ONLY A CHOSEN FEW CAN BECOME PRO SOCCER PLAYERS."
THERE'S ONE RIGHT HERE...
A CHOSEN ONE...
I...
...WANT THIS GUY!!!

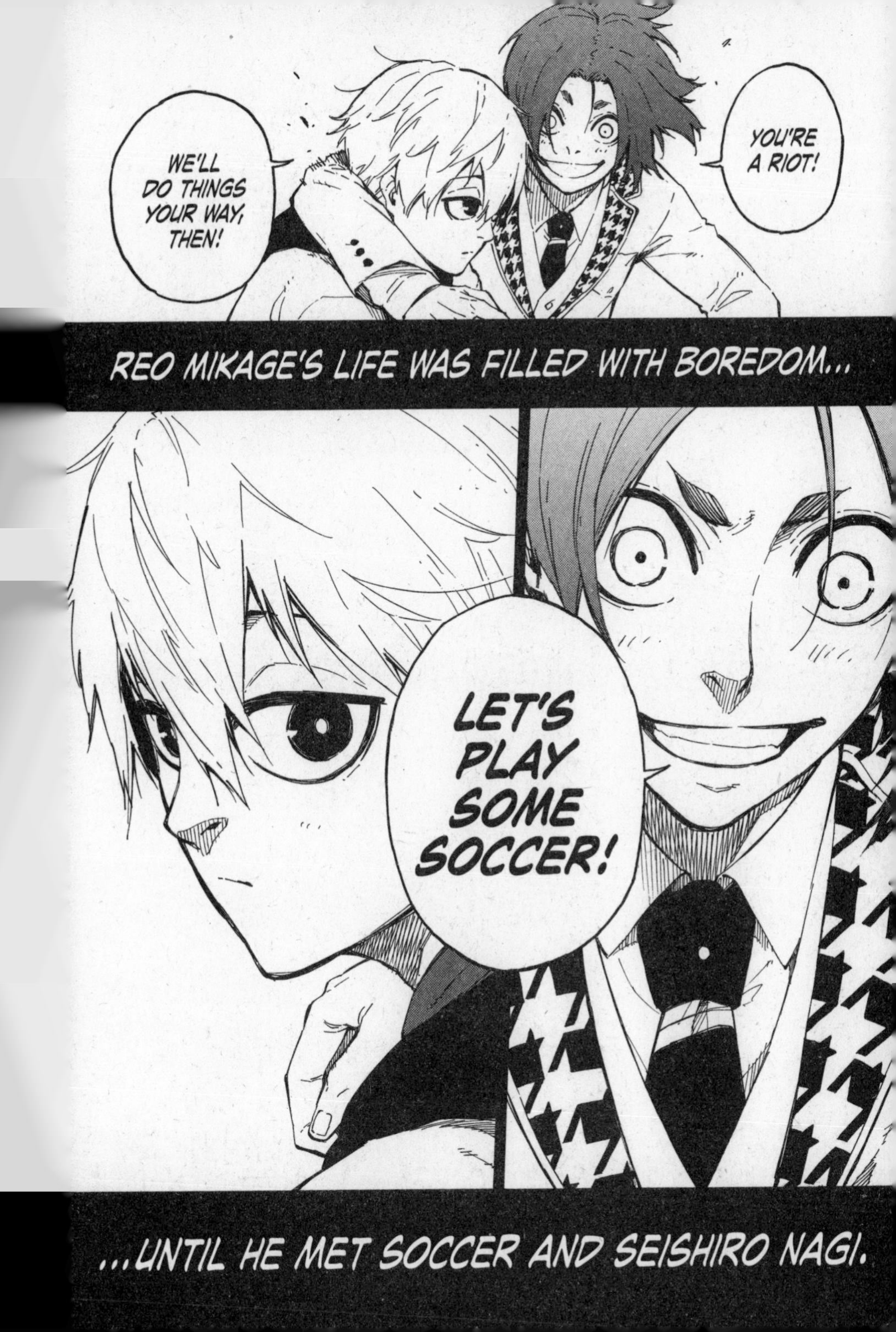
YOU'RE A RIOT!
WE'LL DO THINGS YOUR WAY, THEN!
REO MIKAGE'S LIFE WAS FILLED WITH BOREDOM...
LET'S PLAY SOME SOCCER!
...UNTIL HE MET SOCCER AND SEISHIRO NAGI.

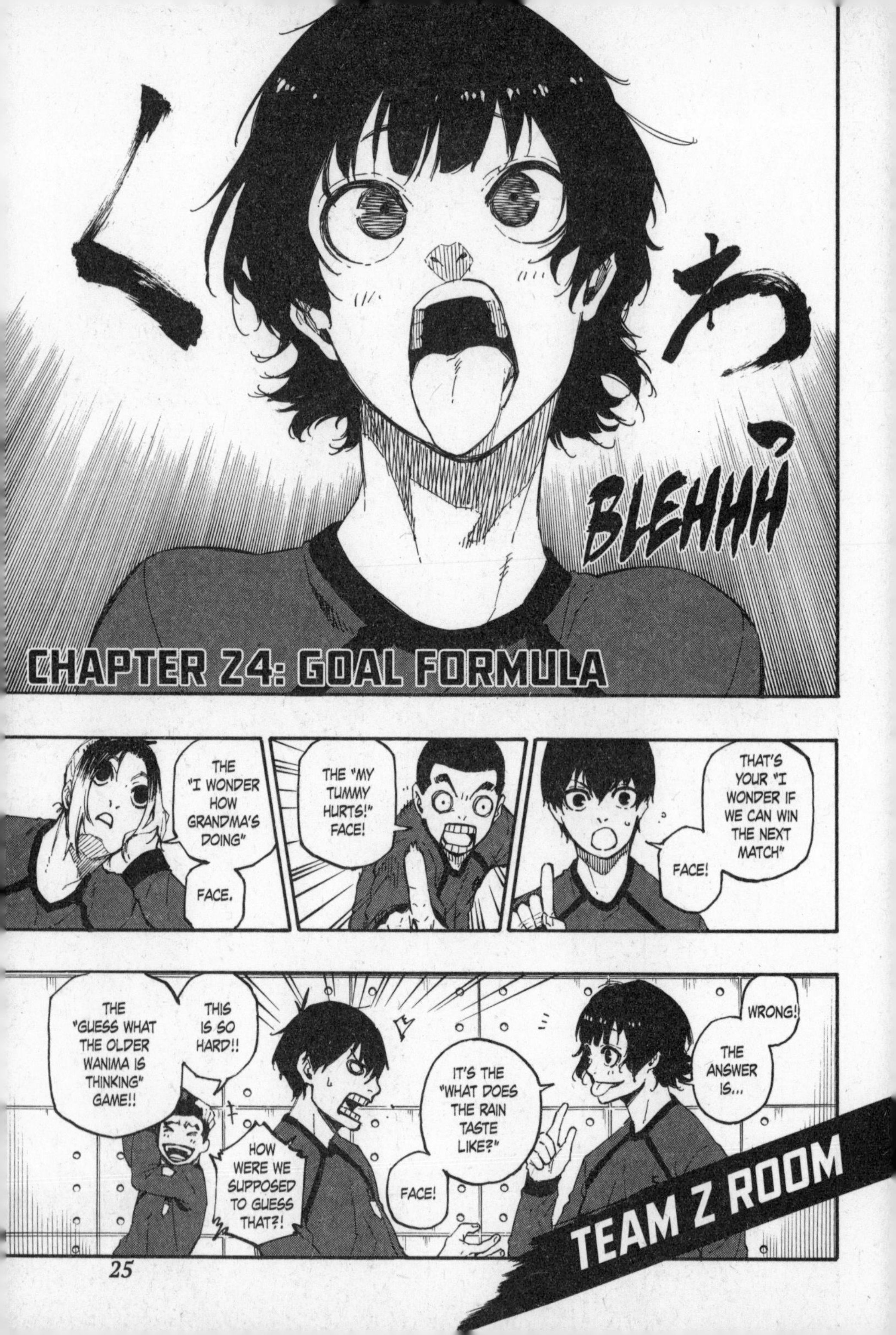
BLEHHH
CHAPTER 24: GOAL FORMULA
THAT'S YOUR "I WONDER IF WE CAN WIN THE NEXT MATCH"
FACE!
THE "MY TUMMY HURTS!" FACE!
THE "I WONDER HOW GRANDMA'S DOING"
FACE.
WRONG!
THE ANSWER IS...
IT'S THE "WHAT DOES THE RAIN TASTE LIKE?"
FACE!
HOW WERE WE SUPPOSED TO GUESS THAT?!
THIS IS SO HARD!!
THE "GUESS WHAT THE OLDER WANIMA IS THINKING" GAME!!
TEAM Z ROOM

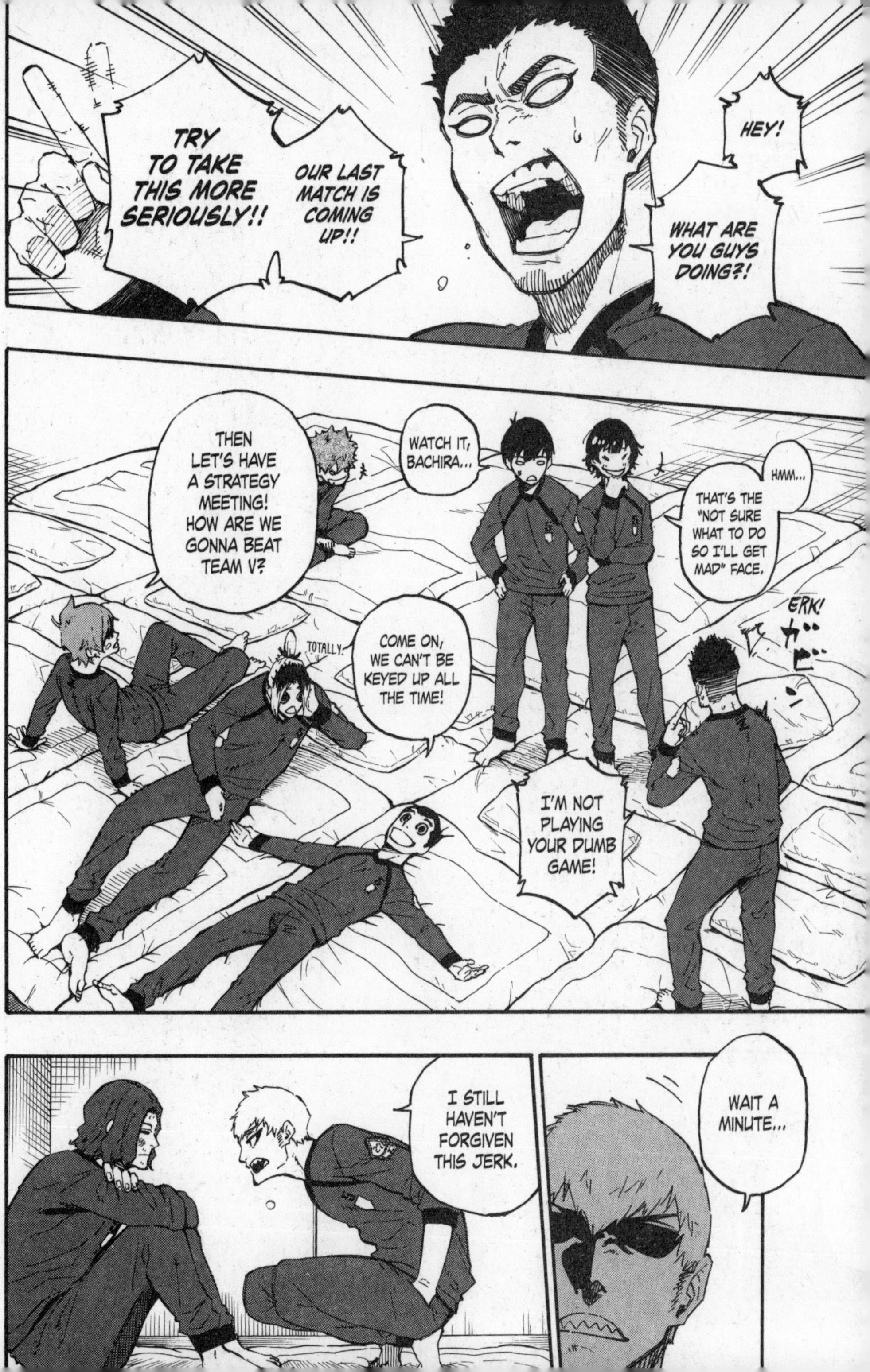
HEY!
WHAT ARE YOU GUYS DOING?!
OUR LAST MATCH IS COMING UP!!
TRY TO TAKE THIS MORE SERIOUSLY!!
HMM...
THAT'S THE "NOT SURE WHAT TO DO SO I'LL GET MAD" FACE.
ERK!
WATCH IT, BACHIRA...
THEN LET'S HAVE A STRATEGY MEETING! HOW ARE WE GONNA BEAT TEAM V?
COME ON, WE CAN'T BE KEYED UP ALL THE TIME!
TOTALLY.
I'M NOT PLAYING YOUR DUMB GAME!
WAIT A MINUTE...
I STILL HAVEN'T FORGIVEN THIS JERK.

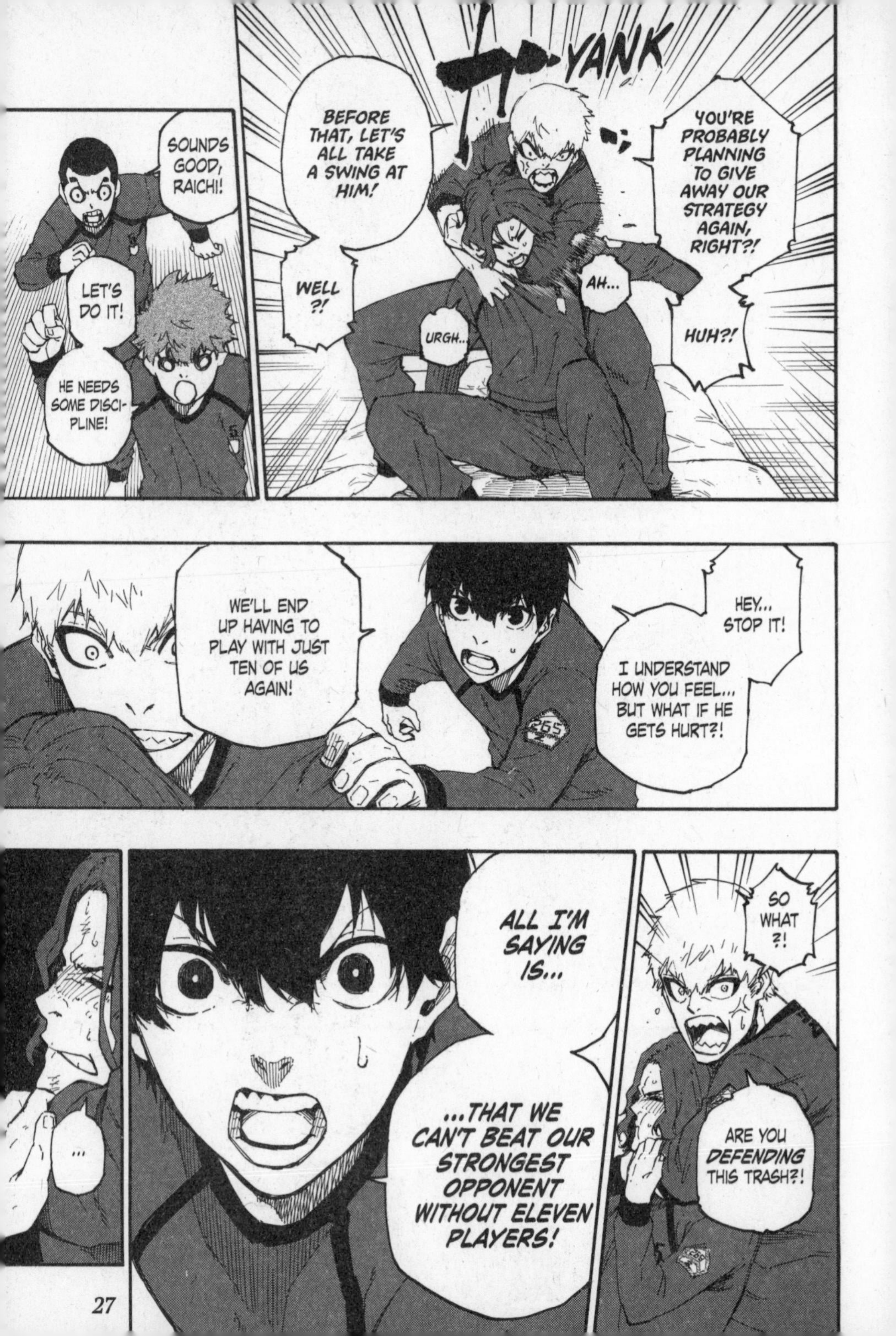
YANK
YOU'RE PROBABLY PLANNING TO GIVE AWAY OUR STRATEGY AGAIN, RIGHT?!
HUH?!
BEFORE THAT, LET'S ALL TAKE A SWING AT HIM!
WELL?!
AH...
URGH...
SOUNDS GOOD, RAICHI!
LET'S DO IT!
HE NEEDS SOME DISCI-PLINE!
HEY... STOP IT!
I UNDERSTAND HOW YOU FEEL... BUT WHAT IF HE GETS HURT?!
WE'LL END UP HAVING TO PLAY WITH JUST TEN OF US AGAIN!
SO WHAT?!
ARE YOU DEFENDING THIS TRASH?!
ALL I'M SAYING IS...
...THAT WE CAN'T BEAT OUR STRONGEST OPPONENT WITHOUT ELEVEN PLAYERS!
...

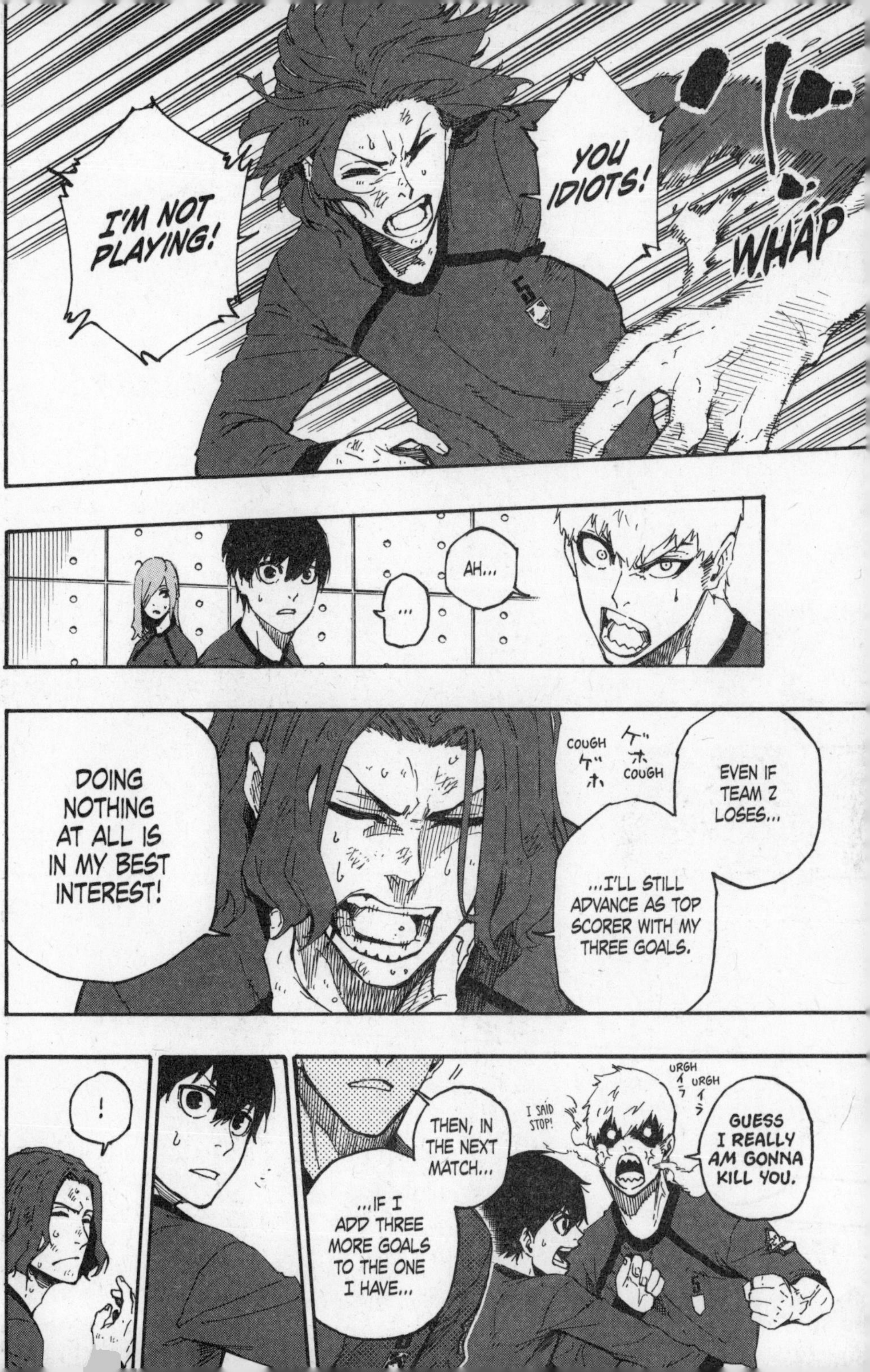
WHAP
YOU IDIOTS!
I'M NOT PLAYING!
AH...
...
COUGH ゲホ COUGH ゲホ
EVEN IF TEAM Z LOSES...
...I'LL STILL ADVANCE AS TOP SCORER WITH MY THREE GOALS.
DOING NOTHING AT ALL IS IN MY BEST INTEREST!
URGH イラ URGH イラ
GUESS I REALLY AM GONNA KILL YOU.
I SAID STOP!
THEN, IN THE NEXT MATCH...
...IF I ADD THREE MORE GOALS TO THE ONE I HAVE...
!

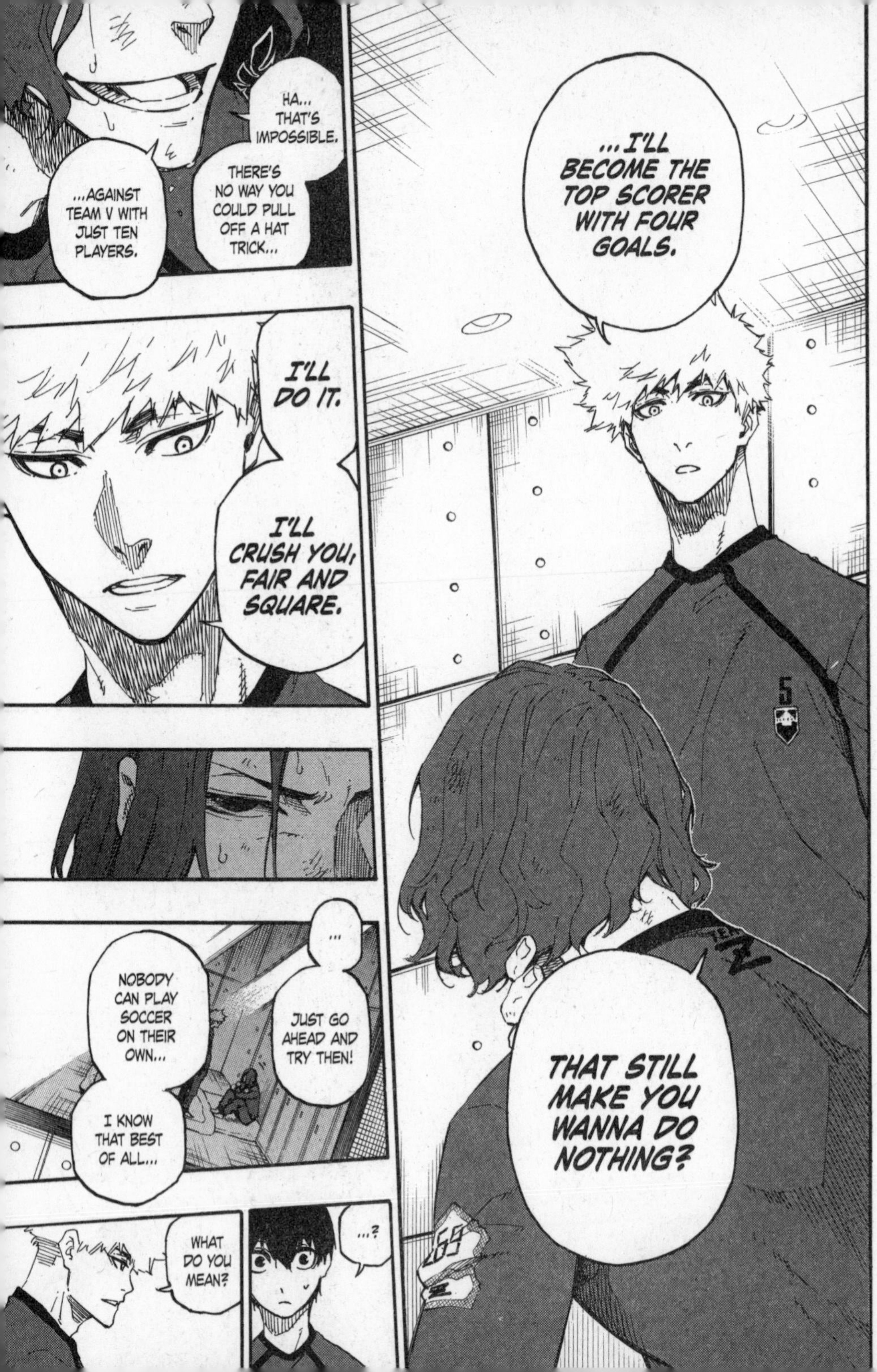
...I'LL BECOME THE TOP SCORER WITH FOUR GOALS.
THAT STILL MAKE YOU WANNA DO NOTHING?
HA... THAT'S IMPOSSIBLE.
THERE'S NO WAY YOU COULD PULL OFF A HAT TRICK...
...AGAINST TEAM V WITH JUST TEN PLAYERS.
I'LL DO IT.
I'LL CRUSH YOU, FAIR AND SQUARE.
...
JUST GO AHEAD AND TRY THEN!
NOBODY CAN PLAY SOCCER ON THEIR OWN...
I KNOW THAT BEST OF ALL...
...?
WHAT DO YOU MEAN?

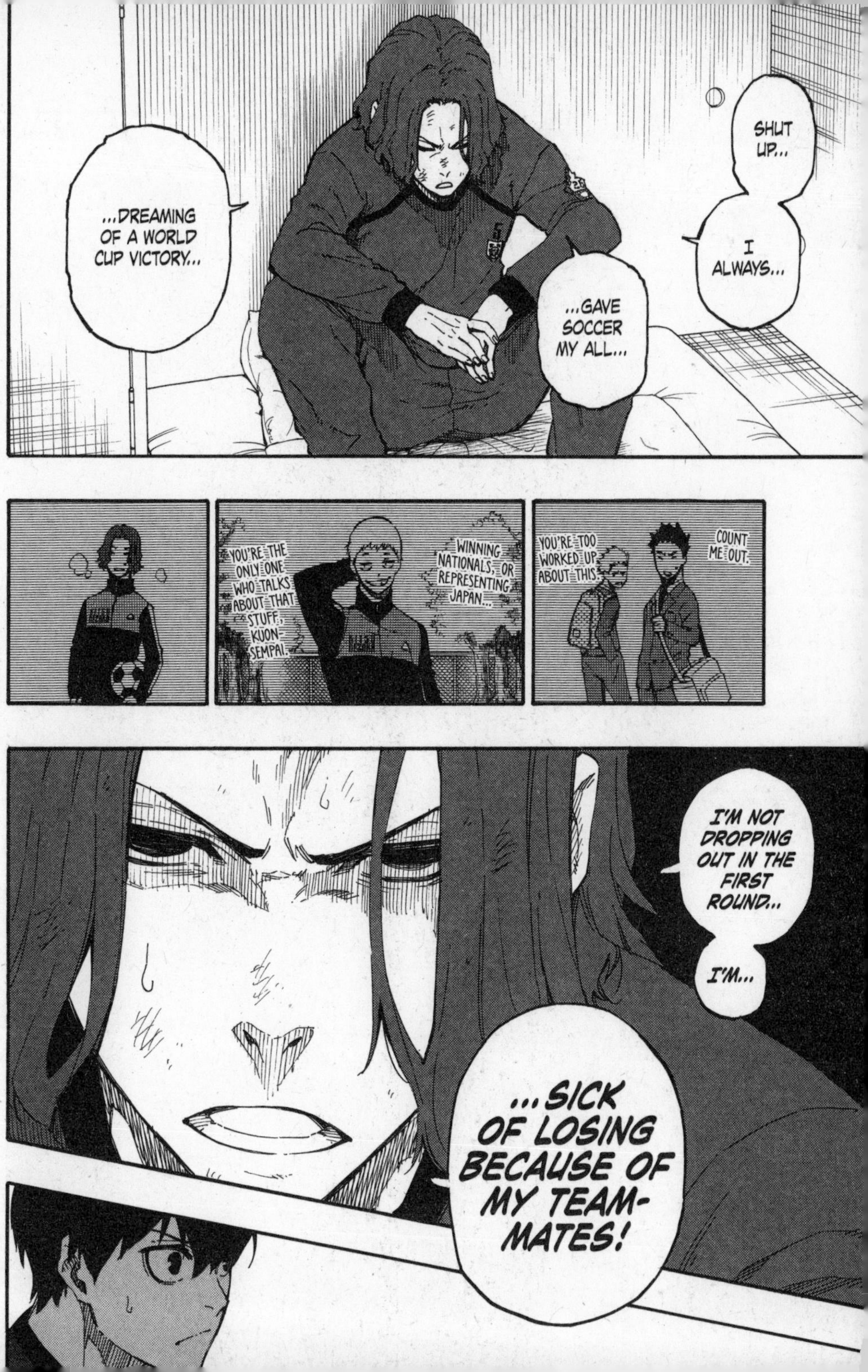
SHUT UP...
I ALWAYS...
...GAVE SOCCER MY ALL...
...DREAMING OF A WORLD CUP VICTORY...
COUNT ME OUT.
YOU'RE TOO WORKED UP ABOUT THIS.
WINNING NATIONALS, OR REPRESENTING JAPAN...
YOU'RE THE ONLY ONE WHO TALKS ABOUT THAT STUFF, KUON-SEMPAI.
I'M NOT DROPPING OUT IN THE FIRST ROUND...
I'M...
...SICK OF LOSING BECAUSE OF MY TEAM-MATES!

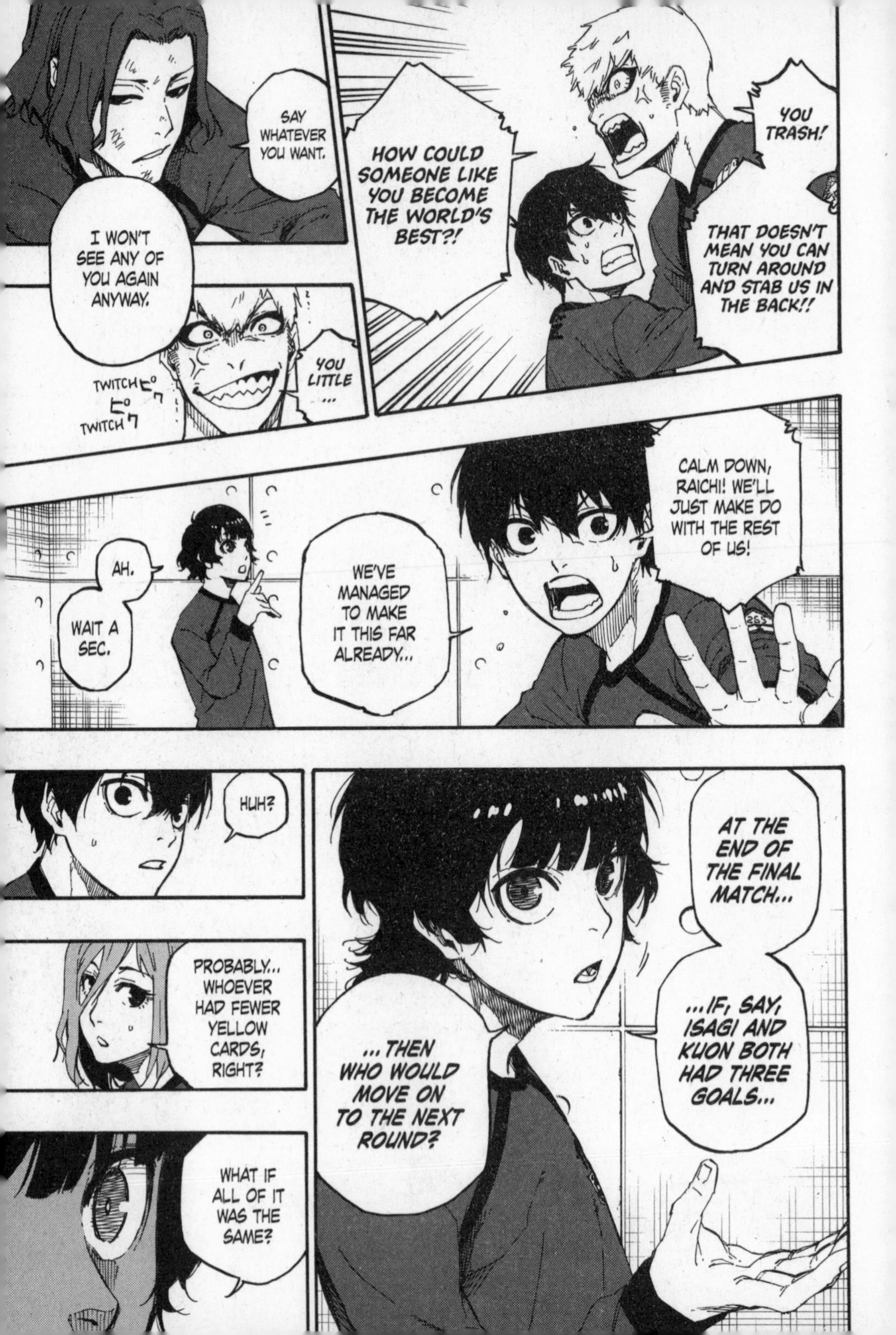
YOU TRASH!
THAT DOESN'T MEAN YOU CAN TURN AROUND AND STAB US IN THE BACK!!
HOW COULD SOMEONE LIKE YOU BECOME THE WORLD'S BEST?!
SAY WHATEVER YOU WANT.
I WON'T SEE ANY OF YOU AGAIN ANYWAY.
YOU LITTLE...
TWITCH
TWITCH
CALM DOWN, RAICHI! WE'LL JUST MAKE DO WITH THE REST OF US!
WE'VE MANAGED TO MAKE IT THIS FAR ALREADY...
AH.
WAIT A SEC.
AT THE END OF THE FINAL MATCH...
...IF, SAY, ISAGI AND KUON BOTH HAD THREE GOALS...
...THEN WHO WOULD MOVE ON TO THE NEXT ROUND?
HUH?
PROBABLY... WHOEVER HAD FEWER YELLOW CARDS, RIGHT?
WHAT IF ALL OF IT WAS THE SAME?

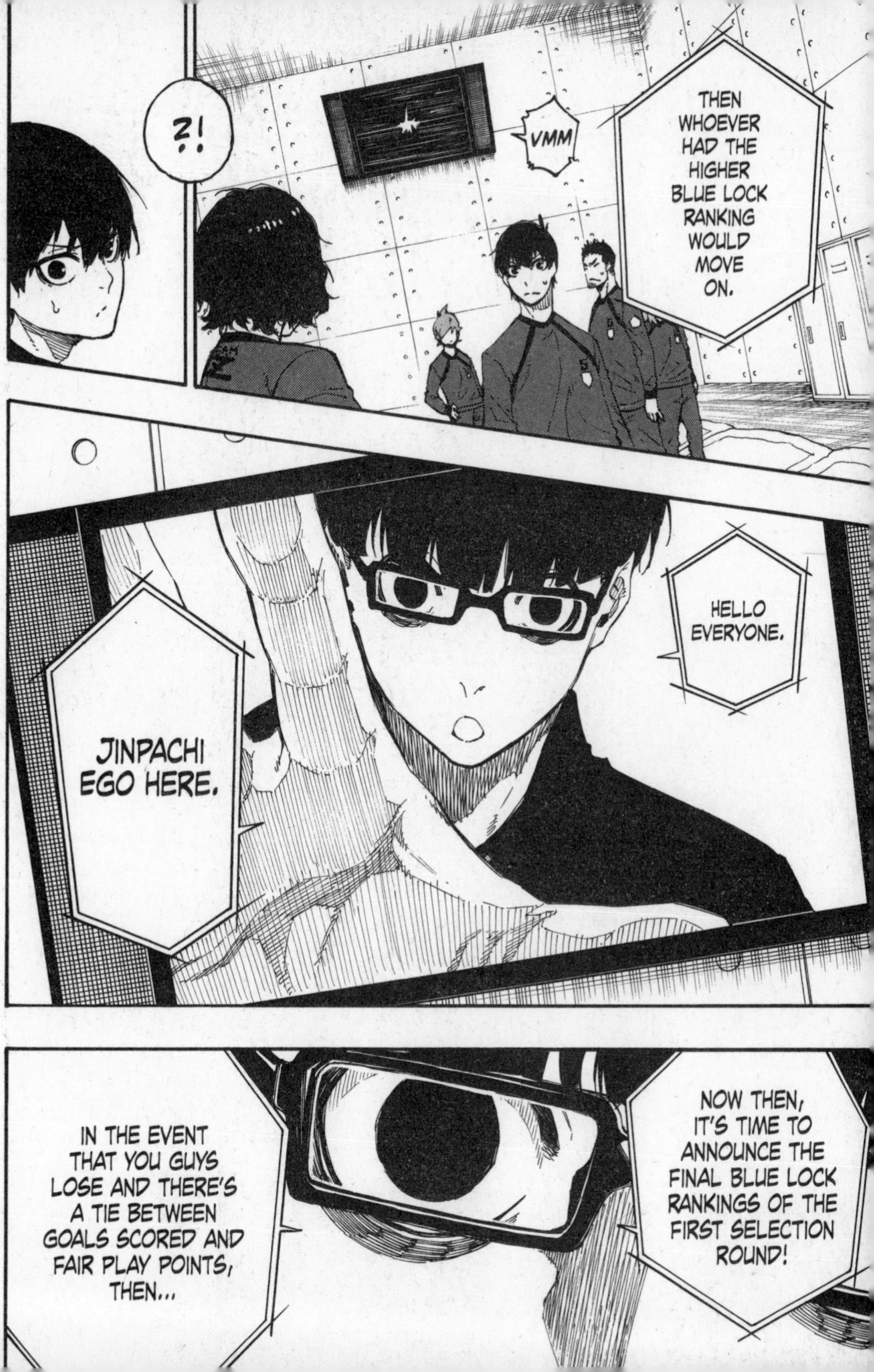
THEN WHOEVER HAD THE HIGHER BLUE LOCK RANKING WOULD MOVE ON.
VMM
?!
HELLO EVERYONE.
JINPACHI EGO HERE.
NOW THEN, IT'S TIME TO ANNOUNCE THE FINAL BLUE LOCK RANKINGS OF THE FIRST SELECTION ROUND!
IN THE EVENT THAT YOU GUYS LOSE AND THERE'S A TIE BETWEEN GOALS SCORED AND FAIR PLAY POINTS, THEN...

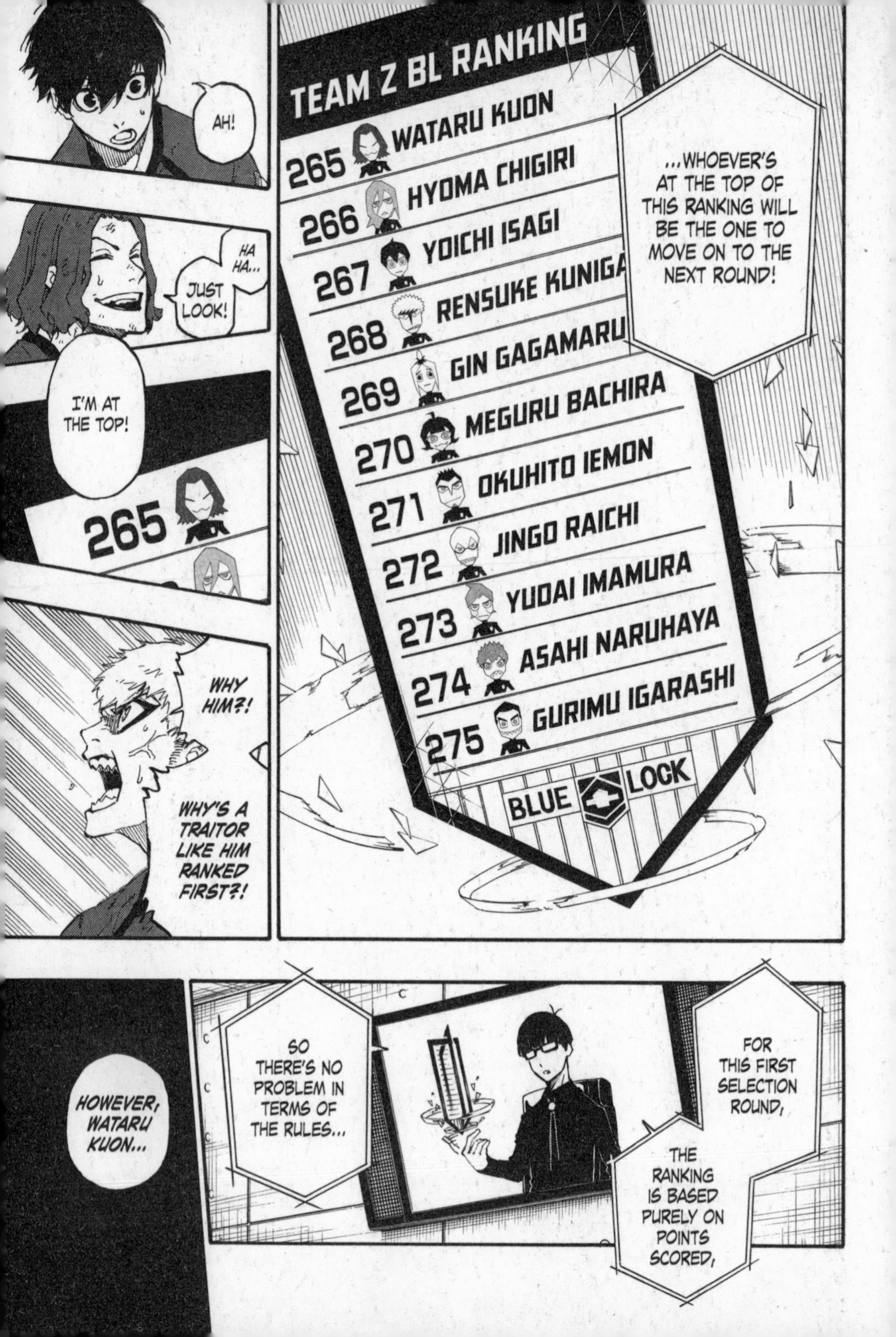
...WHOEVER'S AT THE TOP OF THIS RANKING WILL BE THE ONE TO MOVE ON TO THE NEXT ROUND!
TEAM Z BL RANKING
265 WATARU KUON
266 HYOMA CHIGIRI
267 YOICHI ISAGI
268 RENSUKE KUNIGA
269 GIN GAGAMARU
270 MEGURU BACHIRA
271 OKUHITO IEMON
272 JINGO RAICHI
273 YUDAI IMAMURA
274 ASAHI NARUHAYA
275 GURIMU IGARASHI
BLUE LOCK
AH!
HA HA... JUST LOOK!
I'M AT THE TOP!
265
WHY HIM?!
WHY'S A TRAITOR LIKE HIM RANKED FIRST?!
FOR THIS FIRST SELECTION ROUND,
THE RANKING IS BASED PURELY ON POINTS SCORED,
SO THERE'S NO PROBLEM IN TERMS OF THE RULES...
HOWEVER, WATARU KUON...

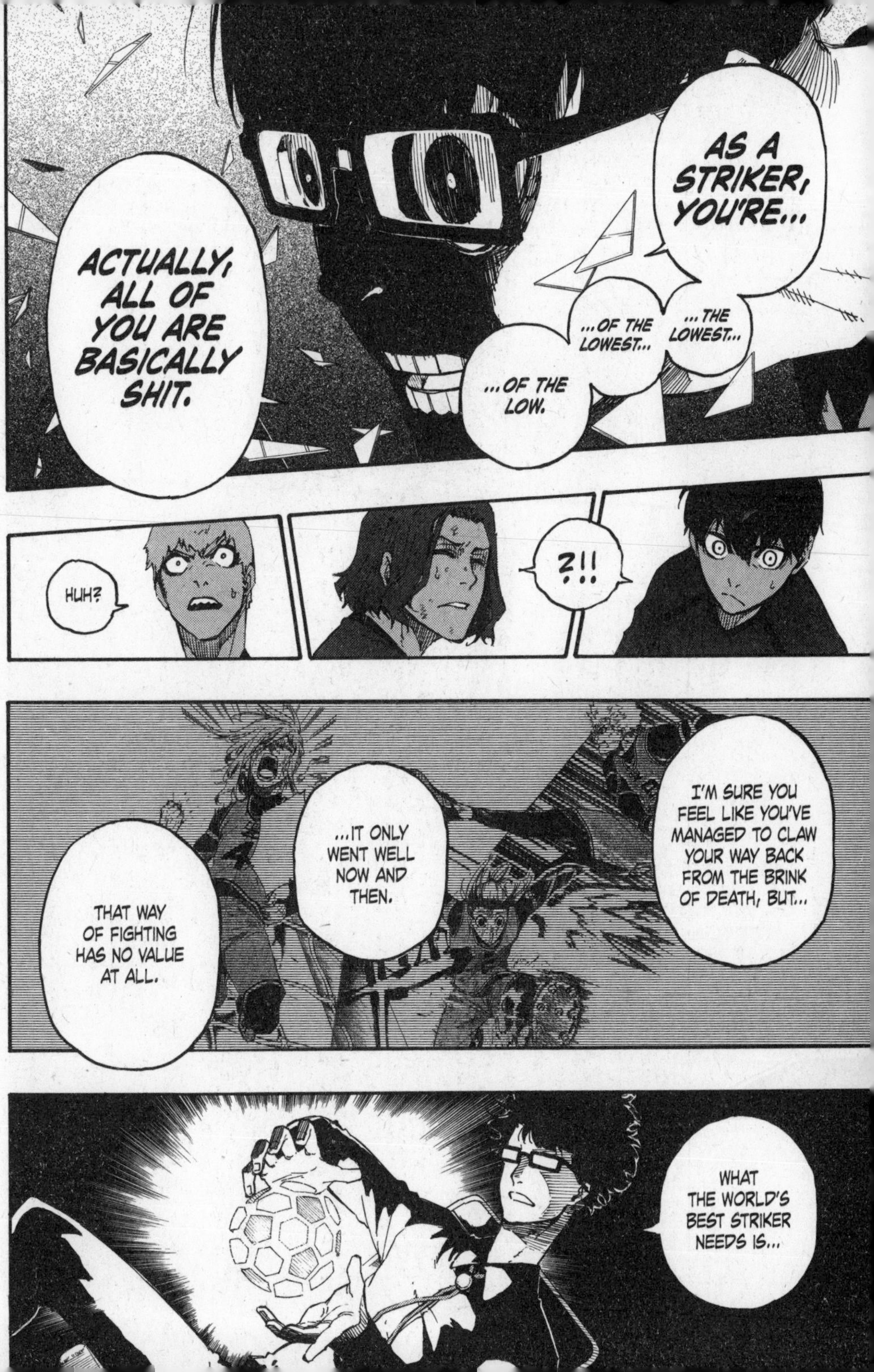
AS A STRIKER, YOU'RE...
...THE LOWEST...
...OF THE LOWEST...
...OF THE LOW.
ACTUALLY, ALL OF YOU ARE BASICALLY SHIT.
?!!
HUH?
I'M SURE YOU FEEL LIKE YOU'VE MANAGED TO CLAW YOUR WAY BACK FROM THE BRINK OF DEATH, BUT...
...IT ONLY WENT WELL NOW AND THEN.
THAT WAY OF FIGHTING HAS NO VALUE AT ALL.
WHAT THE WORLD'S BEST STRIKER NEEDS IS...

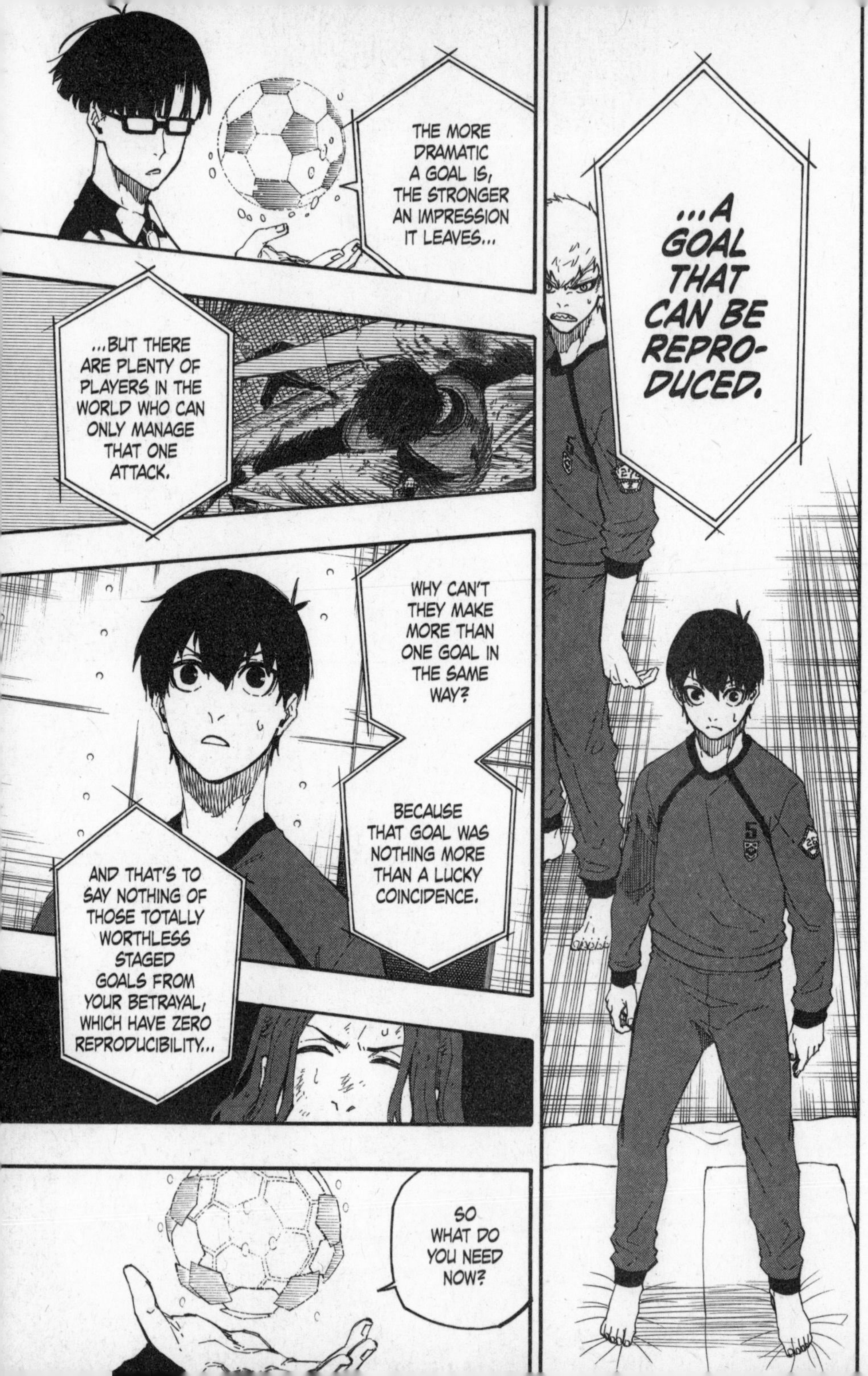
...A GOAL THAT CAN BE REPRODUCED.
THE MORE DRAMATIC A GOAL IS, THE STRONGER AN IMPRESSION IT LEAVES...
...BUT THERE ARE PLENTY OF PLAYERS IN THE WORLD WHO CAN ONLY MANAGE THAT ONE ATTACK.
WHY CAN'T THEY MAKE MORE THAN ONE GOAL IN THE SAME WAY?
BECAUSE THAT GOAL WAS NOTHING MORE THAN A LUCKY COINCIDENCE.
AND THAT'S TO SAY NOTHING OF THOSE TOTALLY WORTHLESS STAGED GOALS FROM YOUR BETRAYAL, WHICH HAVE ZERO REPRODUCIBILITY...
SO WHAT DO YOU NEED NOW?

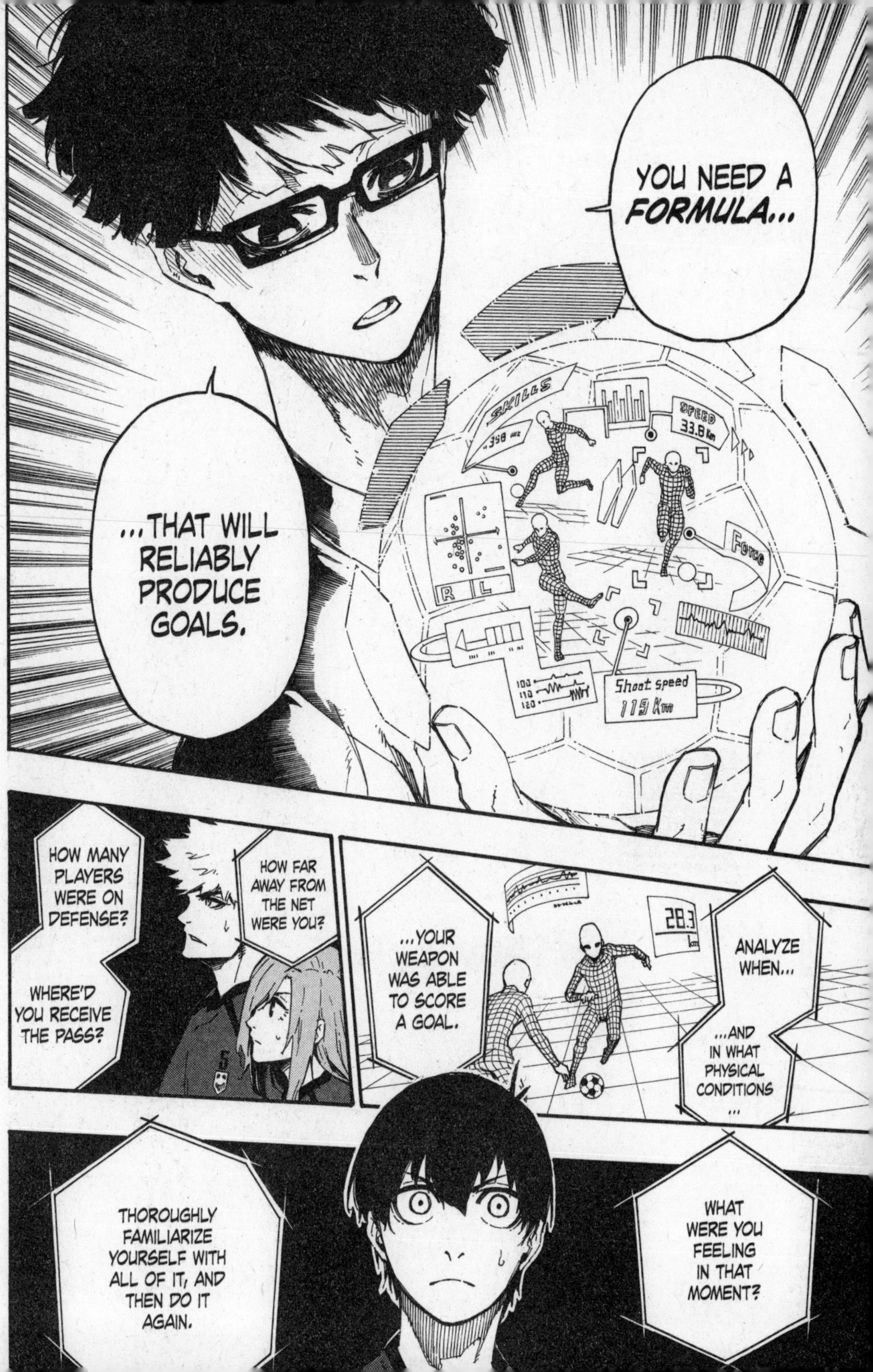
YOU NEED A *FORMULA*...
...THAT WILL RELIABLY PRODUCE GOALS.
SKILLS
SPEED 33.8 Km
Force
R L
Shoot speed 119 Km
ANALYZE WHEN...
...YOUR WEAPON WAS ABLE TO SCORE A GOAL.
28.3 km
...AND IN WHAT PHYSICAL CONDITIONS ...
HOW FAR AWAY FROM THE NET WERE YOU?
HOW MANY PLAYERS WERE ON DEFENSE?
WHERE'D YOU RECEIVE THE PASS?
WHAT WERE YOU FEELING IN THAT MOMENT?
THOROUGHLY FAMILIARIZE YOURSELF WITH ALL OF IT, AND THEN DO IT AGAIN.

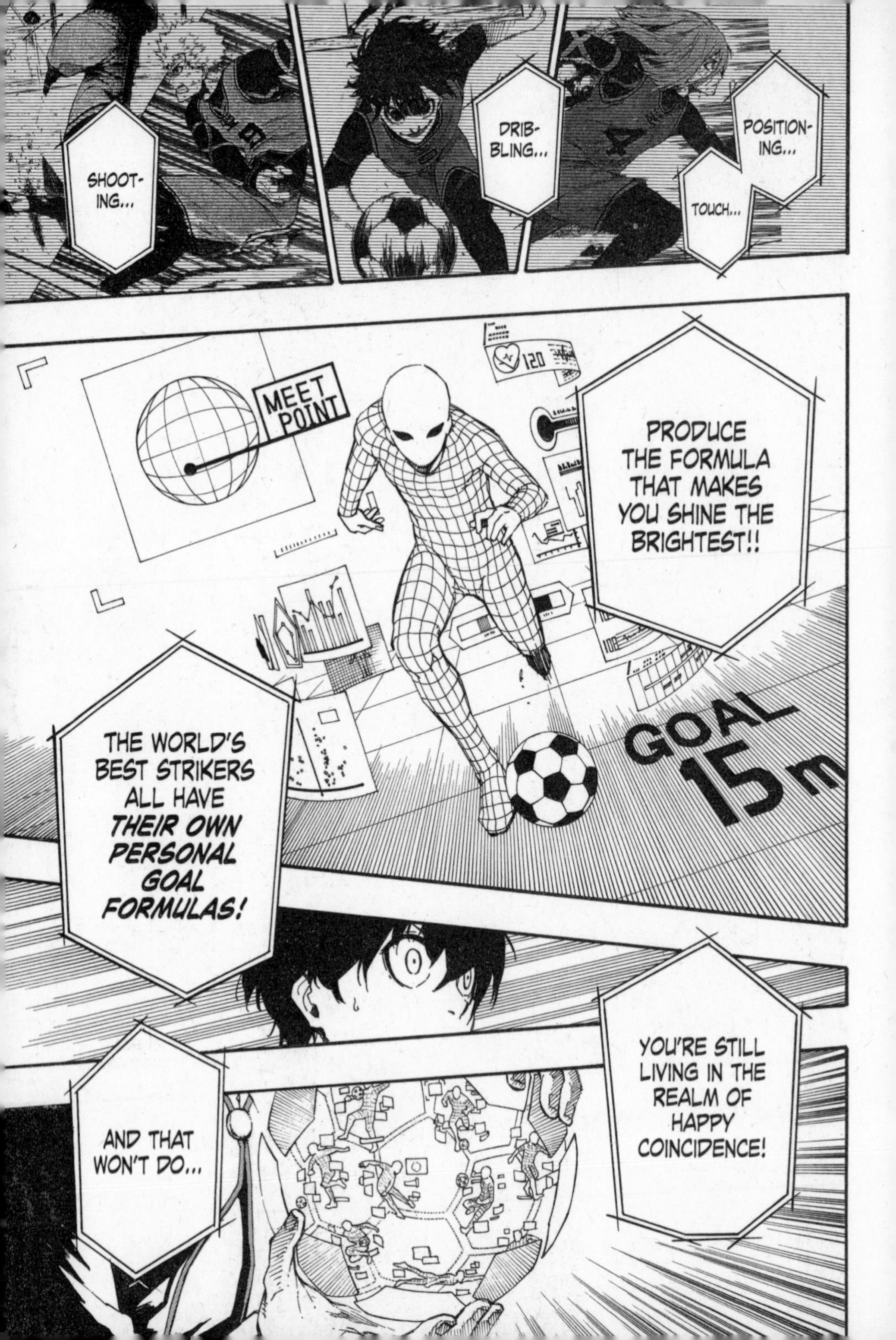
POSITION-ING...
TOUCH...
DRIB-BLING...
SHOOT-ING...
PRODUCE THE FORMULA THAT MAKES YOU SHINE THE BRIGHTEST!!
120
MEET POINT
GOAL 15m
THE WORLD'S BEST STRIKERS ALL HAVE *THEIR OWN PERSONAL GOAL FORMULAS!*
YOU'RE STILL LIVING IN THE REALM OF HAPPY COINCIDENCE!
AND THAT WON'T DO...

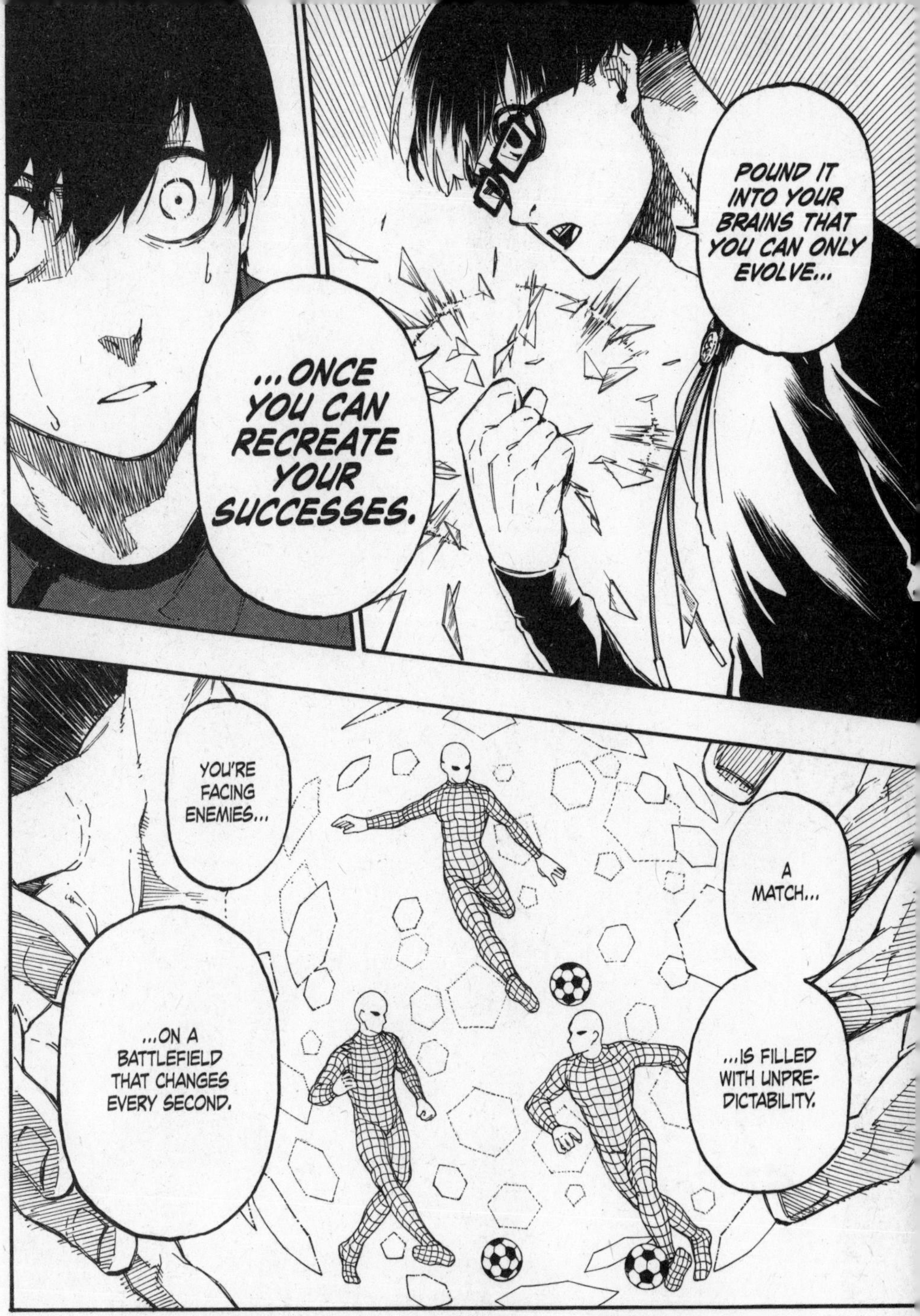
POUND IT INTO YOUR BRAINS THAT YOU CAN ONLY EVOLVE...
...ONCE YOU CAN RECREATE YOUR SUCCESSES.
A MATCH...
...IS FILLED WITH UNPRE-DICTABILITY.
YOU'RE FACING ENEMIES...
...ON A BATTLEFIELD THAT CHANGES EVERY SECOND.

THE ONE WHO CAN PROVE THE FORMULA THEY'VE CREATED FOR THEMSELVES...

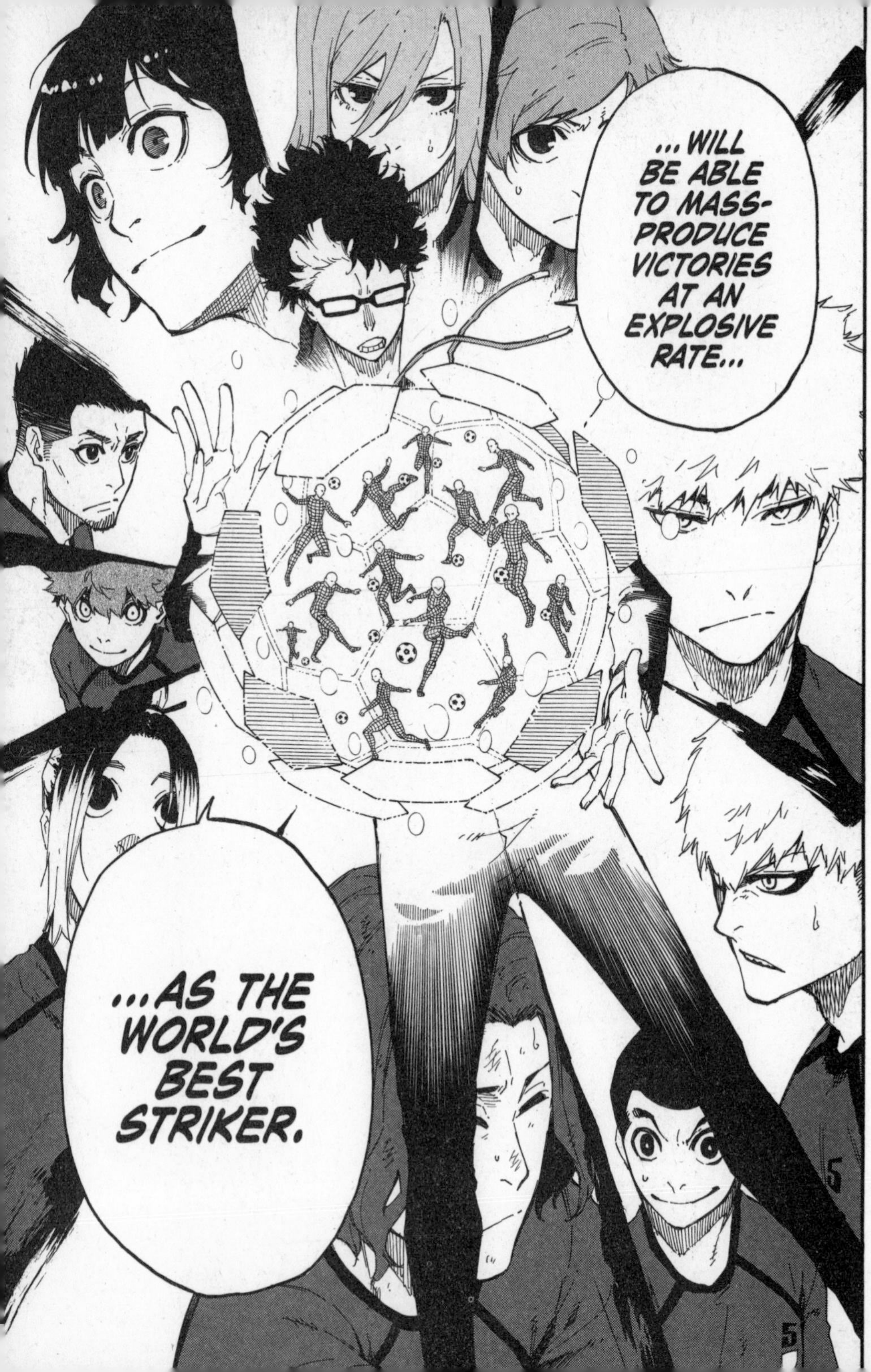
...WILL BE ABLE TO MASS-PRODUCE VICTORIES AT AN EXPLOSIVE RATE...
...AS THE WORLD'S BEST STRIKER.

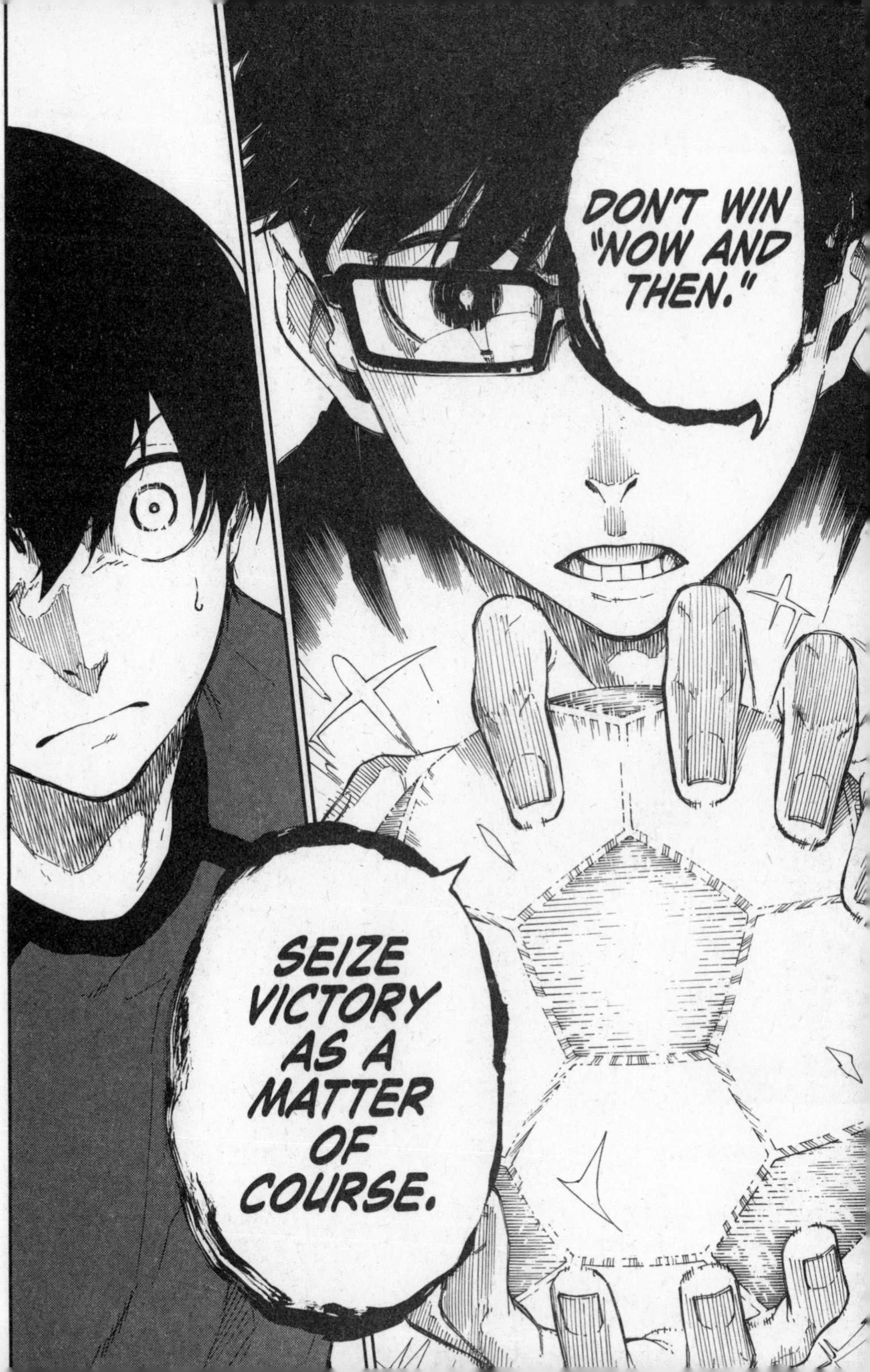
DON'T WIN "NOW AND THEN."
SEIZE VICTORY AS A MATTER OF COURSE.

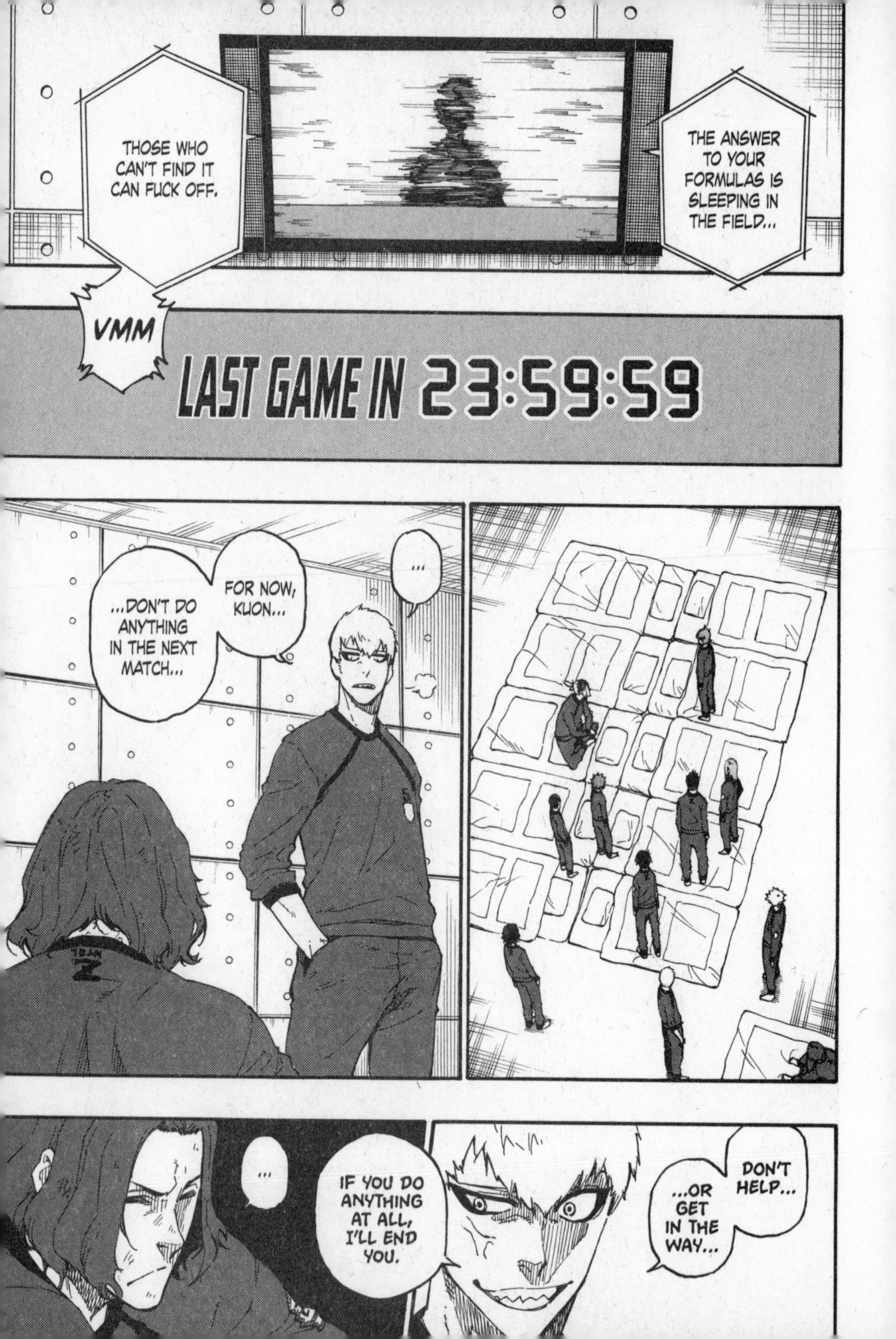
THE ANSWER TO YOUR FORMULAS IS SLEEPING IN THE FIELD...
THOSE WHO CAN'T FIND IT CAN FUCK OFF.
VMM
LAST GAME IN 23:59:59
...
FOR NOW, KUON...
...DON'T DO ANYTHING IN THE NEXT MATCH...
DON'T HELP...
...OR GET IN THE WAY...
IF YOU DO ANYTHING AT ALL, I'LL END YOU.
...

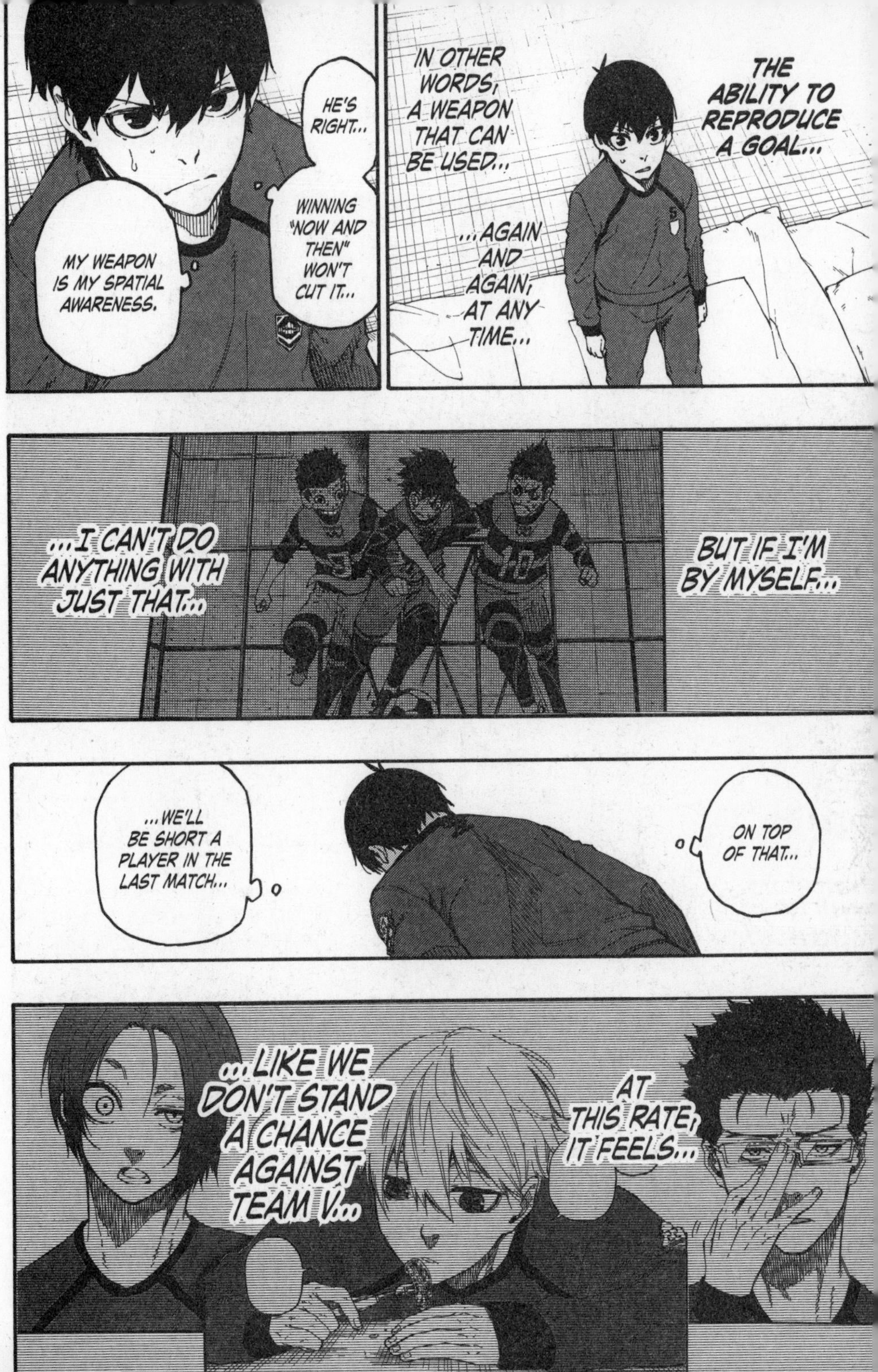
THE ABILITY TO REPRODUCE A GOAL...
IN OTHER WORDS, A WEAPON THAT CAN BE USED...
...AGAIN AND AGAIN, AT ANY TIME...
HE'S RIGHT...
WINNING "NOW AND THEN" WON'T CUT IT...
MY WEAPON IS MY SPATIAL AWARENESS.
BUT IF I'M BY MYSELF...
...I CAN'T DO ANYTHING WITH JUST THAT...
ON TOP OF THAT...
...WE'LL BE SHORT A PLAYER IN THE LAST MATCH...
AT THIS RATE, IT FEELS...
...LIKE WE DON'T STAND A CHANCE AGAINST TEAM V...

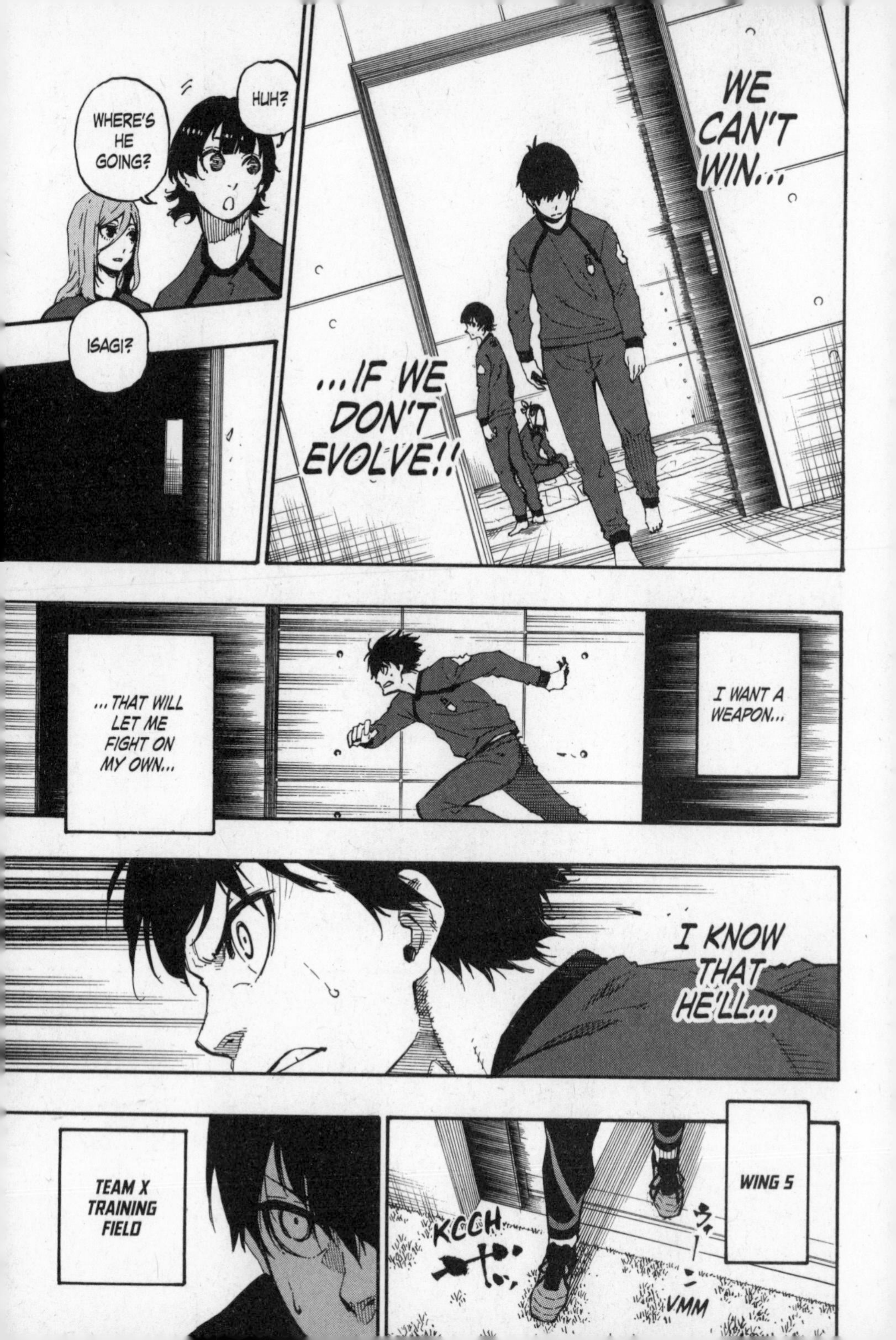
WE CAN'T WIN...
...IF WE DON'T EVOLVE!!
HUH?
WHERE'S HE GOING?
ISAGI?
I WANT A WEAPON...
...THAT WILL LET ME FIGHT ON MY OWN...
I KNOW THAT HE'LL...
WING 5
KCCH
VMM
TEAM X TRAINING FIELD

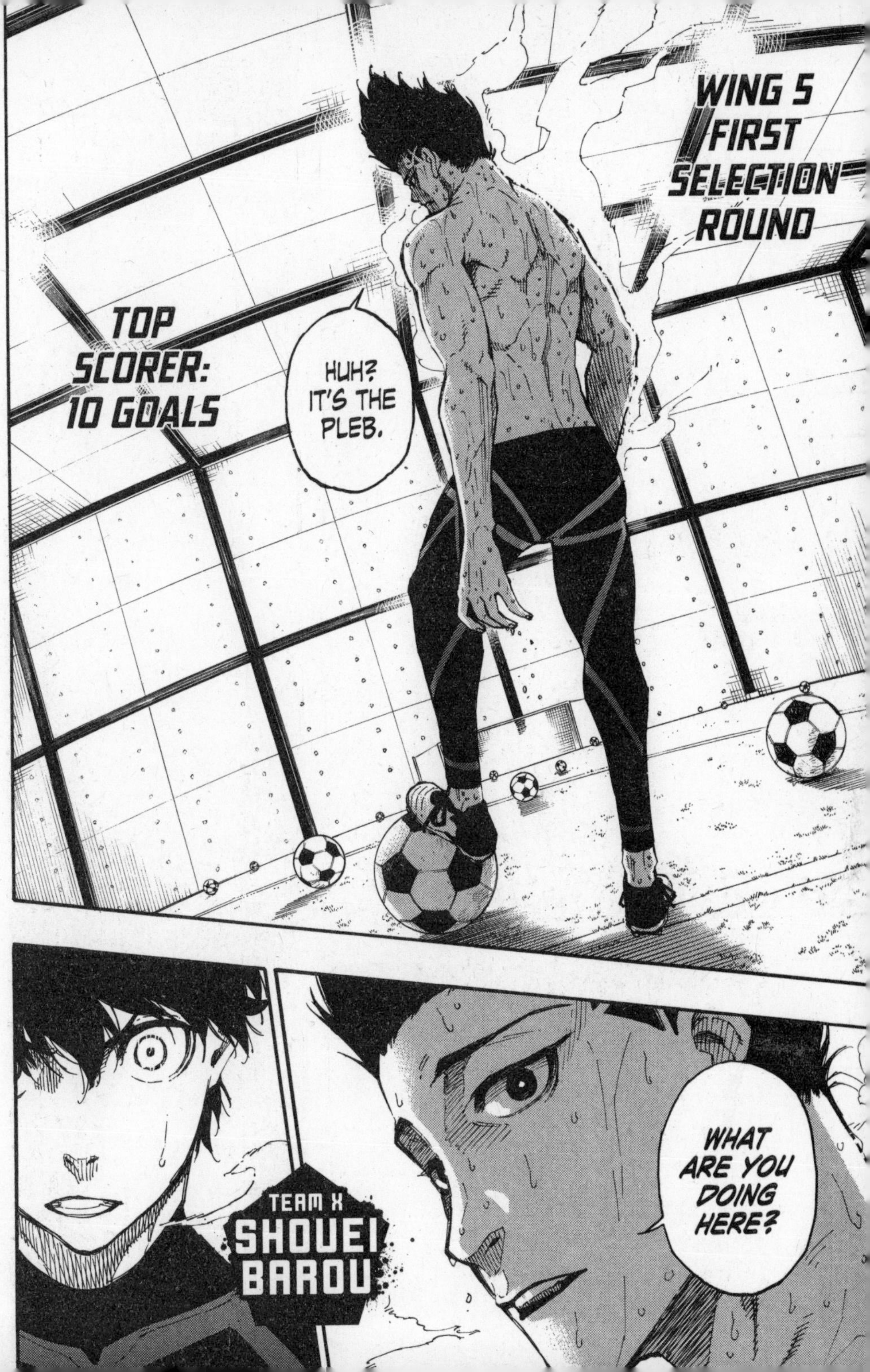
WING 5 / FIRST SELECTION ROUND
HUH? IT'S THE PLEB.
TOP SCORER: 10 GOALS
WHAT ARE YOU DOING HERE?
TEAM X SHOUEI BAROU

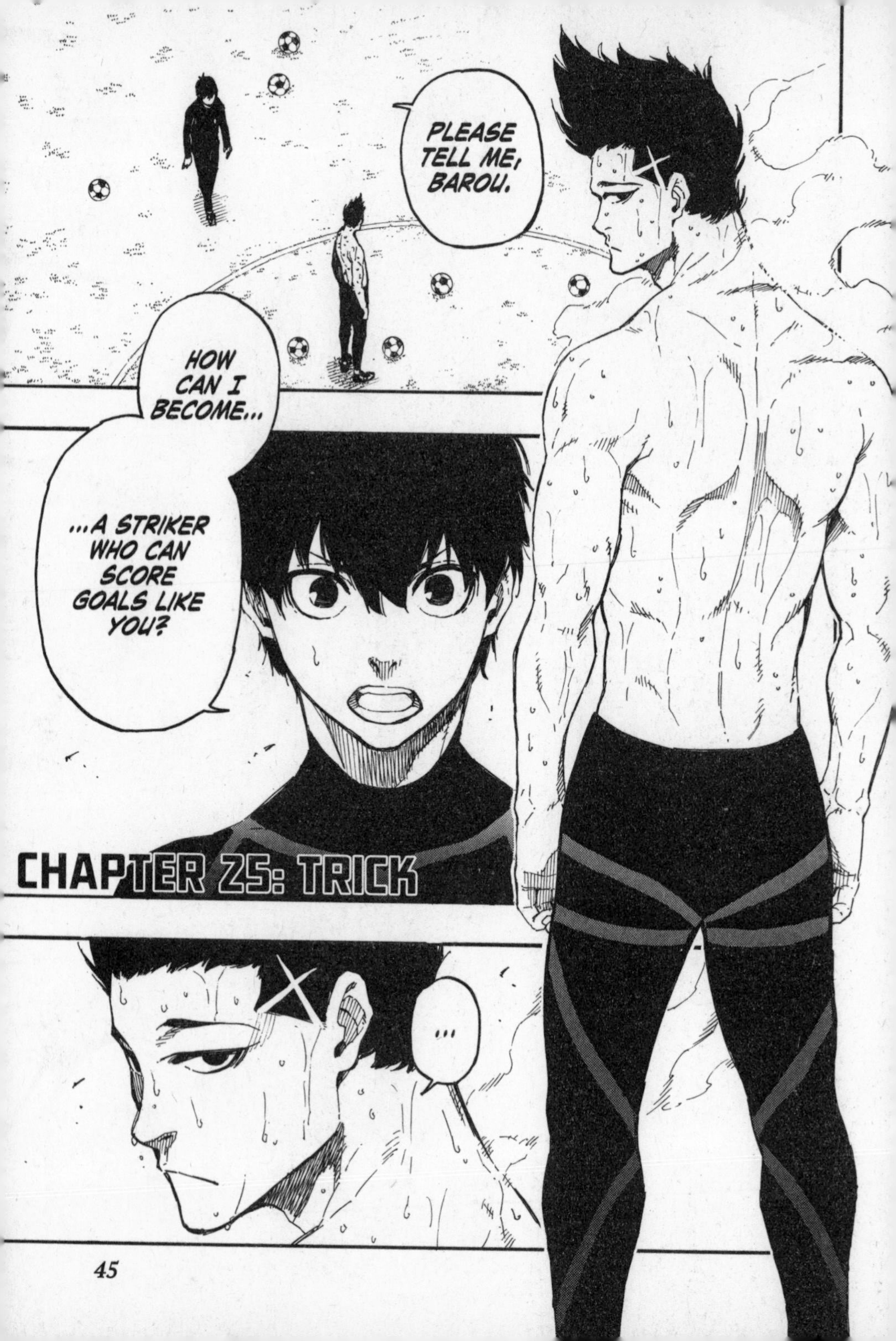
PLEASE TELL ME, BAROU.
HOW CAN I BECOME...
...A STRIKER WHO CAN SCORE GOALS LIKE YOU?
CHAPTER 25: TRICK
...

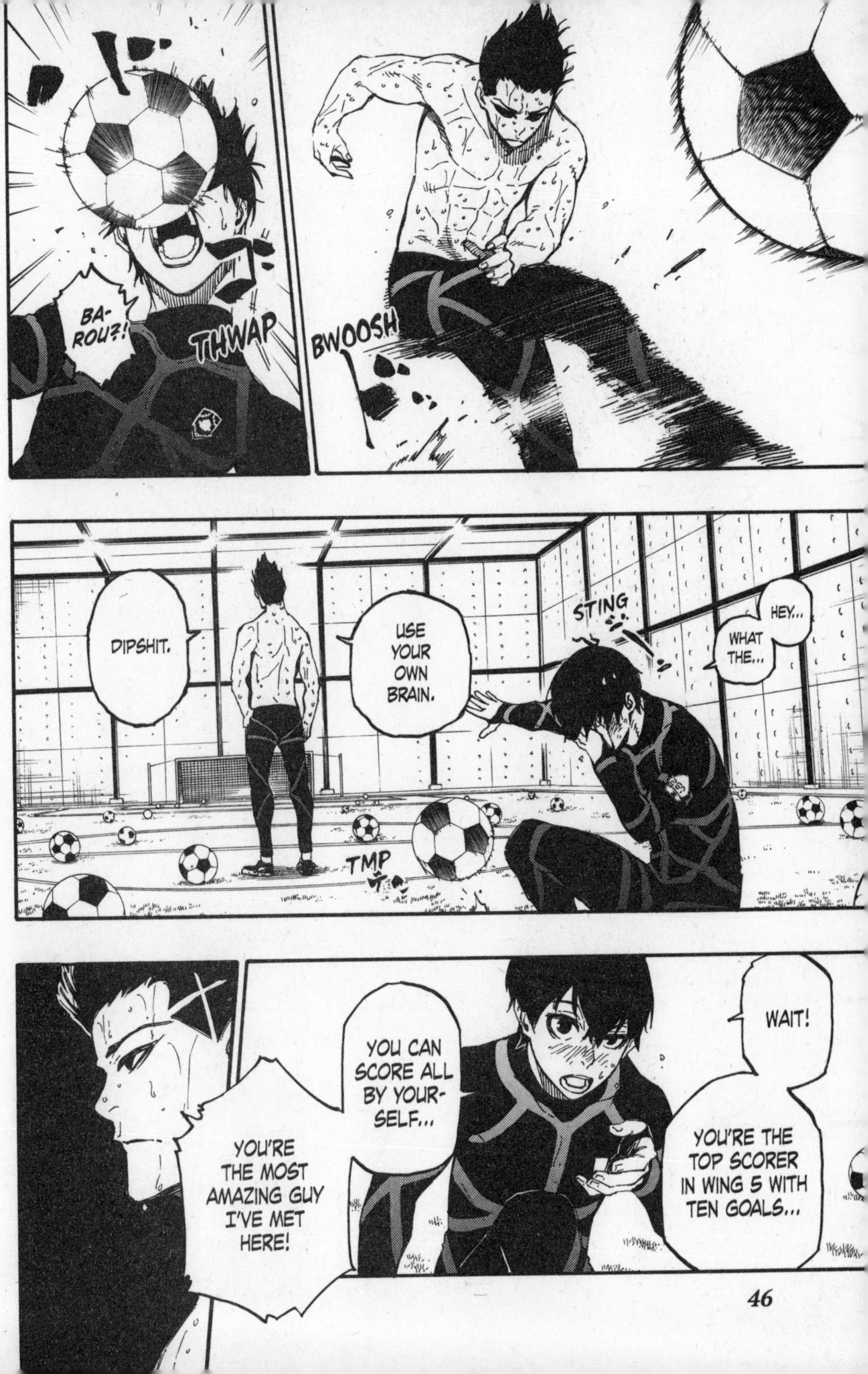
BWOOSH
THWAP
BA-
ROU?!
HEY...
WHAT THE...
STING
USE YOUR OWN BRAIN.
DIPSHIT.
TMP
WAIT!
YOU'RE THE TOP SCORER IN WING 5 WITH TEN GOALS...
YOU CAN SCORE ALL BY YOUR-SELF...
YOU'RE THE MOST AMAZING GUY I'VE MET HERE!

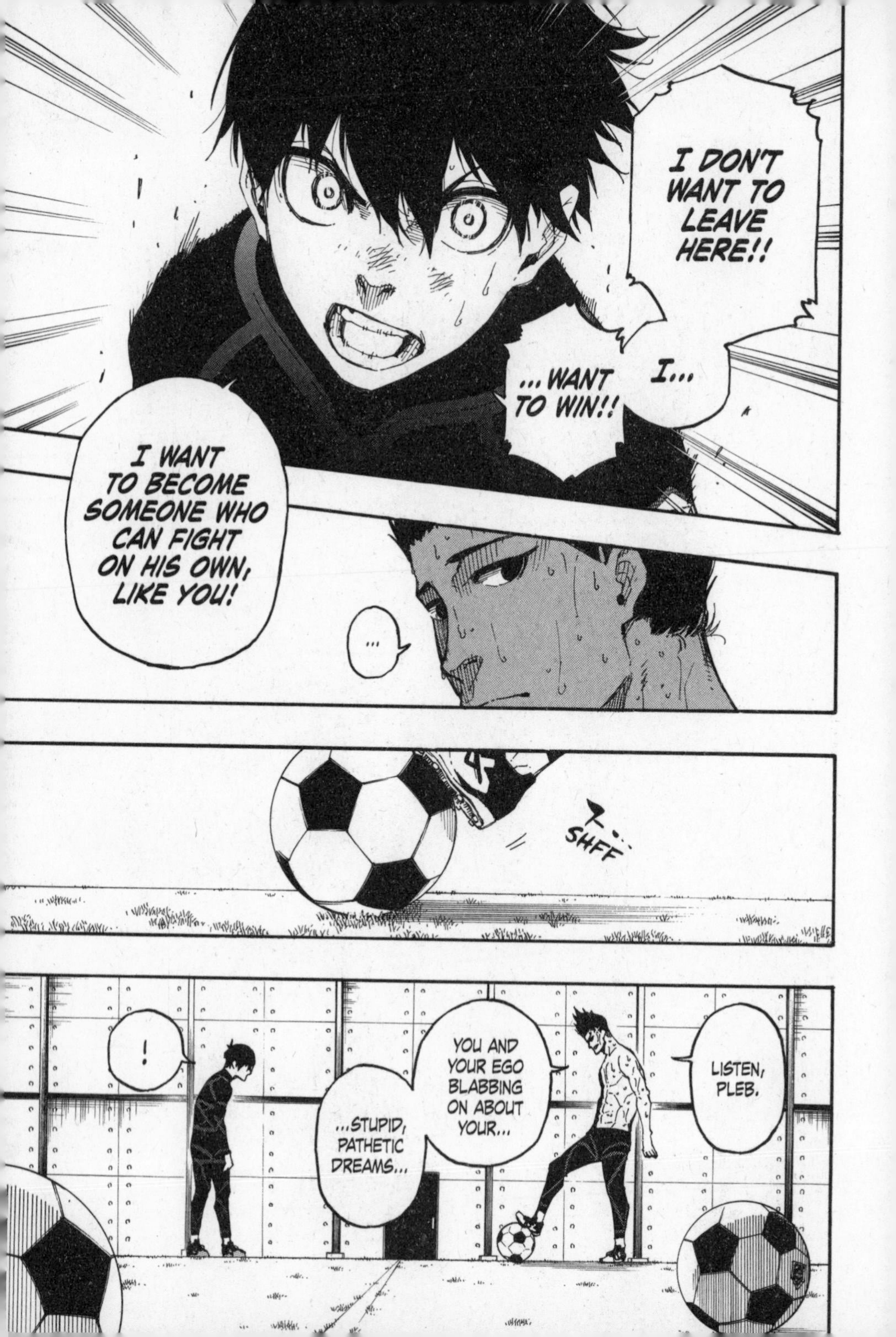
I DON'T WANT TO LEAVE HERE!!
I...
...WANT TO WIN!!
I WANT TO BECOME SOMEONE WHO CAN FIGHT ON HIS OWN, LIKE YOU!
...
SHFF
LISTEN, PLEB.
YOU AND YOUR EGO BLABBING ON ABOUT YOUR...
...STUPID, PATHETIC DREAMS...
!

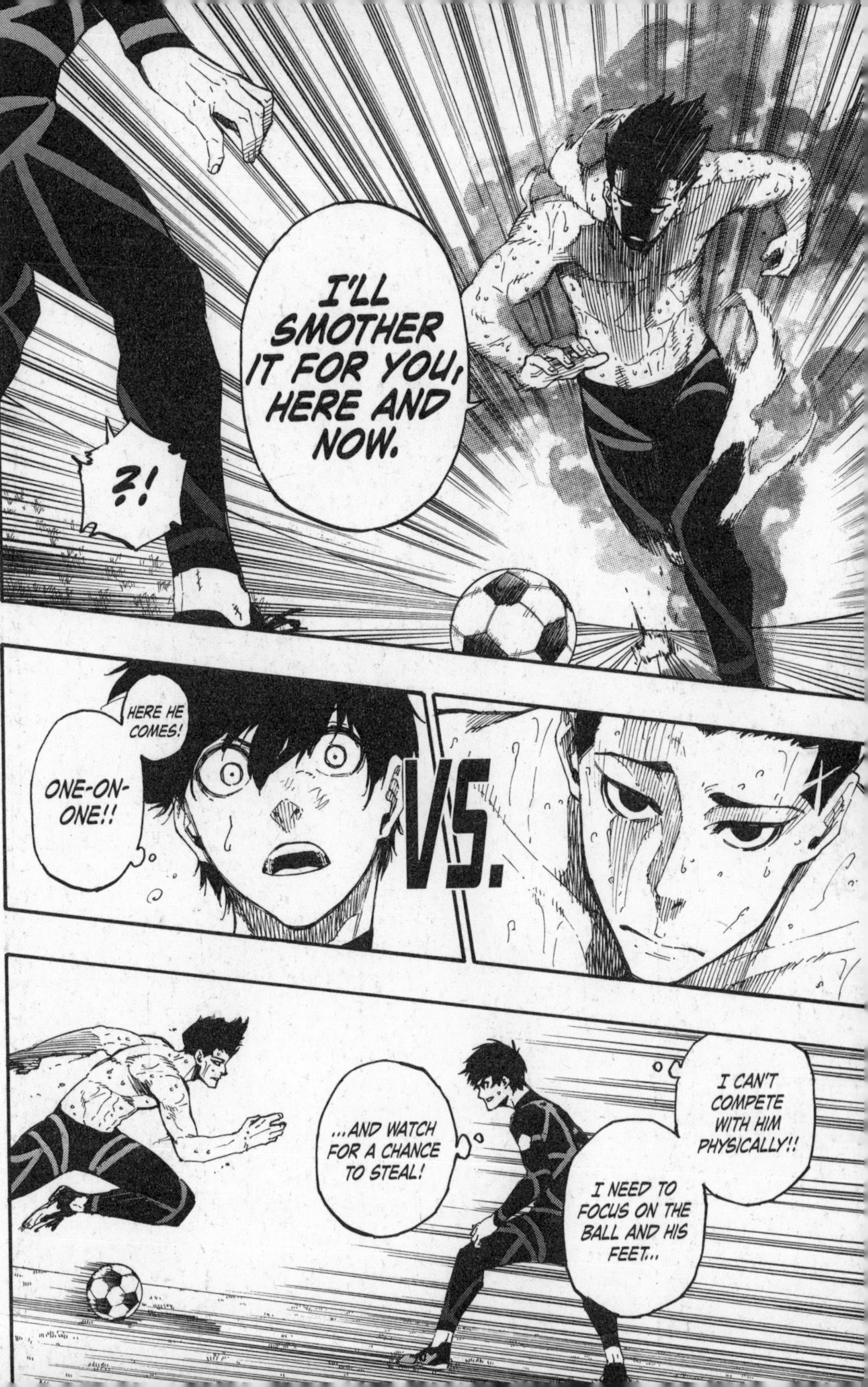
I'LL SMOTHER IT FOR YOU, HERE AND NOW.
?!
VS.
HERE HE COMES!
ONE-ON-ONE!!
I CAN'T COMPETE WITH HIM PHYSICALLY!!
I NEED TO FOCUS ON THE BALL AND HIS FEET...
...AND WATCH FOR A CHANCE TO STEAL!

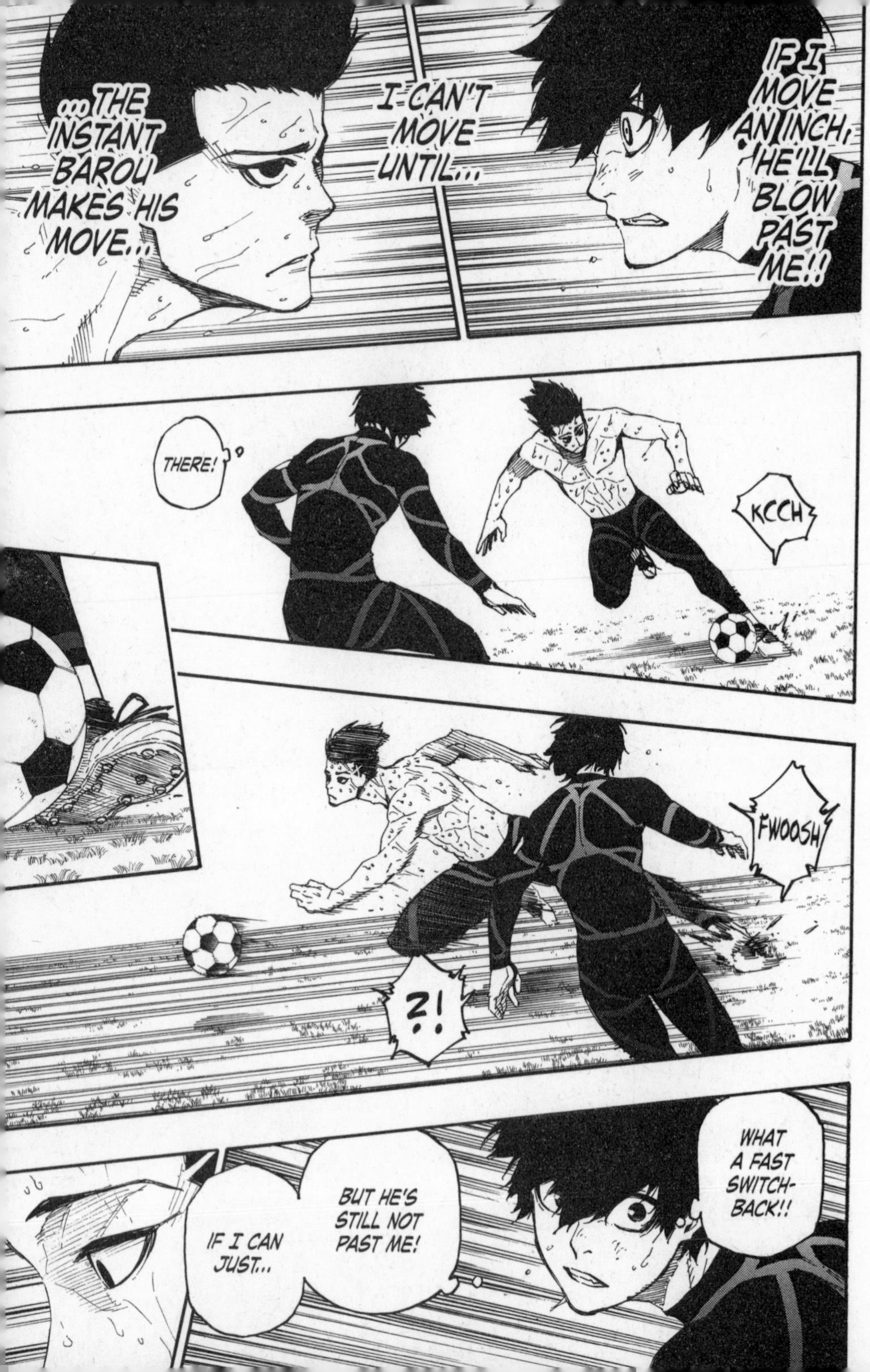
IF I MOVE AN INCH, HE'LL BLOW PAST ME!!
I CAN'T MOVE UNTIL...
...THE INSTANT BAROU MAKES HIS MOVE...
THERE!
KCCH
FWOOSH
?!
WHAT A FAST SWITCH-BACK!!
BUT HE'S STILL NOT PAST ME!
IF I CAN JUST...

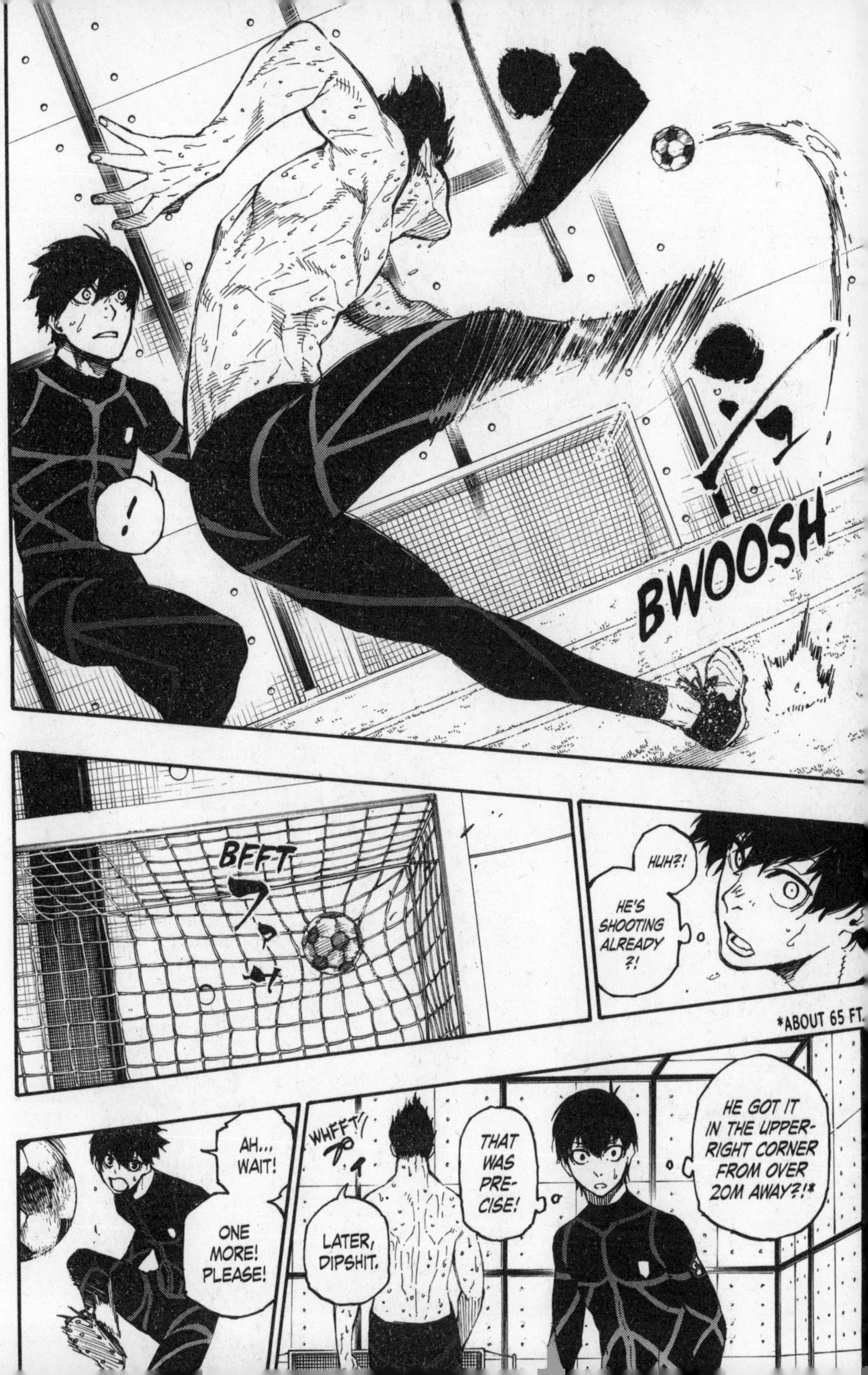
!
BWOOSH
HUH?!
HE'S SHOOTING ALREADY?!
BFFT
HE GOT IT IN THE UPPER-RIGHT CORNER FROM OVER 20M AWAY?!*
THAT WAS PRECISE!
WHFFT
LATER, DIPSHIT.
AH... WAIT!
ONE MORE! PLEASE!
*ABOUT 65 FT.

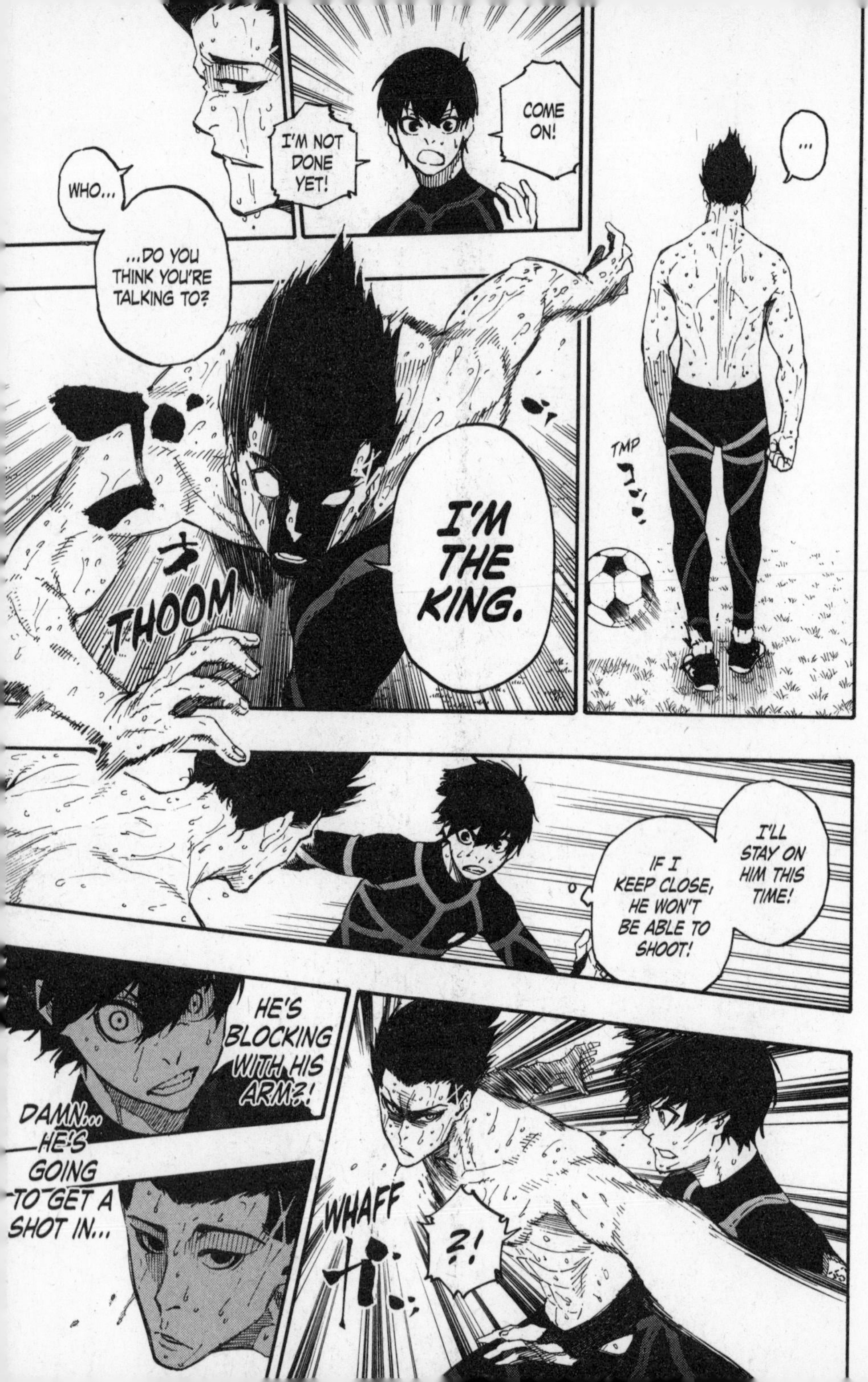
...
TMP
COME ON!
I'M NOT DONE YET!
WHO...
...DO YOU THINK YOU'RE TALKING TO?
I'M THE KING.
THOOM
I'LL STAY ON HIM THIS TIME!
IF I KEEP CLOSE, HE WON'T BE ABLE TO SHOOT!
?!
WHAFF
HE'S BLOCKING WITH HIS ARM?!
DAMN... HE'S GOING TO GET A SHOT IN...

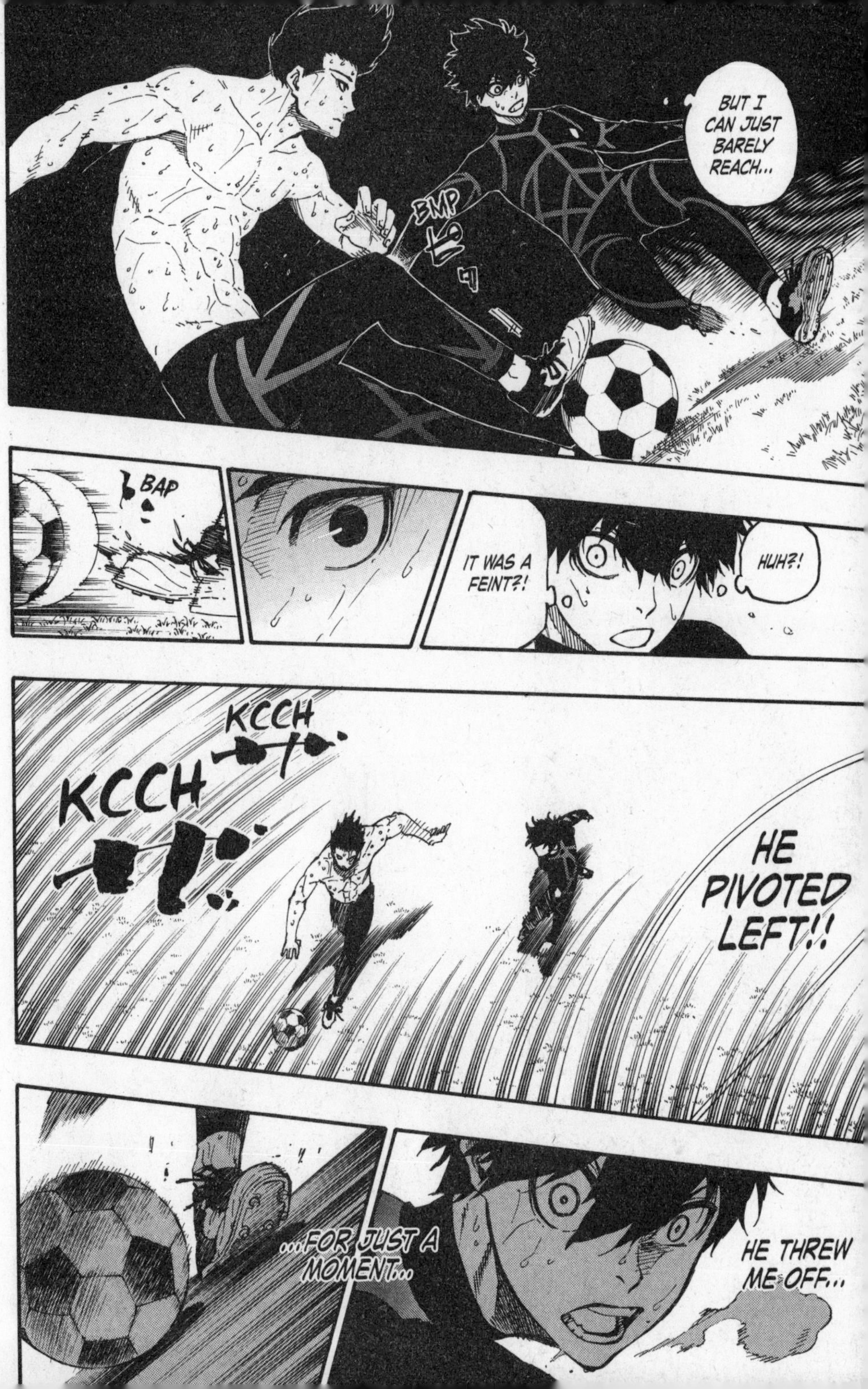
BUT I CAN JUST BARELY REACH...
BMP
HUH?!
IT WAS A FEINT?!
BAP
HE PIVOTED LEFT!!
KCCH
KCCH
HE THREW ME OFF...
...FOR JUST A MOMENT...

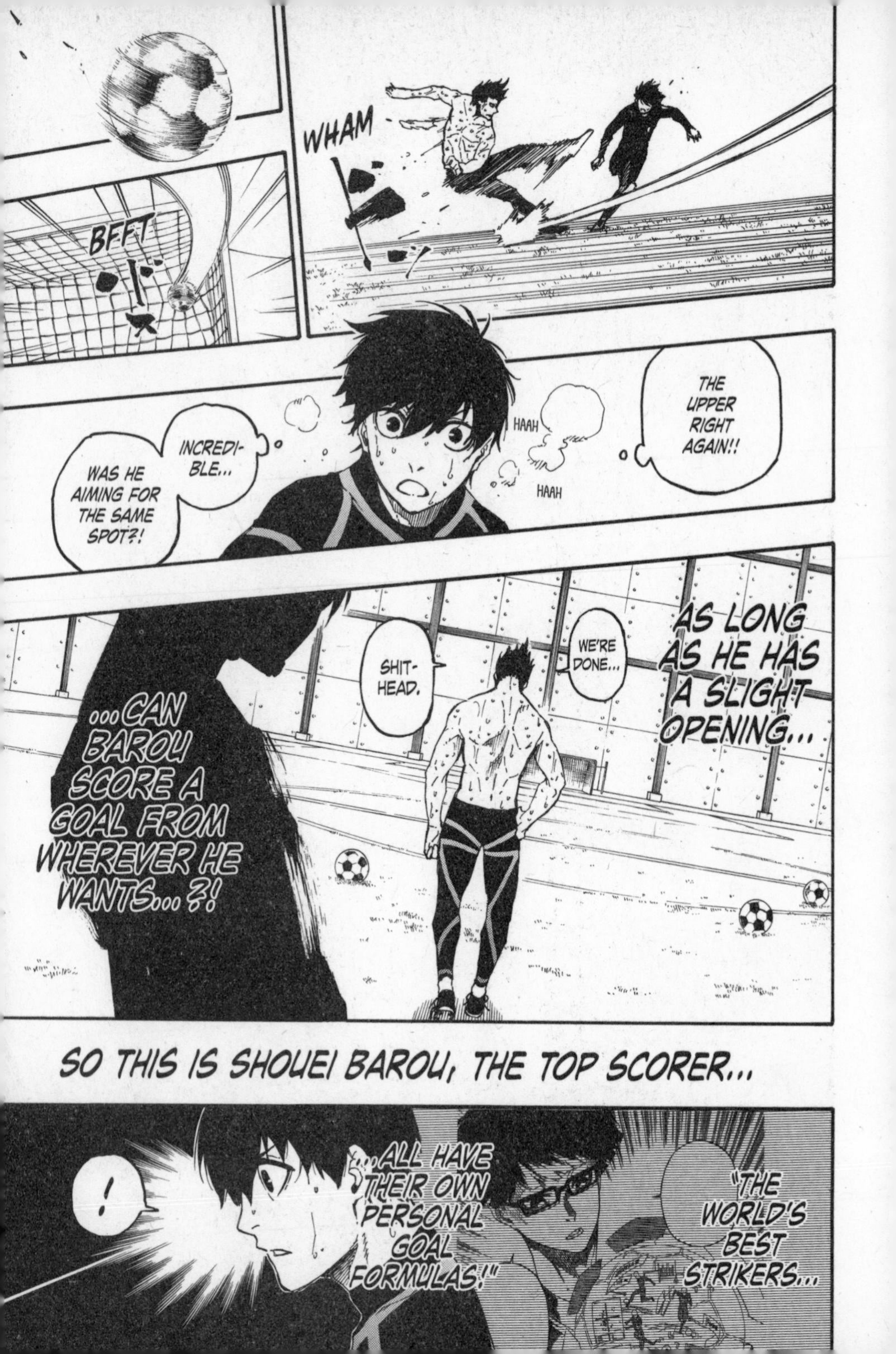
WHAM
BFFT
THE UPPER RIGHT AGAIN!!
HAAH
HAAH
INCREDIBLE...
WAS HE AIMING FOR THE SAME SPOT?!
AS LONG AS HE HAS A SLIGHT OPENING...
WE'RE DONE...
SHIT-HEAD.
...CAN BAROU SCORE A GOAL FROM WHEREVER HE WANTS...?!
SO THIS IS SHOUEI BAROU, THE TOP SCORER...
"THE WORLD'S BEST STRIKERS...
...ALL HAVE THEIR OWN PERSONAL GOAL FORMULAS!"
!

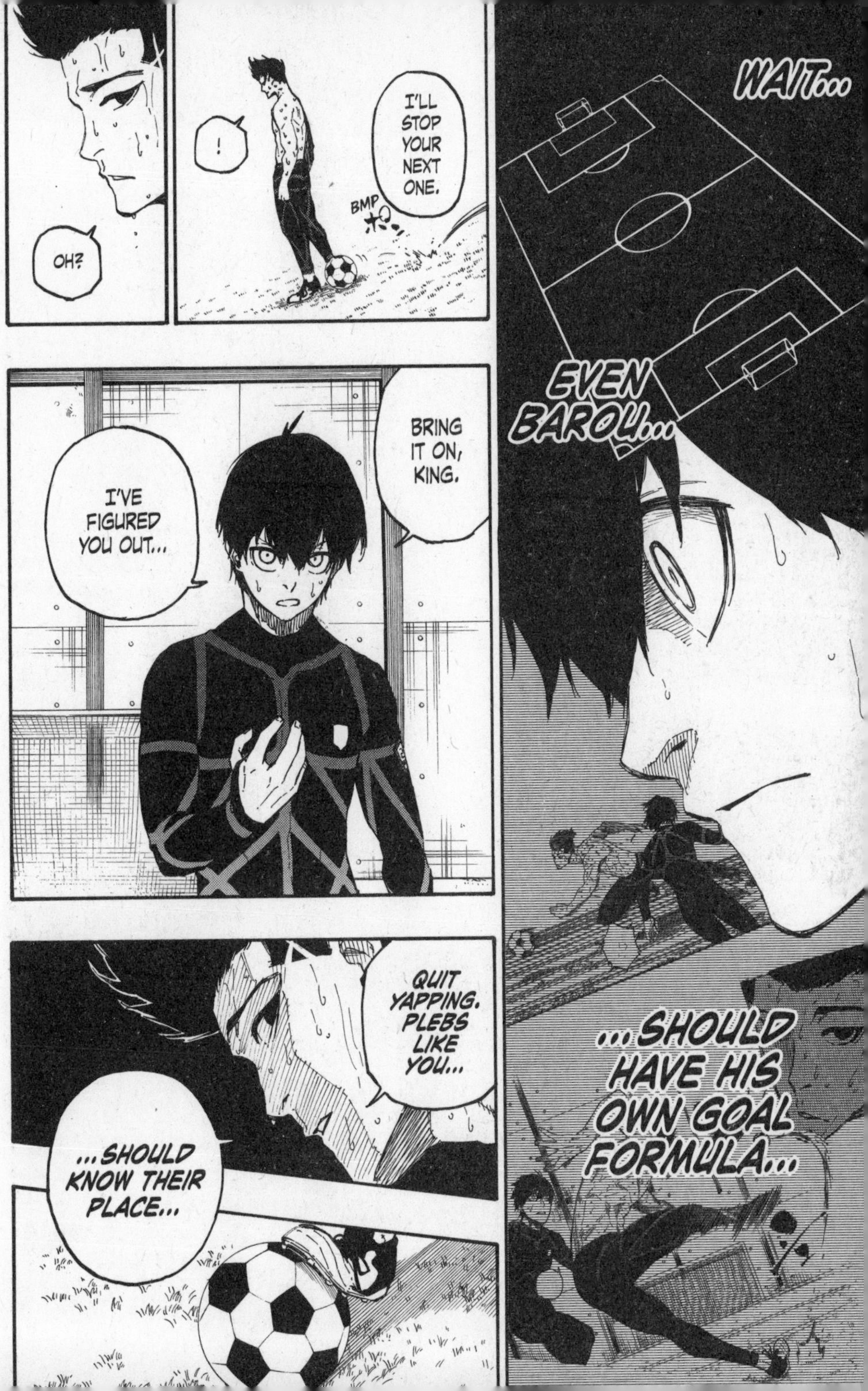
WAIT...
EVEN BAROU...
...SHOULD HAVE HIS OWN GOAL FORMULA...
I'LL STOP YOUR NEXT ONE.
!
BMP
OH?
BRING IT ON, KING.
I'VE FIGURED YOU OUT...
QUIT YAPPING. PLEBS LIKE YOU...
...SHOULD KNOW THEIR PLACE...

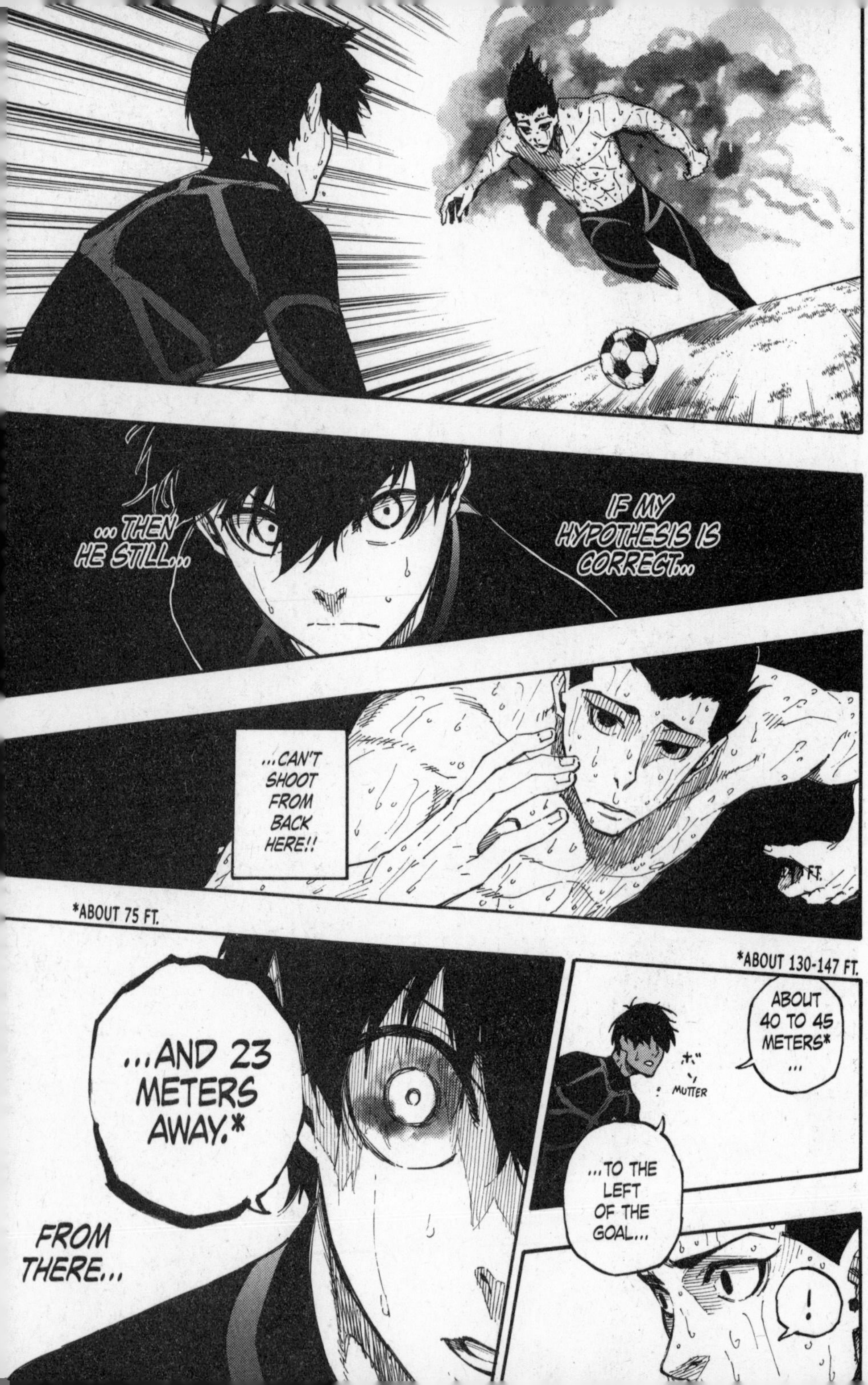
IF MY HYPOTHESIS IS CORRECT...
...THEN HE STILL...
...CAN'T SHOOT FROM BACK HERE!!
*ABOUT 130-147 FT.
ABOUT 40 TO 45 METERS* ...
MUTTER
...TO THE LEFT OF THE GOAL...
!
...AND 23 METERS AWAY.*
FROM THERE...
*ABOUT 75 FT.

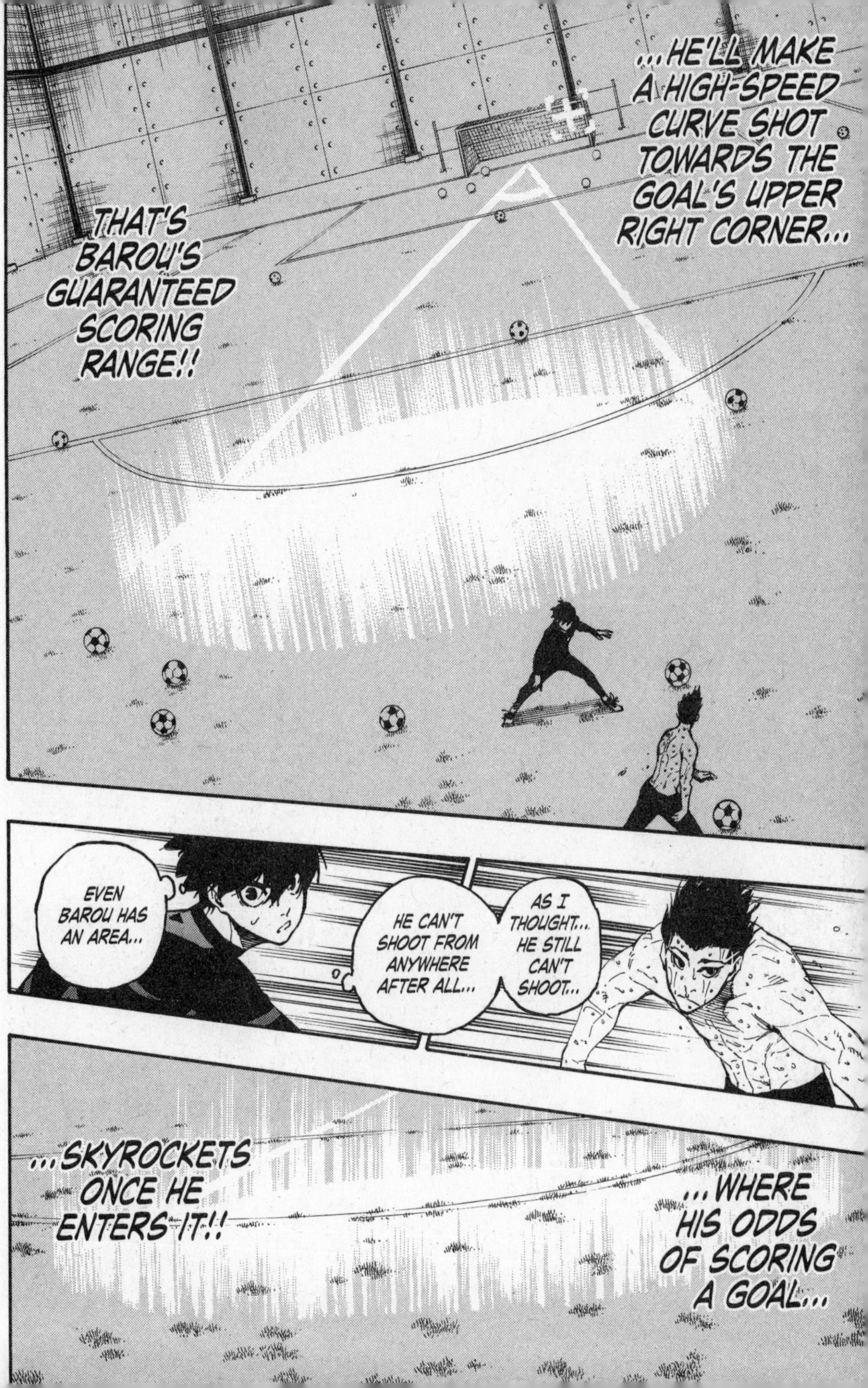
...HE'LL MAKE A HIGH-SPEED CURVE SHOT TOWARDS THE GOAL'S UPPER RIGHT CORNER...
THAT'S BAROU'S GUARANTEED SCORING RANGE!!
AS I THOUGHT... HE STILL CAN'T SHOOT...
HE CAN'T SHOOT FROM ANYWHERE AFTER ALL...
EVEN BAROU HAS AN AREA...
...WHERE HIS ODDS OF SCORING A GOAL...
...SKYROCKETS ONCE HE ENTERS IT!!

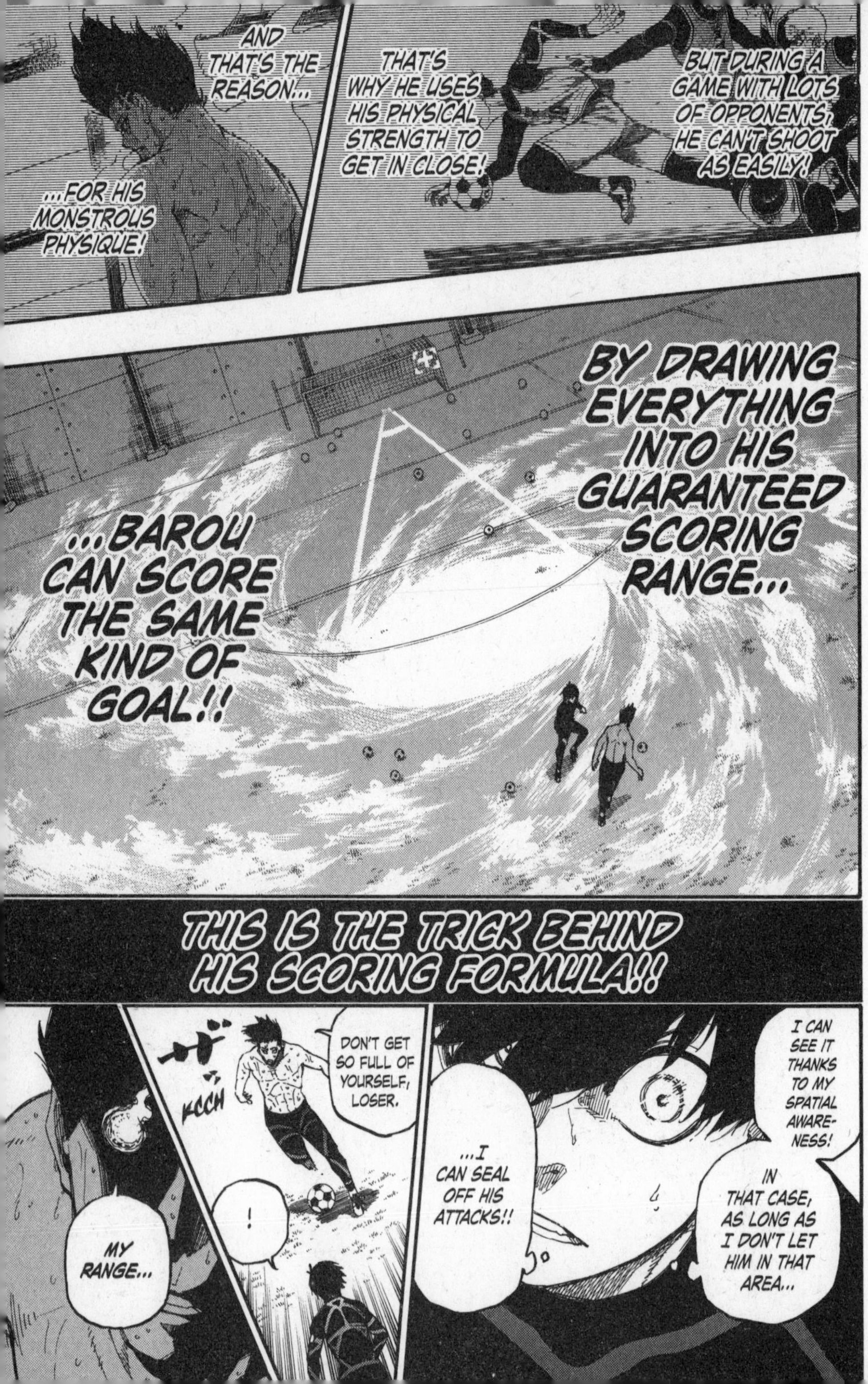
BUT DURING A GAME WITH LOTS OF OPPONENTS, HE CAN'T SHOOT AS EASILY!
THAT'S WHY HE USES HIS PHYSICAL STRENGTH TO GET IN CLOSE!
AND THAT'S THE REASON...
...FOR HIS MONSTROUS PHYSIQUE!
BY DRAWING EVERYTHING INTO HIS GUARANTEED SCORING RANGE...
...BAROU CAN SCORE THE SAME KIND OF GOAL!!
THIS IS THE TRICK BEHIND HIS SCORING FORMULA!!
I CAN SEE IT THANKS TO MY SPATIAL AWARE-NESS!
IN THAT CASE, AS LONG AS I DON'T LET HIM IN THAT AREA...
...I CAN SEAL OFF HIS ATTACKS!!
DON'T GET SO FULL OF YOURSELF, LOSER.
KCCH
!
MY RANGE...

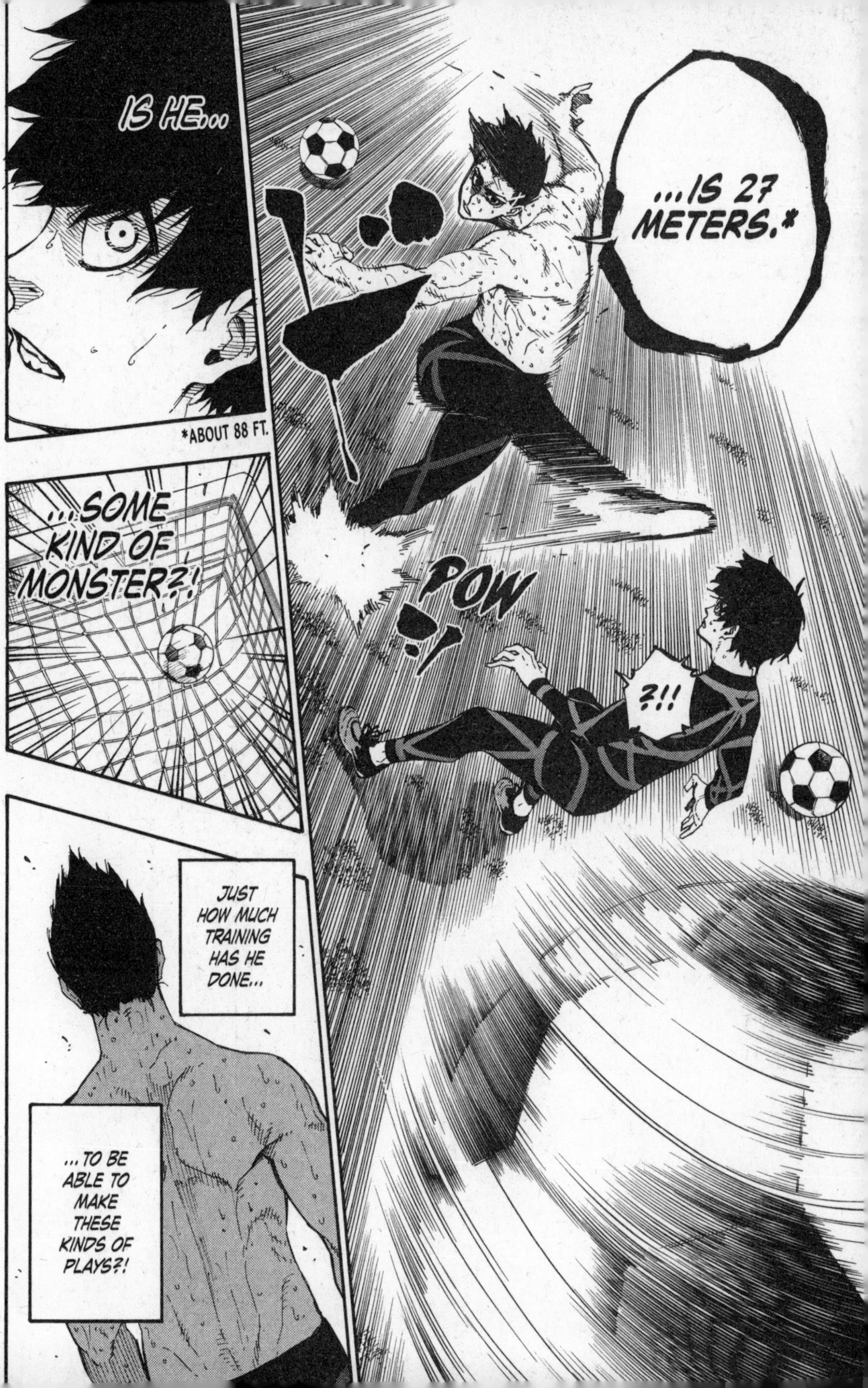
...IS 27 METERS.*
POW
?!!
IS HE...
*ABOUT 88 FT.
...SOME KIND OF MONSTER?!
JUST HOW MUCH TRAINING HAS HE DONE...
...TO BE ABLE TO MAKE THESE KINDS OF PLAYS?!

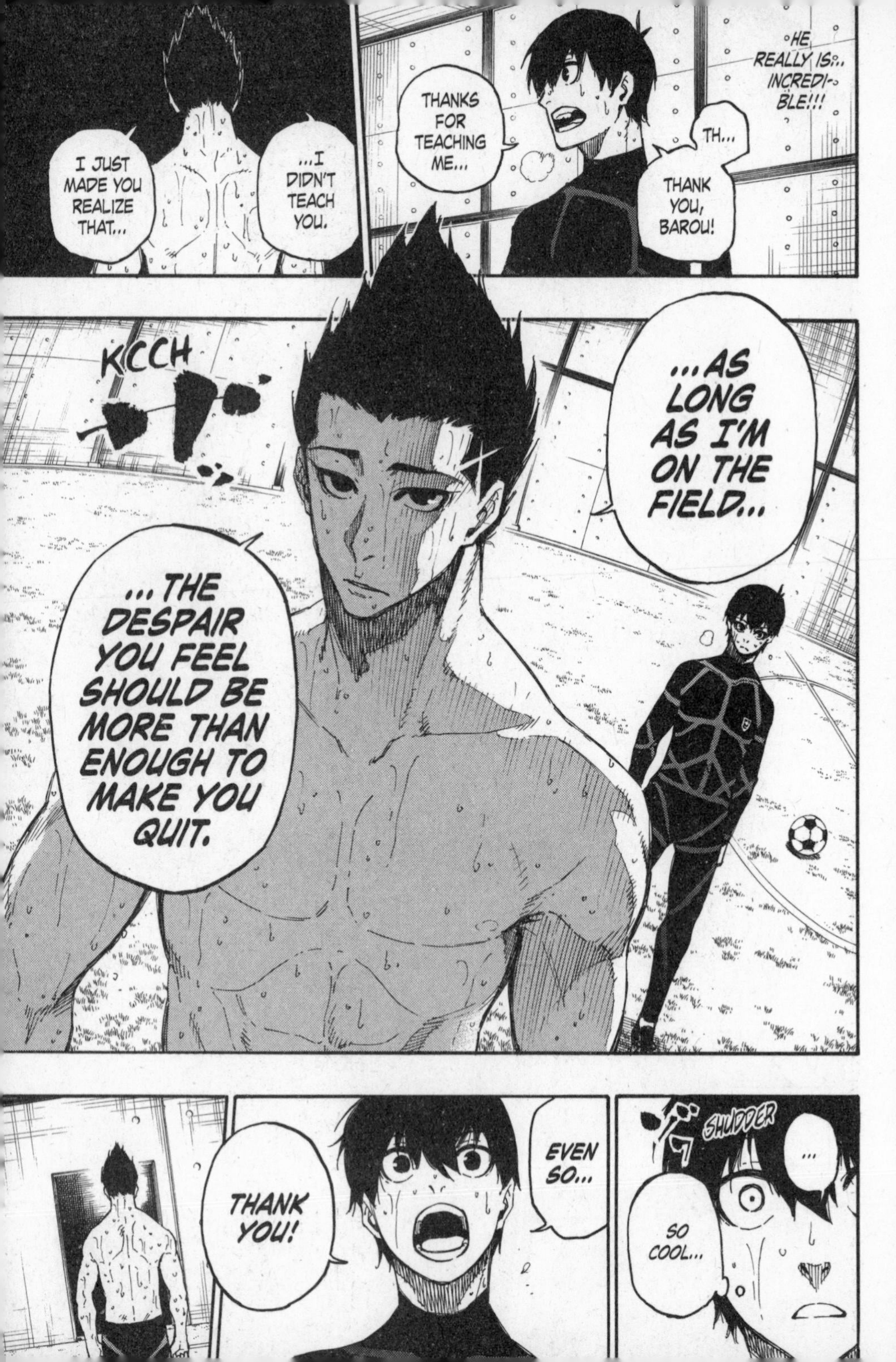
HE REALLY IS... INCREDI-BLE!!!
TH...
THANK YOU, BAROU!
THANKS FOR TEACHING ME...
...I DIDN'T TEACH YOU.
I JUST MADE YOU REALIZE THAT...
...AS LONG AS I'M ON THE FIELD...
KICCH
...THE DESPAIR YOU FEEL SHOULD BE MORE THAN ENOUGH TO MAKE YOU QUIT.
SHUDDER
...
SO COOL...
EVEN SO...
THANK YOU!

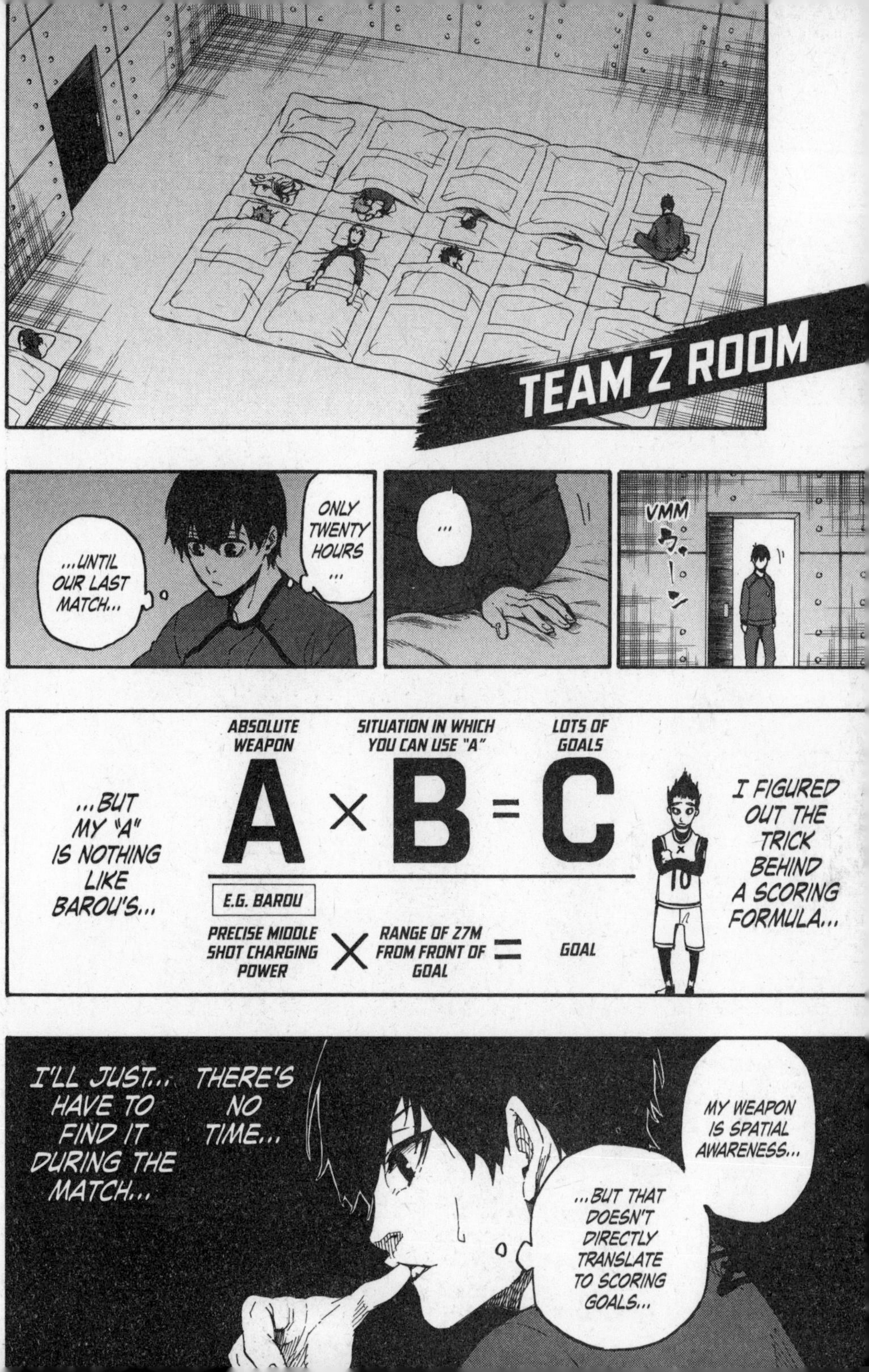
TEAM Z ROOM
VMM
...
ONLY TWENTY HOURS...
...UNTIL OUR LAST MATCH...
I FIGURED OUT THE TRICK BEHIND A SCORING FORMULA...
ABSOLUTE WEAPON
SITUATION IN WHICH YOU CAN USE "A"
LOTS OF GOALS
A × B = C
E.G. BAROU
PRECISE MIDDLE SHOT CHARGING POWER × RANGE OF 27M FROM FRONT OF GOAL = GOAL
...BUT MY "A" IS NOTHING LIKE BAROU'S...
MY WEAPON IS SPATIAL AWARENESS...
...BUT THAT DOESN'T DIRECTLY TRANSLATE TO SCORING GOALS...
THERE'S NO TIME...
I'LL JUST... HAVE TO FIND IT DURING THE MATCH...

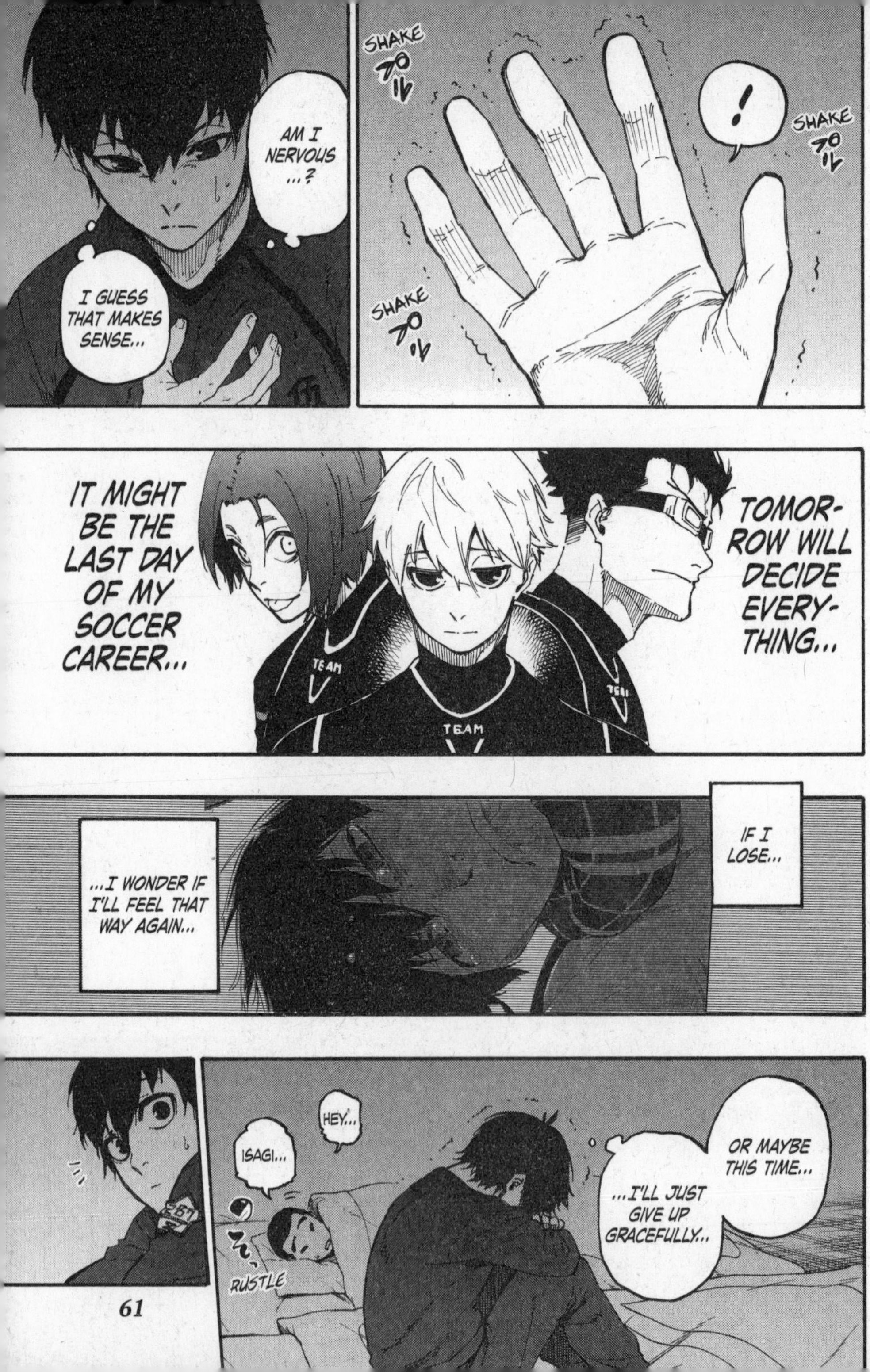
SHAKE
!
SHAKE
SHAKE
AM I NERVOUS ...?
I GUESS THAT MAKES SENSE...
TOMOR-ROW WILL DECIDE EVERY-THING...
IT MIGHT BE THE LAST DAY OF MY SOCCER CAREER...
IF I LOSE...
...I WONDER IF I'LL FEEL THAT WAY AGAIN...
OR MAYBE THIS TIME...
...I'LL JUST GIVE UP GRACEFULLY...
HEY...
ISAGI...
RUSTLE

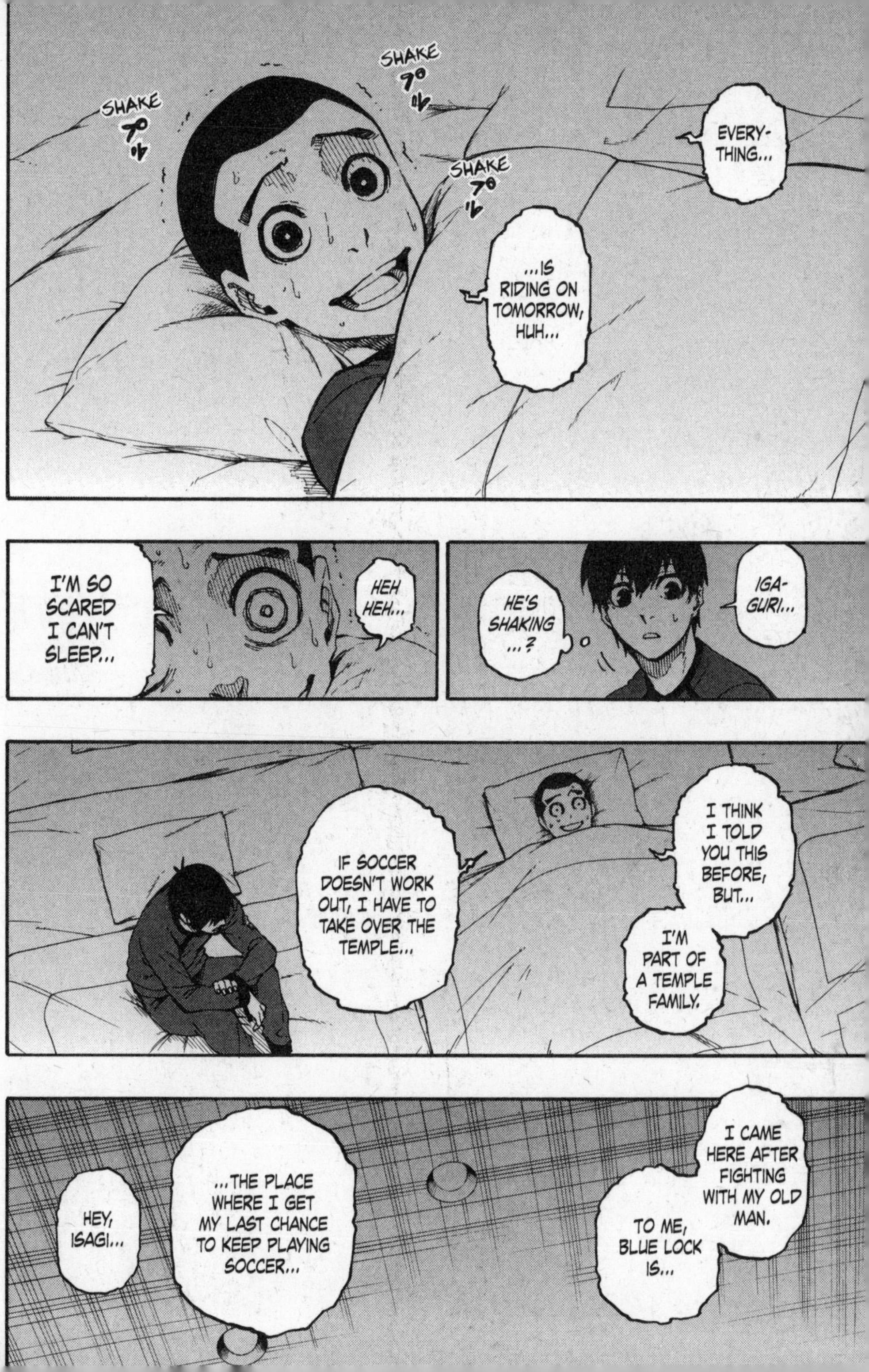
EVERYTHING...
SHAKE
SHAKE
SHAKE
...IS RIDING ON TOMORROW, HUH...
IGAGURI...
HE'S SHAKING...?
HEH HEH...
I'M SO SCARED I CAN'T SLEEP...
I THINK I TOLD YOU THIS BEFORE, BUT...
I'M PART OF A TEMPLE FAMILY.
IF SOCCER DOESN'T WORK OUT, I HAVE TO TAKE OVER THE TEMPLE...
I CAME HERE AFTER FIGHTING WITH MY OLD MAN.
TO ME, BLUE LOCK IS...
...THE PLACE WHERE I GET MY LAST CHANCE TO KEEP PLAYING SOCCER...
HEY, ISAGI...

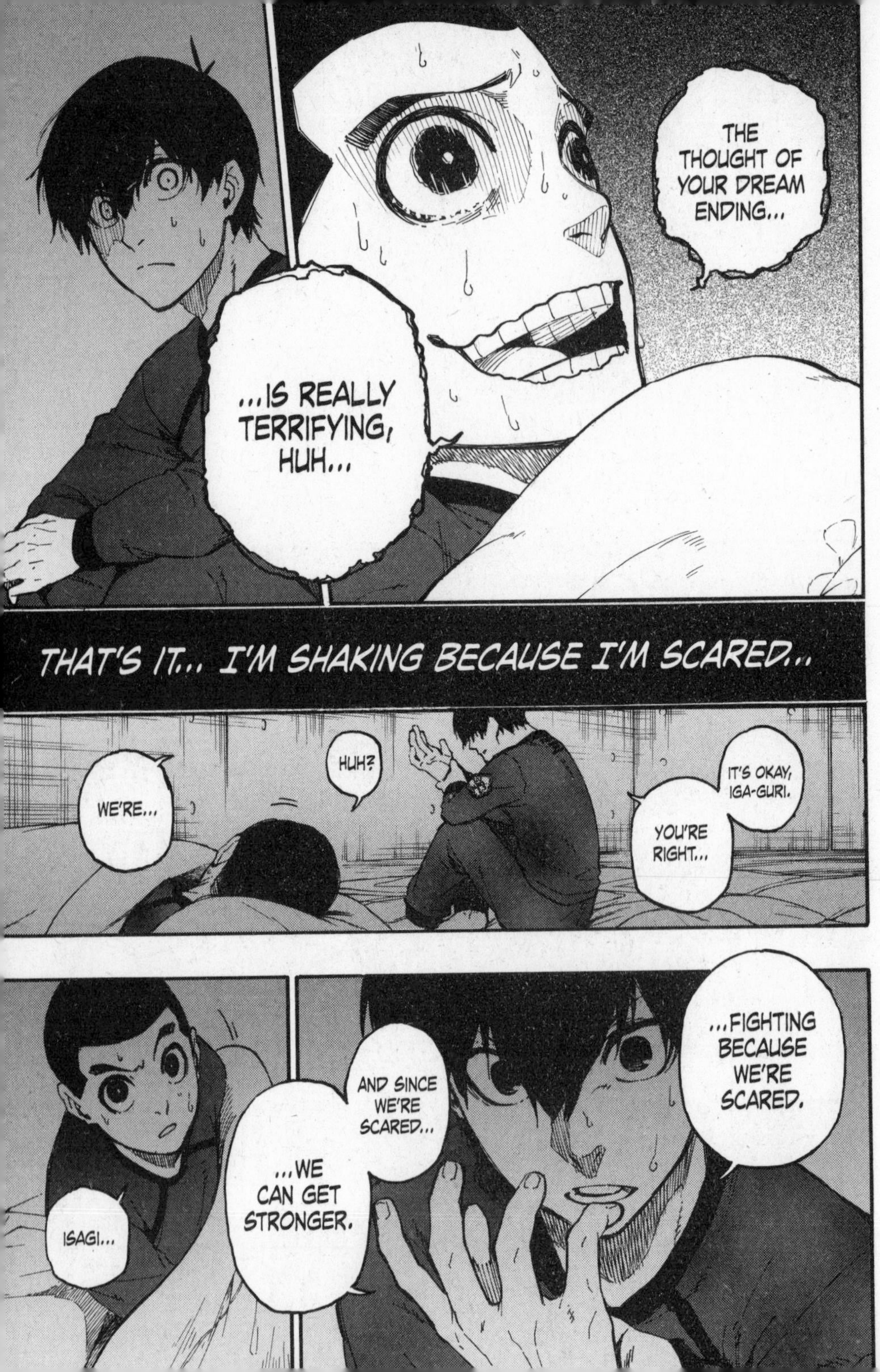
THE THOUGHT OF YOUR DREAM ENDING...
...IS REALLY TERRIFYING, HUH...
THAT'S IT... I'M SHAKING BECAUSE I'M SCARED...
IT'S OKAY, IGA-GURI.
YOU'RE RIGHT...
HUH?
WE'RE...
...FIGHTING BECAUSE WE'RE SCARED.
AND SINCE WE'RE SCARED...
...WE CAN GET STRONGER.
ISAGI...

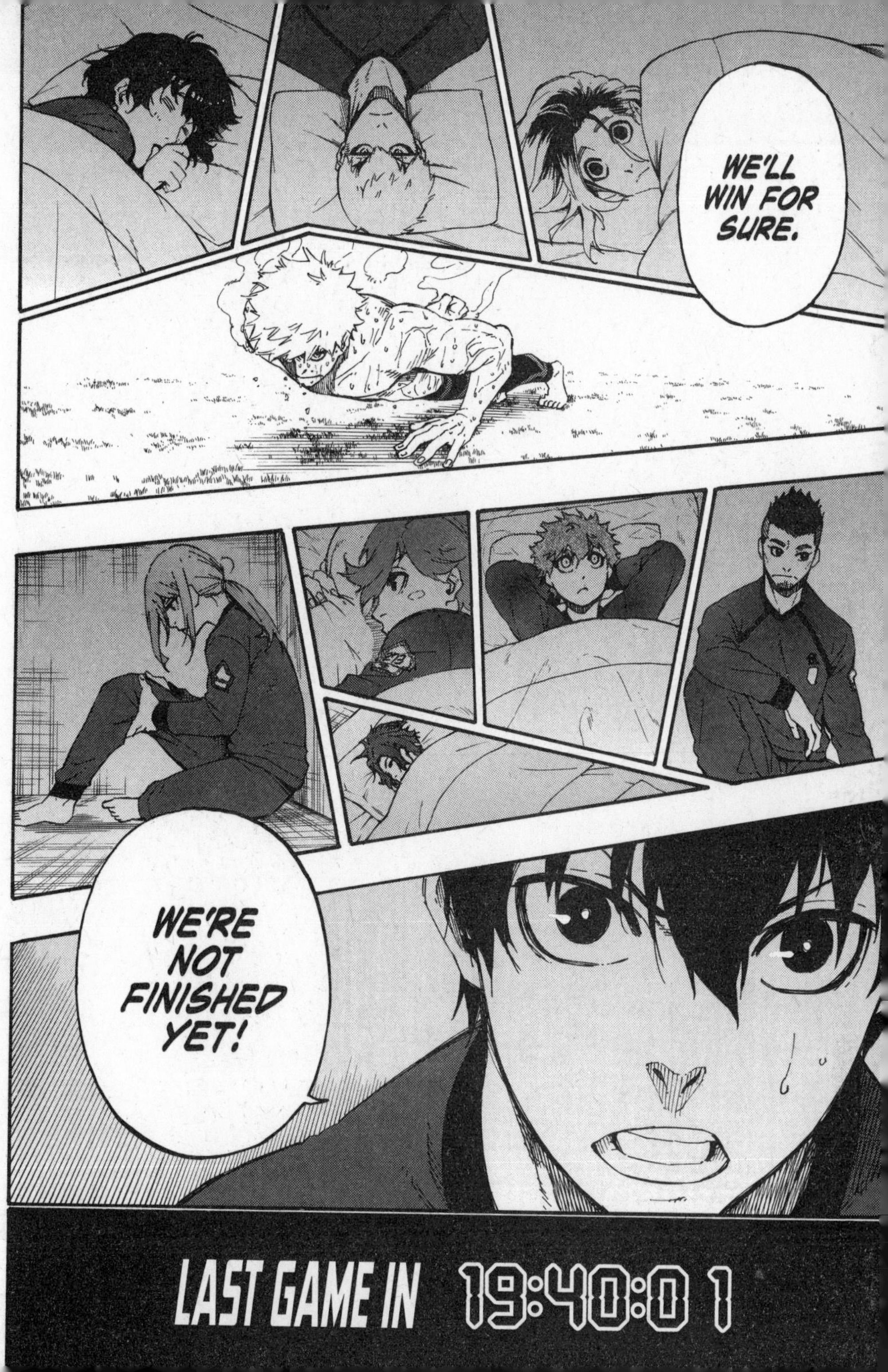
WE'LL WIN FOR SURE.
WE'RE NOT FINISHED YET!
LAST GAME IN 19:40:01

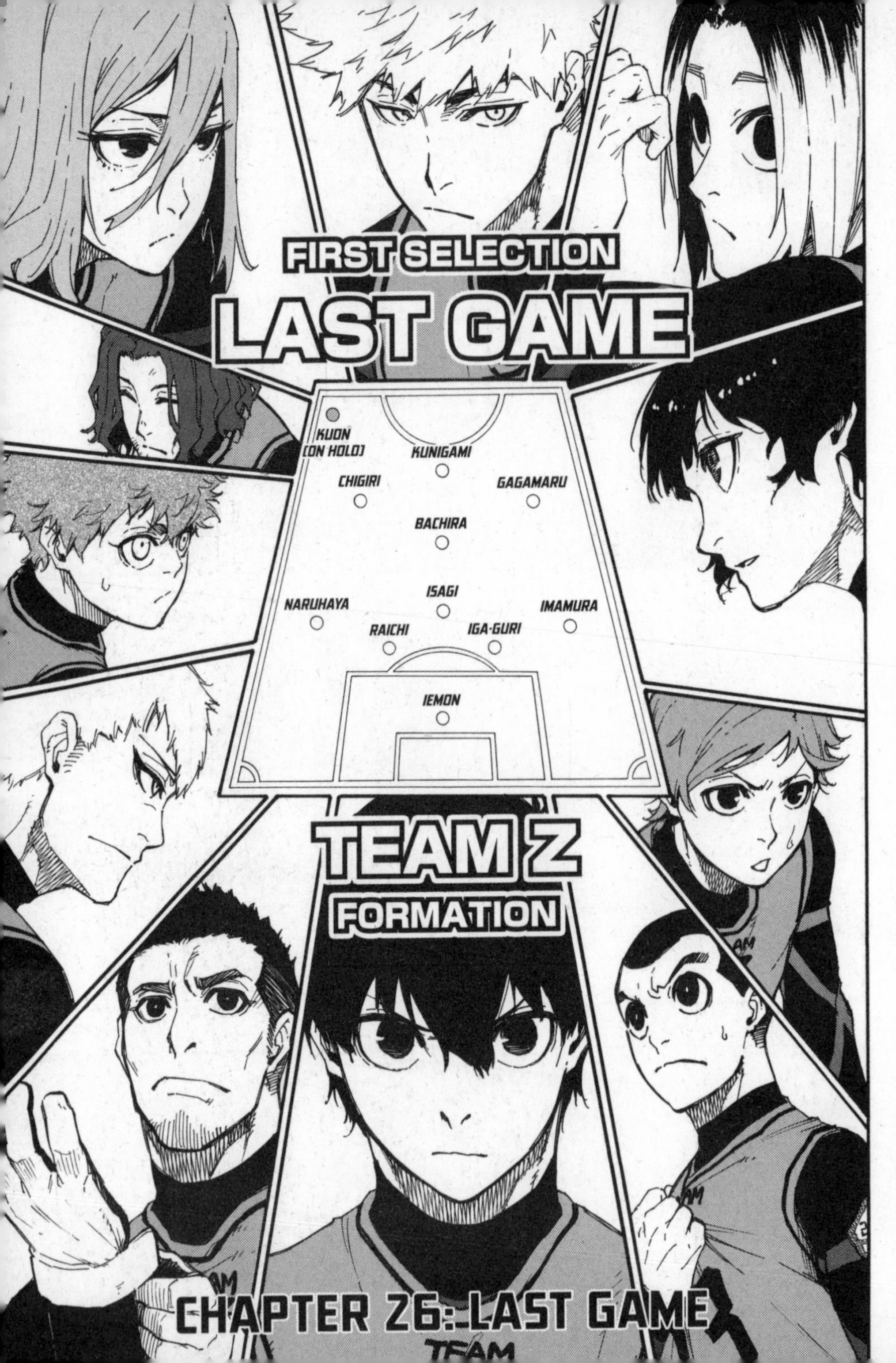
FIRST SELECTION
LAST GAME
KUON (ON HOLD)
KUNIGAMI
CHIGIRI
GAGAMARU
BACHIRA
ISAGI
NARUHAYA
IMAMURA
RAICHI
IGA-GURI
IEMON
TEAM Z
FORMATION
CHAPTER 26: LAST GAME

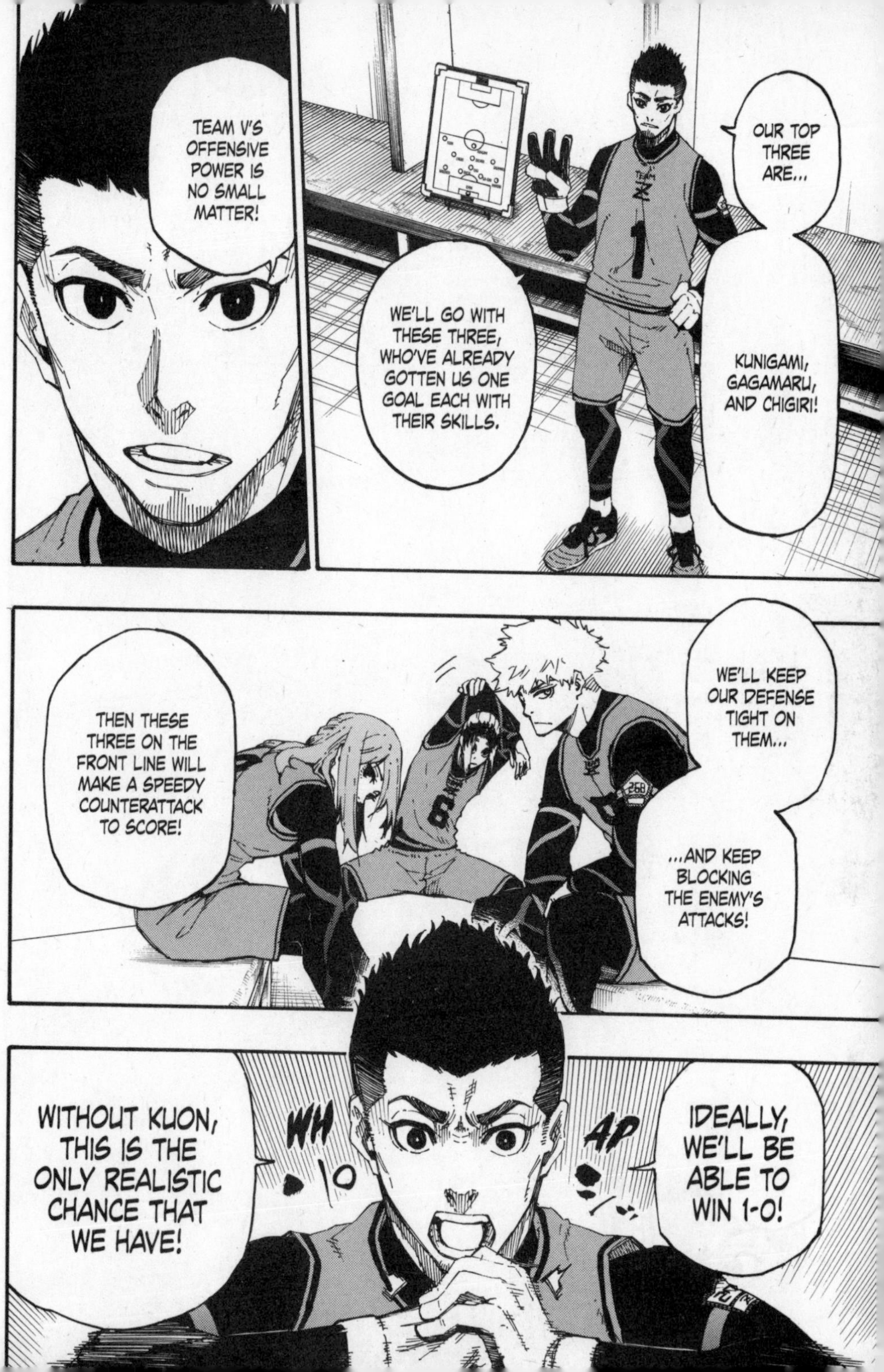
OUR TOP THREE ARE...
KUNIGAMI, GAGAMARU, AND CHIGIRI!
WE'LL GO WITH THESE THREE, WHO'VE ALREADY GOTTEN US ONE GOAL EACH WITH THEIR SKILLS.
TEAM V'S OFFENSIVE POWER IS NO SMALL MATTER!
WE'LL KEEP OUR DEFENSE TIGHT ON THEM...
...AND KEEP BLOCKING THE ENEMY'S ATTACKS!
THEN THESE THREE ON THE FRONT LINE WILL MAKE A SPEEDY COUNTERATTACK TO SCORE!
IDEALLY, WE'LL BE ABLE TO WIN 1-0!
AP
WH
WITHOUT KUON, THIS IS THE ONLY REALISTIC CHANCE THAT WE HAVE!

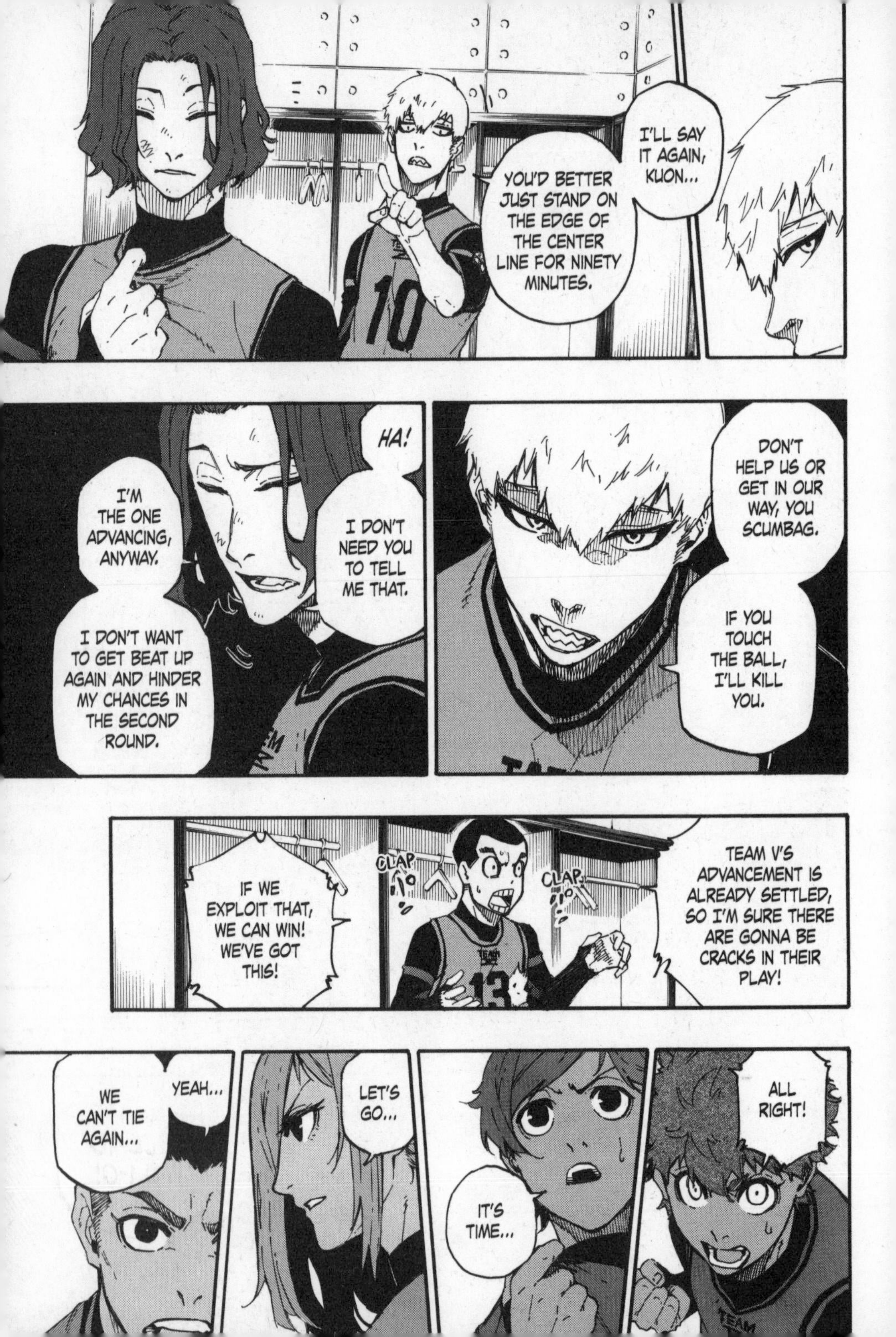
I'LL SAY IT AGAIN, KUON...
YOU'D BETTER JUST STAND ON THE EDGE OF THE CENTER LINE FOR NINETY MINUTES.
DON'T HELP US OR GET IN OUR WAY, YOU SCUMBAG.
IF YOU TOUCH THE BALL, I'LL KILL YOU.
HA!
I DON'T NEED YOU TO TELL ME THAT.
I'M THE ONE ADVANCING, ANYWAY.
I DON'T WANT TO GET BEAT UP AGAIN AND HINDER MY CHANCES IN THE SECOND ROUND.
TEAM V'S ADVANCEMENT IS ALREADY SETTLED, SO I'M SURE THERE ARE GONNA BE CRACKS IN THEIR PLAY!
CLAP
CLAP
IF WE EXPLOIT THAT, WE CAN WIN! WE'VE GOT THIS!
ALL RIGHT!
IT'S TIME...
LET'S GO...
YEAH...
WE CAN'T TIE AGAIN...

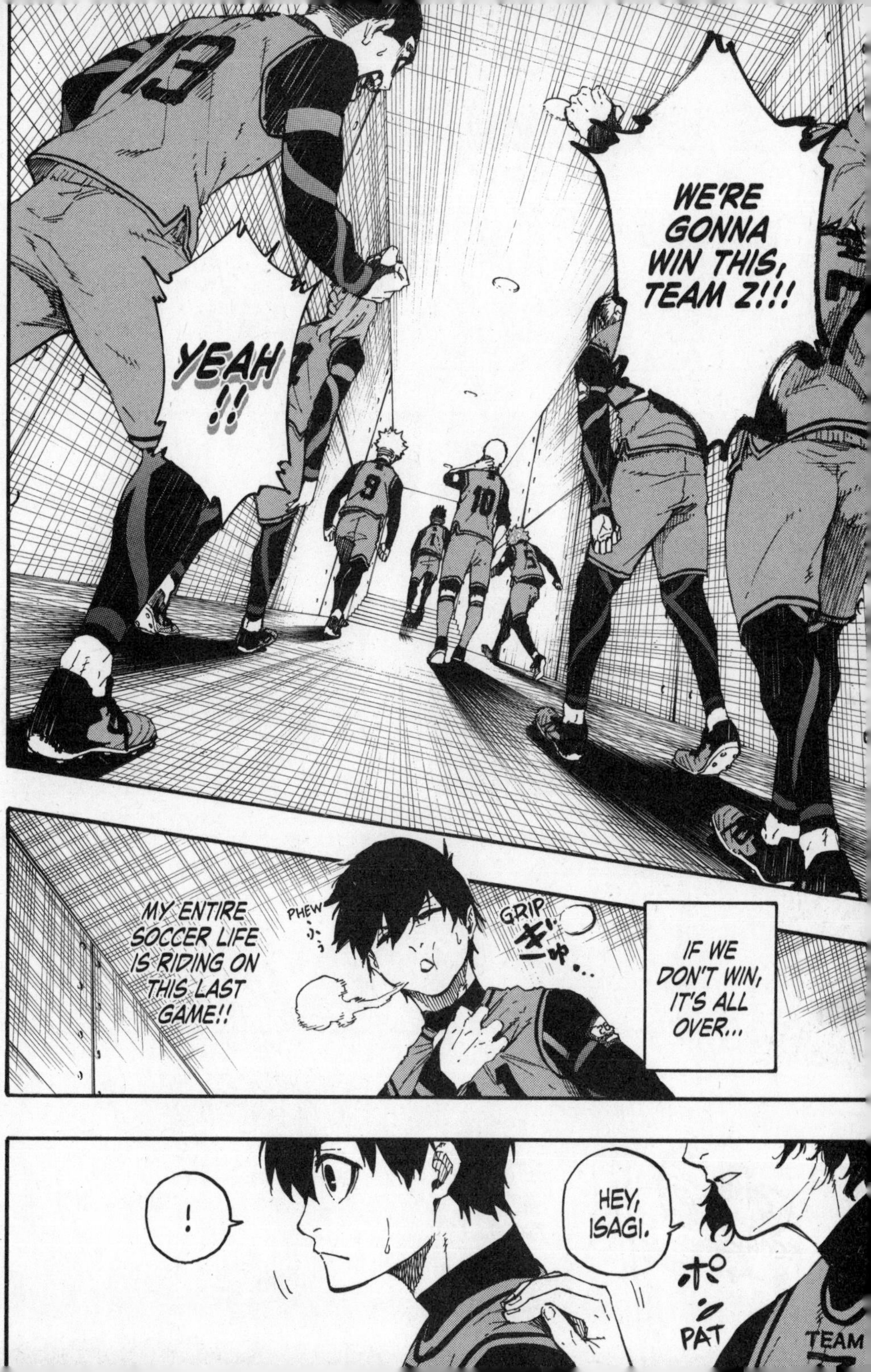
WE'RE GONNA WIN THIS, TEAM Z!!!
YEAH!!
IF WE DON'T WIN, IT'S ALL OVER...
GRIP
MY ENTIRE SOCCER LIFE IS RIDING ON THIS LAST GAME!!
PHEW
PAT
TEAM
HEY, ISAGI.
!

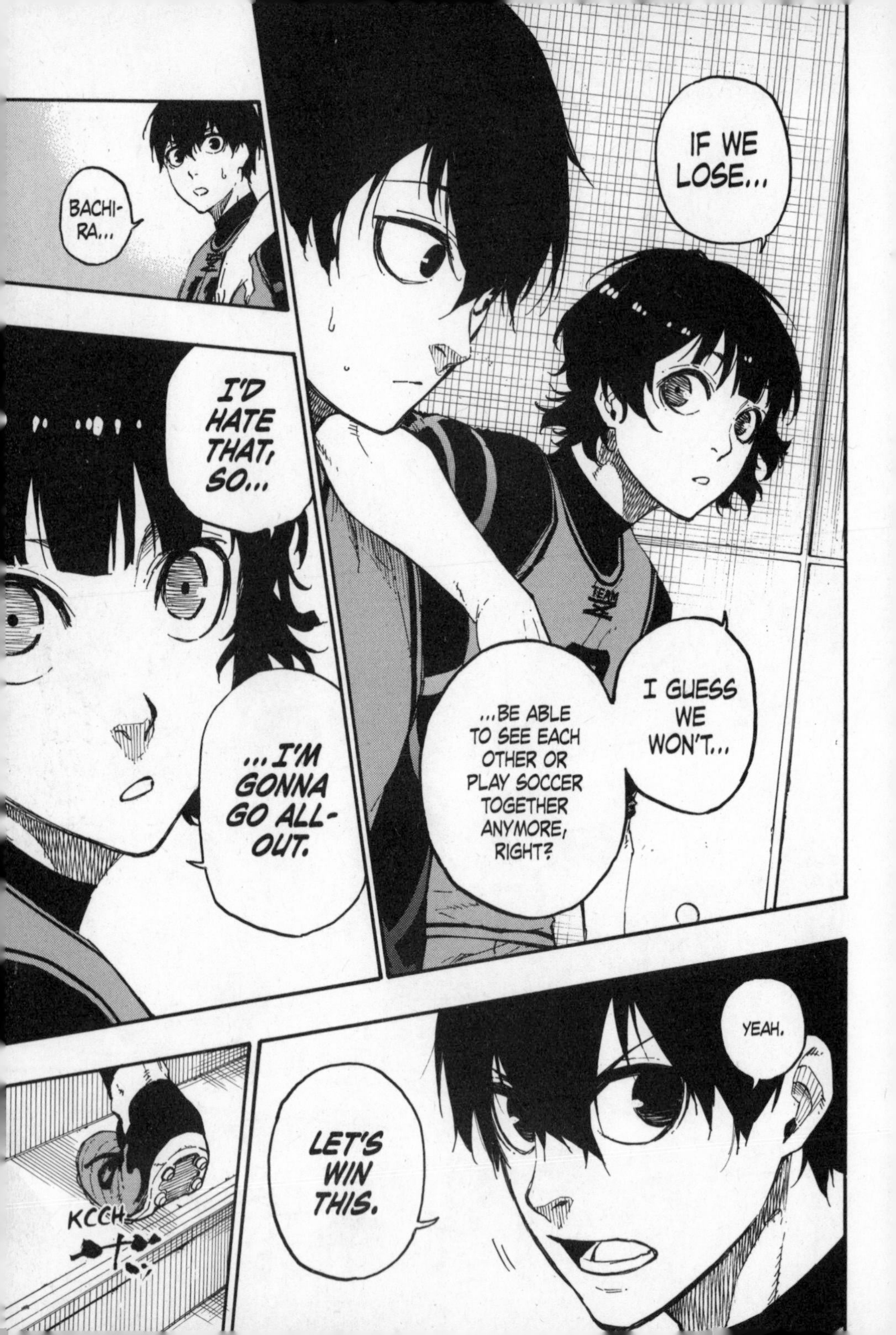
IF WE LOSE...
I GUESS WE WON'T...
...BE ABLE TO SEE EACH OTHER OR PLAY SOCCER TOGETHER ANYMORE, RIGHT?
BACHIRA...
I'D HATE THAT, SO...
...I'M GONNA GO ALL-OUT.
YEAH.
LET'S WIN THIS.
KCCH

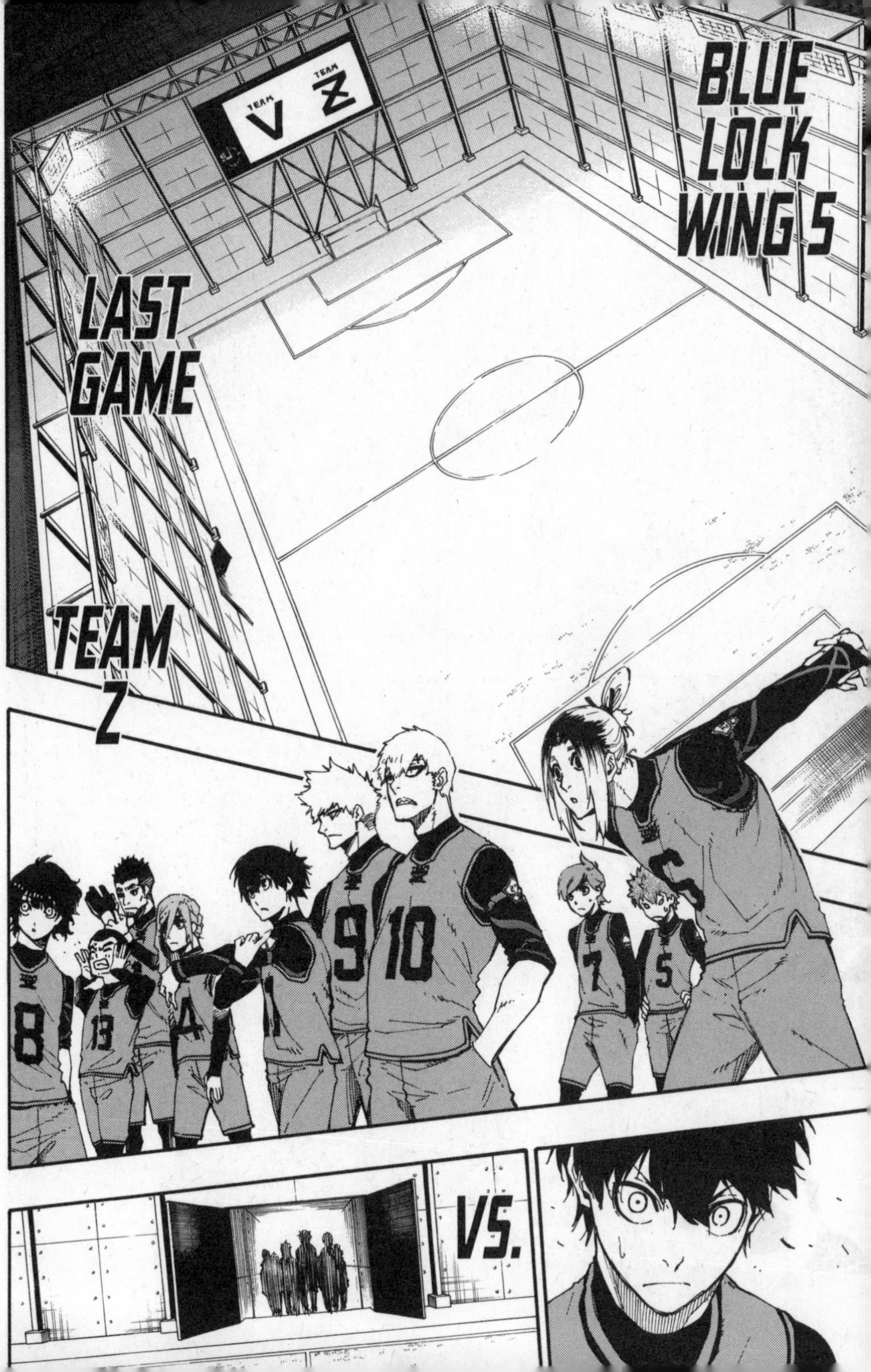

BLUE LOCK WING 5
TEAM V
TEAM Z
LAST GAME
TEAM Z
VS.

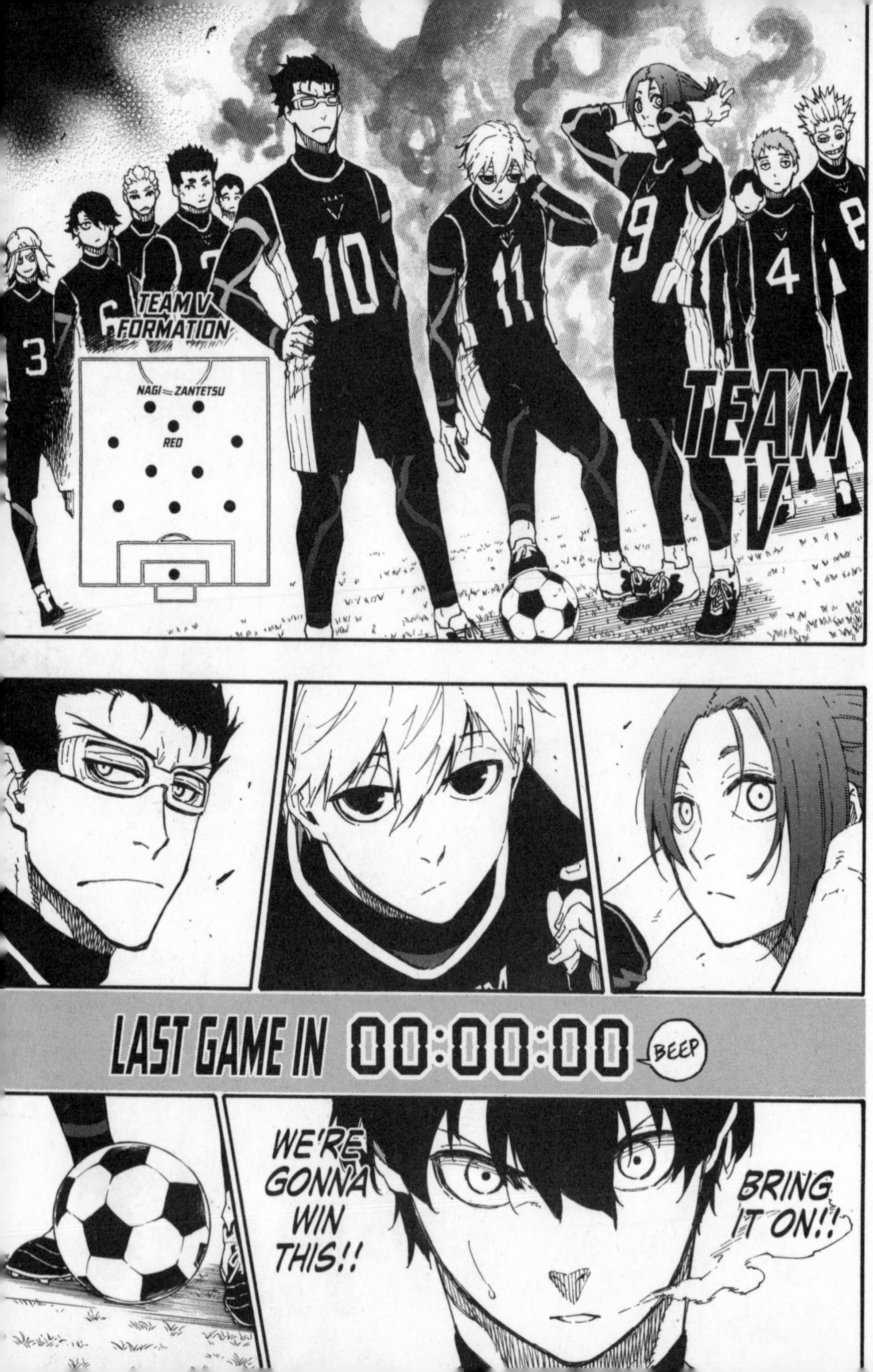

TEAM V
TEAM V FORMATION
NAGI
ZANTETSU
REO
LAST GAME IN 00:00:00
BEEP
BRING IT ON!!
WE'RE GONNA WIN THIS!!

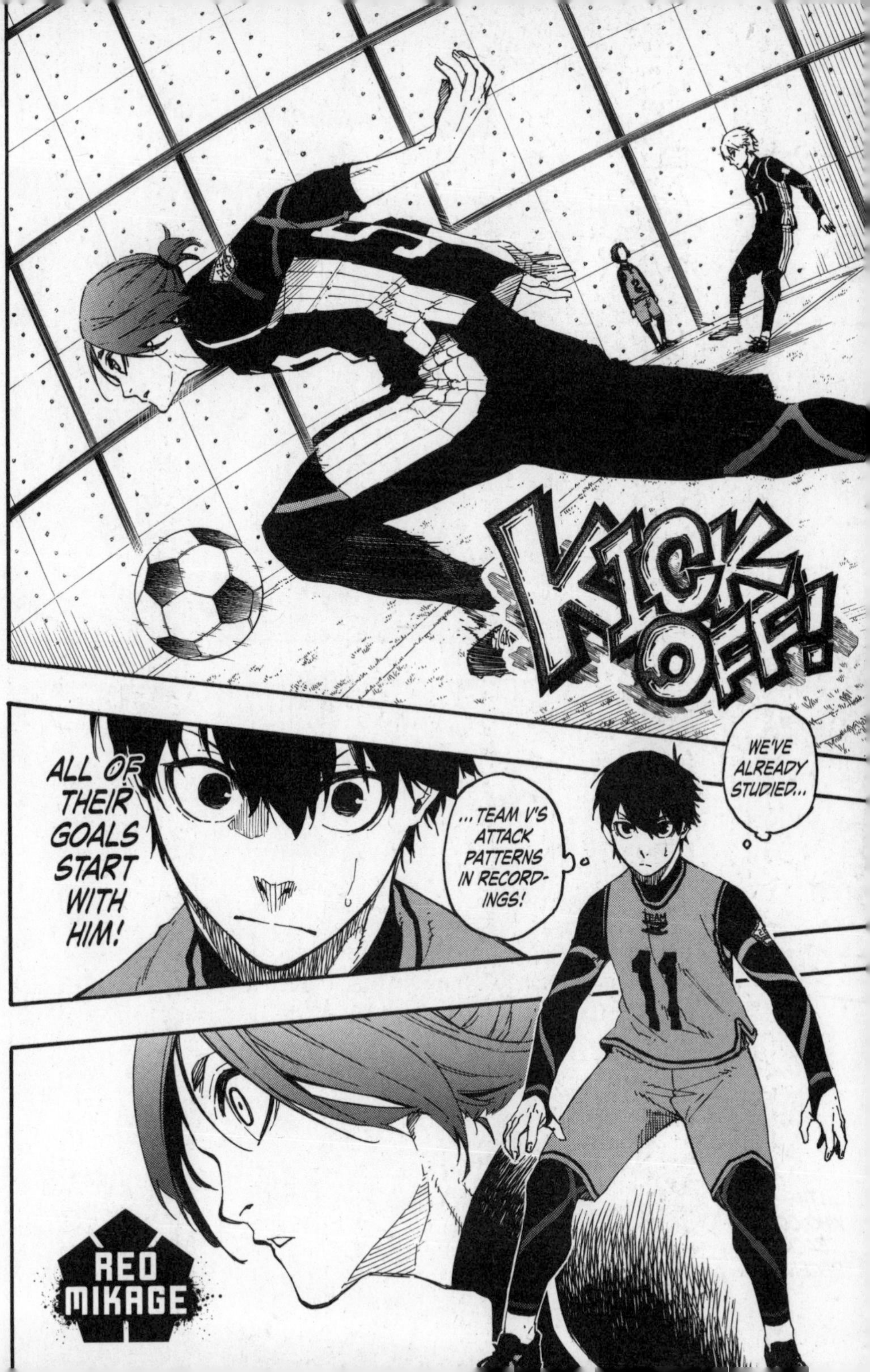
KICK OFF!
WE'VE ALREADY STUDIED...
...TEAM V'S ATTACK PATTERNS IN RECORD-INGS!
ALL OF THEIR GOALS START WITH HIM!
REO MIKAGE

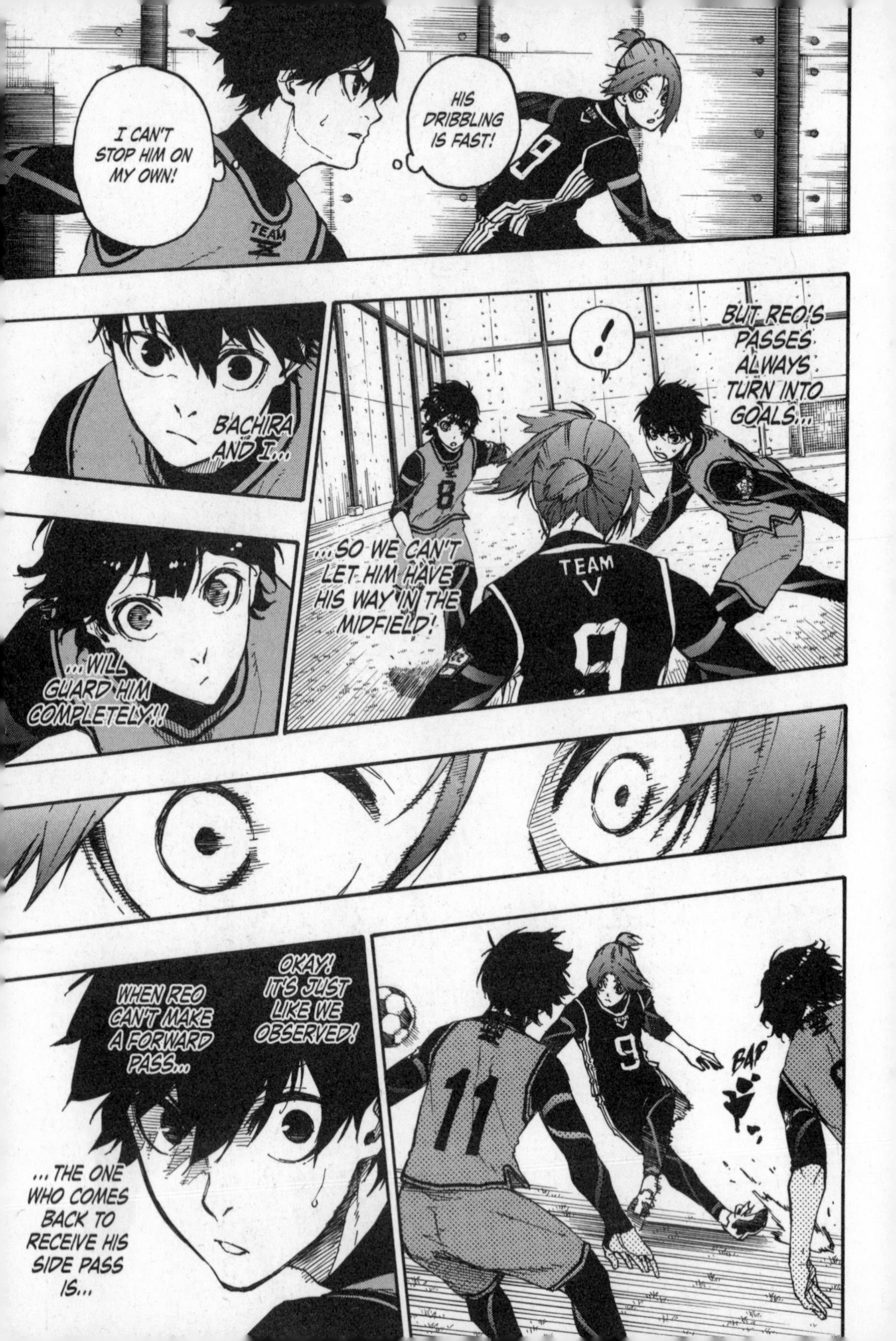
HIS DRIBBLING IS FAST!
I CAN'T STOP HIM ON MY OWN!
BUT REO'S PASSES ALWAYS TURN INTO GOALS...
!
...SO WE CAN'T LET HIM HAVE HIS WAY IN THE MIDFIELD!
BACHIRA AND I...
...WILL GUARD HIM COMPLETELY!!
BAP
OKAY! IT'S JUST LIKE WE OBSERVED!
WHEN REO CAN'T MAKE A FORWARD PASS...
...THE ONE WHO COMES BACK TO RECEIVE HIS SIDE PASS IS...

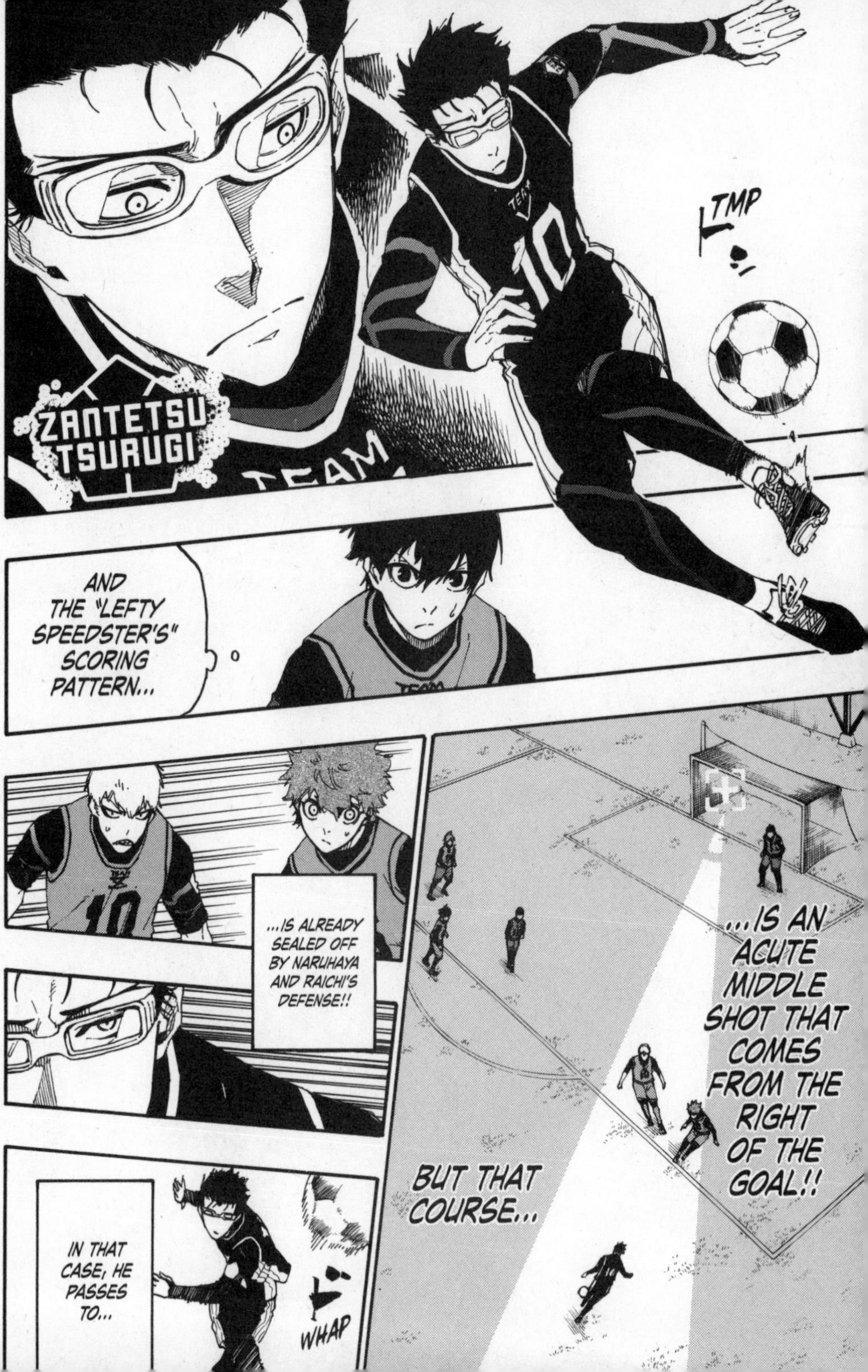
TMP
ZANTETSU TSURUGI
AND THE "LEFTY SPEEDSTER'S" SCORING PATTERN...
...IS AN ACUTE MIDDLE SHOT THAT COMES FROM THE RIGHT OF THE GOAL!!
BUT THAT COURSE...
...IS ALREADY SEALED OFF BY NARUHAYA AND RAICHI'S DEFENSE!!
IN THAT CASE, HE PASSES TO...
WHAP

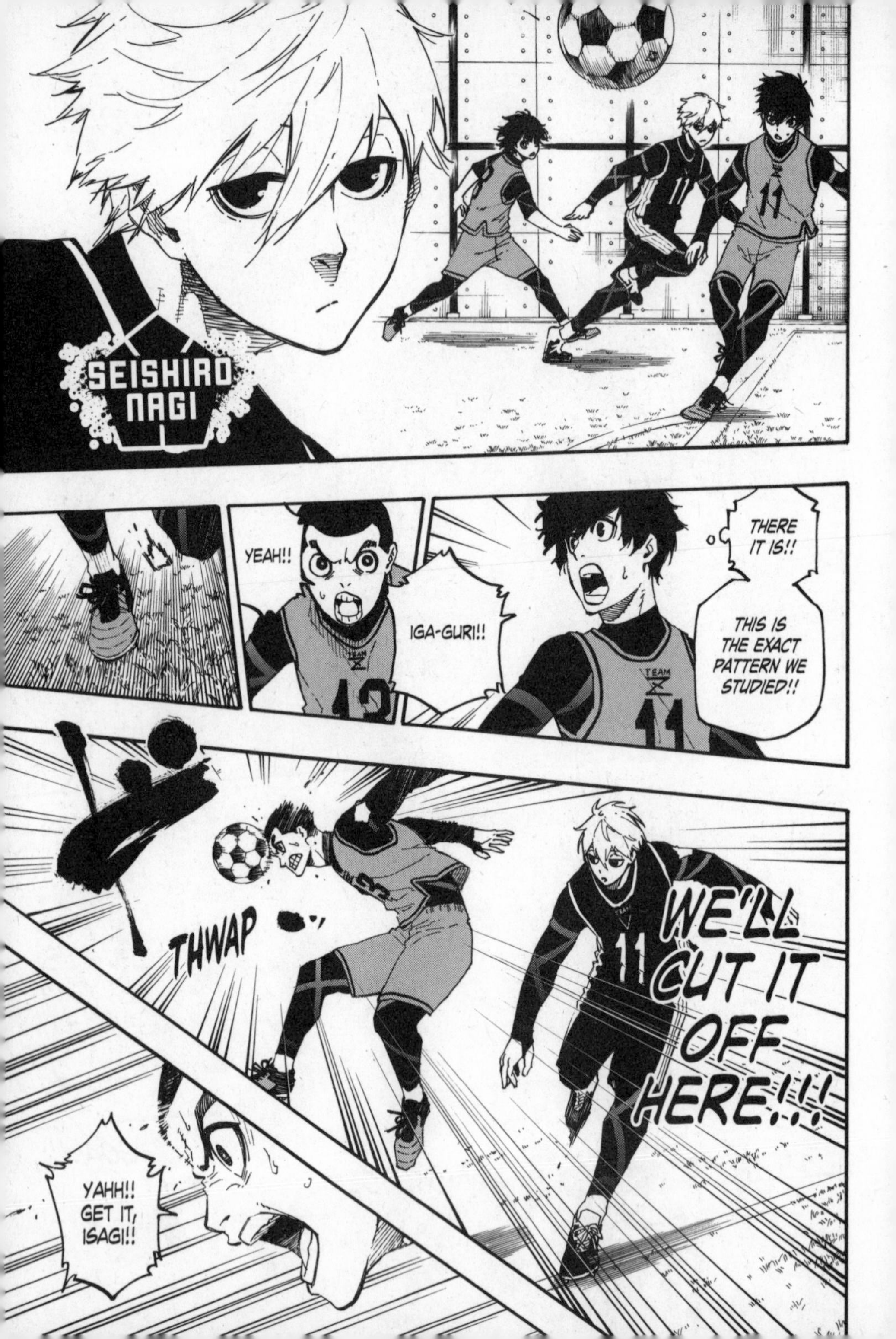
SEISHIRO NAGI
THERE IT IS!!
THIS IS THE EXACT PATTERN WE STUDIED!!
IGA-GURI!!
YEAH!!
WE'LL CUT IT OFF HERE!!!
THWAP
YAHH!! GET IT, ISAGI!!

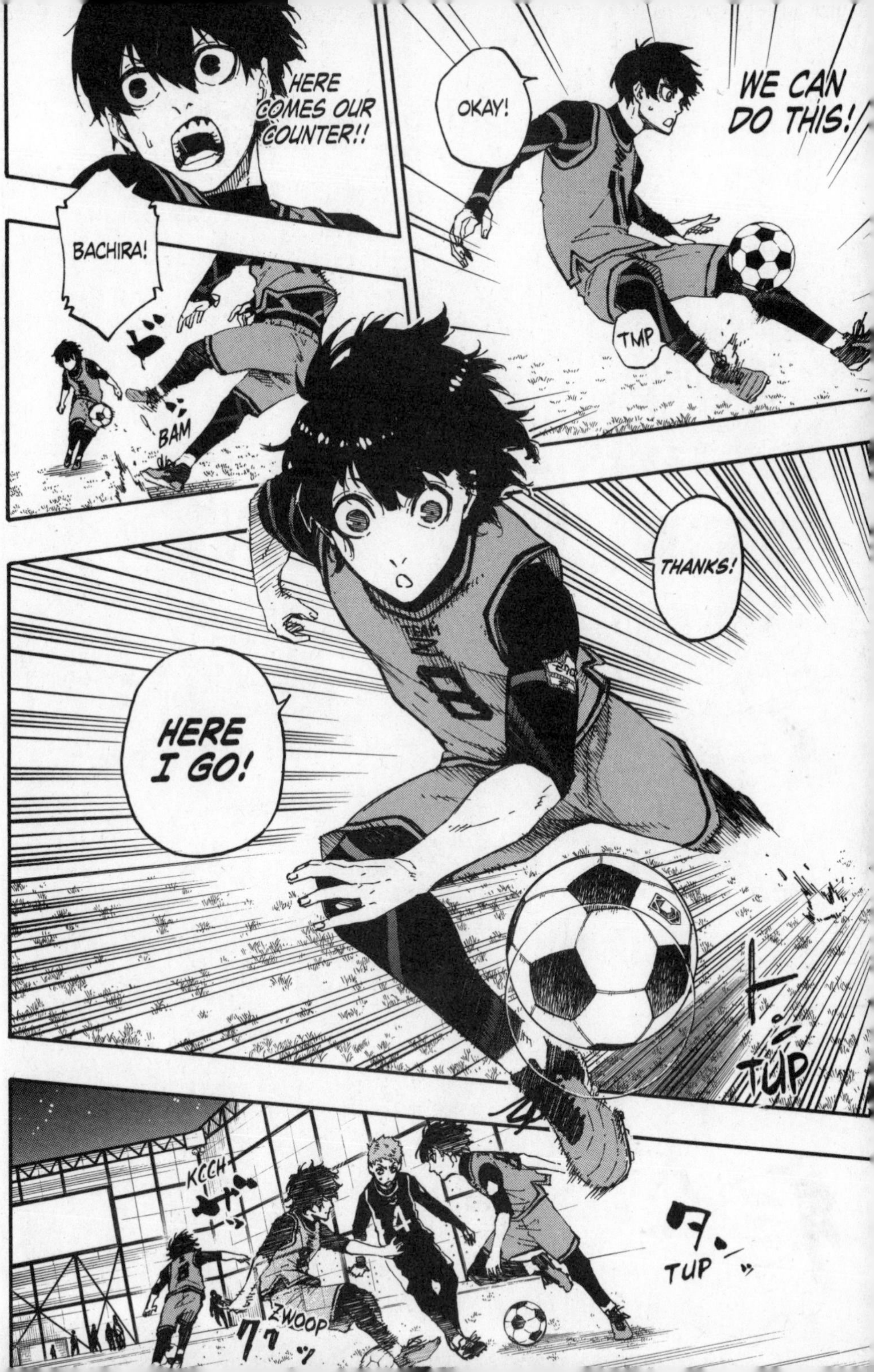

OKAY!
WE CAN DO THIS!
TMP
HERE COMES OUR COUNTER!!
BACHIRA!
BAM
THANKS!
HERE I GO!
TUP
TUP
KCCH
ZWOOP

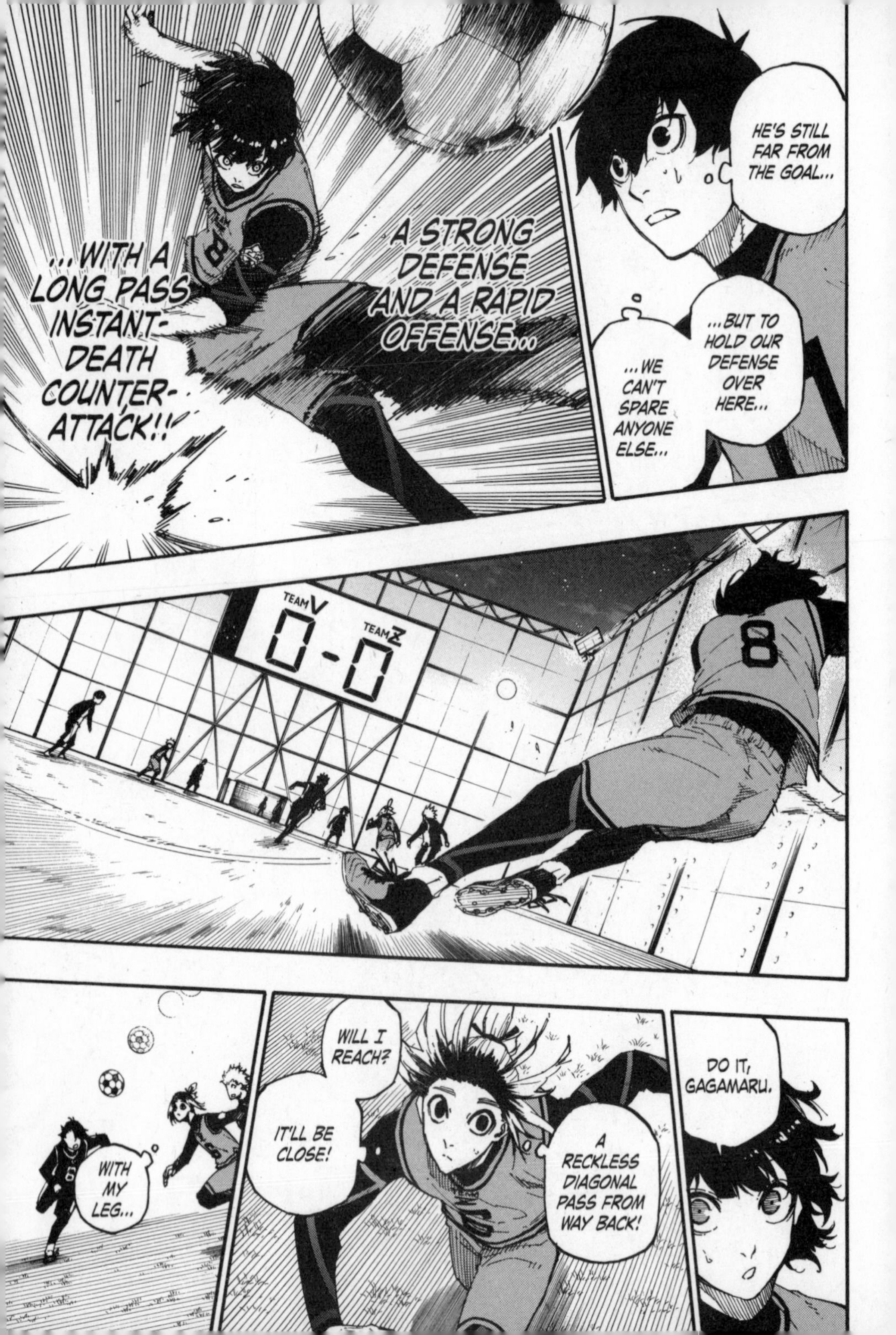
HE'S STILL FAR FROM THE GOAL...
...BUT TO HOLD OUR DEFENSE OVER HERE...
...WE CAN'T SPARE ANYONE ELSE...
A STRONG DEFENSE AND A RAPID OFFENSE...
...WITH A LONG PASS INSTANT-DEATH COUNTER-ATTACK!!
TEAM V
TEAM Z
0-0
DO IT, GAGAMARU.
A RECKLESS DIAGONAL PASS FROM WAY BACK!
WILL I REACH?
IT'LL BE CLOSE!
WITH MY LEG...

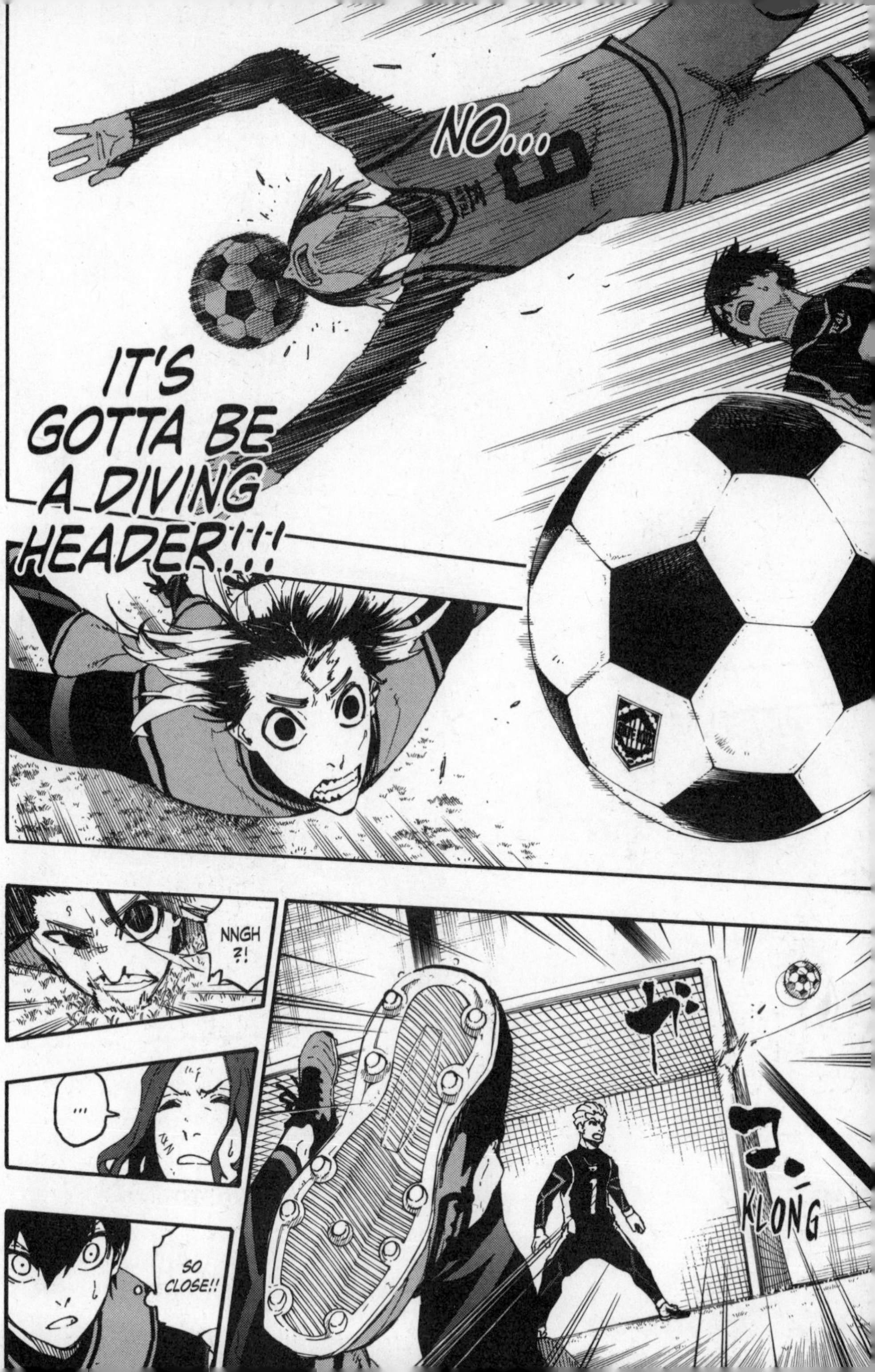
NO...
IT'S GOTTA BE A DIVING HEADER!!!
KLONG
NNGH ?!
...
SO CLOSE!!

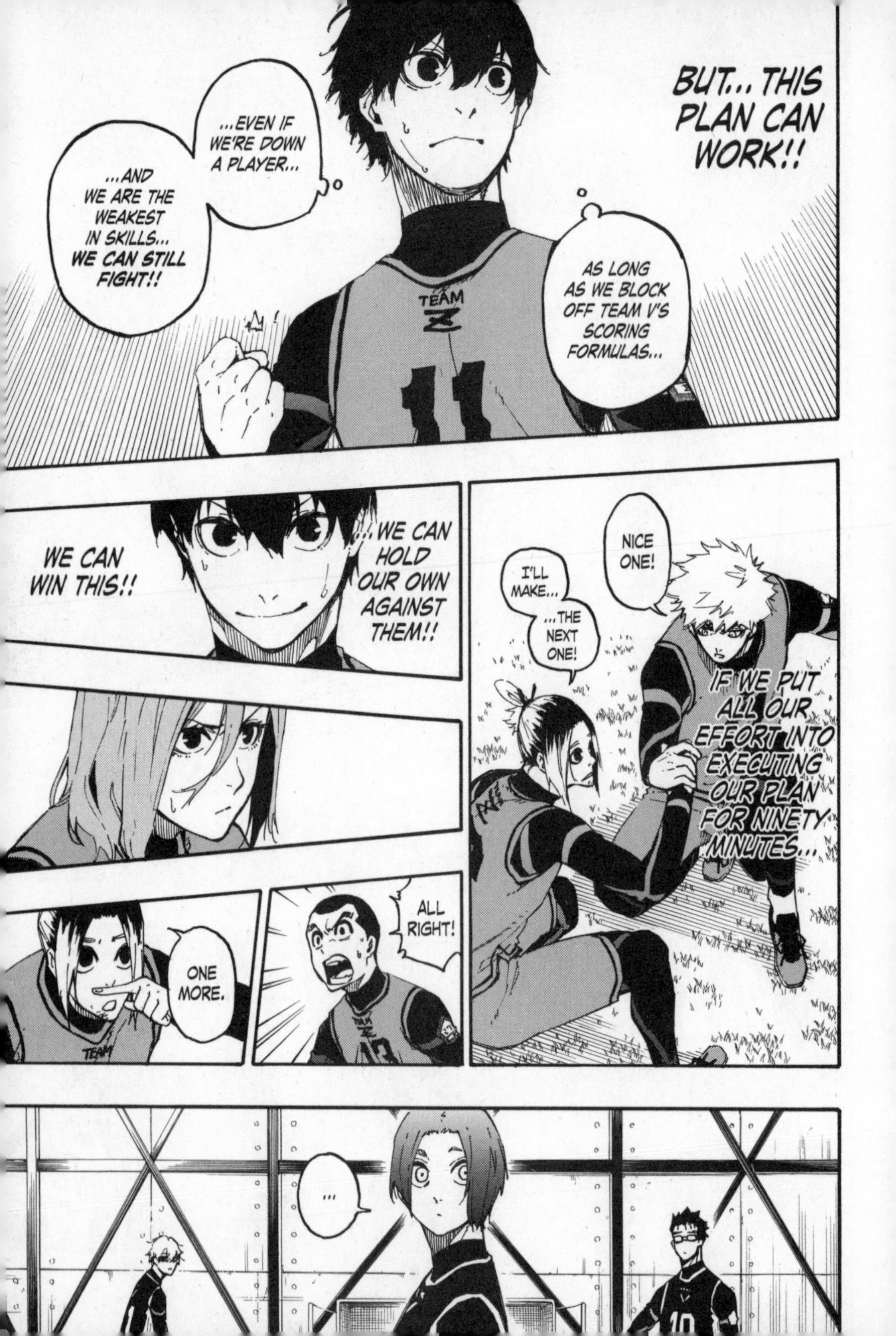
BUT... THIS PLAN CAN WORK!!
AS LONG AS WE BLOCK OFF TEAM V'S SCORING FORMULAS...
...EVEN IF WE'RE DOWN A PLAYER...
...AND WE ARE THE WEAKEST IN SKILLS... WE CAN STILL FIGHT!!
NICE ONE!
I'LL MAKE...
...THE NEXT ONE!
IF WE PUT ALL OUR EFFORT INTO EXECUTING OUR PLAN FOR NINETY MINUTES...
...WE CAN HOLD OUR OWN AGAINST THEM!!
WE CAN WIN THIS!!
ALL RIGHT!
ONE MORE.
...

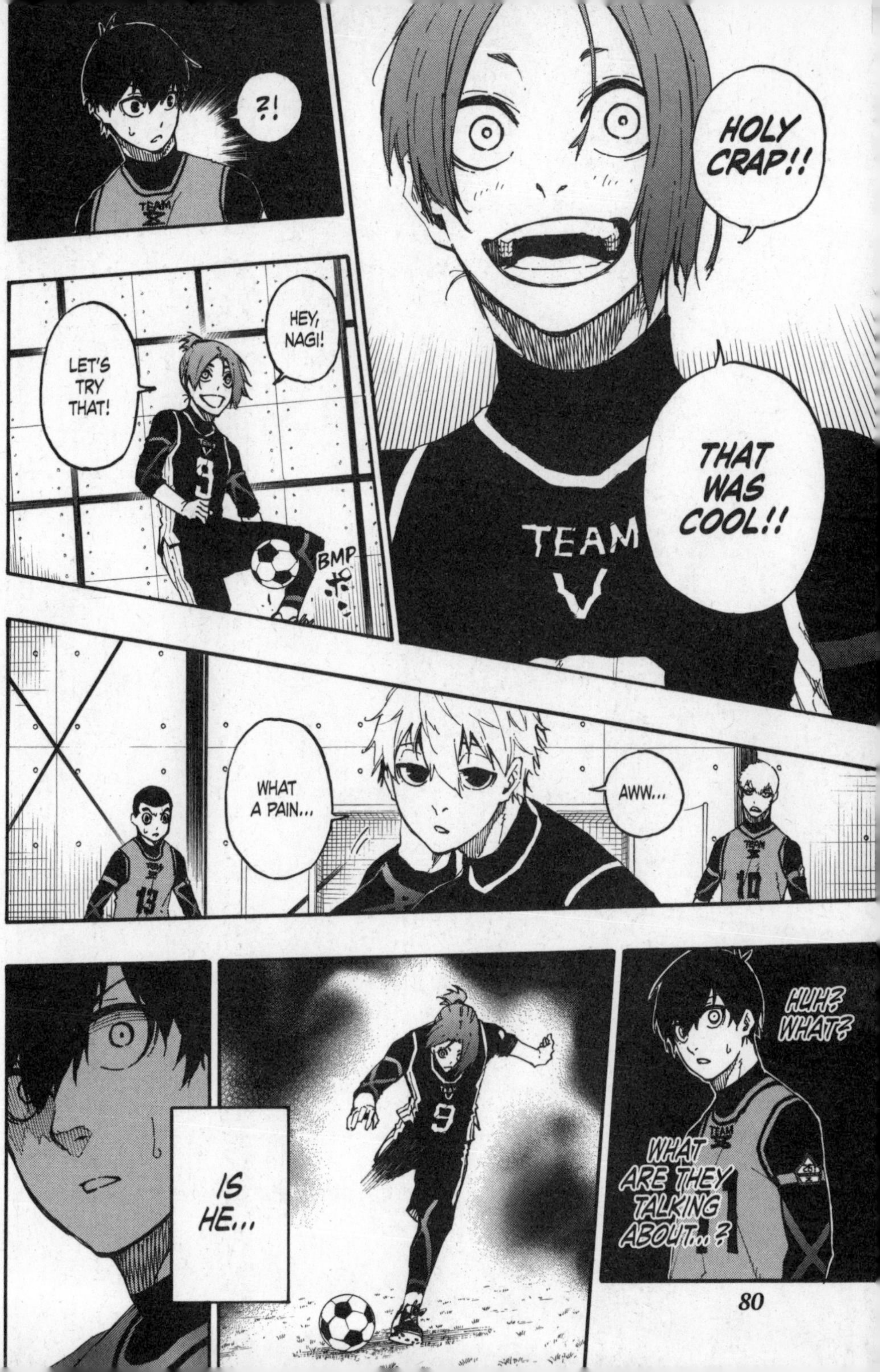
HOLY CRAP!!
THAT WAS COOL!!
?!
HEY, NAGI!
LET'S TRY THAT!
BMP
AWW...
WHAT A PAIN...
HUH? WHAT?
WHAT ARE THEY TALKING ABOUT..?
IS HE...

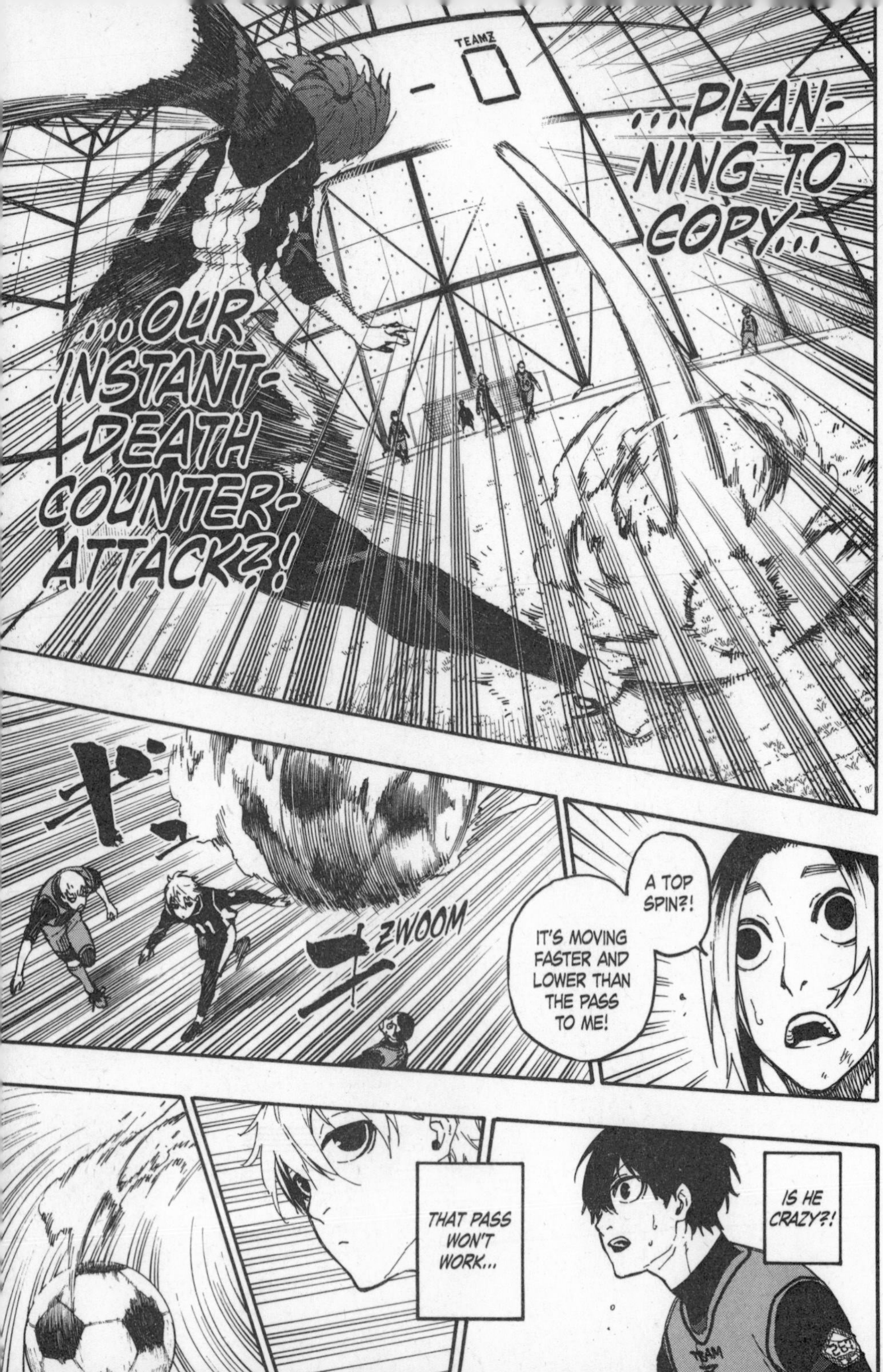
TEAM Z
-0
...PLAN-NING TO COPY...
...OUR INSTANT-DEATH COUNTER-ATTACK?!
A TOP SPIN?!
IT'S MOVING FASTER AND LOWER THAN THE PASS TO ME!
ZWOOM
IS HE CRAZY?!
THAT PASS WON'T WORK...

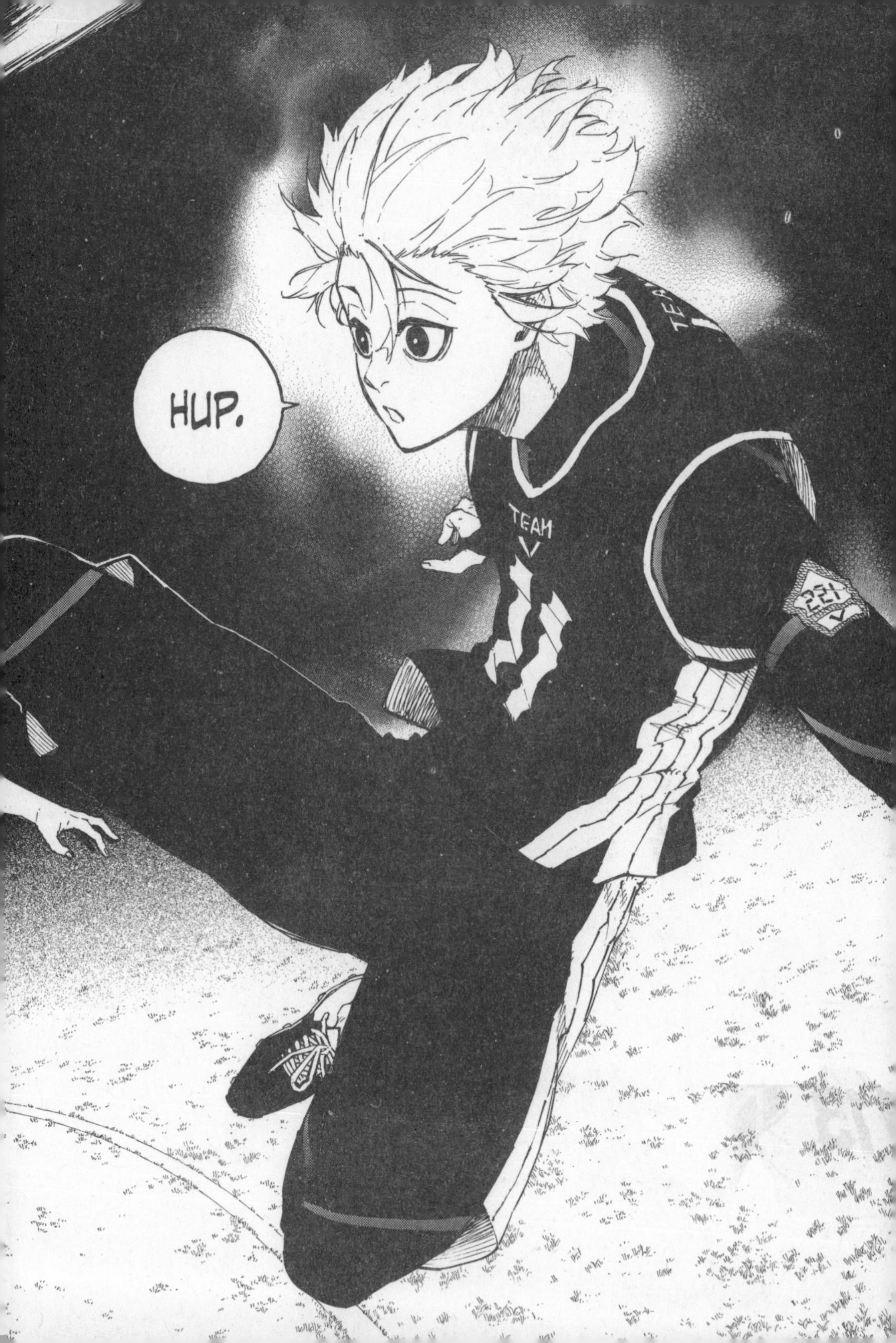
HUP.

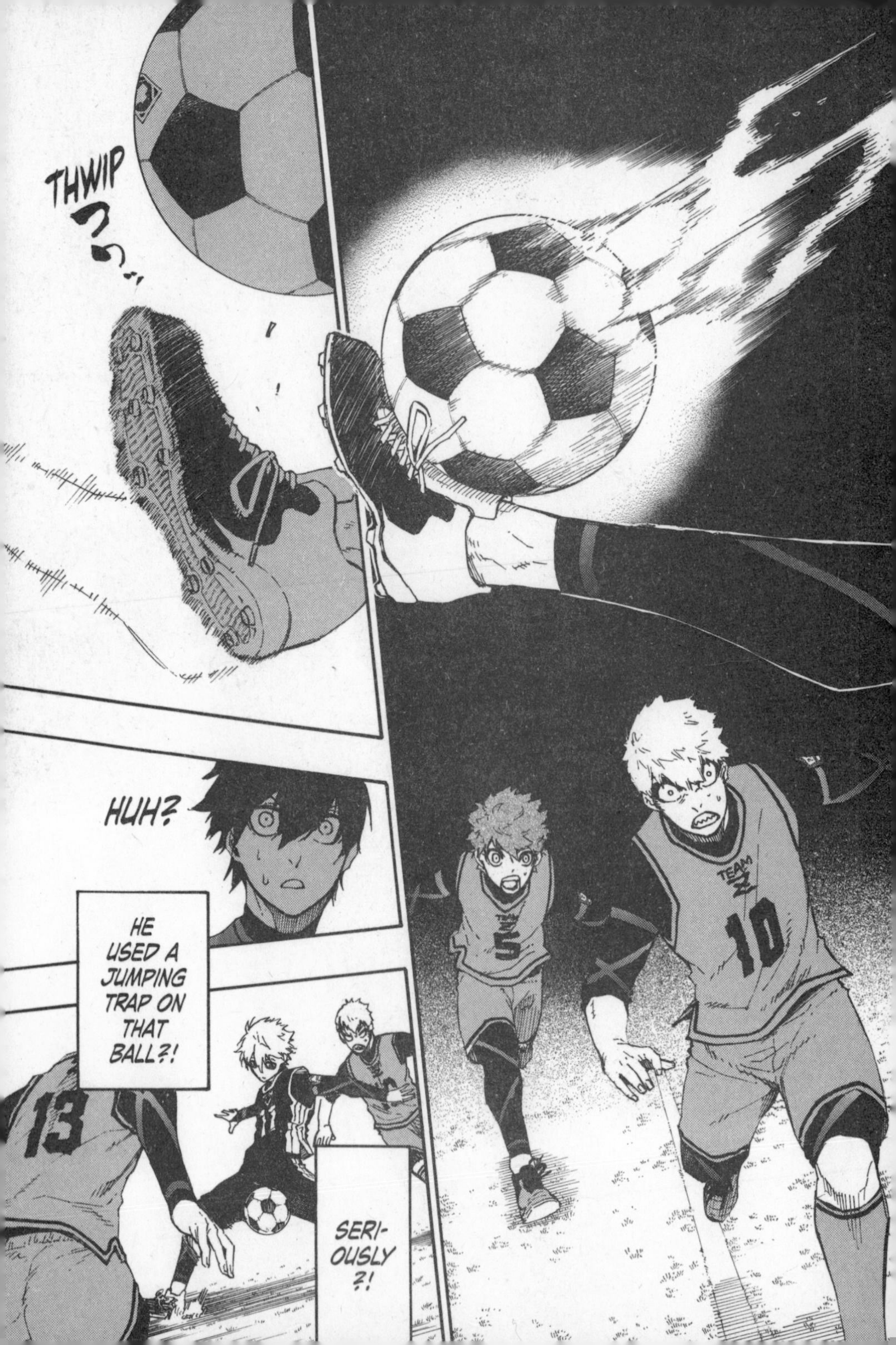
THWIP
HUH?
HE USED A JUMPING TRAP ON THAT BALL?!
SERI-OUSLY?!

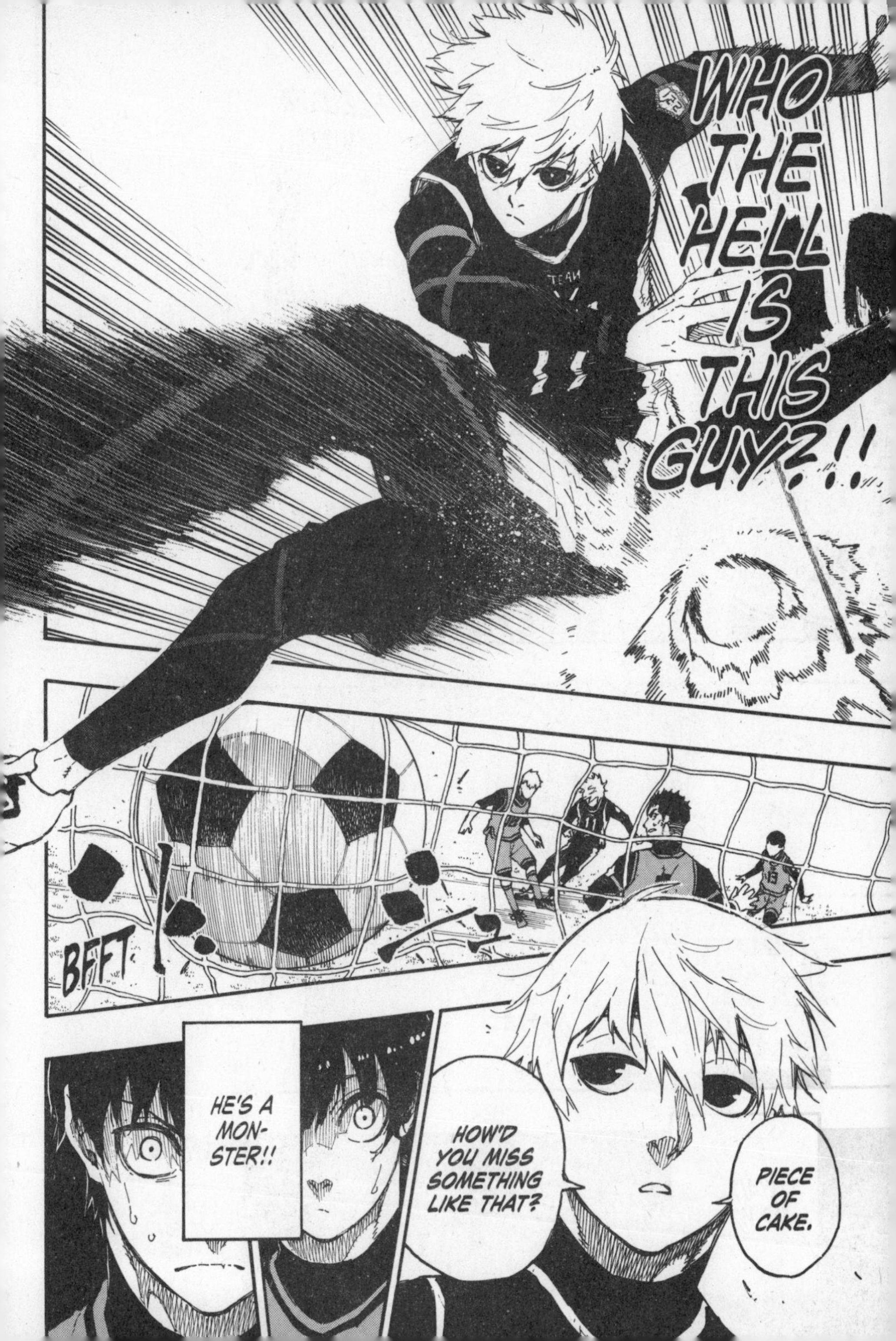
WHO THE HELL IS THIS GUY?!!
BFFT
PIECE OF CAKE.
HOW'D YOU MISS SOMETHING LIKE THAT?
HE'S A MON-STER!!

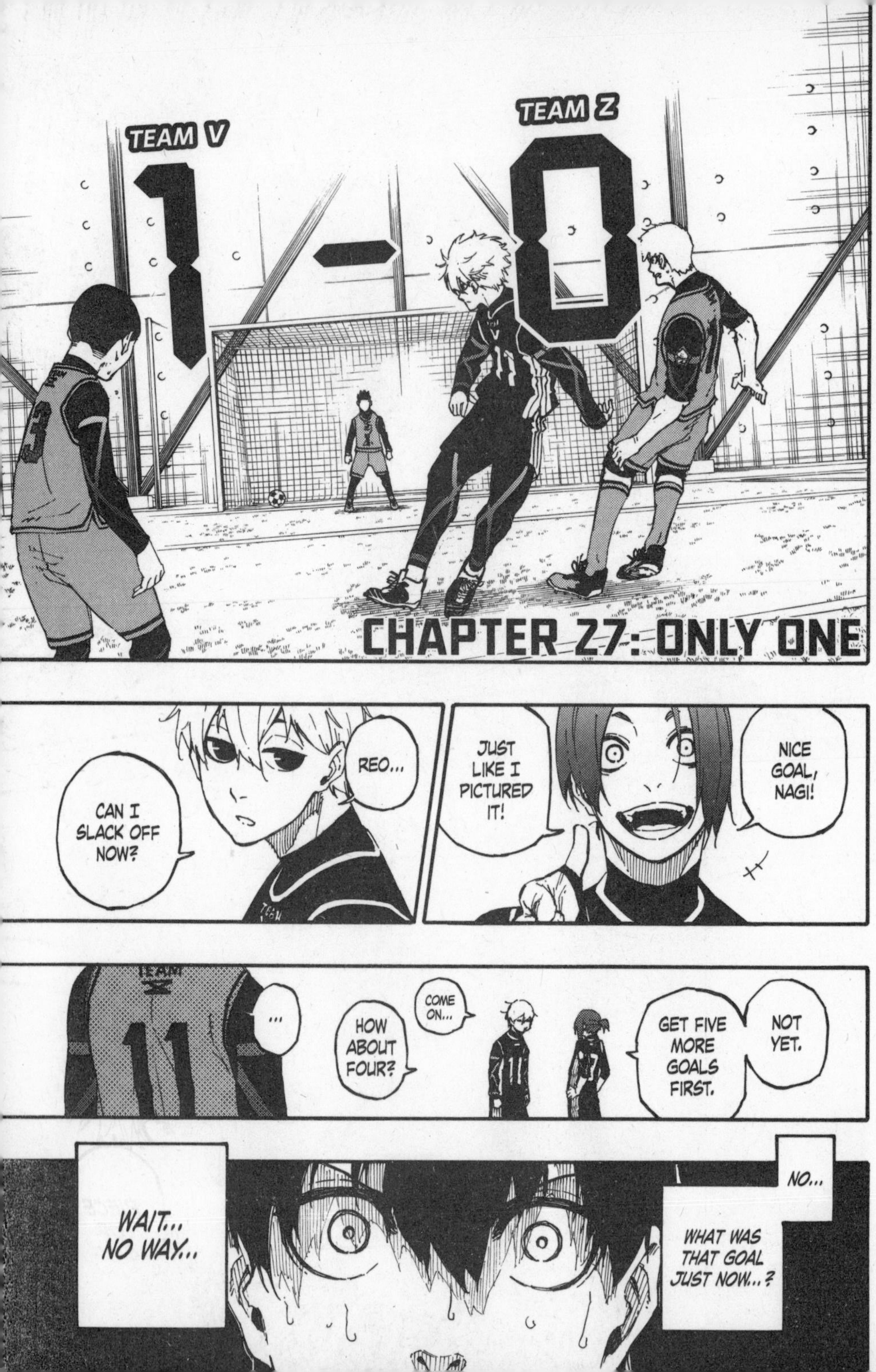
TEAM V
1 - 0
TEAM Z
CHAPTER 27: ONLY ONE
NICE GOAL, NAGI!
JUST LIKE I PICTURED IT!
REO...
CAN I SLACK OFF NOW?
NOT YET.
GET FIVE MORE GOALS FIRST.
COME ON...
HOW ABOUT FOUR?
...
NO...
WHAT WAS THAT GOAL JUST NOW...?
WAIT... NO WAY...

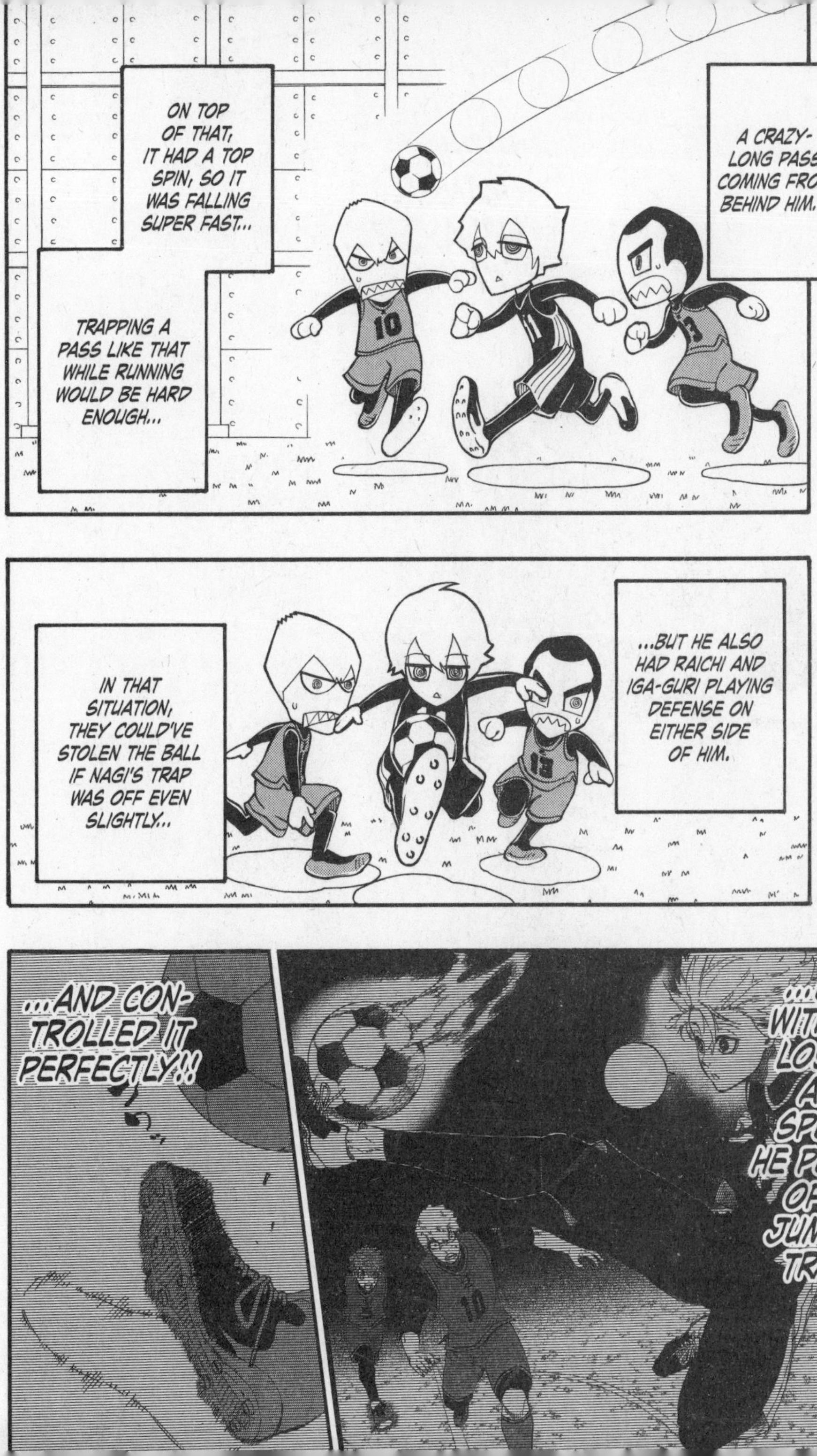
A CRAZY-LONG PASS COMING FROM BEHIND HIM...
ON TOP OF THAT, IT HAD A TOP SPIN, SO IT WAS FALLING SUPER FAST...
TRAPPING A PASS LIKE THAT WHILE RUNNING WOULD BE HARD ENOUGH...
...BUT HE ALSO HAD RAICHI AND IGA-GURI PLAYING DEFENSE ON EITHER SIDE OF HIM.
IN THAT SITUATION, THEY COULD'VE STOLEN THE BALL IF NAGI'S TRAP WAS OFF EVEN SLIGHTLY...
...BUT WITHOUT LOSING ANY SPEED, HE PULLED OFF A JUMPING TRAP...
...AND CON-TROLLED IT PERFECTLY!!

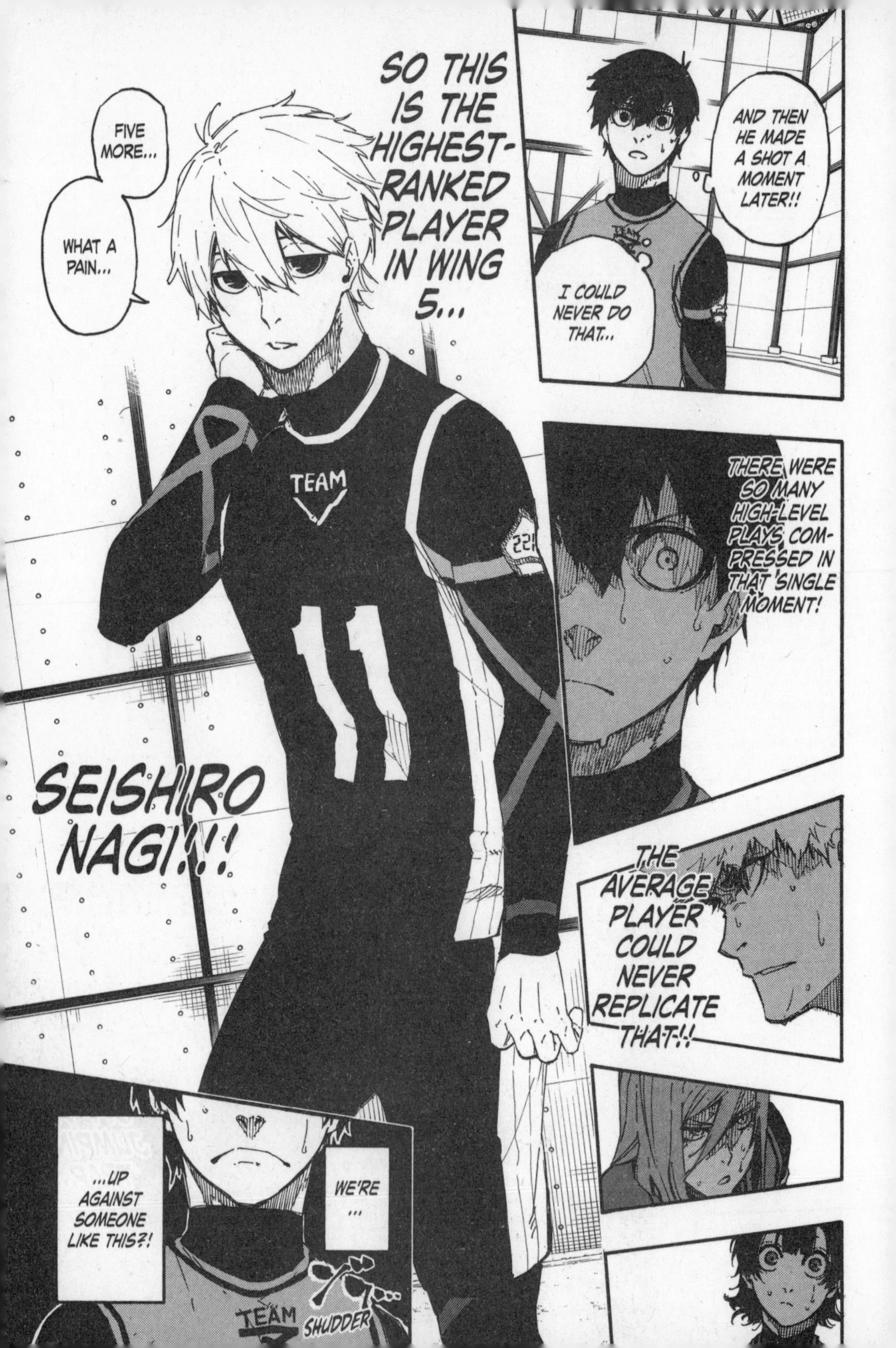

AND THEN HE MADE A SHOT A MOMENT LATER!!
I COULD NEVER DO THAT...
THERE WERE SO MANY HIGH-LEVEL PLAYS, COMPRESSED IN THAT SINGLE MOMENT!
THE AVERAGE PLAYER COULD NEVER REPLICATE THAT!!
SO THIS IS THE HIGHEST-RANKED PLAYER IN WING 5...
FIVE MORE...
WHAT A PAIN...
SEISHIRO NAGI!!!
WE'RE ...
...UP AGAINST SOMEONE LIKE THIS?!
SHUDDER

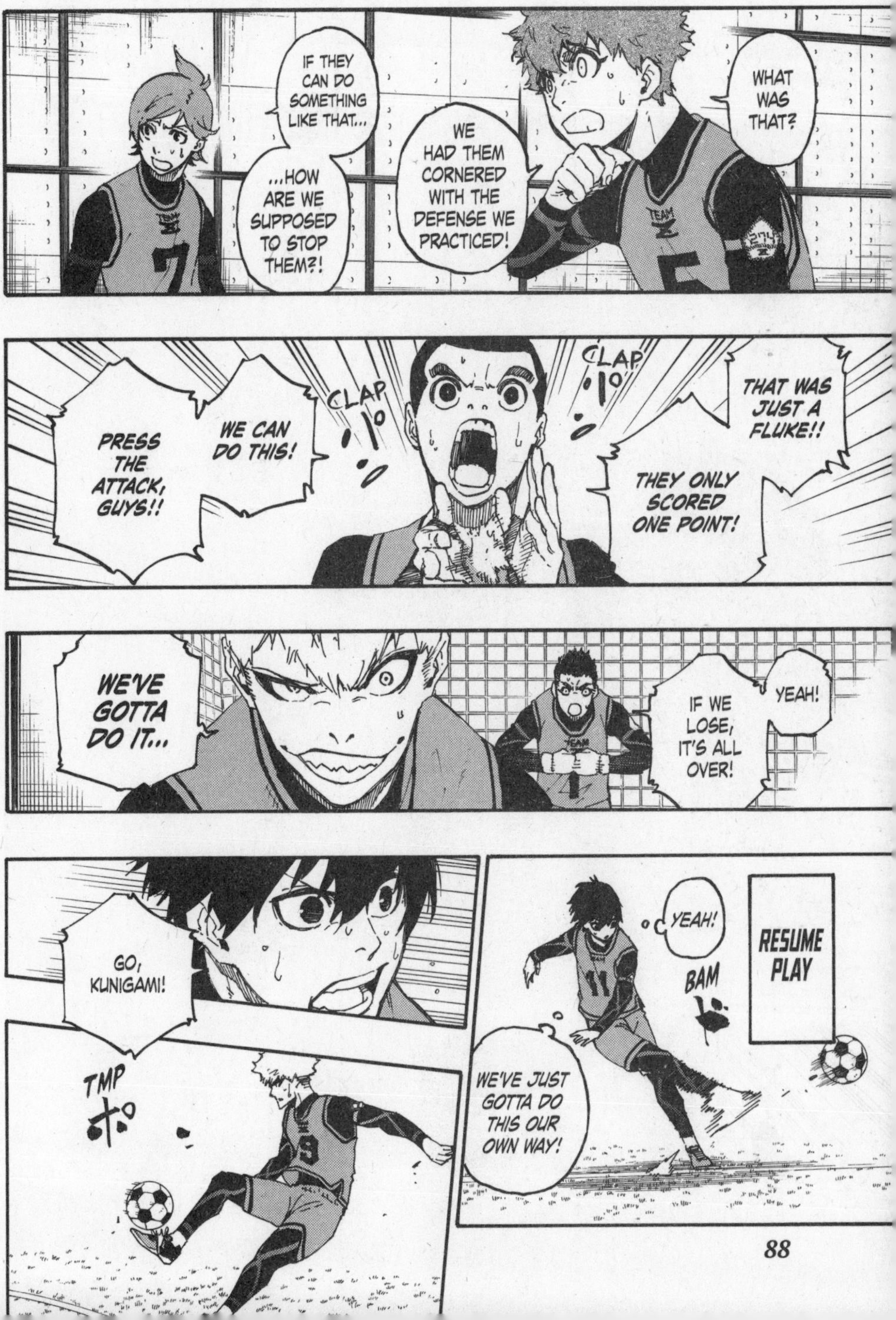
WHAT WAS THAT?
WE HAD THEM CORNERED WITH THE DEFENSE WE PRACTICED!
IF THEY CAN DO SOMETHING LIKE THAT...
...HOW ARE WE SUPPOSED TO STOP THEM?!
THAT WAS JUST A FLUKE!!
THEY ONLY SCORED ONE POINT!
CLAP
CLAP
WE CAN DO THIS!
PRESS THE ATTACK, GUYS!!
YEAH!
IF WE LOSE, IT'S ALL OVER!
WE'VE GOTTA DO IT...
RESUME PLAY
YEAH!
BAM
WE'VE JUST GOTTA DO THIS OUR OWN WAY!
GO, KUNIGAMI!
TMP

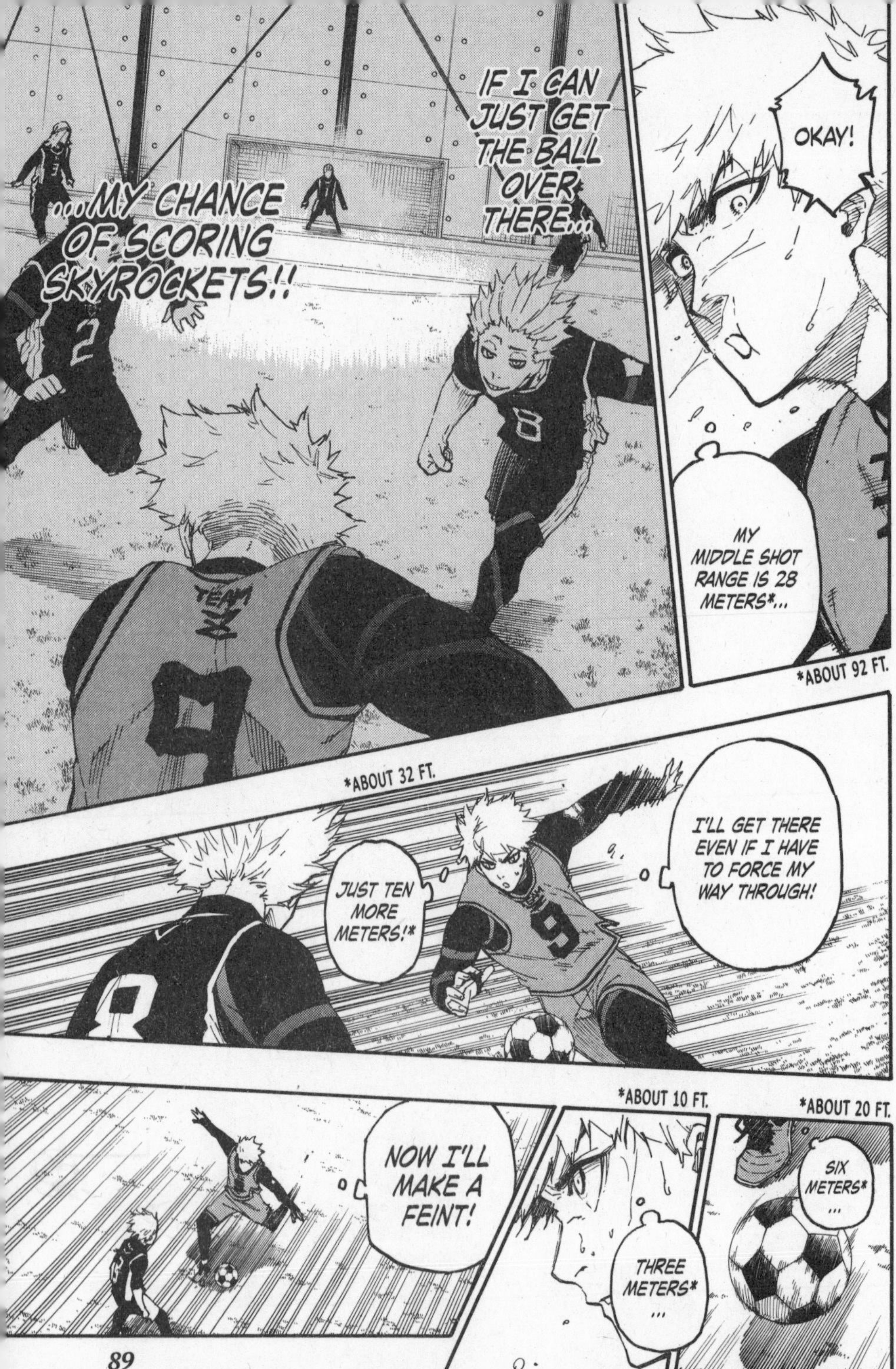
OKAY!
MY MIDDLE SHOT RANGE IS 28 METERS*...
*ABOUT 92 FT.
IF I CAN JUST GET THE BALL OVER THERE...
...MY CHANCE OF SCORING SKYROCKETS!!
I'LL GET THERE EVEN IF I HAVE TO FORCE MY WAY THROUGH!
JUST TEN MORE METERS!*
*ABOUT 32 FT.
SIX METERS* ...
*ABOUT 20 FT.
THREE METERS* ...
*ABOUT 10 FT.
NOW I'LL MAKE A FEINT!

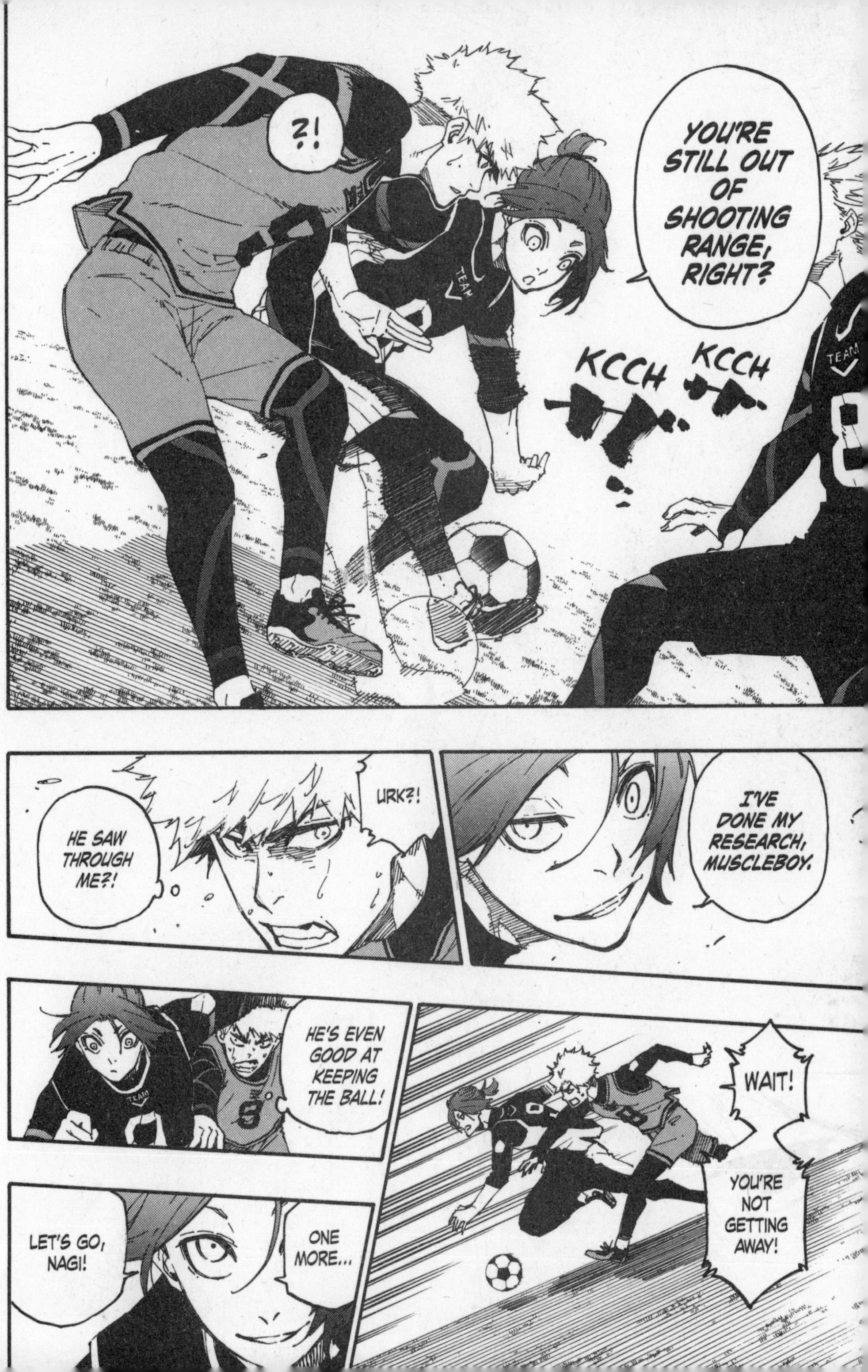
YOU'RE STILL OUT OF SHOOTING RANGE, RIGHT?
KCCH KCCH
?!
I'VE DONE MY RESEARCH, MUSCLEBOY.
URK?!
HE SAW THROUGH ME?!
WAIT!
YOU'RE NOT GETTING AWAY!
HE'S EVEN GOOD AT KEEPING THE BALL!
ONE MORE...
LET'S GO, NAGI!

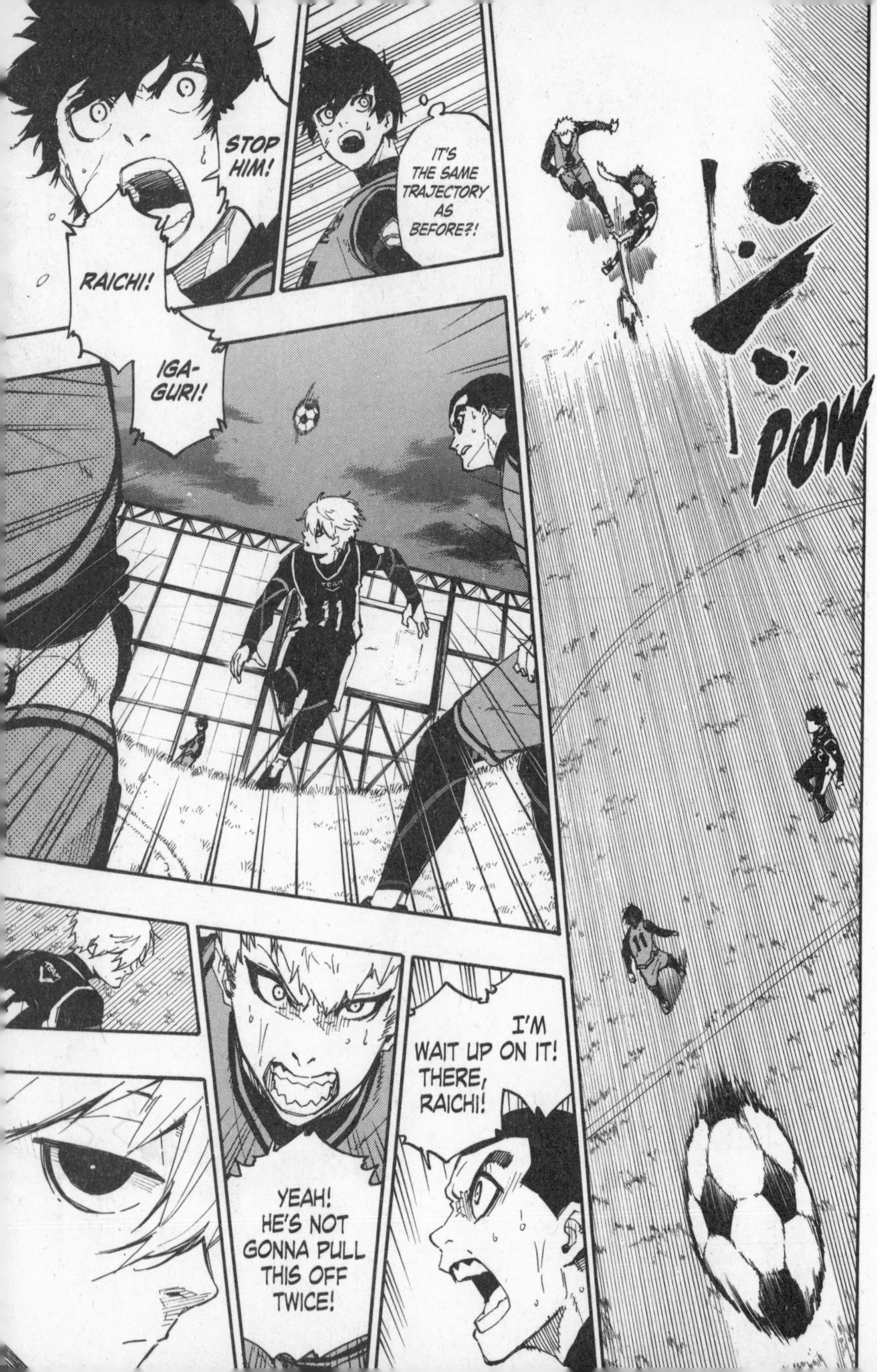
POW
IT'S THE SAME TRAJECTORY AS BEFORE?!
STOP HIM!
RAICHI!
IGA-GURI!
I'M WAIT UP ON IT! THERE, RAICHI!
YEAH! HE'S NOT GONNA PULL THIS OFF TWICE!

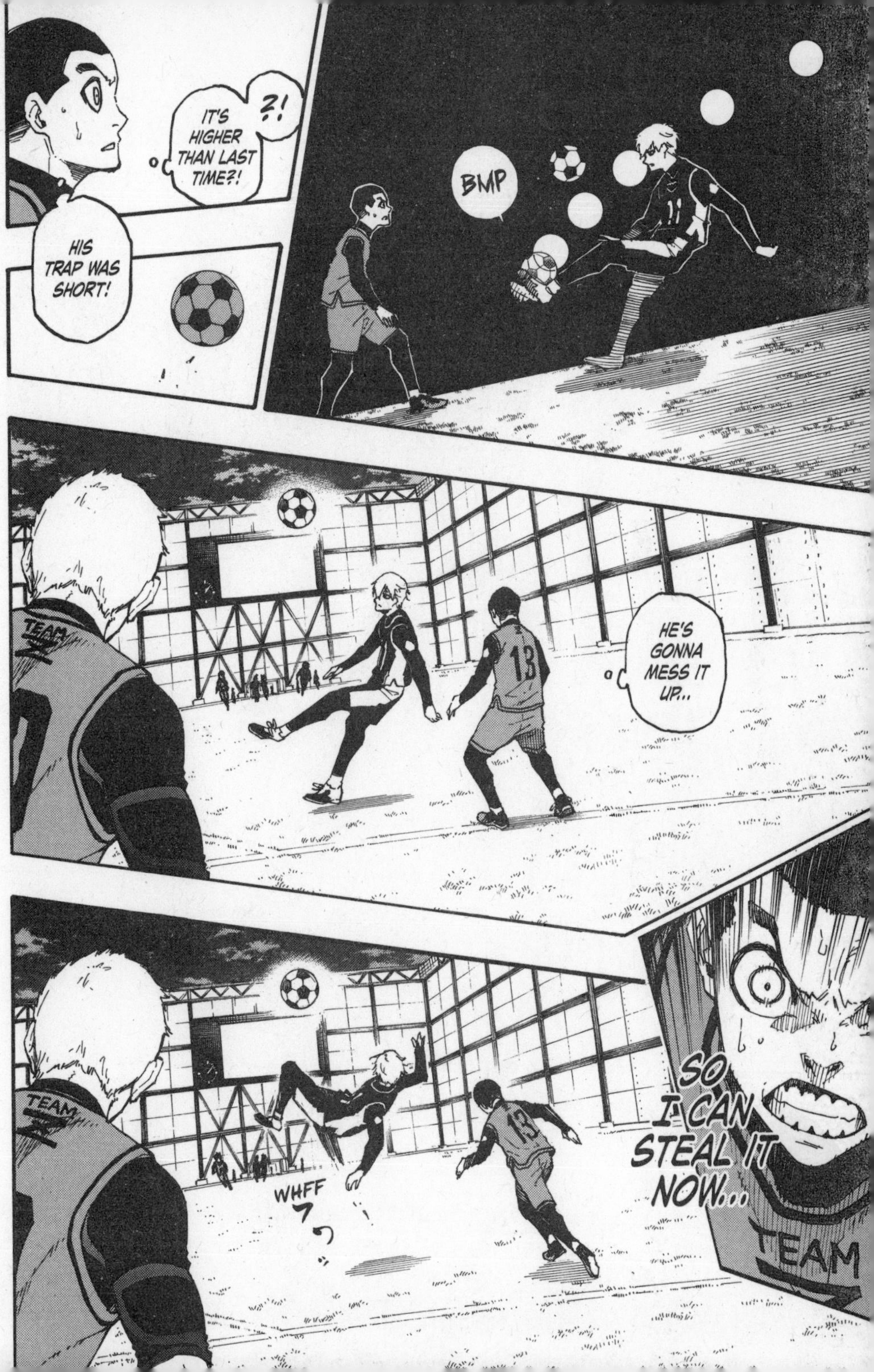
BMP
?!
IT'S HIGHER THAN LAST TIME?!
HIS TRAP WAS SHORT!
HE'S GONNA MESS IT UP...
SO I CAN STEAL IT NOW...
WHFF

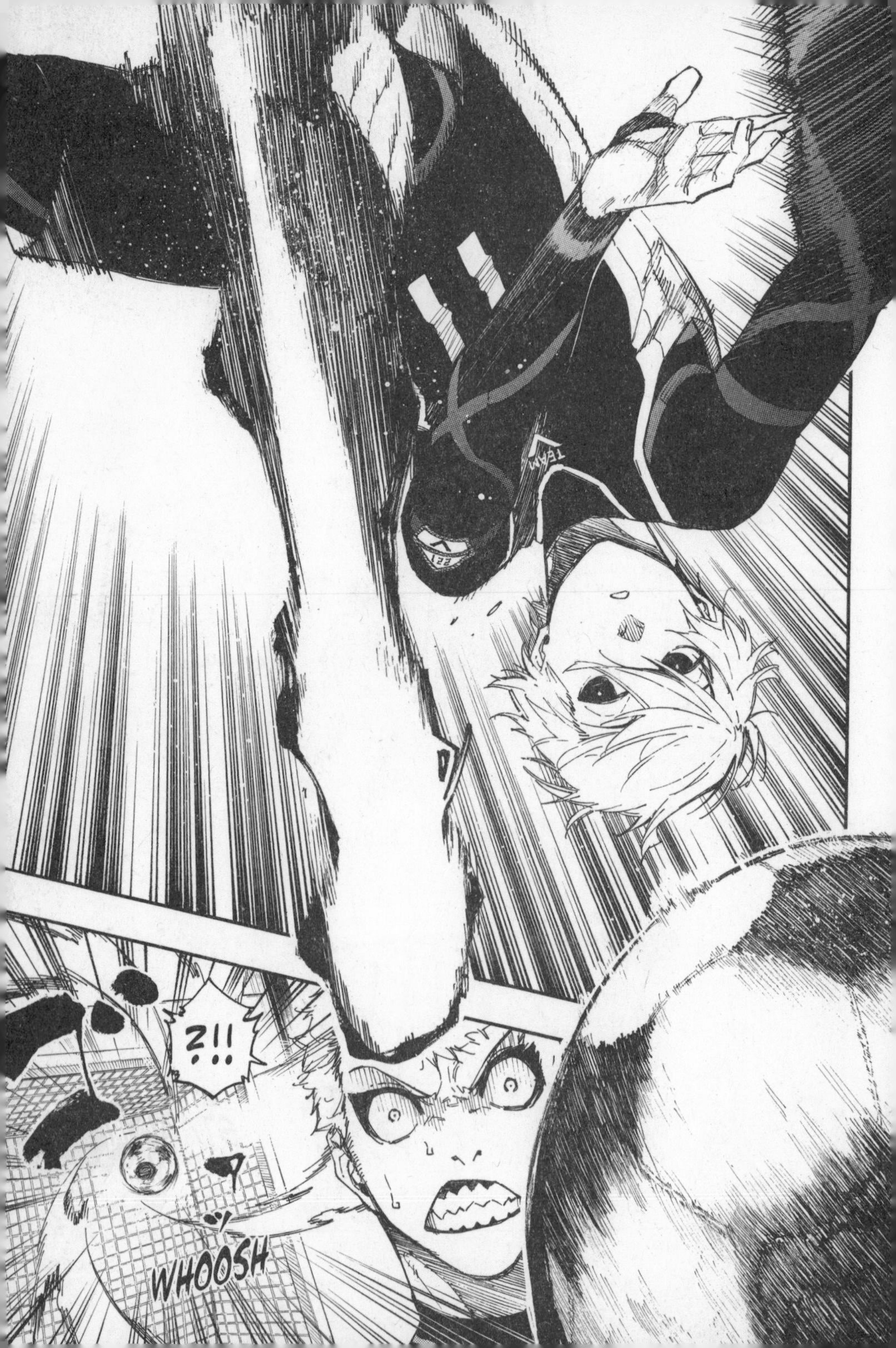
?!!
WHOOSH

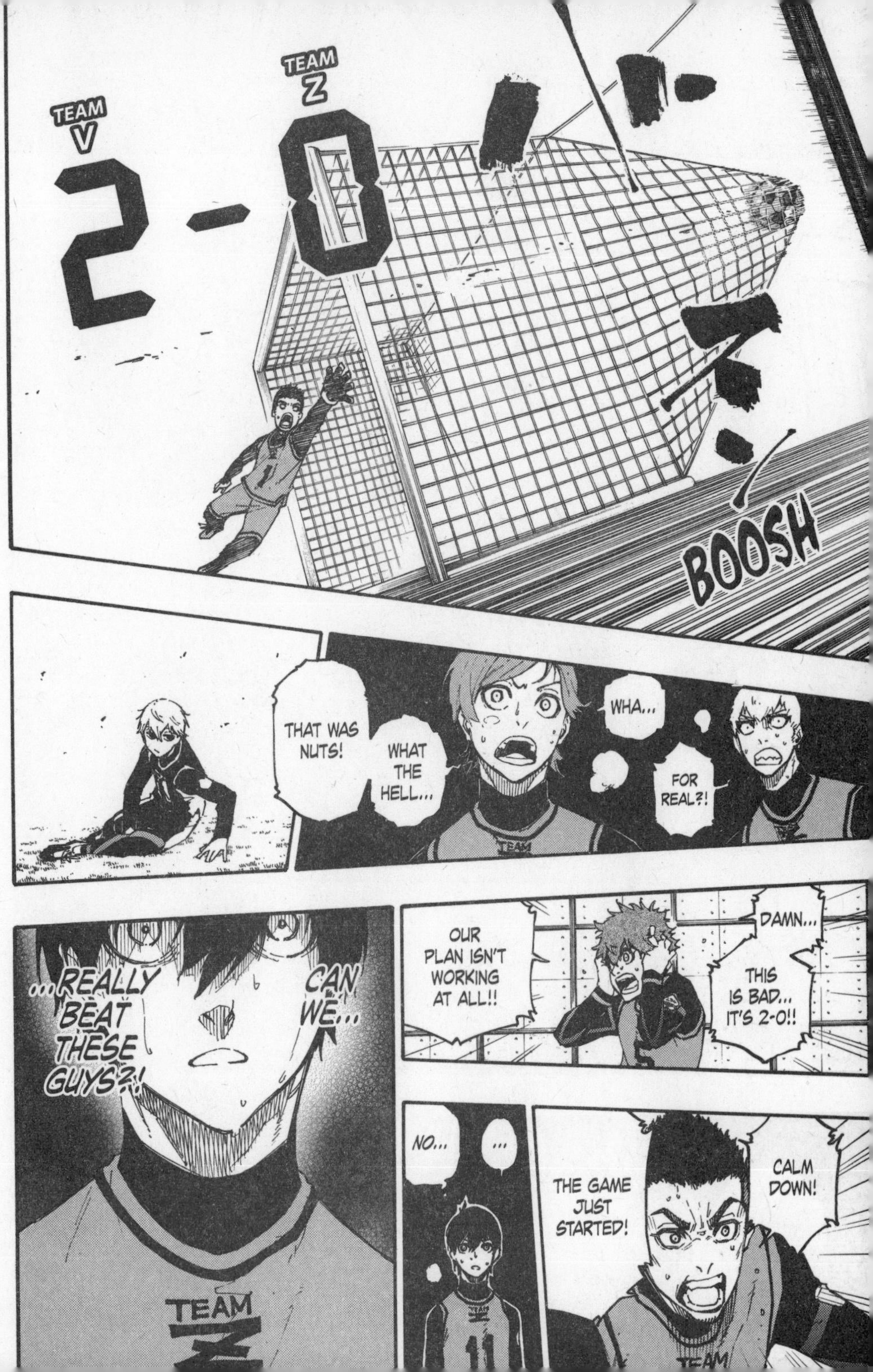
TEAM V
TEAM Z
2-0
BOOSH
WHA...
FOR REAL?!
WHAT THE HELL...
THAT WAS NUTS!
DAMN...
THIS IS BAD... IT'S 2-0!!
OUR PLAN ISN'T WORKING AT ALL!!
CALM DOWN!
THE GAME JUST STARTED!
...
NO...
CAN WE...
...REALLY BEAT THESE GUYS?!
TEAM Z

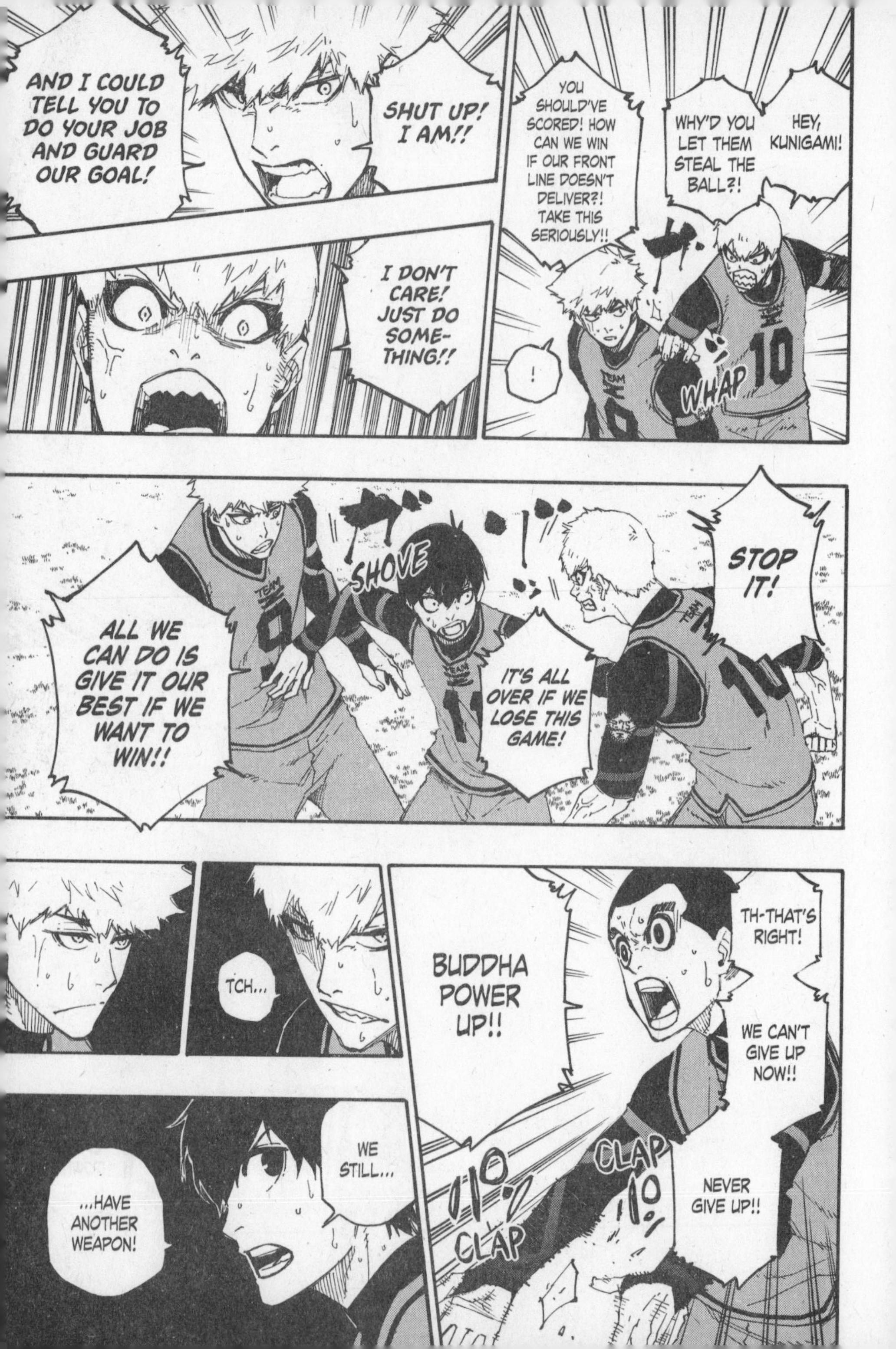
HEY, KUNIGAMI!
WHY'D YOU LET THEM STEAL THE BALL?!
YOU SHOULD'VE SCORED! HOW CAN WE WIN IF OUR FRONT LINE DOESN'T DELIVER?! TAKE THIS SERIOUSLY!!
!
WHAP
SHUT UP! I AM!!
AND I COULD TELL YOU TO DO YOUR JOB AND GUARD OUR GOAL!
I DON'T CARE! JUST DO SOME-THING!!
STOP IT!
IT'S ALL OVER IF WE LOSE THIS GAME!
SHOVE
ALL WE CAN DO IS GIVE IT OUR BEST IF WE WANT TO WIN!!
TH-THAT'S RIGHT!
WE CAN'T GIVE UP NOW!!
BUDDHA POWER UP!!
NEVER GIVE UP!!
CLAP
CLAP
TCH...
WE STILL...
...HAVE ANOTHER WEAPON!

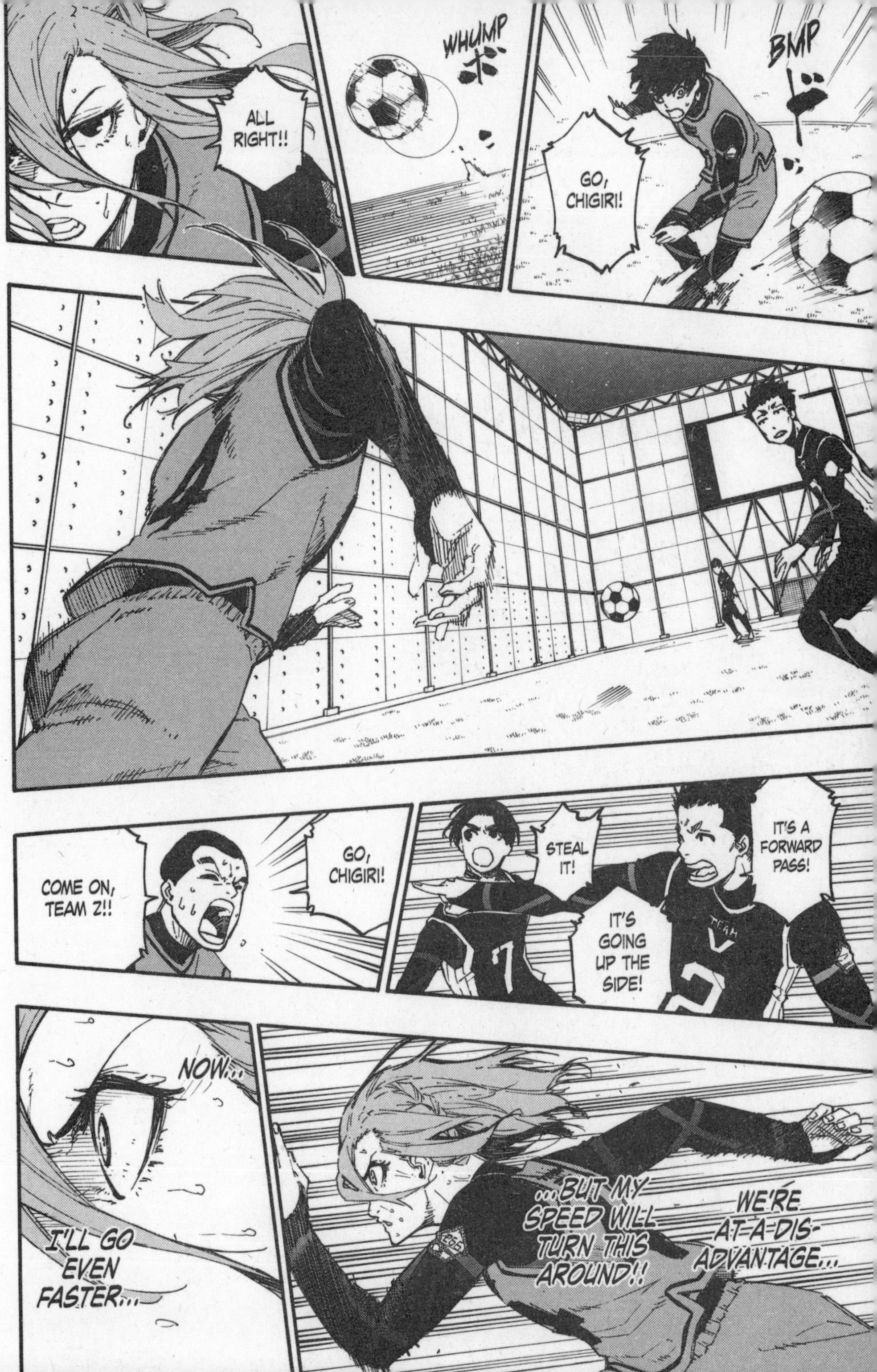
BMP
GO, CHIGIRI!
WHUMP
ALL RIGHT!!
IT'S A FORWARD PASS!
STEAL IT!
IT'S GOING UP THE SIDE!
GO, CHIGIRI!
COME ON, TEAM Z!!
WE'RE AT A DIS-ADVANTAGE...
...BUT MY SPEED WILL TURN THIS AROUND!!
NOW...
I'LL GO EVEN FASTER...

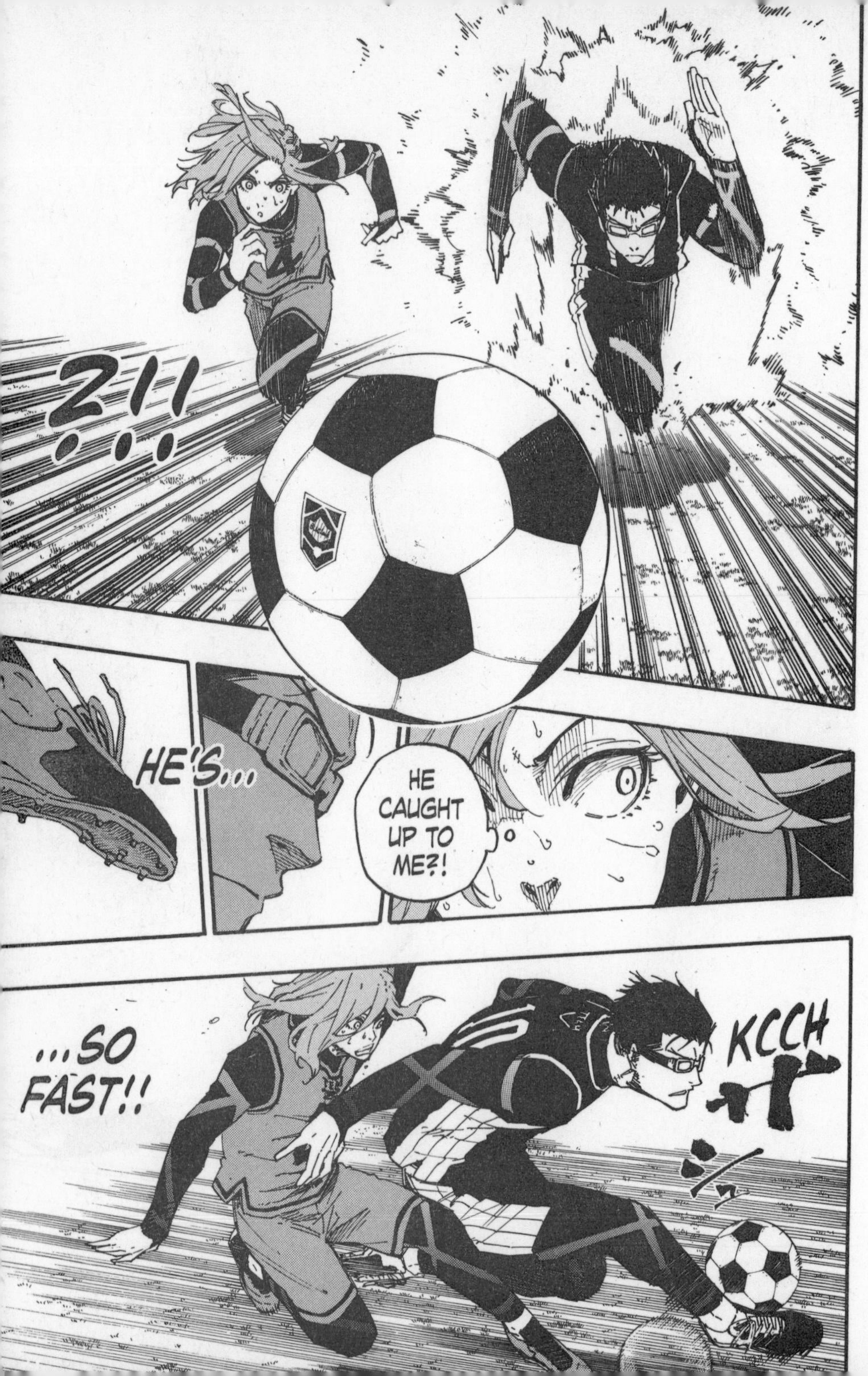
?!!
HE CAUGHT UP TO ME?!
HE'S...
KCCH
...SO FAST!!

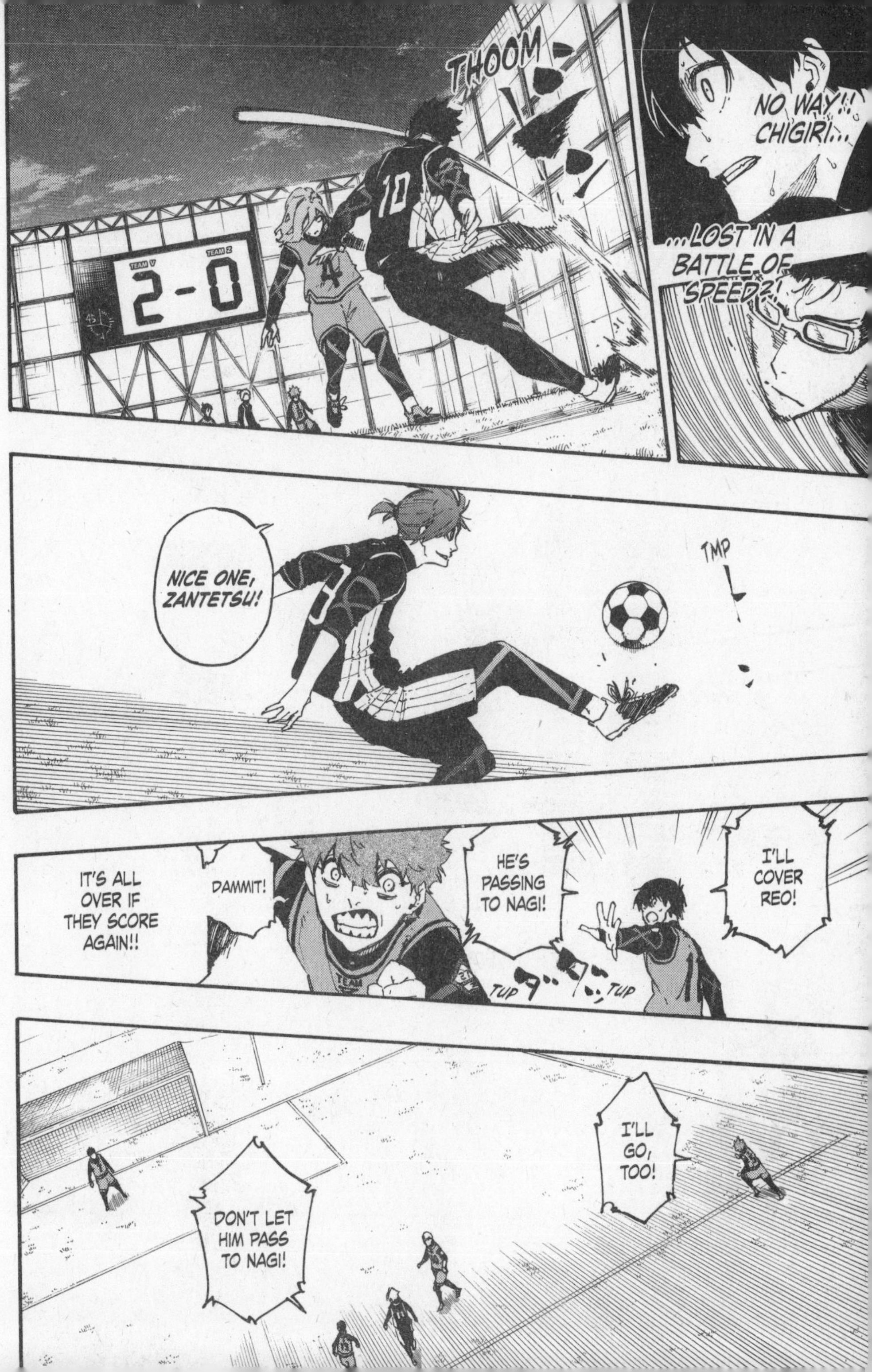
NO WAY!! CHIGIRI...
...LOST IN A BATTLE OF SPEED?!
THOOM
TEAM V
TEAM Z
2-0
TMP
NICE ONE, ZANTETSU!
I'LL COVER REO!
HE'S PASSING TO NAGI!
TUP
TUP
DAMMIT!
IT'S ALL OVER IF THEY SCORE AGAIN!!
I'LL GO, TOO!
DON'T LET HIM PASS TO NAGI!

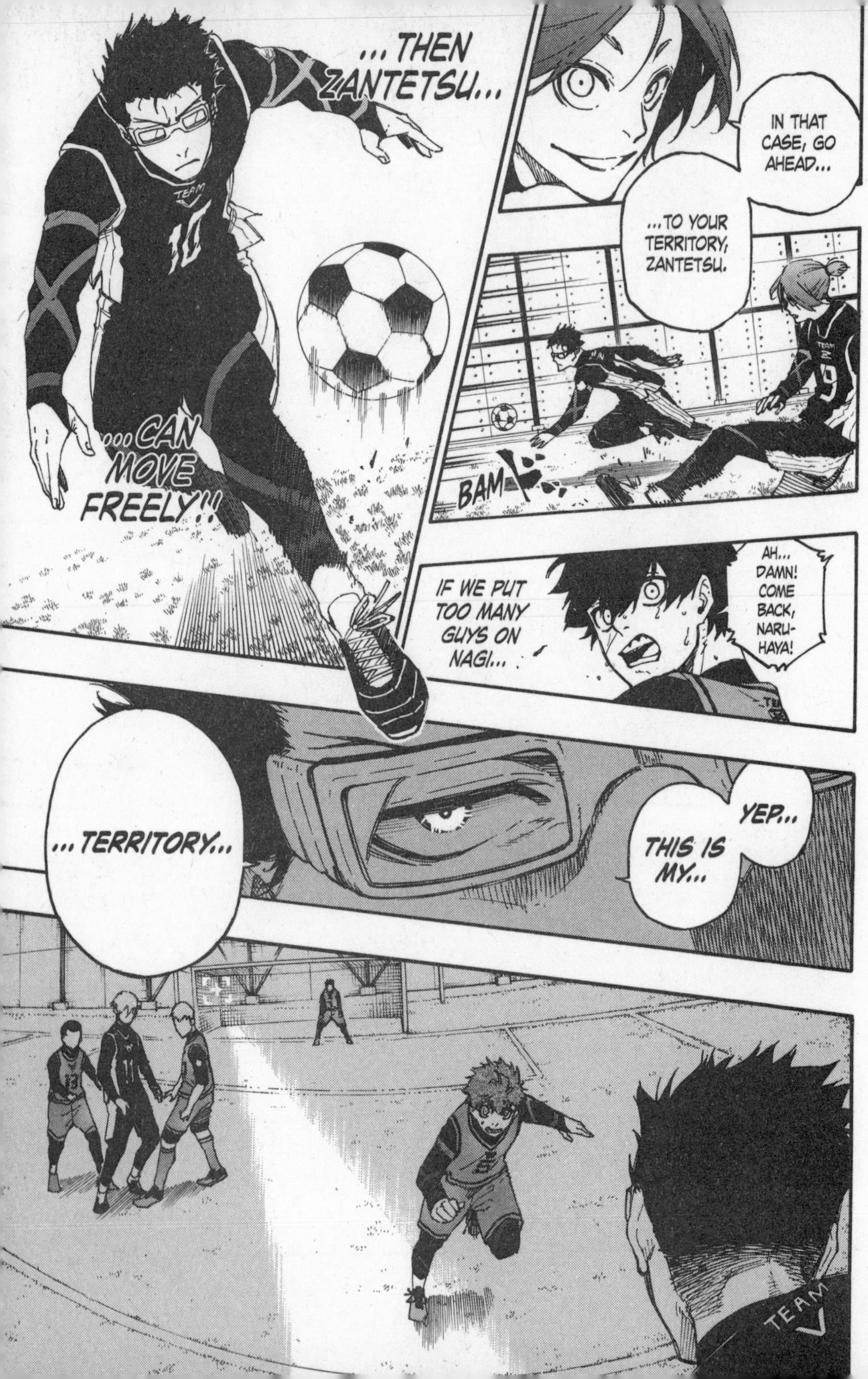
IN THAT CASE, GO AHEAD...
...TO YOUR TERRITORY, ZANTETSU.
BAM
AH... DAMN! COME BACK, NARUHAYA!
IF WE PUT TOO MANY GUYS ON NAGI...
...THEN ZANTETSU...
...CAN MOVE FREELY!!
YEP... THIS IS MY...
...TERRITORY...

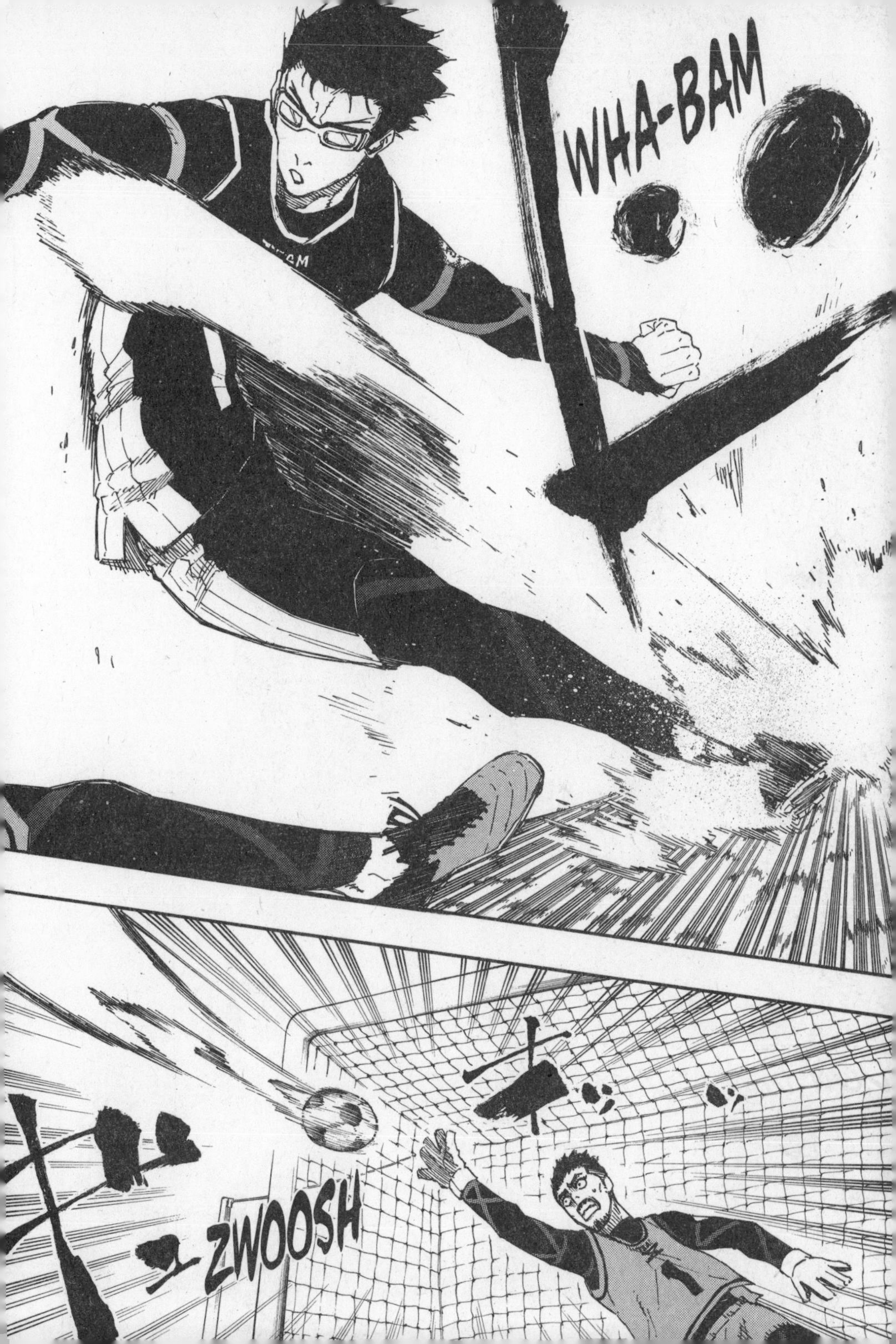
WHA-BAM
ZWOOSH

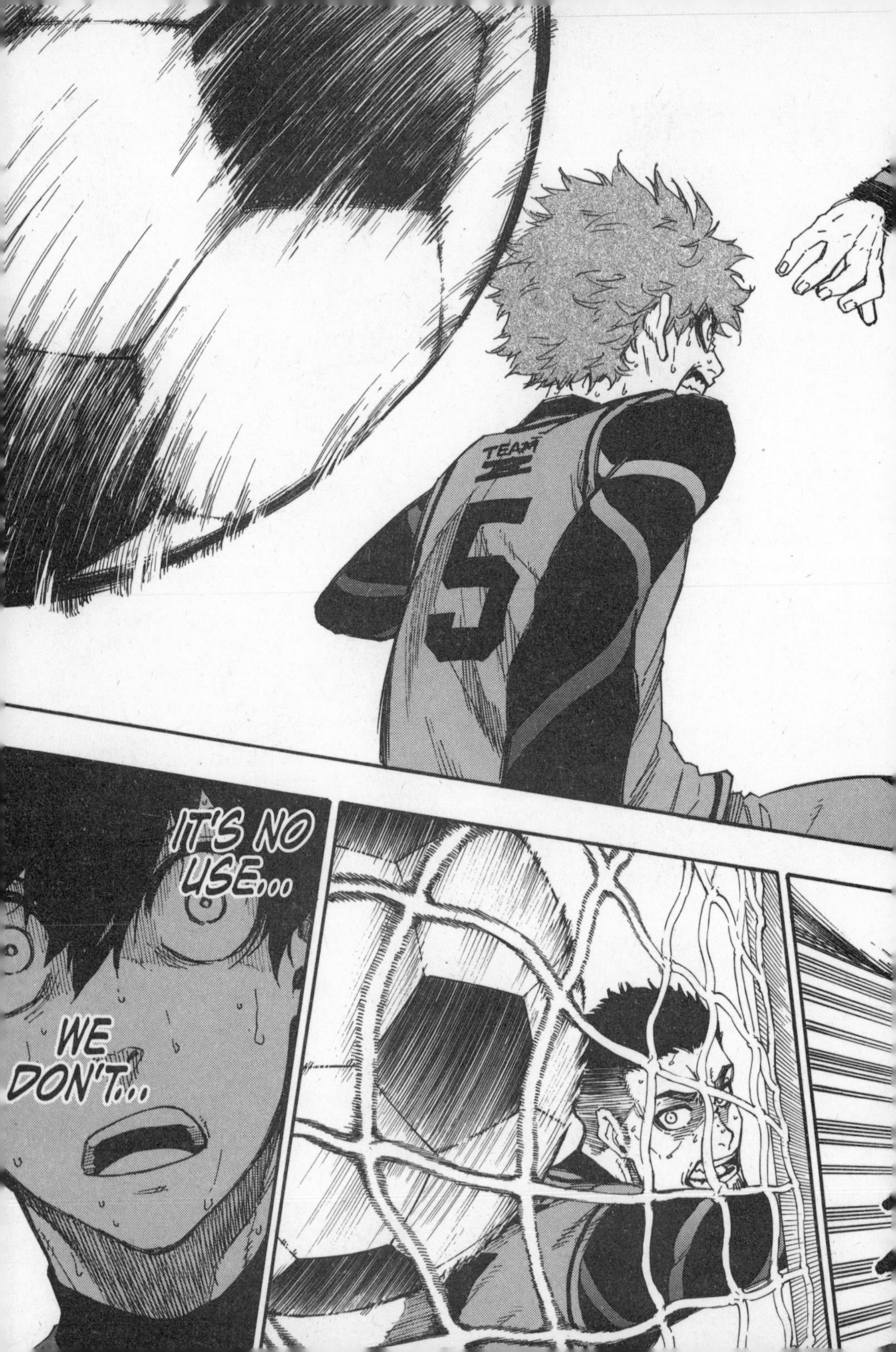
TEAM
5
IT'S NO USE...
WE DON'T...

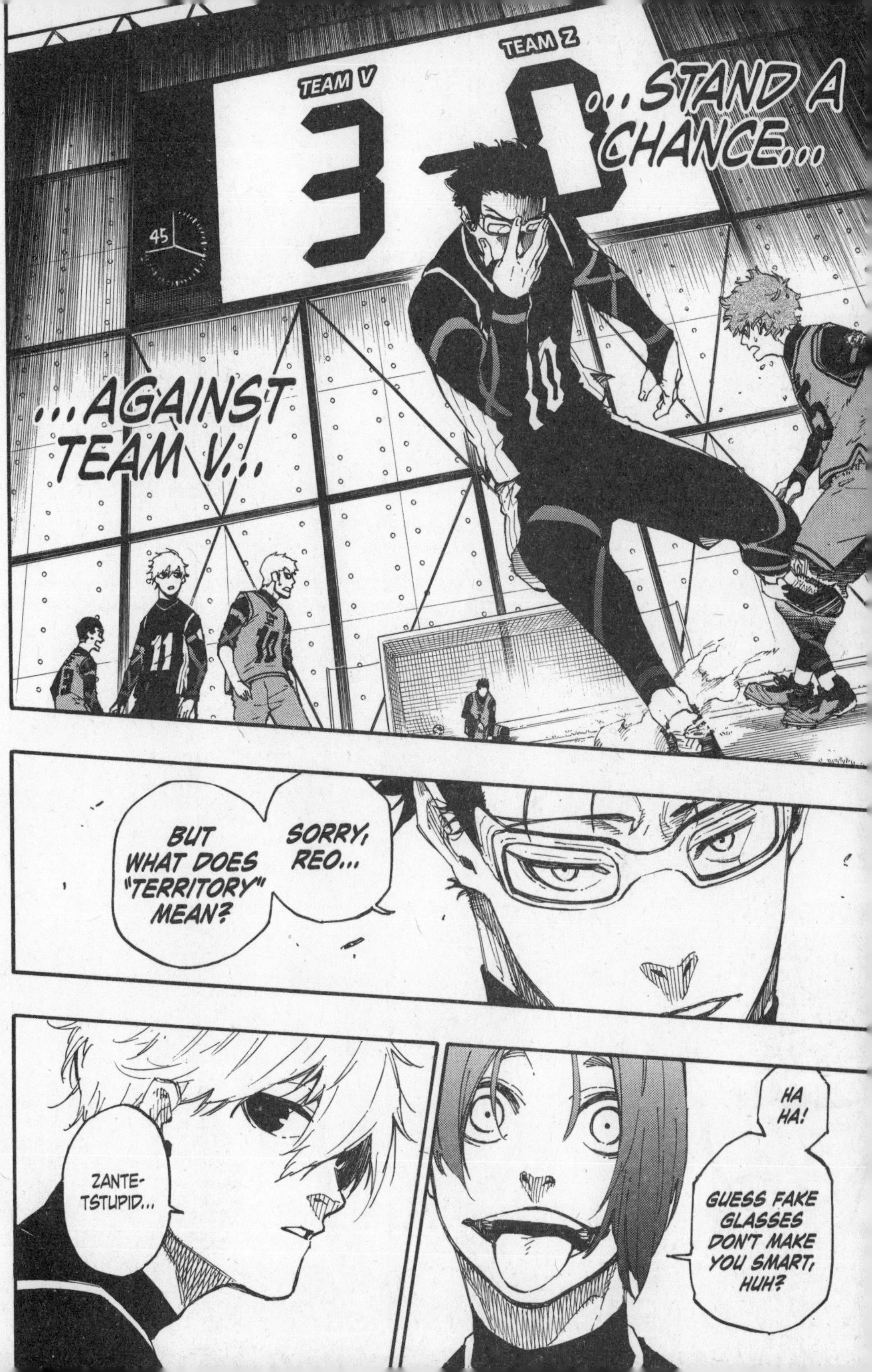
TEAM Z
TEAM V
...STAND A CHANCE...
...AGAINST TEAM V...
SORRY, REO...
BUT WHAT DOES "TERRITORY" MEAN?
HA HA!
GUESS FAKE GLASSES DON'T MAKE YOU SMART, HUH?
ZANTE-TSTUPID...

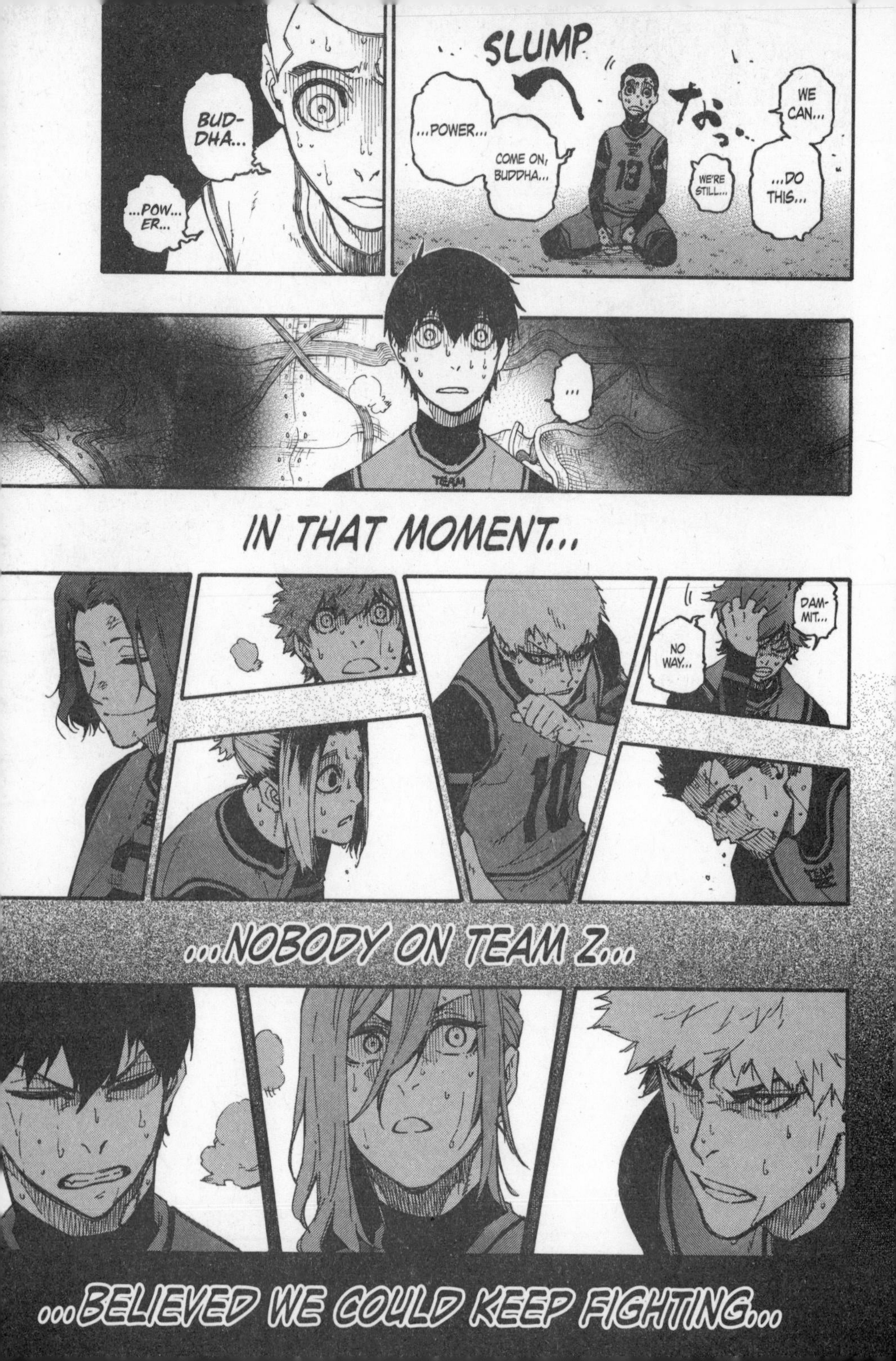

WE CAN...
...DO THIS...
WE'RE STILL...
なっ
SLUMP
...POWER...
COME ON, BUDDHA...
BUD-DHA...
...POW... ER...
...
IN THAT MOMENT...
DAM-MIT...
NO WAY...
...NOBODY ON TEAM Z...
...BELIEVED WE COULD KEEP FIGHTING...

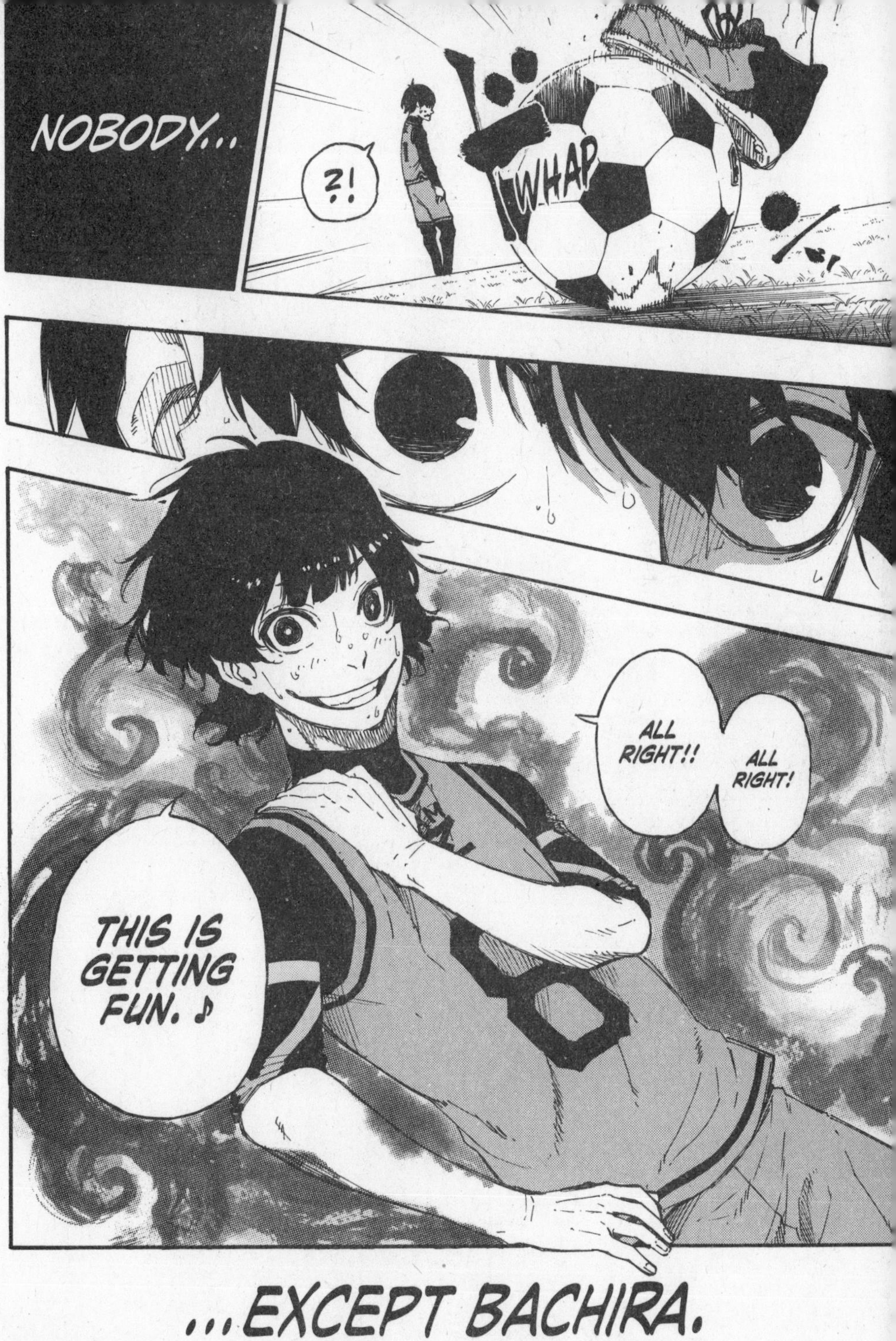
WHAP
?!
NOBODY...
ALL RIGHT!
ALL RIGHT!!
THIS IS GETTING FUN. ♪
...EXCEPT BACHIRA.

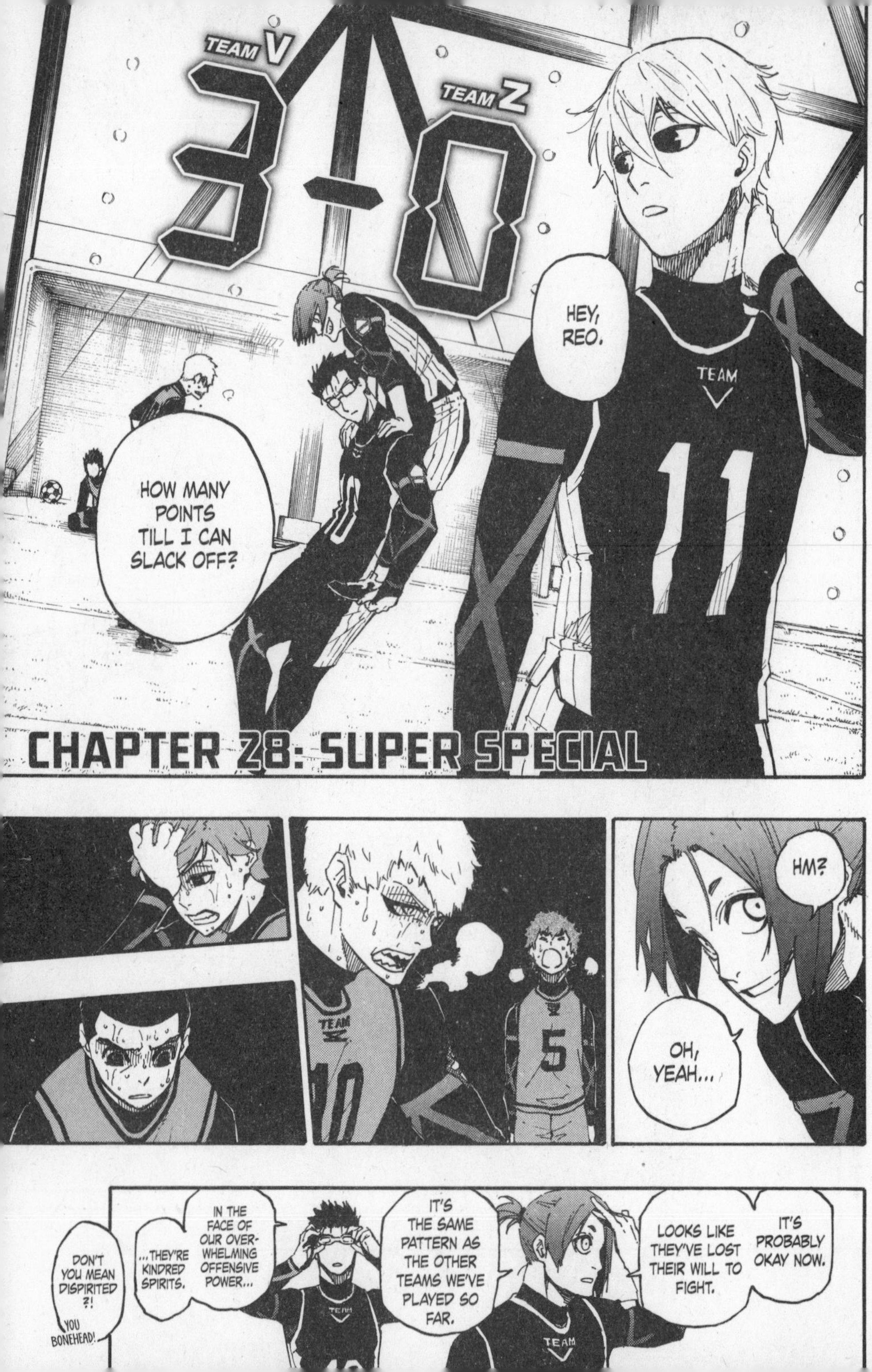
TEAM V
3-8
TEAM Z
HEY, REO.
HOW MANY POINTS TILL I CAN SLACK OFF?
CHAPTER 28: SUPER SPECIAL
HM?
OH, YEAH...
IT'S PROBABLY OKAY NOW.
LOOKS LIKE THEY'VE LOST THEIR WILL TO FIGHT.
IT'S THE SAME PATTERN AS THE OTHER TEAMS WE'VE PLAYED SO FAR.
IN THE FACE OF OUR OVER-WHELMING OFFENSIVE POWER...
...THEY'RE KINDRED SPIRITS.
DON'T YOU MEAN DISPIRITED?!
YOU BONEHEAD!

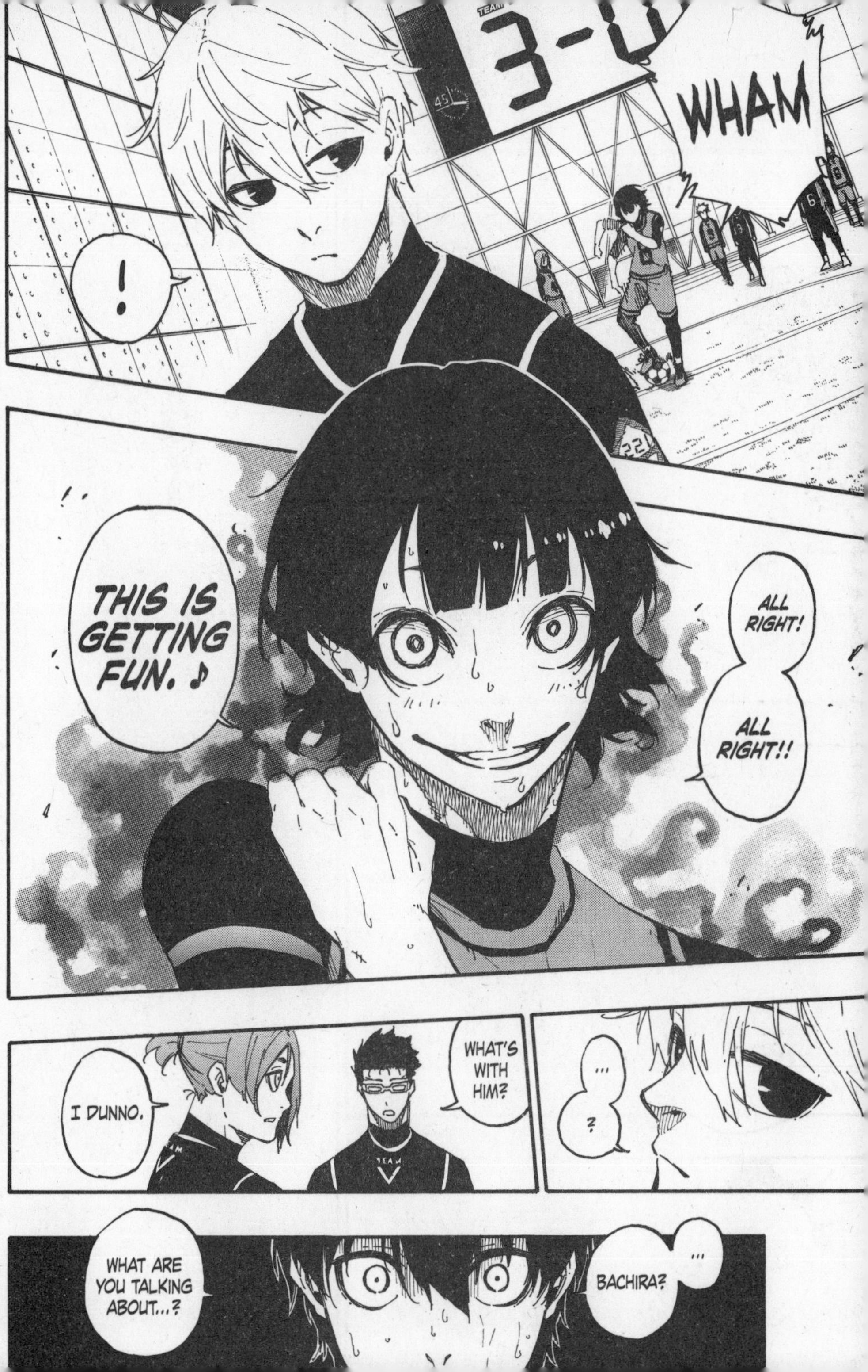
3-0
WHAM
!
ALL RIGHT! ALL RIGHT!!
THIS IS GETTING FUN. ♪
... ?
WHAT'S WITH HIM?
I DUNNO.
... BACHIRA?
WHAT ARE YOU TALKING ABOUT...?

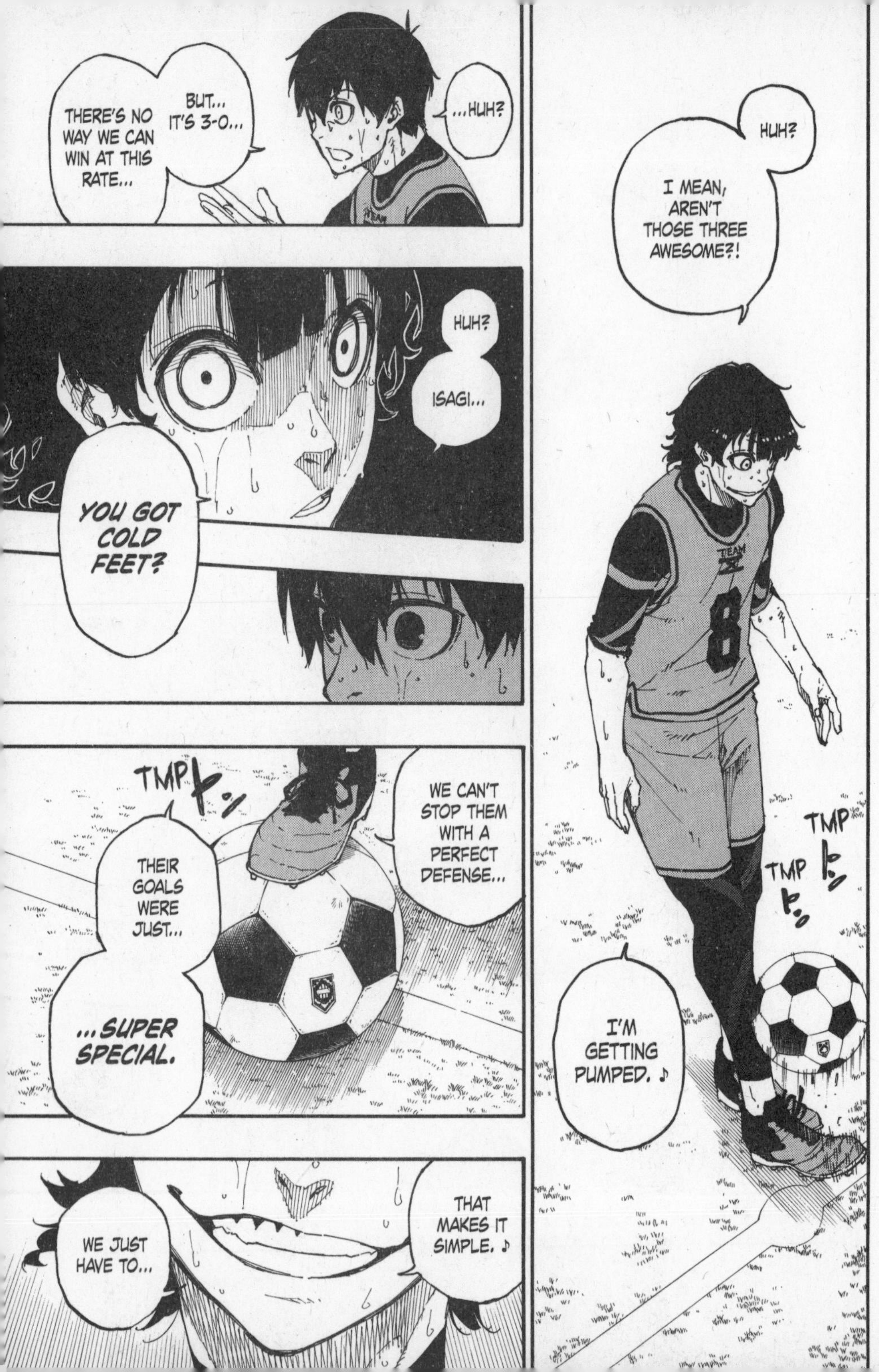
HUH?
I MEAN, AREN'T THOSE THREE AWESOME?!
TMP
TMP
I'M GETTING PUMPED. ♪
...HUH?
BUT... IT'S 3-0...
THERE'S NO WAY WE CAN WIN AT THIS RATE...
HUH?
ISAGI...
YOU GOT COLD FEET?
TMP
WE CAN'T STOP THEM WITH A PERFECT DEFENSE...
THEIR GOALS WERE JUST...
...SUPER SPECIAL.
THAT MAKES IT SIMPLE. ♪
WE JUST HAVE TO...

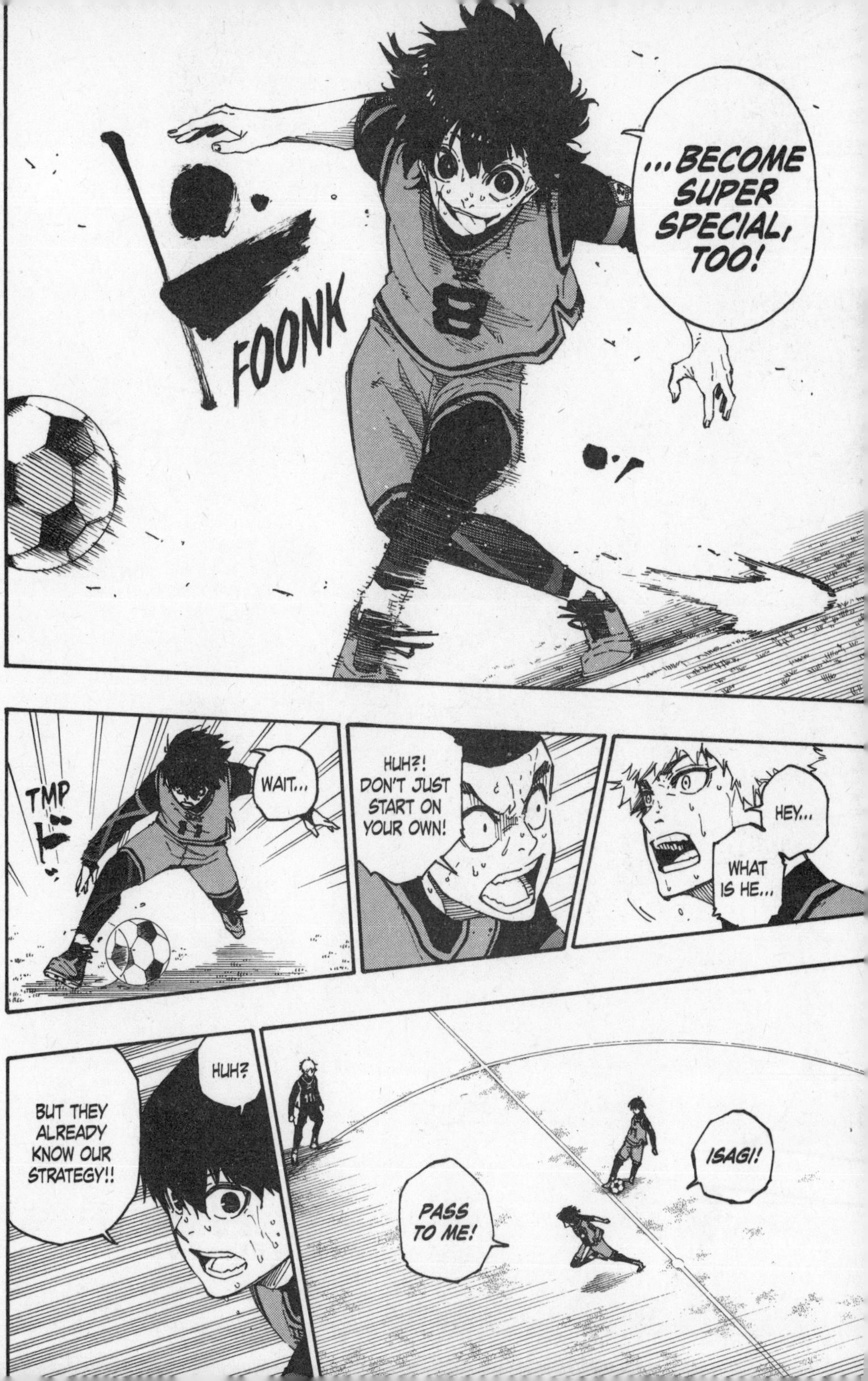
...BECOME SUPER SPECIAL, TOO!
FOONK
HEY...
WHAT IS HE...
HUH?! DON'T JUST START ON YOUR OWN!
WAIT...
TMP
ISAGI!
PASS TO ME!
HUH?
BUT THEY ALREADY KNOW OUR STRATEGY!!

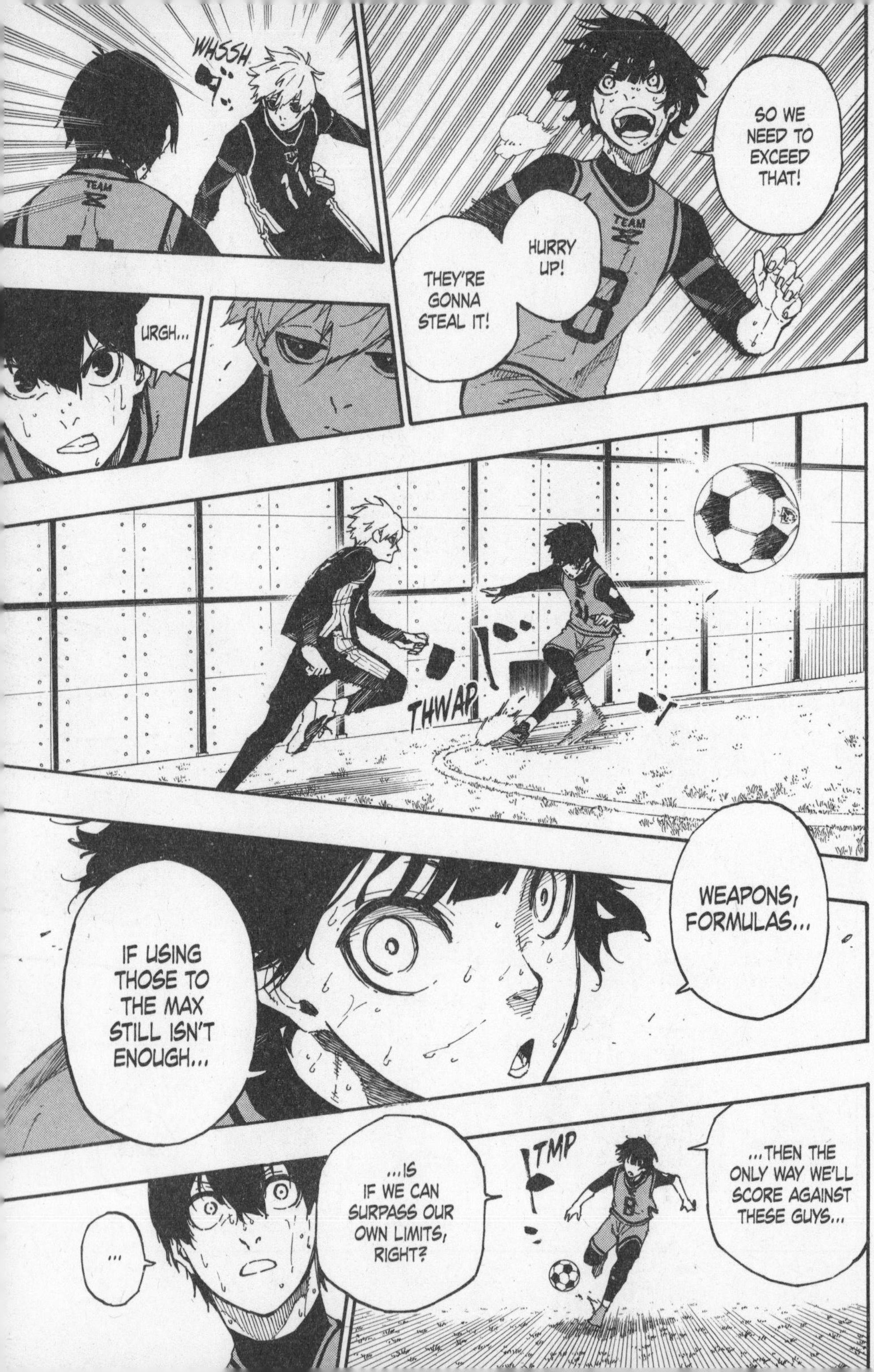
SO WE NEED TO EXCEED THAT!
HURRY UP!
THEY'RE GONNA STEAL IT!
WHSSH
URGH...
THWAP
WEAPONS, FORMULAS...
IF USING THOSE TO THE MAX STILL ISN'T ENOUGH...
...THEN THE ONLY WAY WE'LL SCORE AGAINST THESE GUYS...
TMP
...IS IF WE CAN SURPASS OUR OWN LIMITS, RIGHT?
...

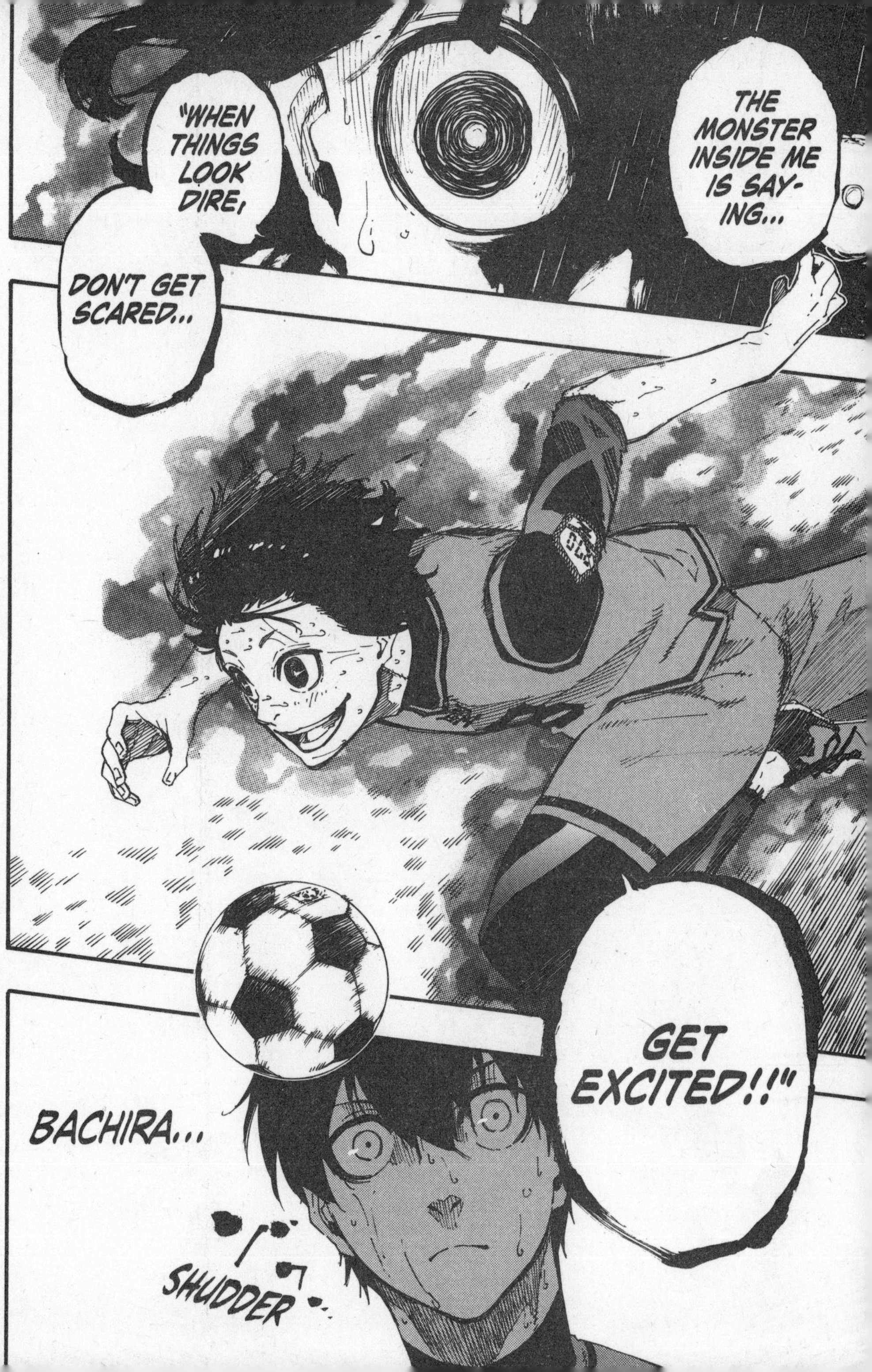
THE MONSTER INSIDE ME IS SAYING...
"WHEN THINGS LOOK DIRE,
DON'T GET SCARED...
GET EXCITED!!"
BACHIRA...
SHUDDER

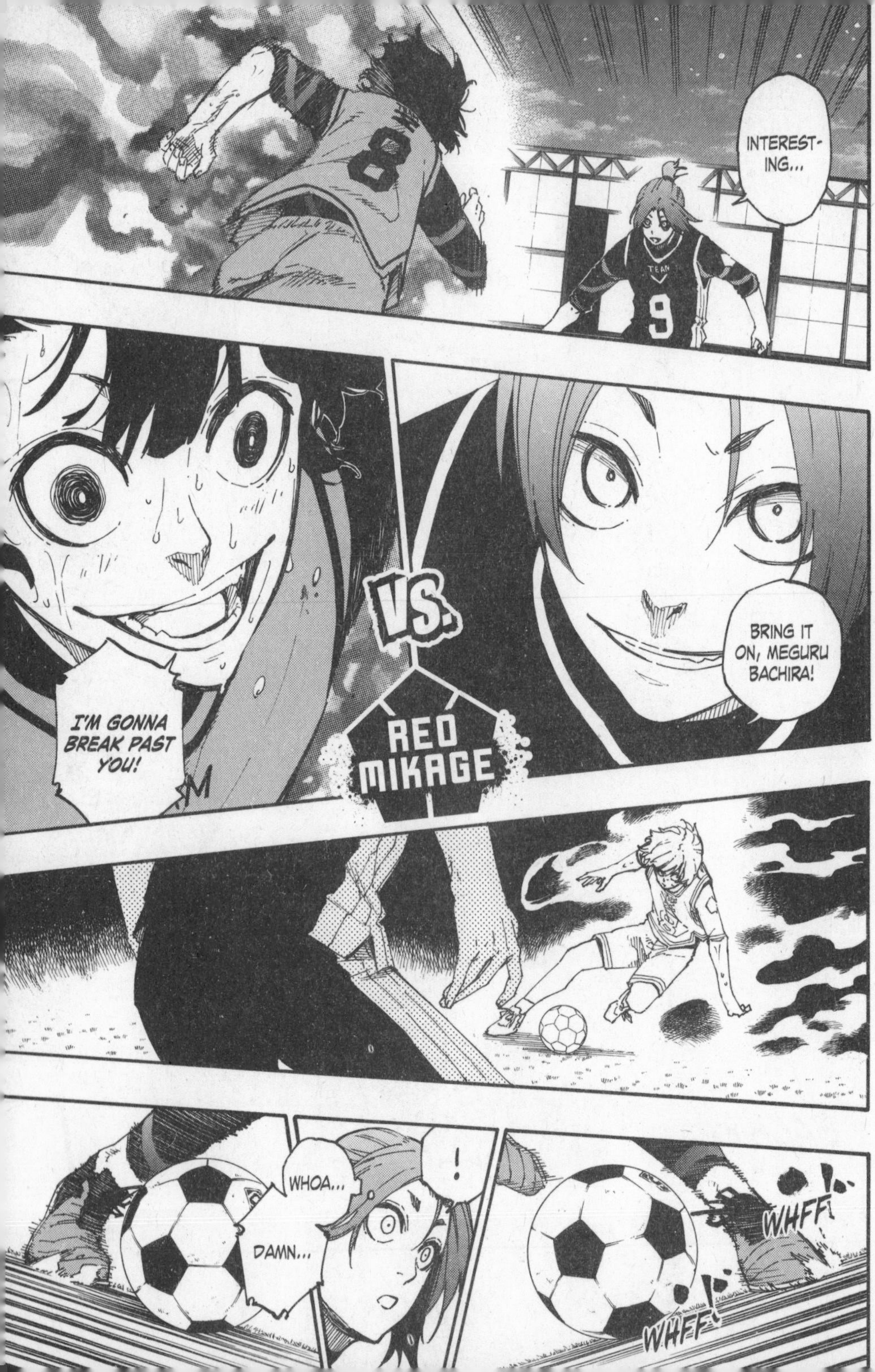
INTERESTING...
BRING IT ON, MEGURU BACHIRA!
VS.
REO MIKAGE
I'M GONNA BREAK PAST YOU!
WHFF
WHFF
!
WHOA...
DAMN...

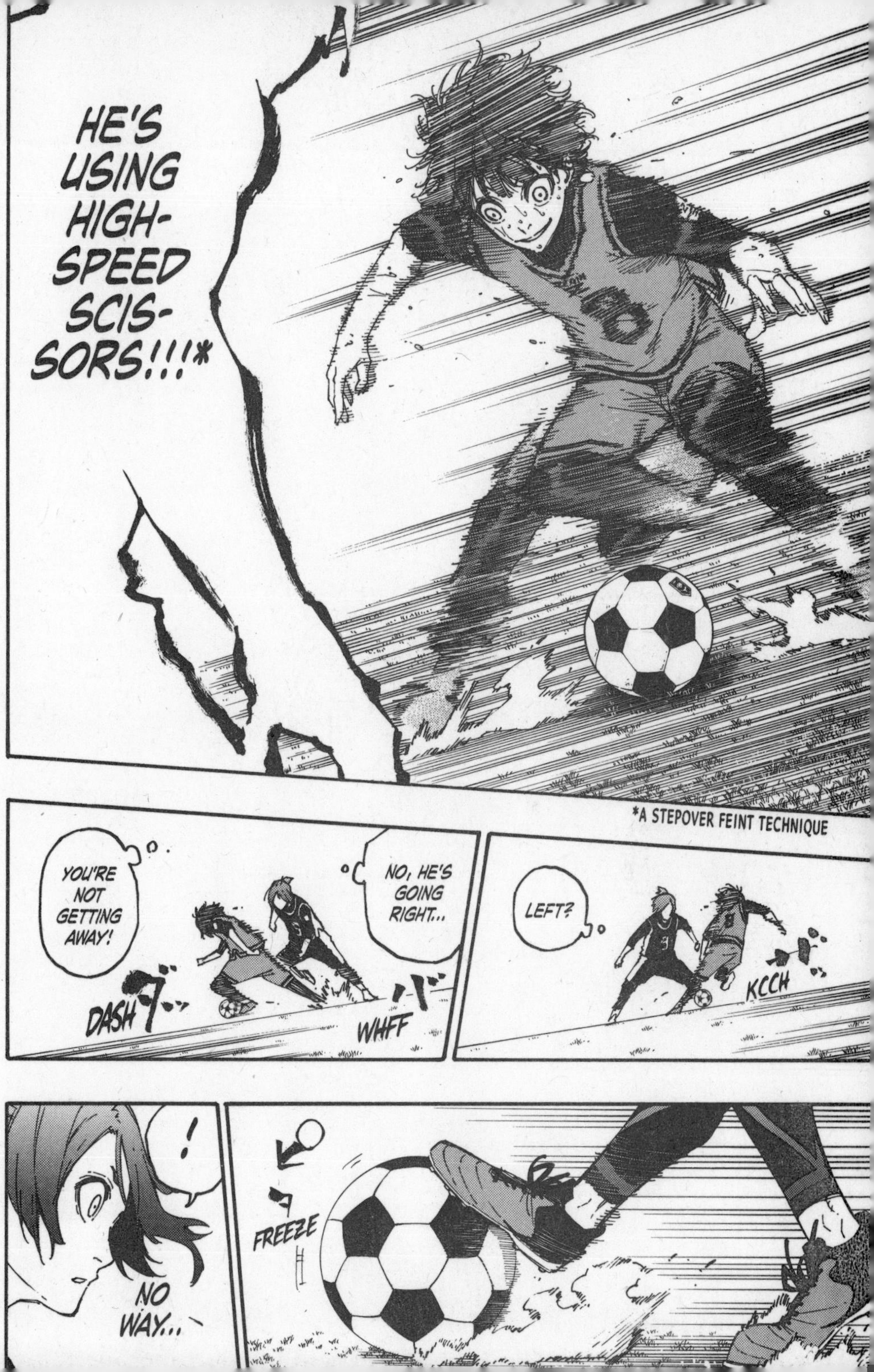
HE'S USING HIGH-SPEED SCISSORS!!!*
*A STEPOVER FEINT TECHNIQUE
LEFT?
KCCH
NO, HE'S GOING RIGHT...
YOU'RE NOT GETTING AWAY!
WHFF
DASH
FREEZE
!
NO WAY...

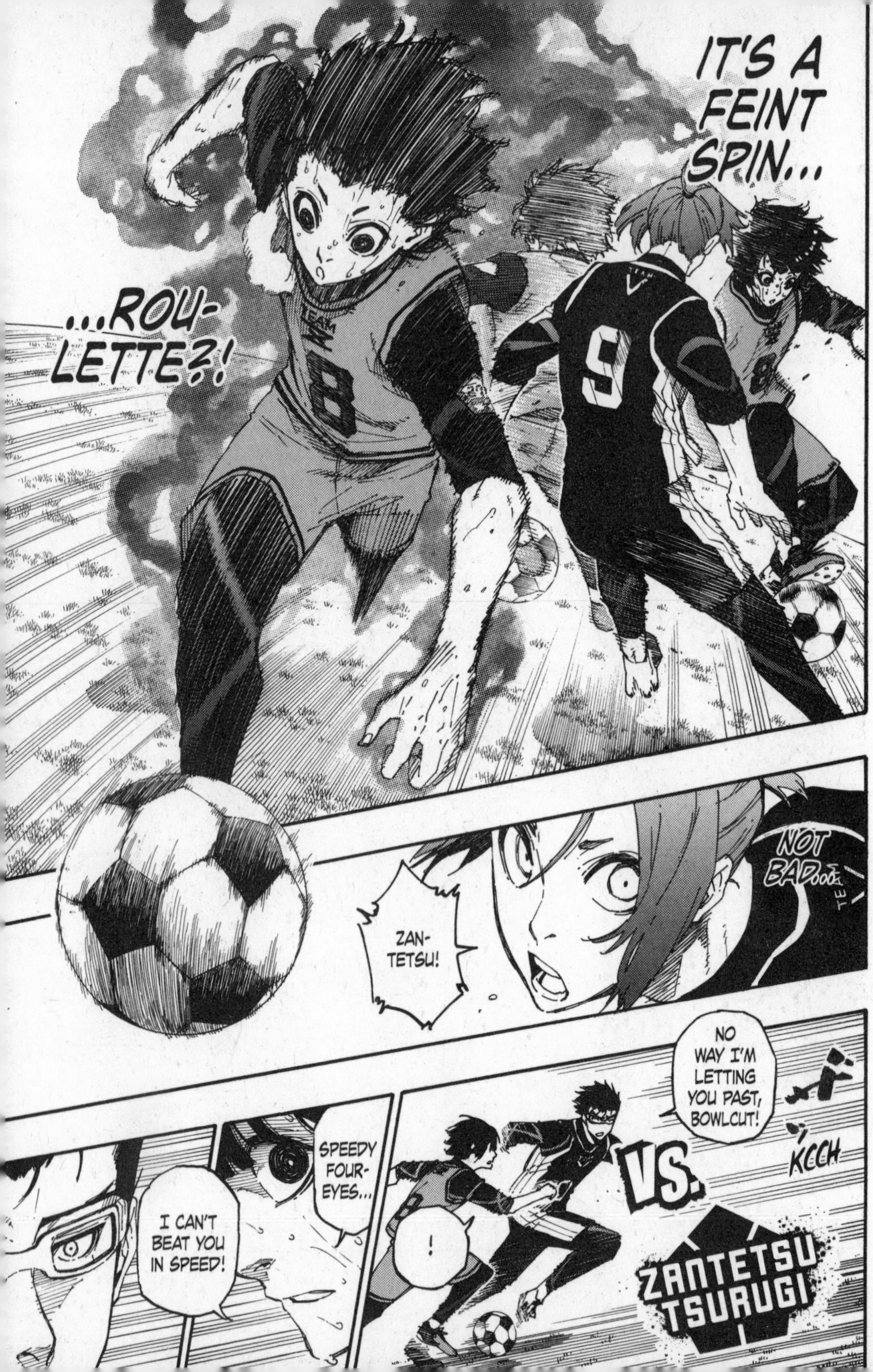
IT'S A FEINT SPIN...
...ROU-LETTE?!
NOT BAD...
ZAN-TETSU!
NO WAY I'M LETTING YOU PAST, BOWLCUT!
KCCH
VS.
ZANTETSU TSURUGI
!
SPEEDY FOUR-EYES...
I CAN'T BEAT YOU IN SPEED!

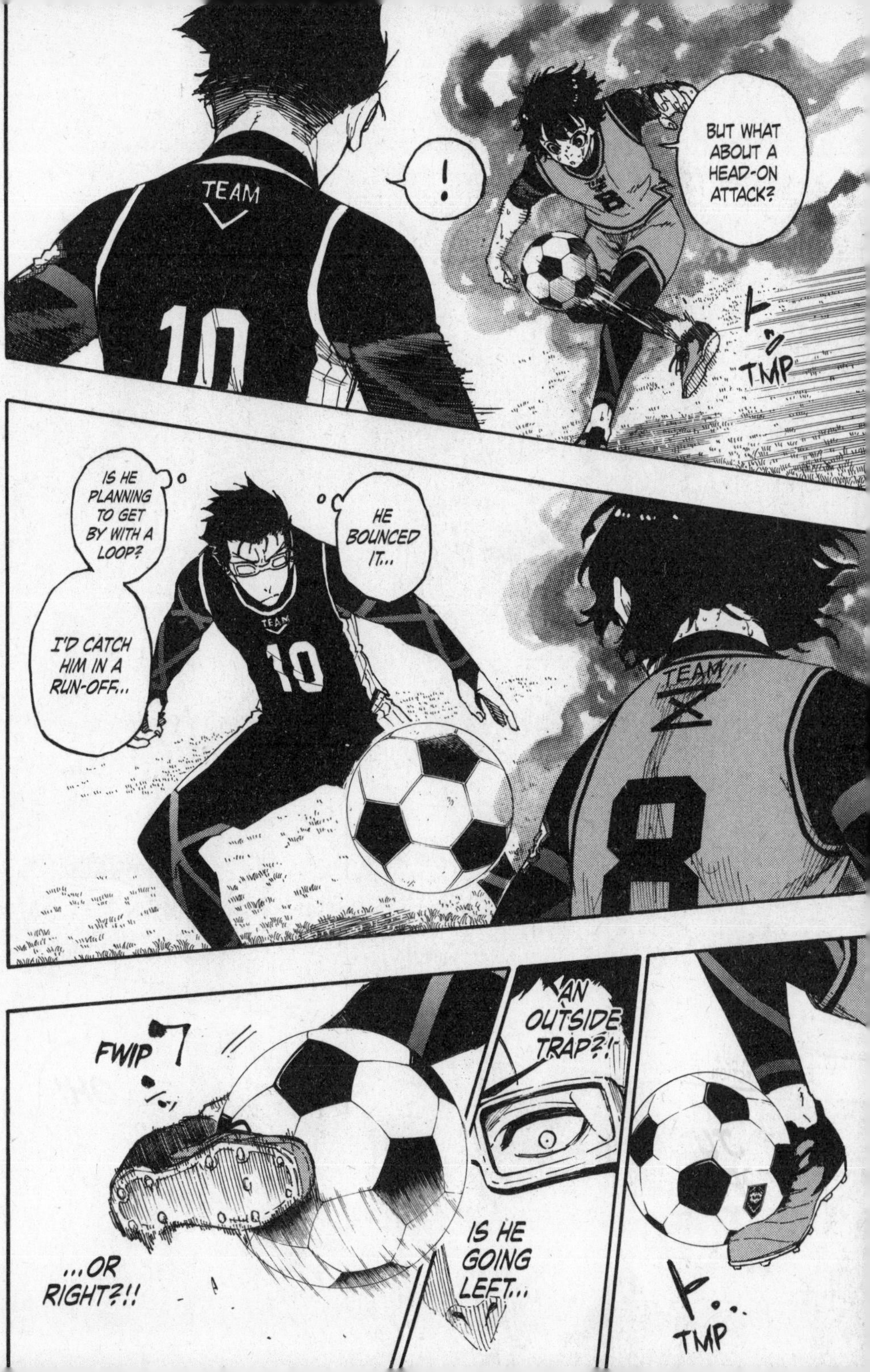
BUT WHAT ABOUT A HEAD-ON ATTACK?
!
TMP
HE BOUNCED IT...
IS HE PLANNING TO GET BY WITH A LOOP?
I'D CATCH HIM IN A RUN-OFF...
TMP
AN OUTSIDE TRAP?!
IS HE GOING LEFT...
FWIP
...OR RIGHT?!!

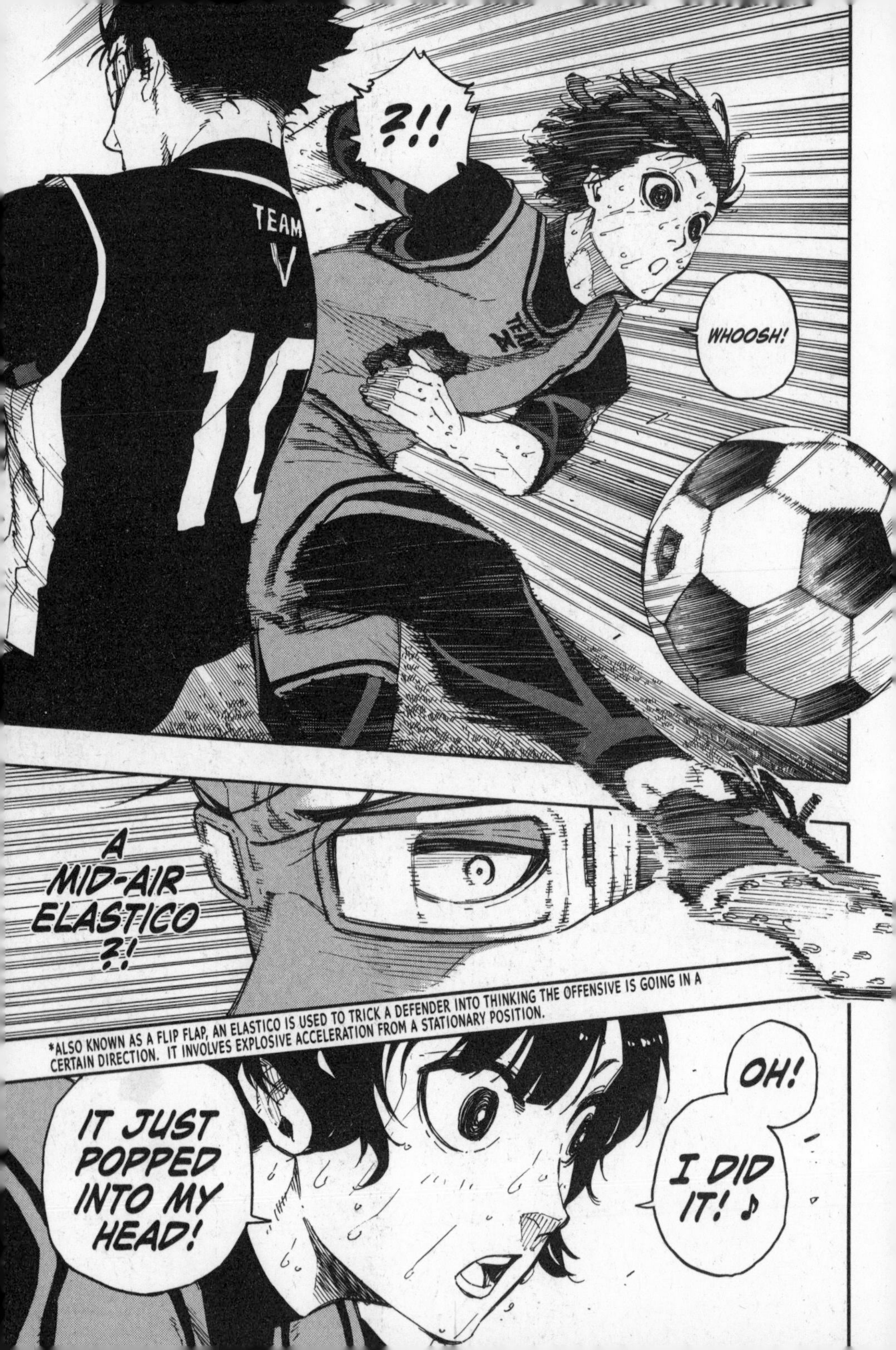
?!!
WHOOSH!
A MID-AIR ELASTICO ?!
*ALSO KNOWN AS A FLIP FLAP, AN ELASTICO IS USED TO TRICK A DEFENDER INTO THINKING THE OFFENSIVE IS GOING IN A CERTAIN DIRECTION. IT INVOLVES EXPLOSIVE ACCELERATION FROM A STATIONARY POSITION.
OH!
I DID IT! ♪
IT JUST POPPED INTO MY HEAD!

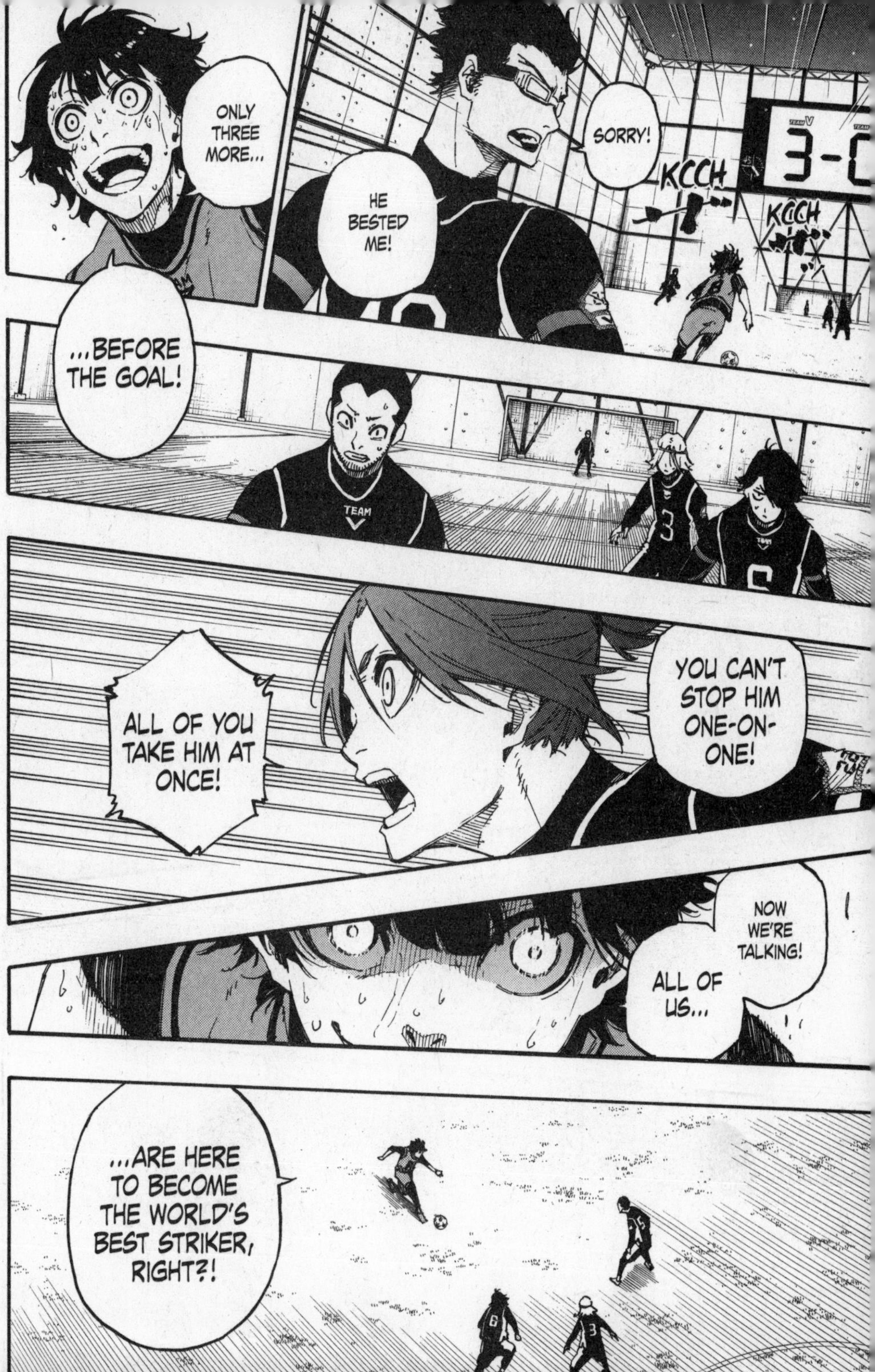
KCCH
KCCH
SORRY!
HE BESTED ME!
ONLY THREE MORE...
...BEFORE THE GOAL!
TEAM V
YOU CAN'T STOP HIM ONE-ON-ONE!
ALL OF YOU TAKE HIM AT ONCE!
NOW WE'RE TALKING!
ALL OF US...
...ARE HERE TO BECOME THE WORLD'S BEST STRIKER, RIGHT?!

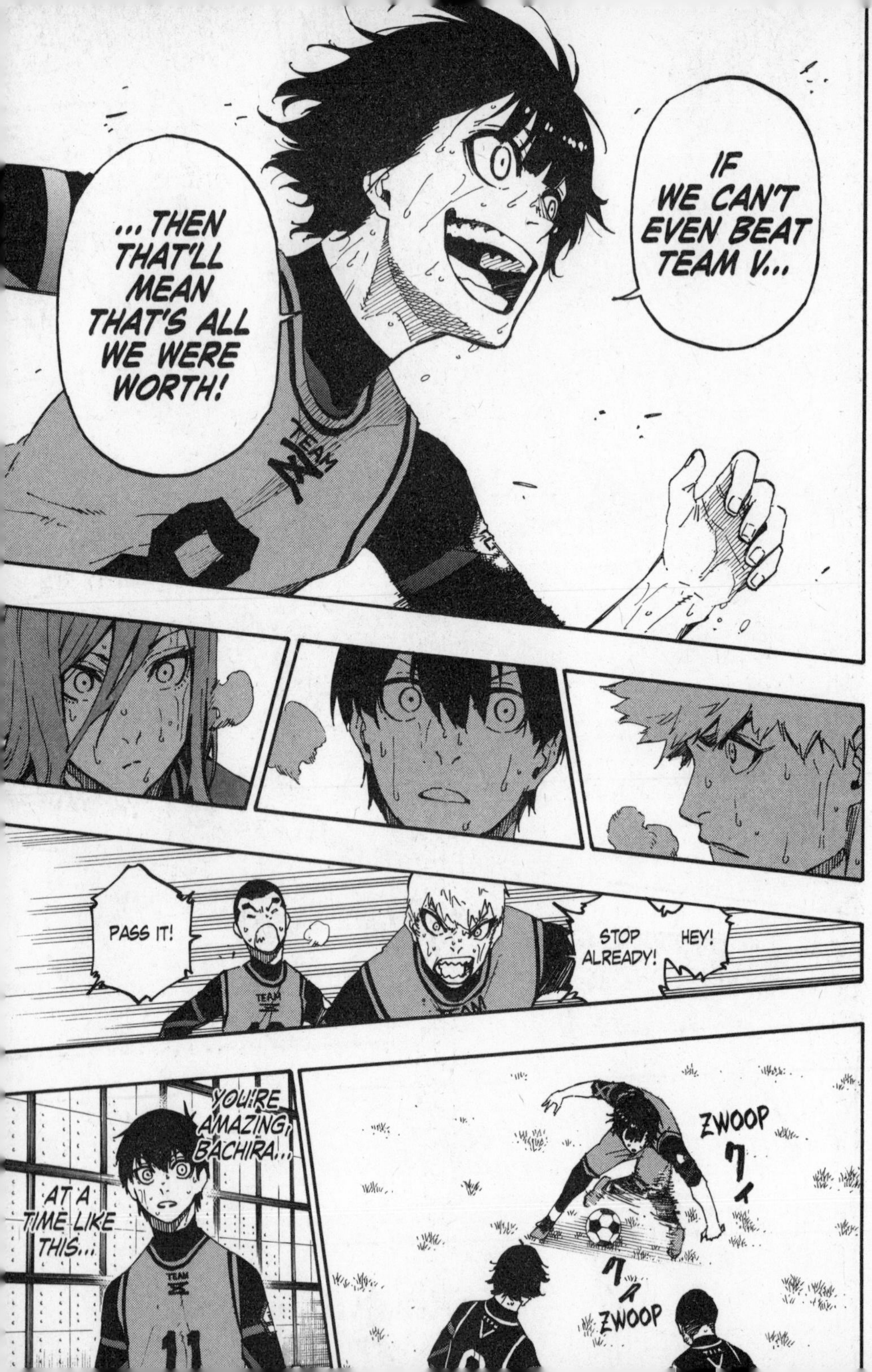
IF WE CAN'T EVEN BEAT TEAM V...
...THEN THAT'LL MEAN THAT'S ALL WE WERE WORTH!
HEY!
STOP ALREADY!
PASS IT!
ZWOOP
クイ
クイ
ZWOOP
YOU'RE AMAZING, BACHIRA...
AT A TIME LIKE THIS...

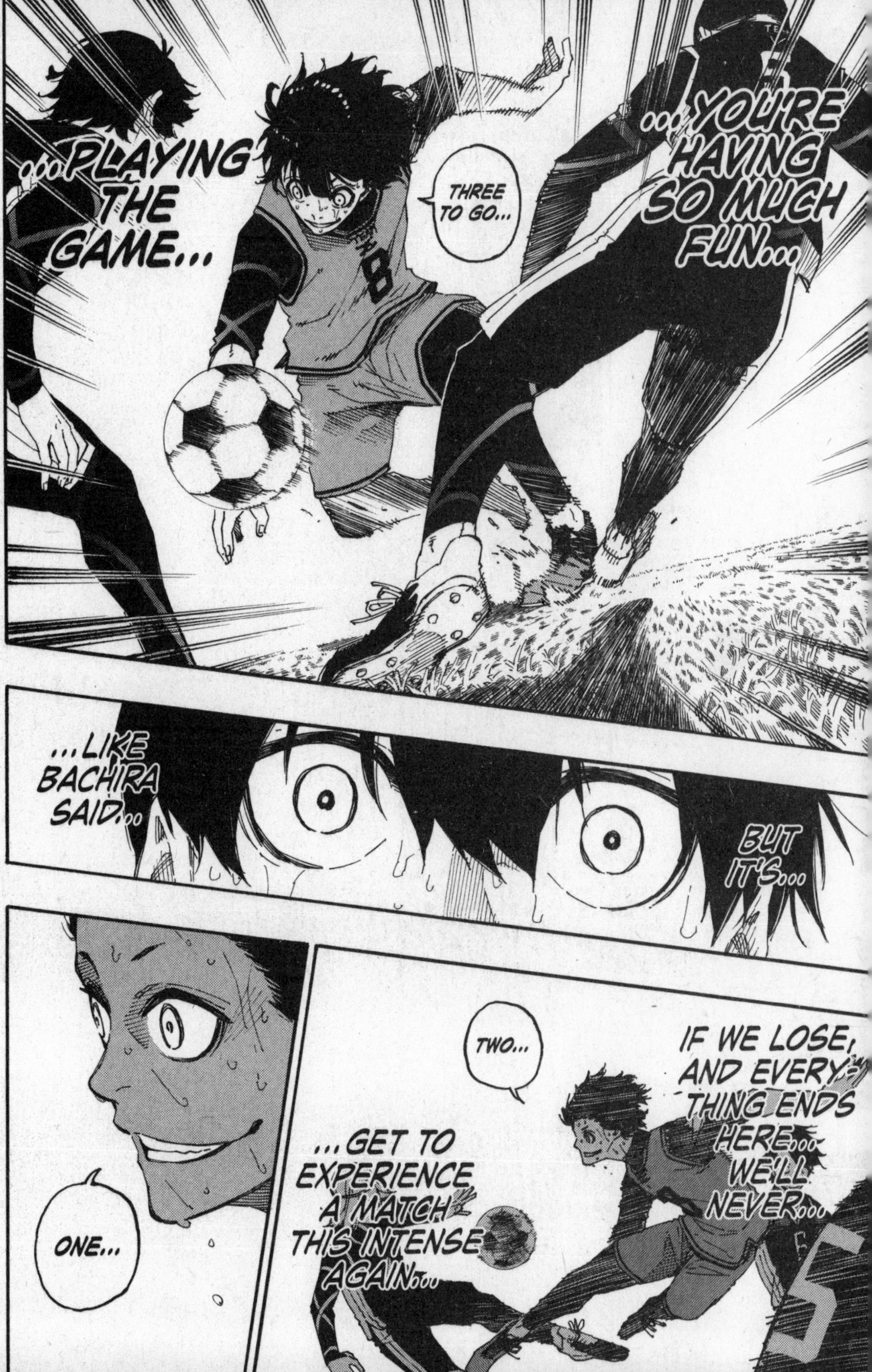
...YOU'RE HAVING SO MUCH FUN...
THREE TO GO...
...PLAYING THE GAME...
BUT IT'S...
...LIKE BACHIRA SAID...
IF WE LOSE, AND EVERY-THING ENDS HERE... WE'LL NEVER...
TWO...
...GET TO EXPERIENCE A MATCH THIS INTENSE AGAIN...
ONE...

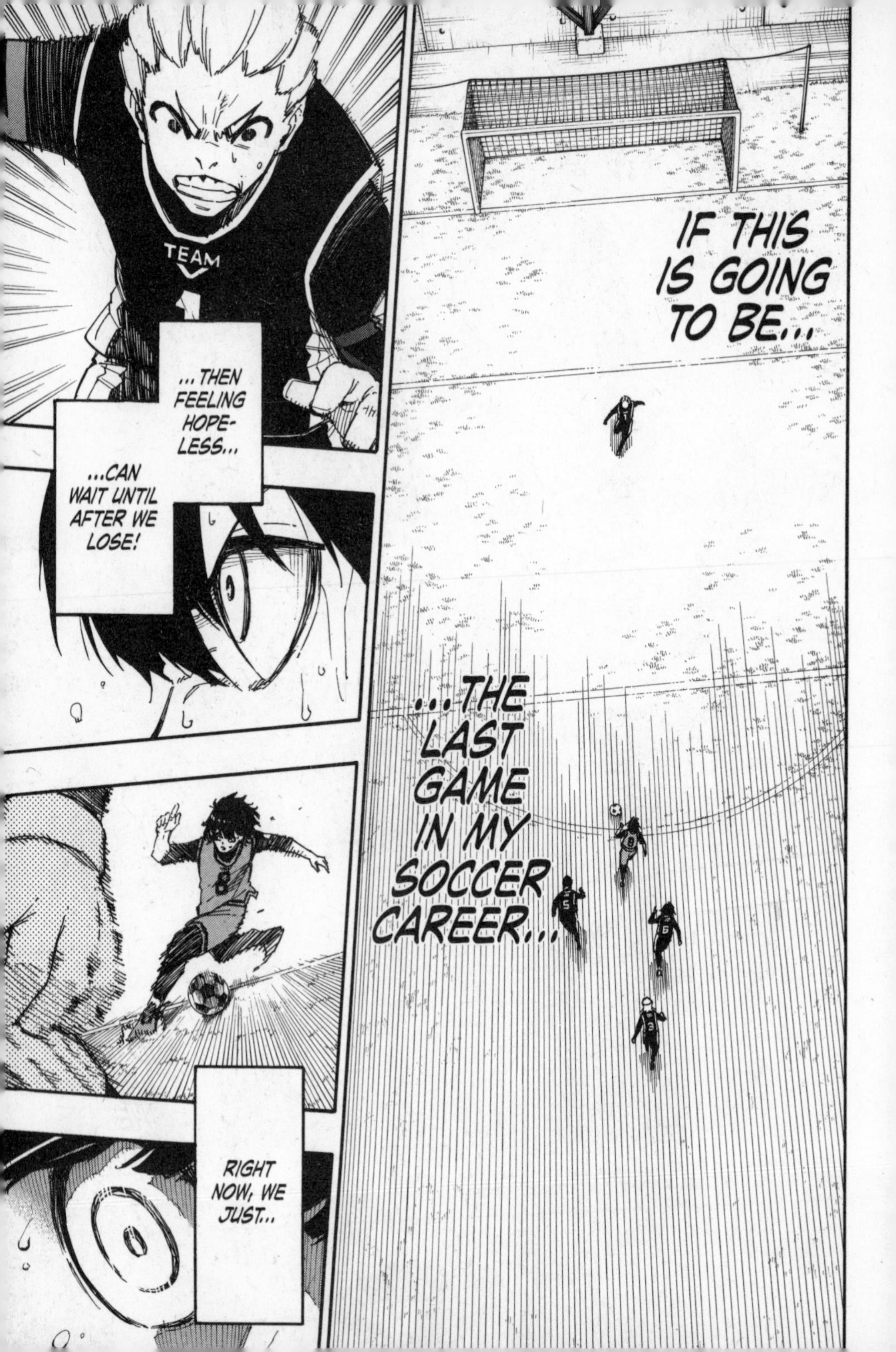
IF THIS IS GOING TO BE...
...THE LAST GAME IN MY SOCCER CAREER...
TEAM
...THEN FEELING HOPE-LESS...
...CAN WAIT UNTIL AFTER WE LOSE!
RIGHT NOW, WE JUST...

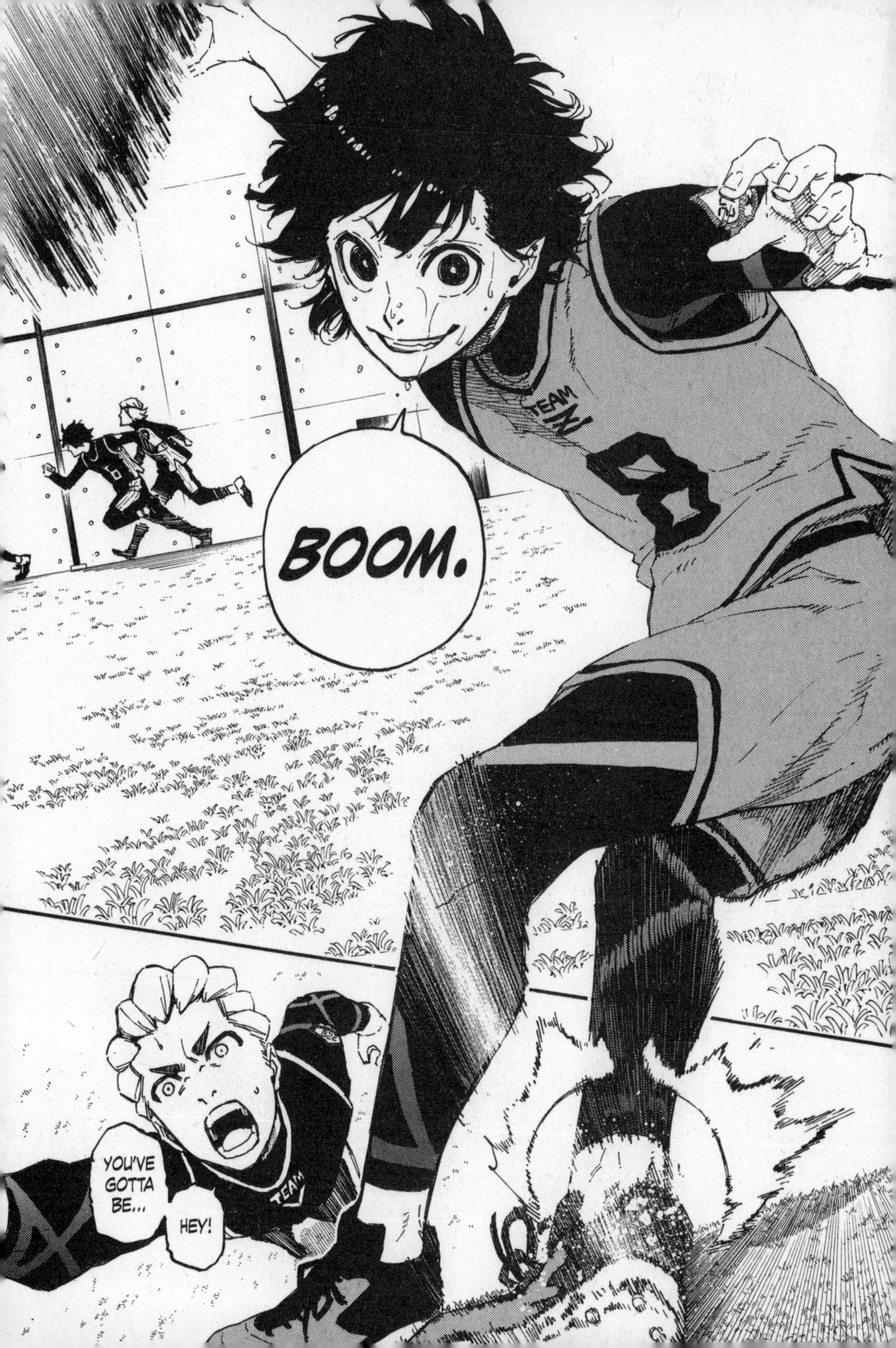
BOOM.
YOU'VE GOTTA BE...
HEY!

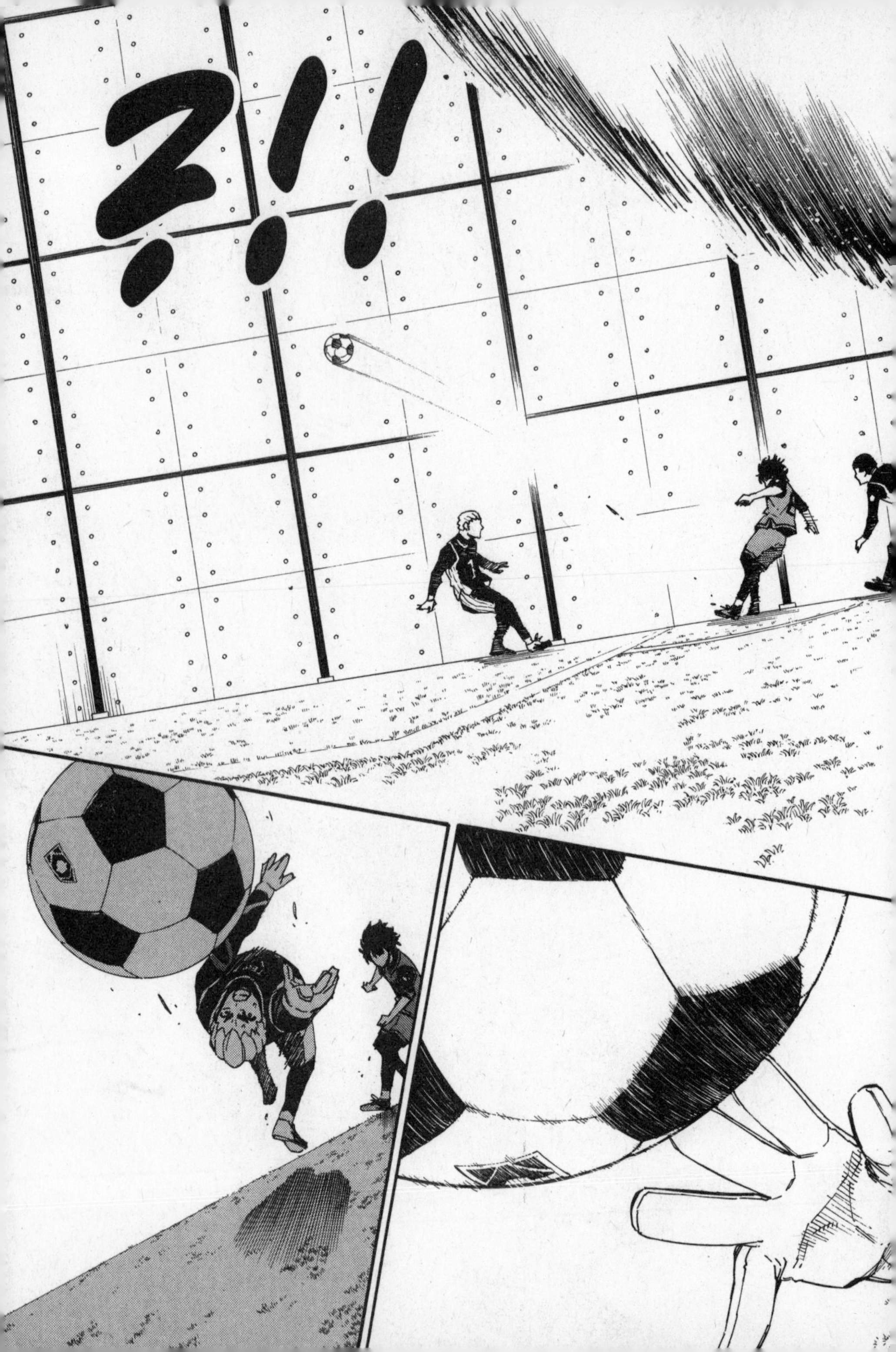
?!!

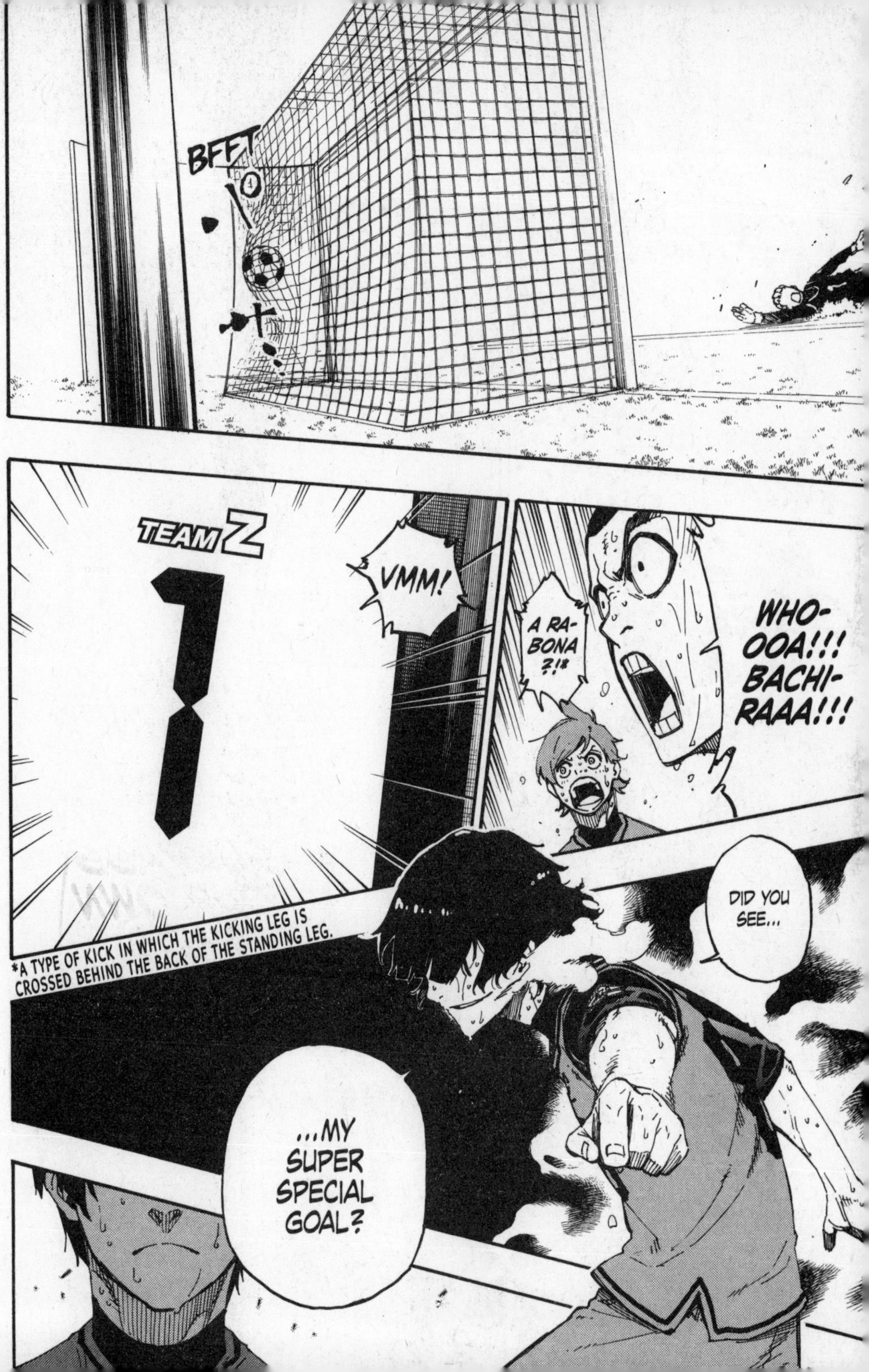
BFFT
WHO-OOA!!! BACHI-RAAA!!!
A RA-BONA?!*
TEAM Z
1
VMM!
*A TYPE OF KICK IN WHICH THE KICKING LEG IS CROSSED BEHIND THE BACK OF THE STANDING LEG.
DID YOU SEE...
...MY SUPER SPECIAL GOAL?

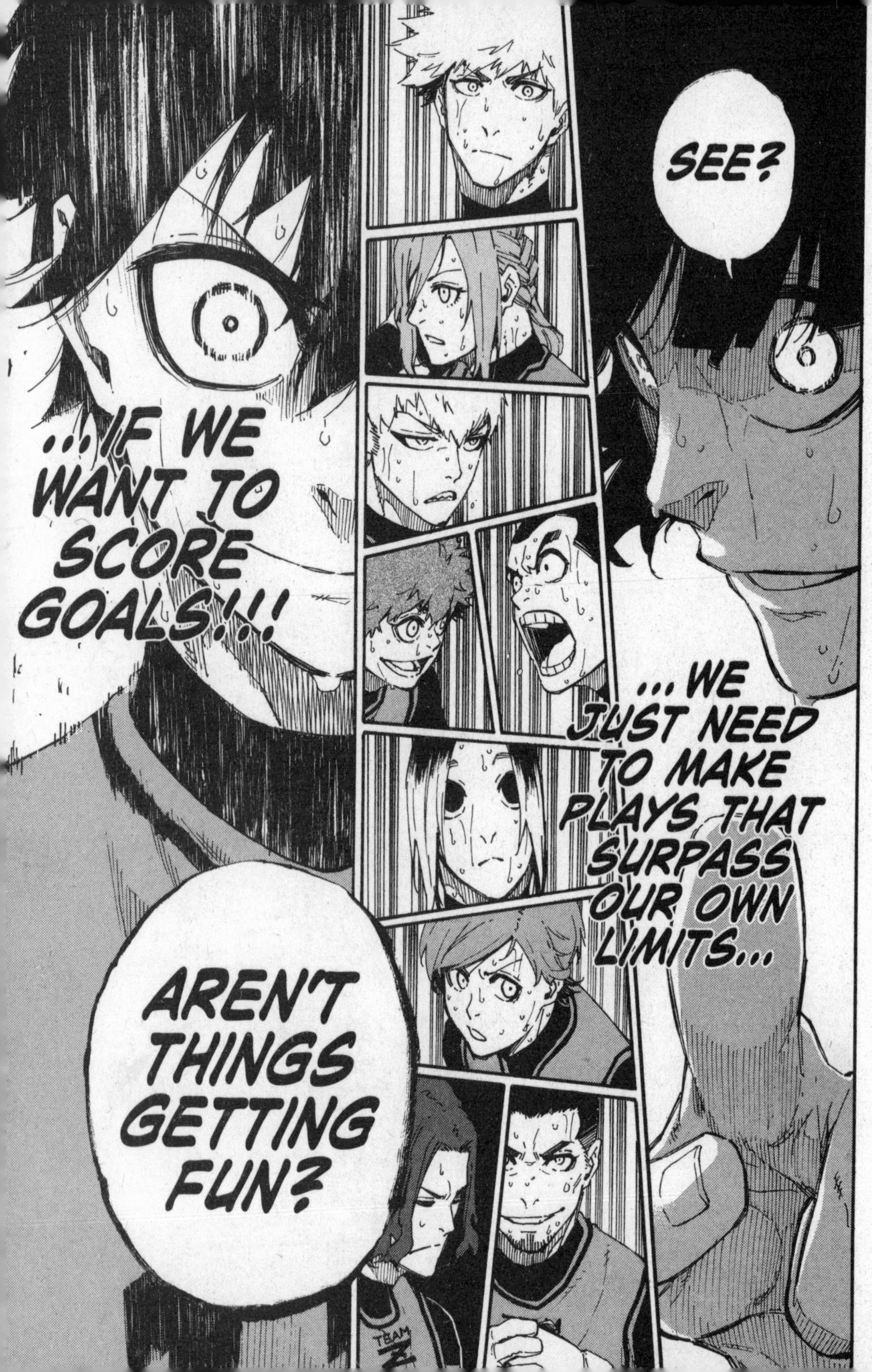
SEE?
...WE JUST NEED TO MAKE PLAYS THAT SURPASS OUR OWN LIMITS...
...IF WE WANT TO SCORE GOALS!!!
AREN'T THINGS GETTING FUN?
TEAM Z

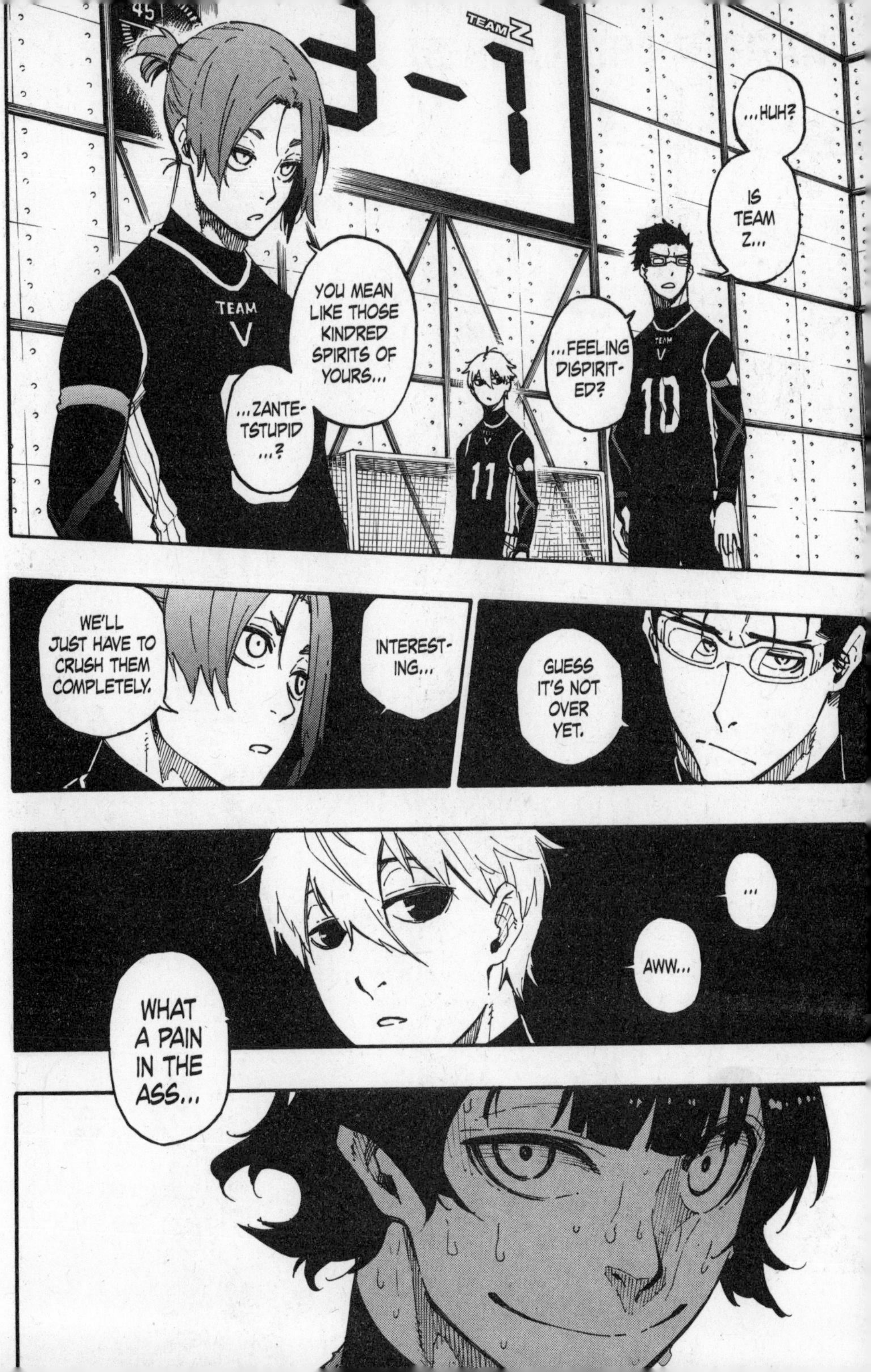
TEAM Z
...HUH?
IS TEAM Z...
...FEELING DISPIRITED?
YOU MEAN LIKE THOSE KINDRED SPIRITS OF YOURS...
...ZANTETSTUPID...?
GUESS IT'S NOT OVER YET.
INTERESTING...
WE'LL JUST HAVE TO CRUSH THEM COMPLETELY.
...
AWW...
WHAT A PAIN IN THE ASS...

CHAPTER 29: FLASH OF EVOLUTION

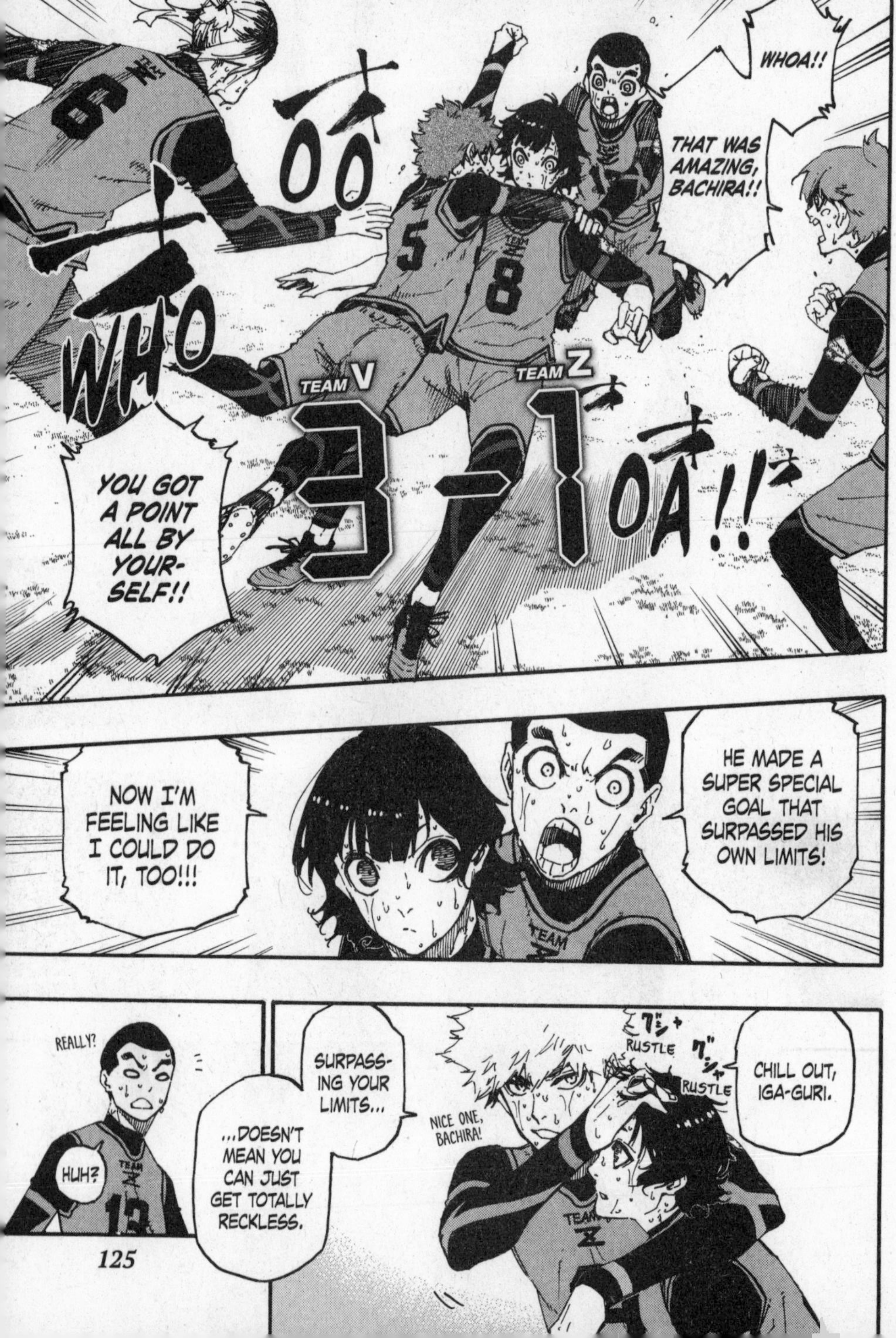
WHOA!!
THAT WAS AMAZING, BACHIRA!!
WHOOOOA!!
TEAM V 3 - 1 TEAM Z
YOU GOT A POINT ALL BY YOURSELF!!
HE MADE A SUPER SPECIAL GOAL THAT SURPASSED HIS OWN LIMITS!
NOW I'M FEELING LIKE I COULD DO IT, TOO!!!
CHILL OUT, IGA-GURI.
RUSTLE
RUSTLE
NICE ONE, BACHIRA!
SURPASSING YOUR LIMITS...
...DOESN'T MEAN YOU CAN JUST GET TOTALLY RECKLESS.
REALLY?
HUH?

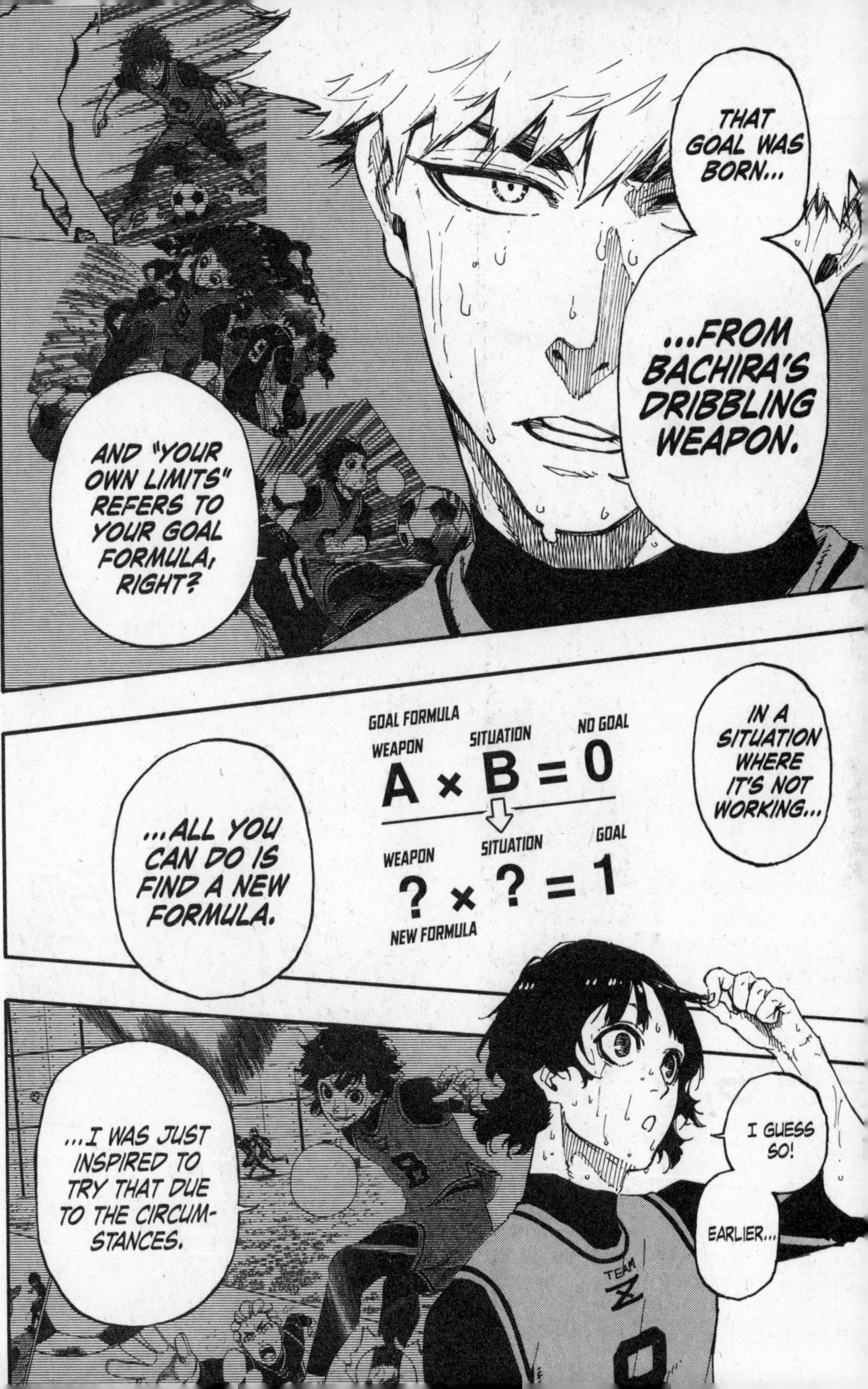
THAT GOAL WAS BORN...
...FROM BACHIRA'S DRIBBLING WEAPON.
AND "YOUR OWN LIMITS" REFERS TO YOUR GOAL FORMULA, RIGHT?
IN A SITUATION WHERE IT'S NOT WORKING...
GOAL FORMULA
WEAPON
SITUATION
NO GOAL
A × B = 0
WEAPON
SITUATION
GOAL
? × ? = 1
NEW FORMULA
...ALL YOU CAN DO IS FIND A NEW FORMULA.
I GUESS SO!
EARLIER...
...I WAS JUST INSPIRED TO TRY THAT DUE TO THE CIRCUM-STANCES.

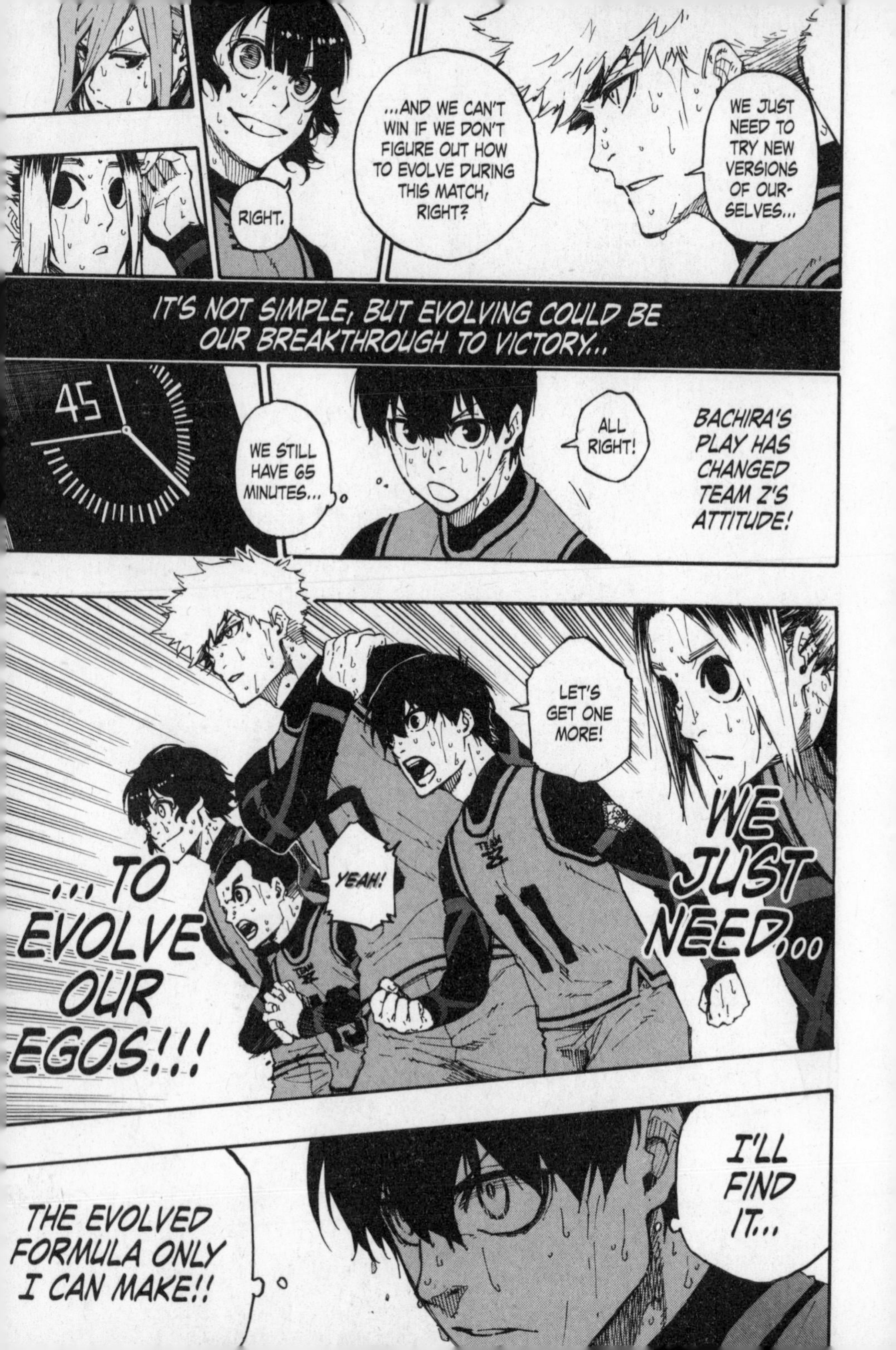

WE JUST NEED TO TRY NEW VERSIONS OF OUR-SELVES...
...AND WE CAN'T WIN IF WE DON'T FIGURE OUT HOW TO EVOLVE DURING THIS MATCH, RIGHT?
RIGHT.
IT'S NOT SIMPLE, BUT EVOLVING COULD BE OUR BREAKTHROUGH TO VICTORY...
BACHIRA'S PLAY HAS CHANGED TEAM Z'S ATTITUDE!
ALL RIGHT!
WE STILL HAVE 65 MINUTES...
45
LET'S GET ONE MORE!
WE JUST NEED...
YEAH!
...TO EVOLVE OUR EGOS!!!
I'LL FIND IT...
THE EVOLVED FORMULA ONLY I CAN MAKE!!

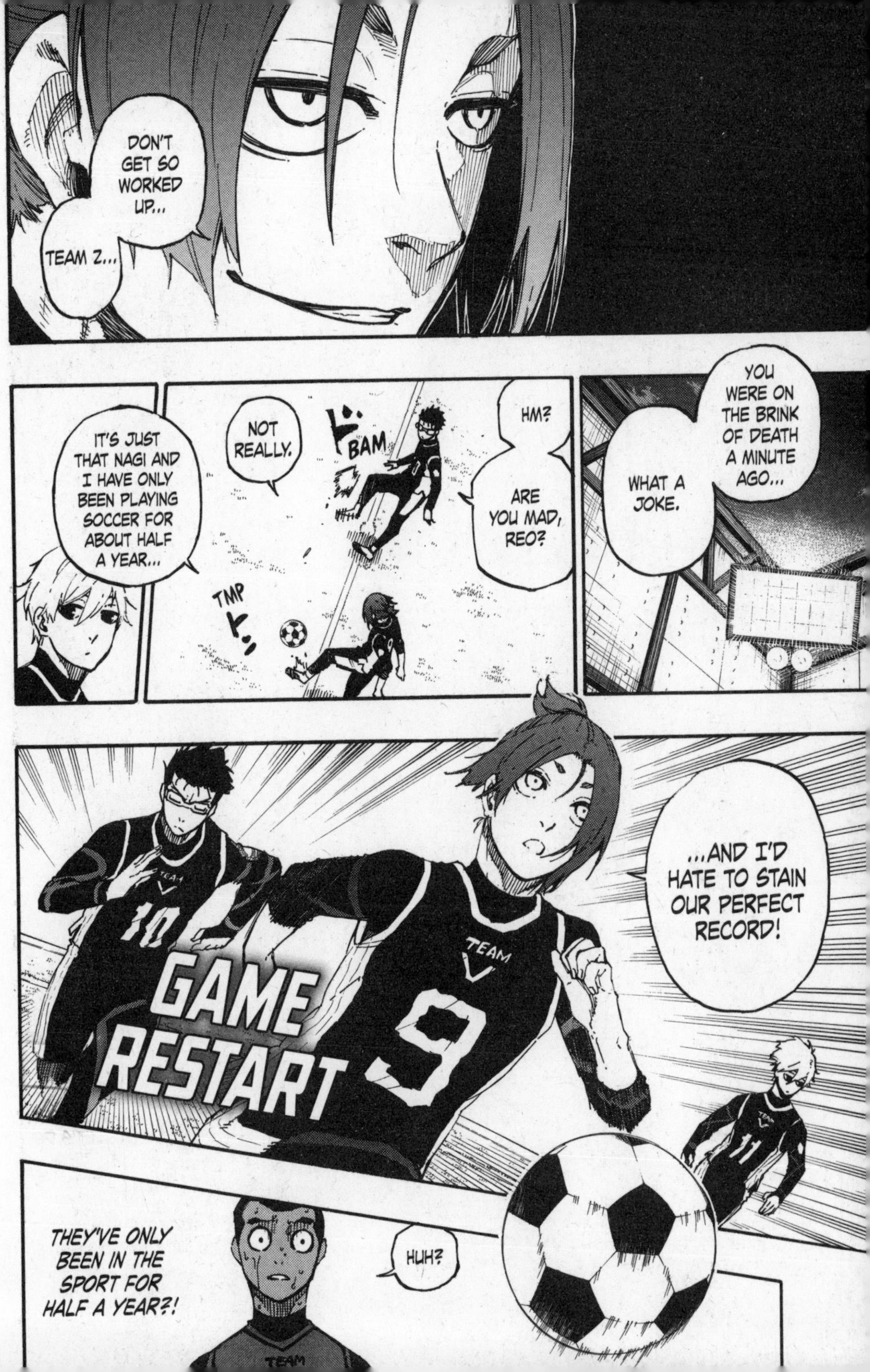
DON'T GET SO WORKED UP...
TEAM Z...
YOU WERE ON THE BRINK OF DEATH A MINUTE AGO...
WHAT A JOKE.
HM?
ARE YOU MAD, REO?
BAM
NOT REALLY.
TMP
IT'S JUST THAT NAGI AND I HAVE ONLY BEEN PLAYING SOCCER FOR ABOUT HALF A YEAR...
...AND I'D HATE TO STAIN OUR PERFECT RECORD!
GAME RESTART
HUH?
THEY'VE ONLY BEEN IN THE SPORT FOR HALF A YEAR?!

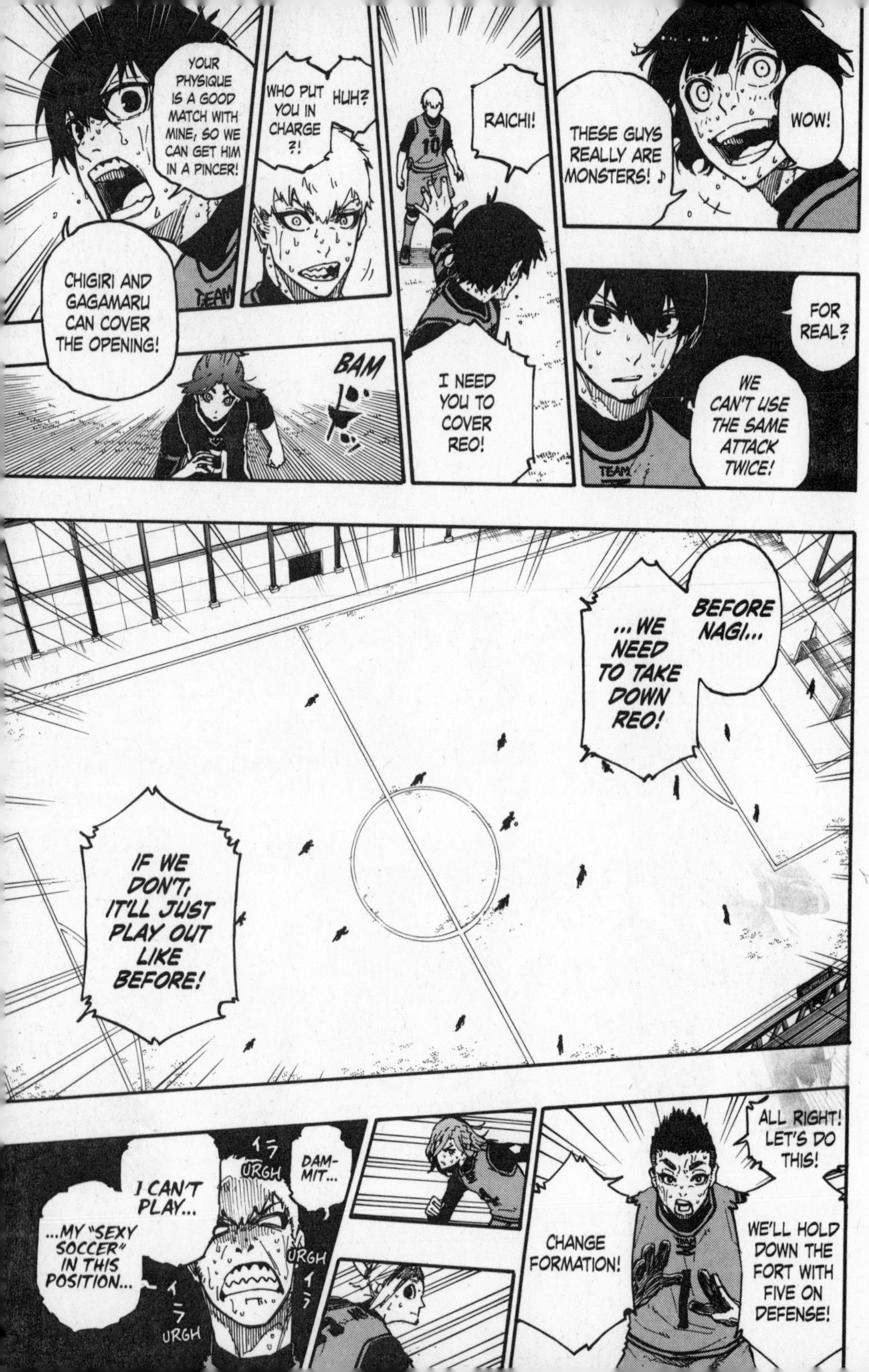
WOW!
THESE GUYS REALLY ARE MONSTERS! ♪
FOR REAL?
WE CAN'T USE THE SAME ATTACK TWICE!
RAICHI!
I NEED YOU TO COVER REO!
HUH?
WHO PUT YOU IN CHARGE?!
YOUR PHYSIQUE IS A GOOD MATCH WITH MINE, SO WE CAN GET HIM IN A PINCER!
CHIGIRI AND GAGAMARU CAN COVER THE OPENING!
BAM
BEFORE NAGI...
...WE NEED TO TAKE DOWN REO!
IF WE DON'T, IT'LL JUST PLAY OUT LIKE BEFORE!
ALL RIGHT! LET'S DO THIS!
CHANGE FORMATION!
WE'LL HOLD DOWN THE FORT WITH FIVE ON DEFENSE!
DAM-MIT...
イラ URGH
I CAN'T PLAY...
...MY "SEXY SOCCER" IN THIS POSITION...
イラ URGH
イラ URGH

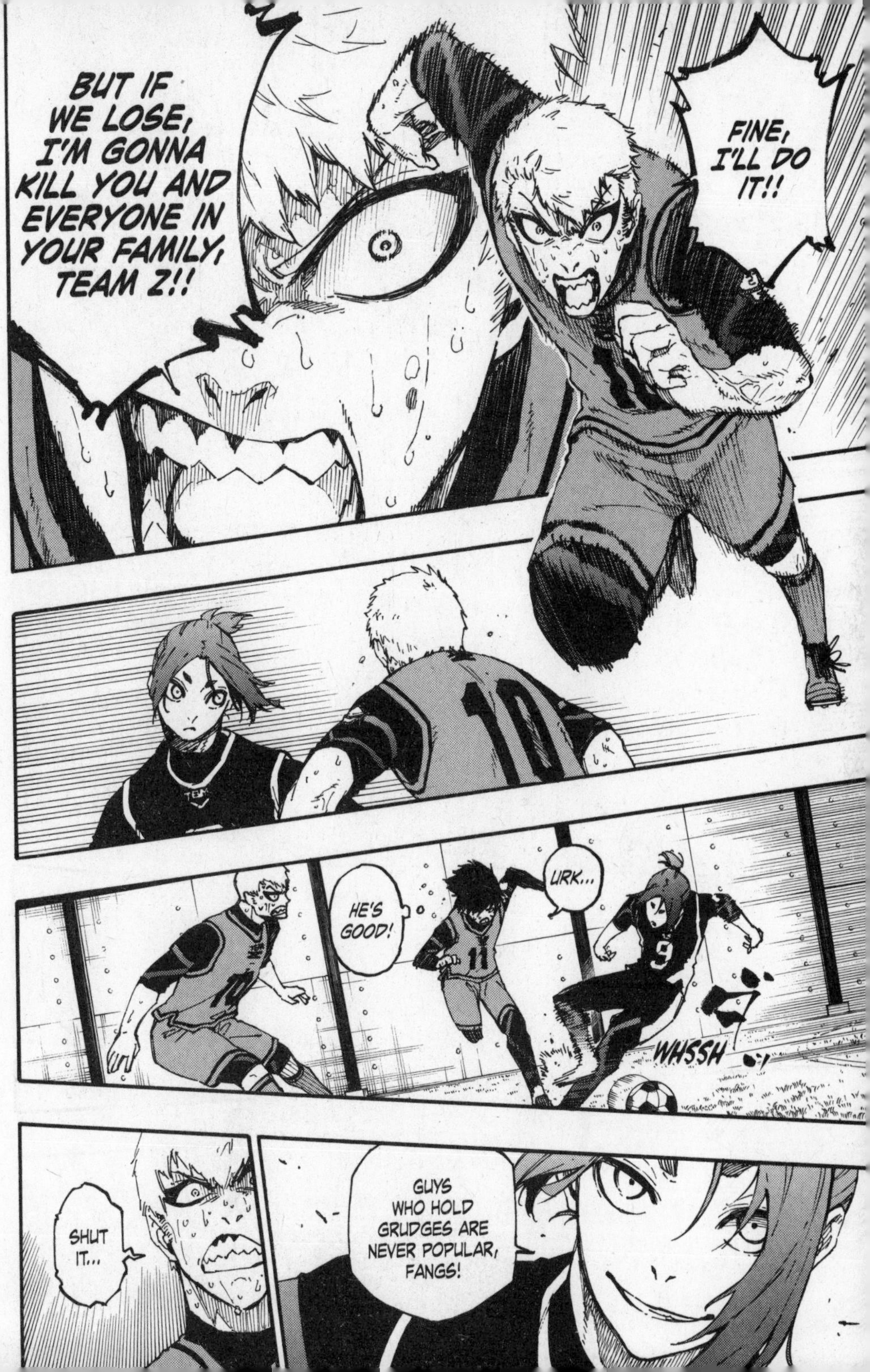
FINE, I'LL DO IT!!
BUT IF WE LOSE, I'M GONNA KILL YOU AND EVERYONE IN YOUR FAMILY, TEAM Z!!
URK...
HE'S GOOD!
WHSSH
GUYS WHO HOLD GRUDGES ARE NEVER POPULAR, FANGS!
SHUT IT...

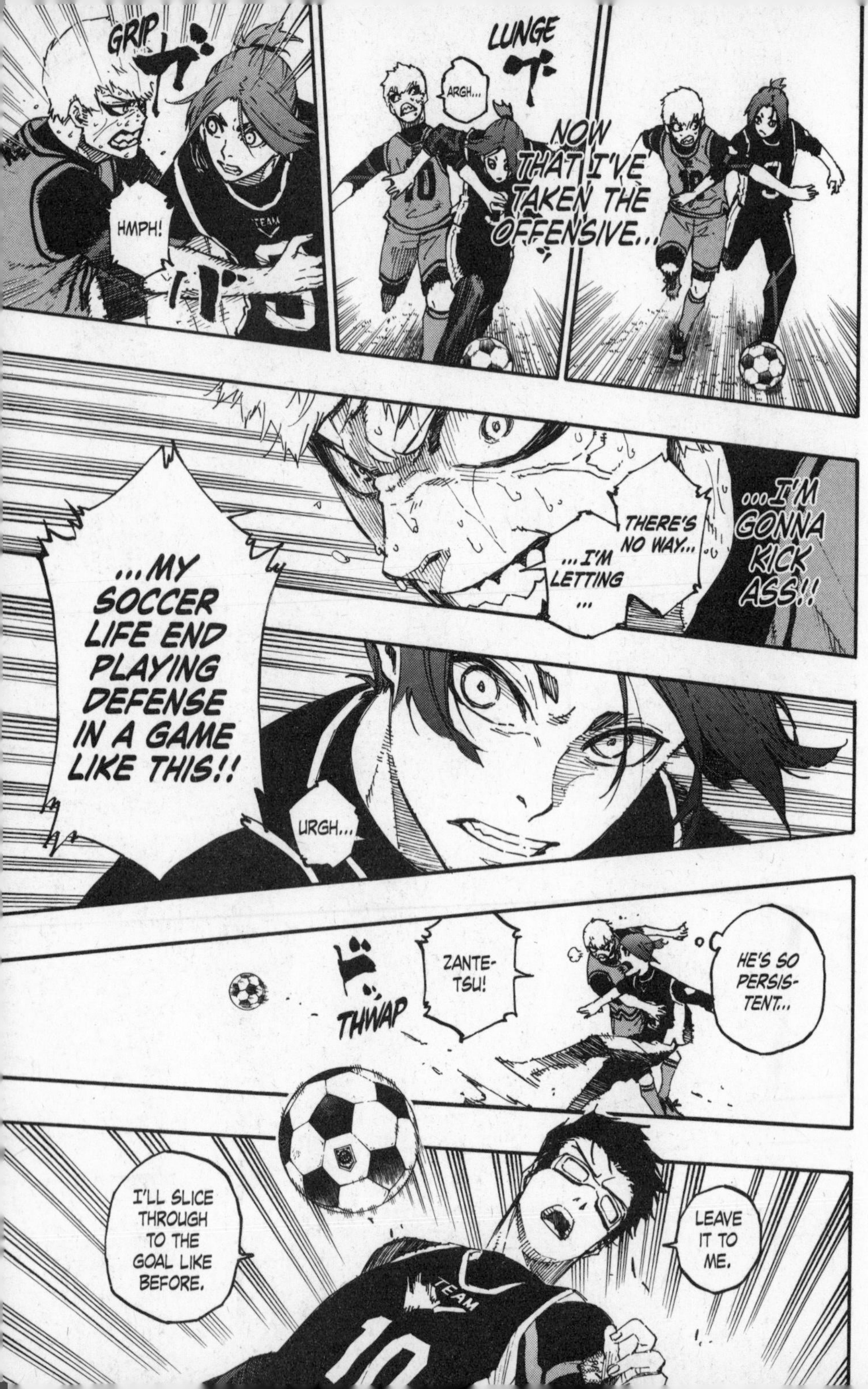
NOW THAT I'VE TAKEN THE OFFENSIVE...
LUNGE
ARGH...
GRIP
HMPH!
...I'M GONNA KICK ASS!!
THERE'S NO WAY...
...I'M LETTING ...
...MY SOCCER LIFE END PLAYING DEFENSE IN A GAME LIKE THIS!!
URGH...
HE'S SO PERSISTENT...
ZANTE-TSU!
THWAP
LEAVE IT TO ME.
I'LL SLICE THROUGH TO THE GOAL LIKE BEFORE.

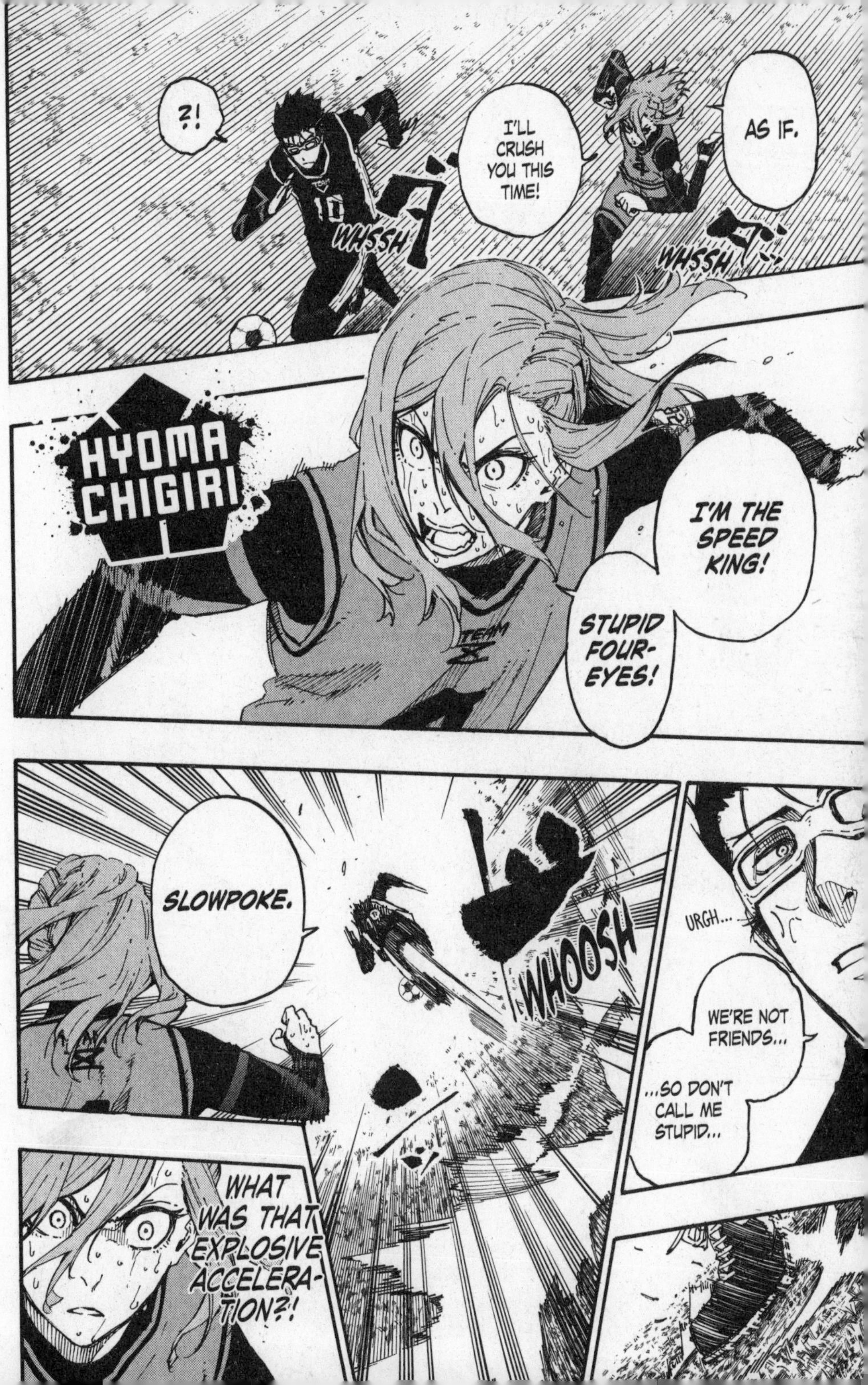
AS IF.
WHSSH
I'LL CRUSH YOU THIS TIME!
?!
WHSSH
I'M THE SPEED KING!
STUPID FOUR-EYES!
HYOMA CHIGIRI
URGH...
WE'RE NOT FRIENDS...
...SO DON'T CALL ME STUPID...
WHOOSH
SLOWPOKE.
WHAT WAS THAT EXPLOSIVE ACCELERA-TION?!

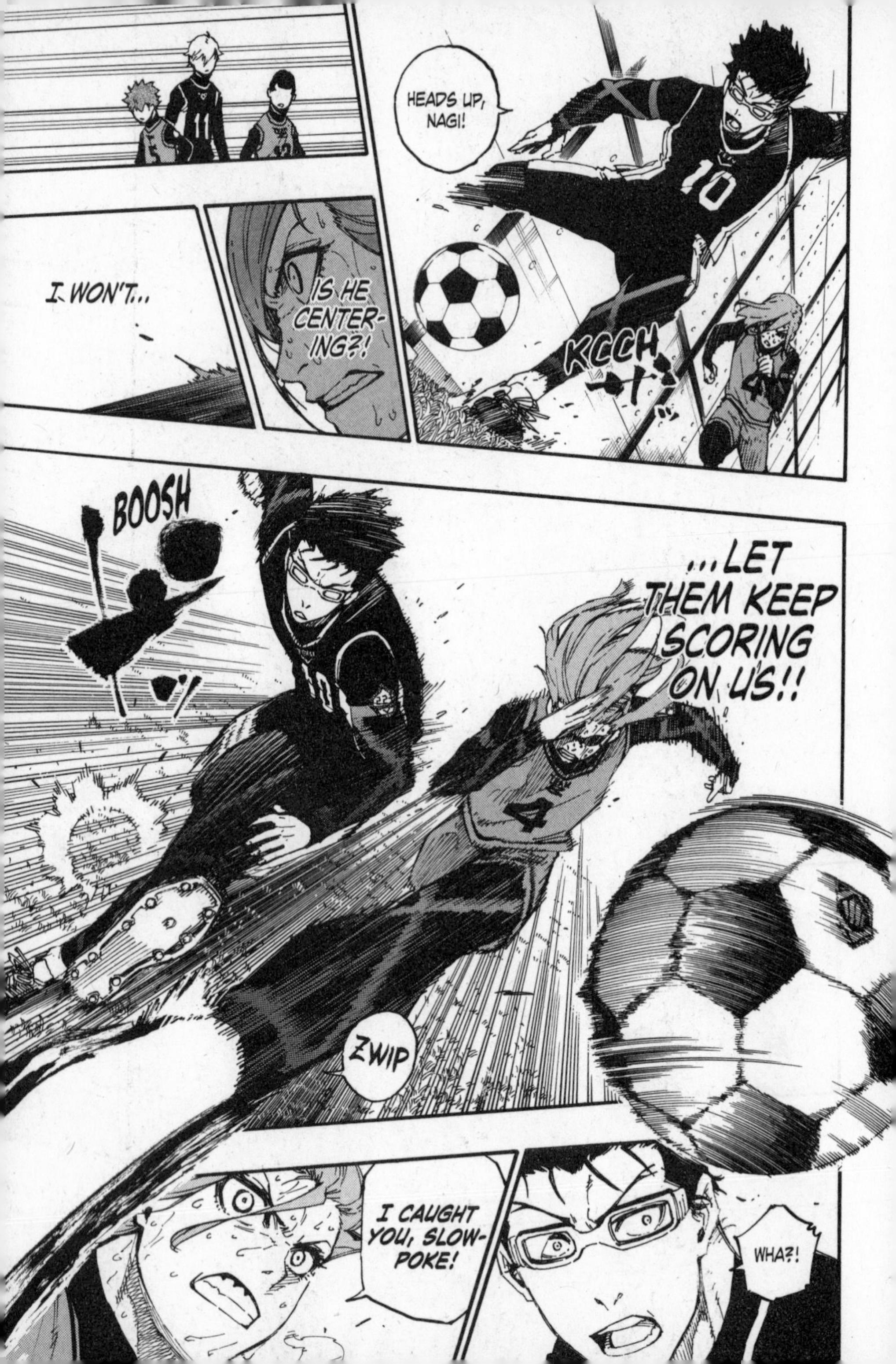
HEADS UP, NAGI!
KCCH
IS HE CENTERING?!
I WON'T...
...LET THEM KEEP SCORING ON US!!
BOOSH
ZWIP
WHA?!
I CAUGHT YOU, SLOW-POKE!

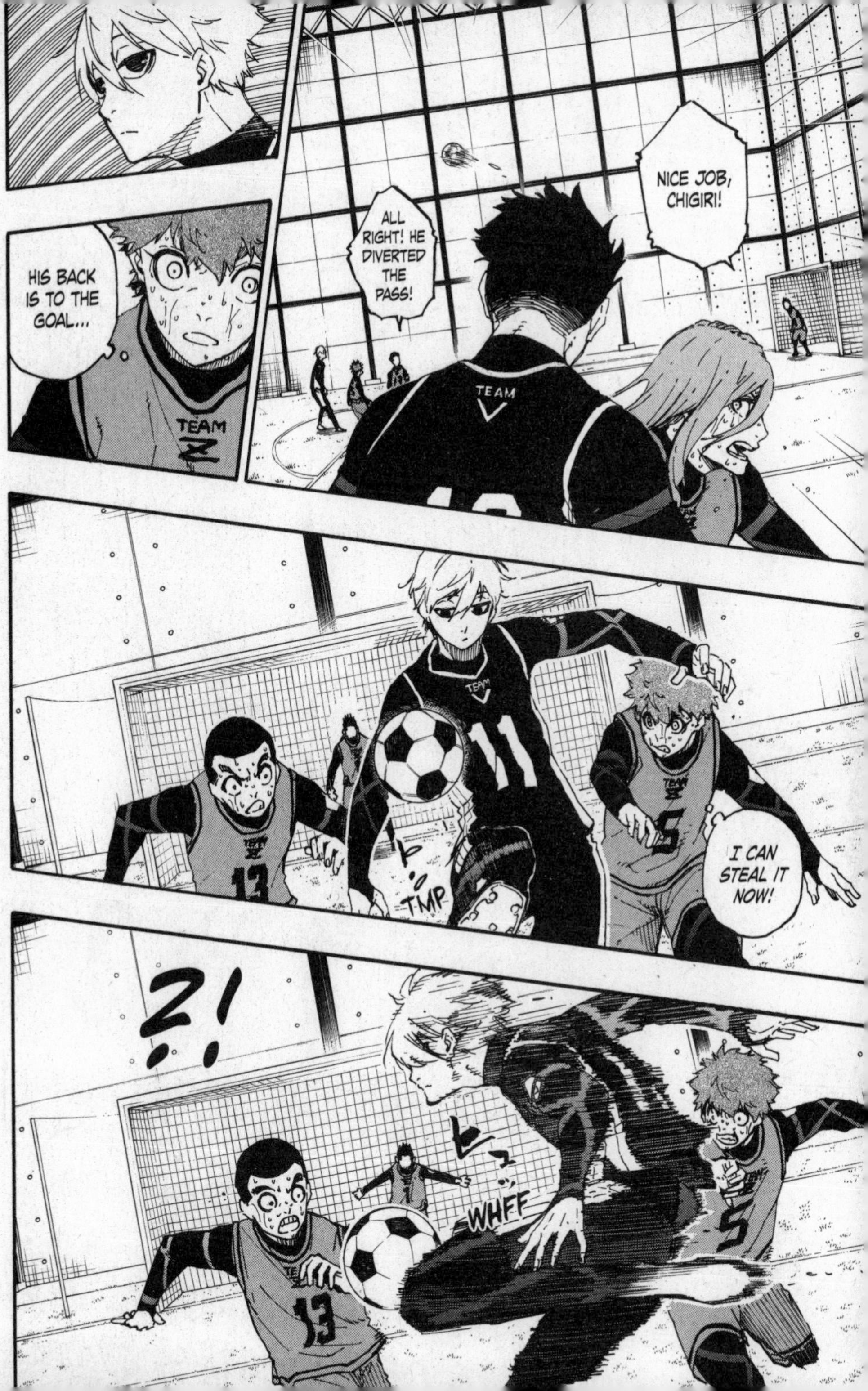
NICE JOB, CHIGIRI!
ALL RIGHT! HE DIVERTED THE PASS!
HIS BACK IS TO THE GOAL...
I CAN STEAL IT NOW!
TMP
?!
WHFF

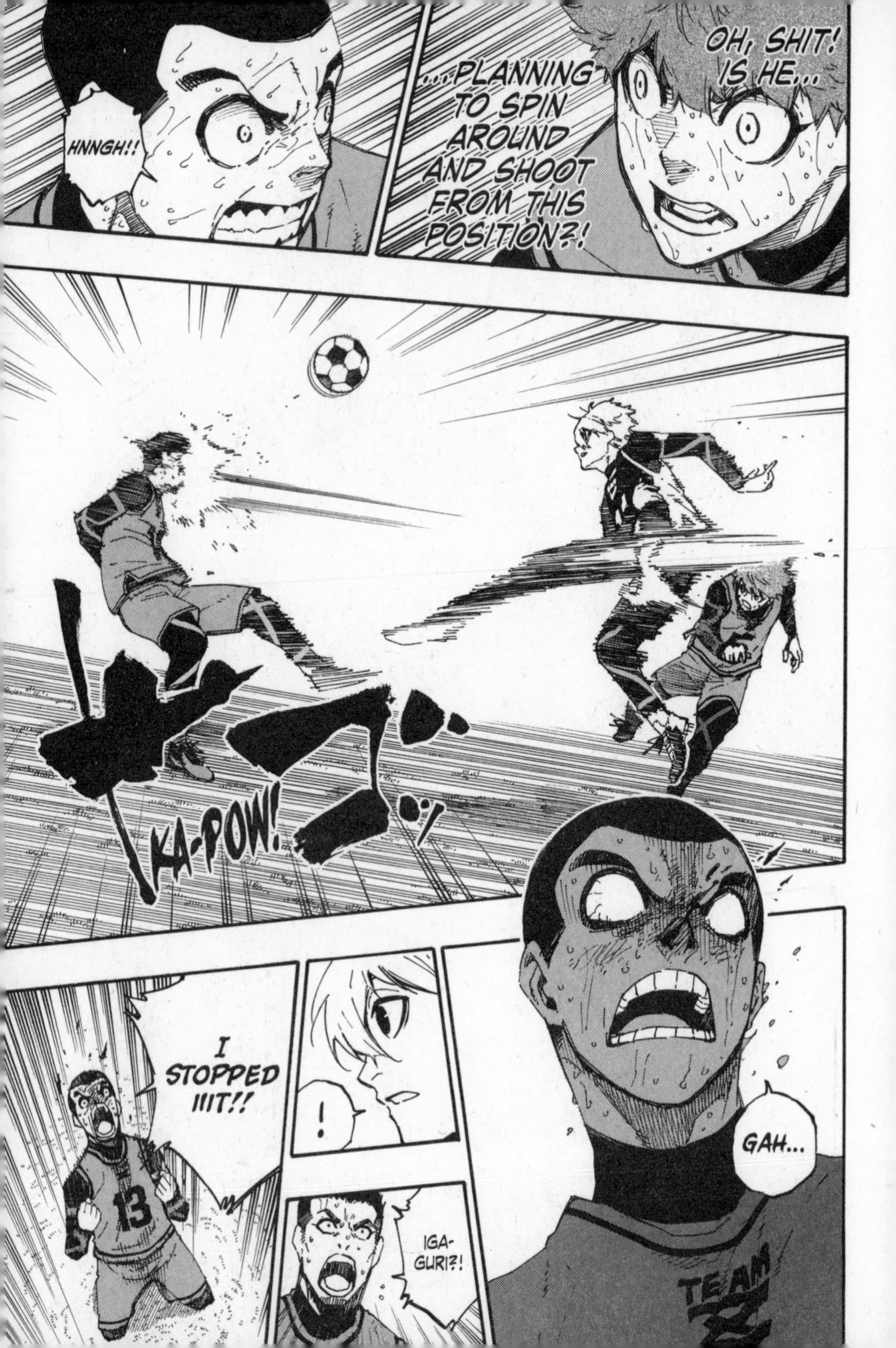
OH, SHIT! IS HE...
...PLANNING TO SPIN AROUND AND SHOOT FROM THIS POSITION?!
HNNGH!!
KA-POW!
GAH...
!
IGA-GURI?!
I STOPPED IIIT!!

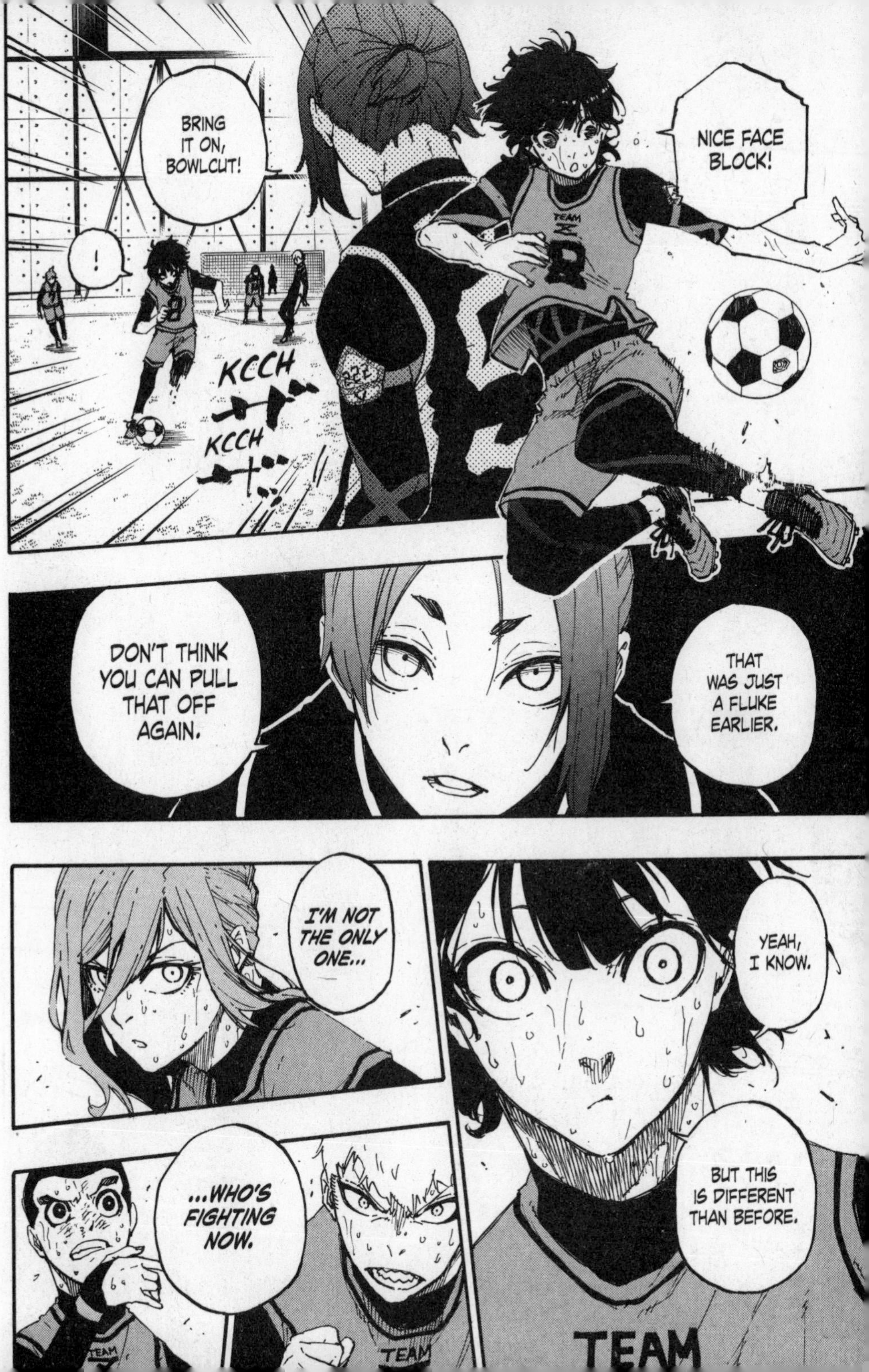
NICE FACE BLOCK!
BRING IT ON, BOWLCUT!
!
KCCH
KCCH
THAT WAS JUST A FLUKE EARLIER.
DON'T THINK YOU CAN PULL THAT OFF AGAIN.
YEAH, I KNOW.
BUT THIS IS DIFFERENT THAN BEFORE.
I'M NOT THE ONLY ONE...
...WHO'S FIGHTING NOW.
TEAM

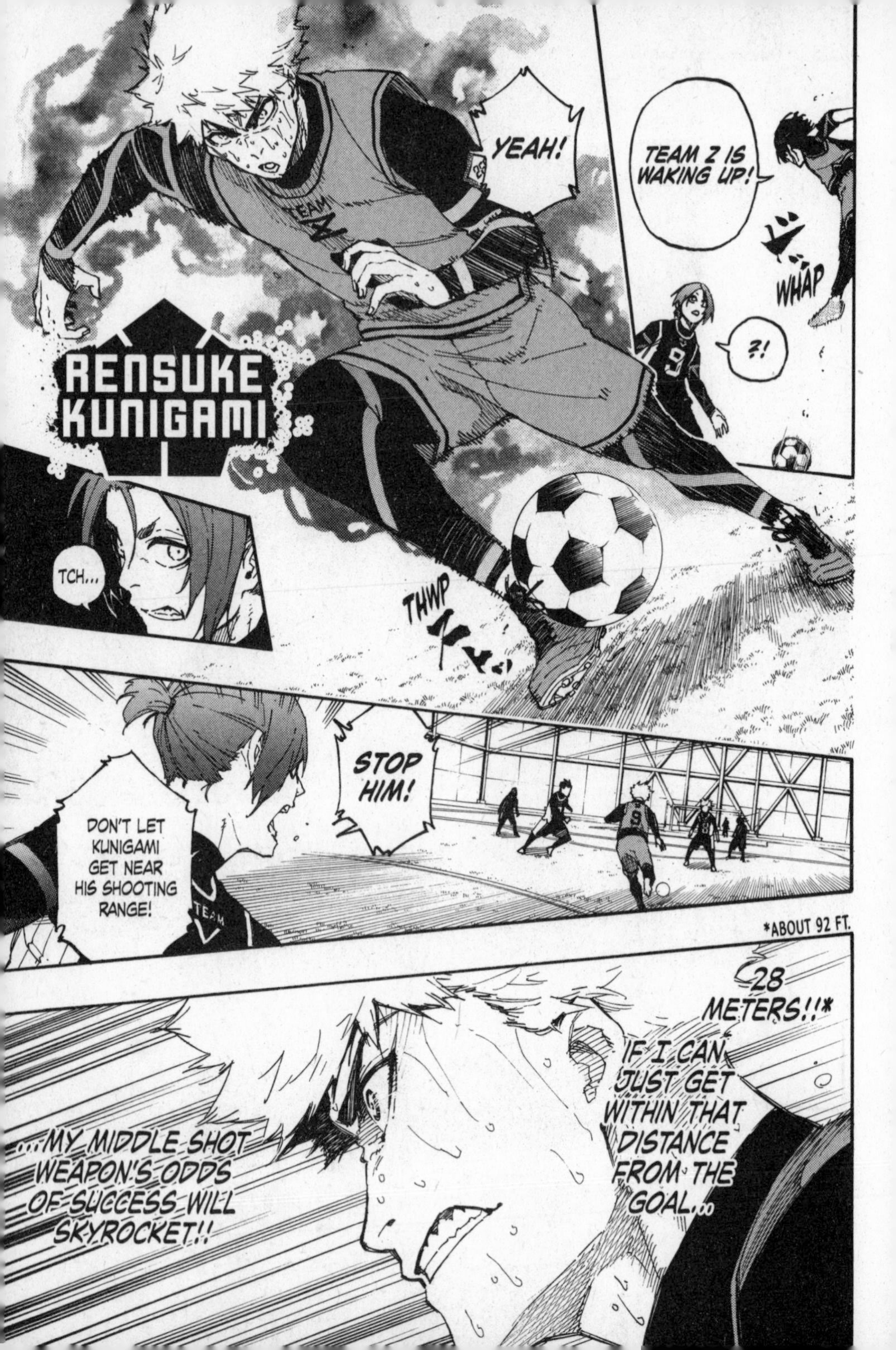
TEAM Z IS WAKING UP!
WHAP
?!
YEAH!
RENSUKE KUNIGAMI
THWP
TCH...
STOP HIM!
DON'T LET KUNIGAMI GET NEAR HIS SHOOTING RANGE!
28 METERS!!*
IF I CAN JUST GET WITHIN THAT DISTANCE FROM THE GOAL...
...MY MIDDLE SHOT WEAPON'S ODDS OF SUCCESS WILL SKYROCKET!!
*ABOUT 92 FT.

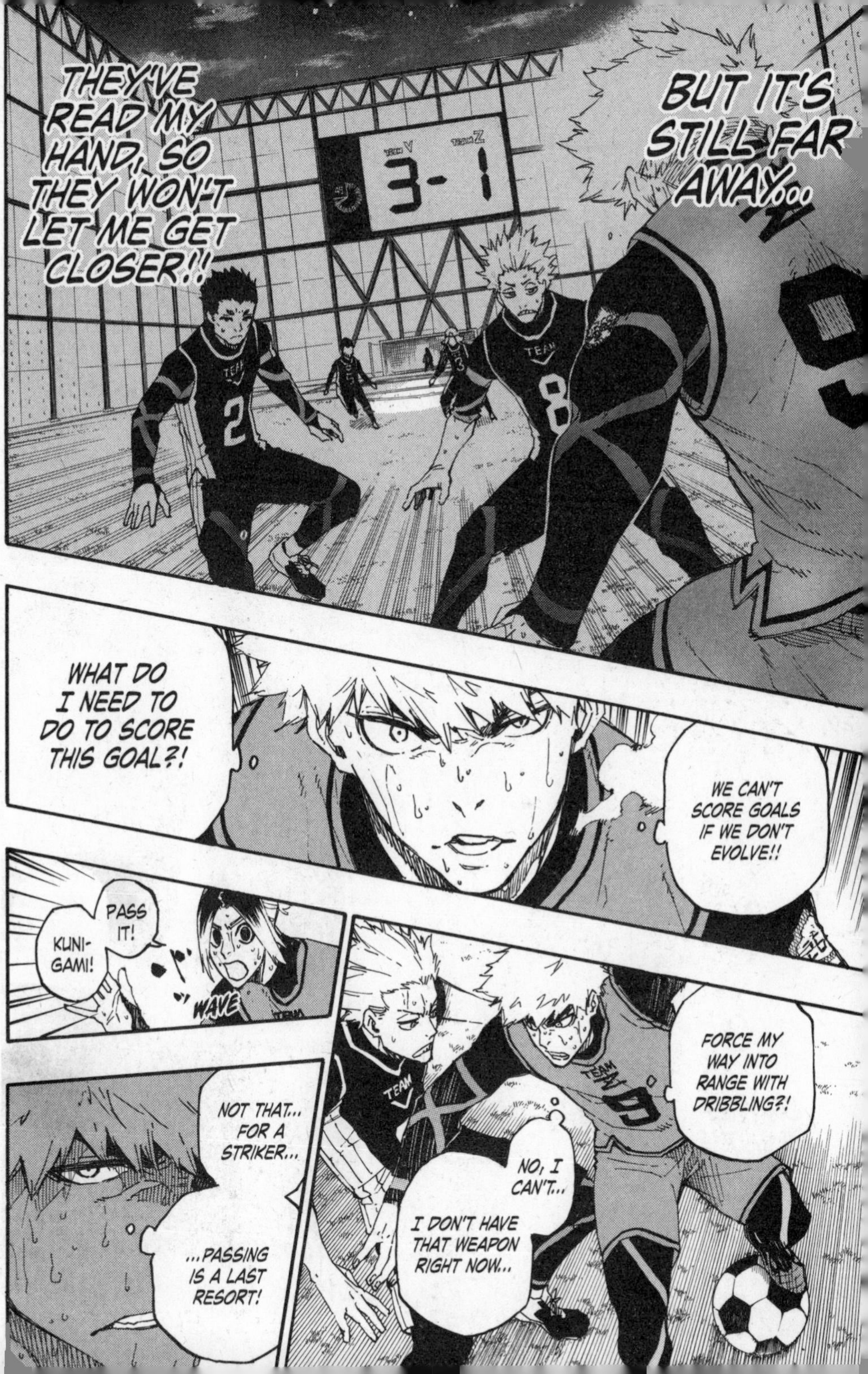
BUT IT'S STILL FAR AWAY...
3-1
THEY'VE READ MY HAND, SO THEY WON'T LET ME GET CLOSER!!
WE CAN'T SCORE GOALS IF WE DON'T EVOLVE!!
WHAT DO I NEED TO DO TO SCORE THIS GOAL?!
FORCE MY WAY INTO RANGE WITH DRIBBLING?!
NO, I CAN'T...
I DON'T HAVE THAT WEAPON RIGHT NOW...
PASS IT!
KUNI-GAMI!
WAVE
NOT THAT... FOR A STRIKER...
...PASSING IS A LAST RESORT!

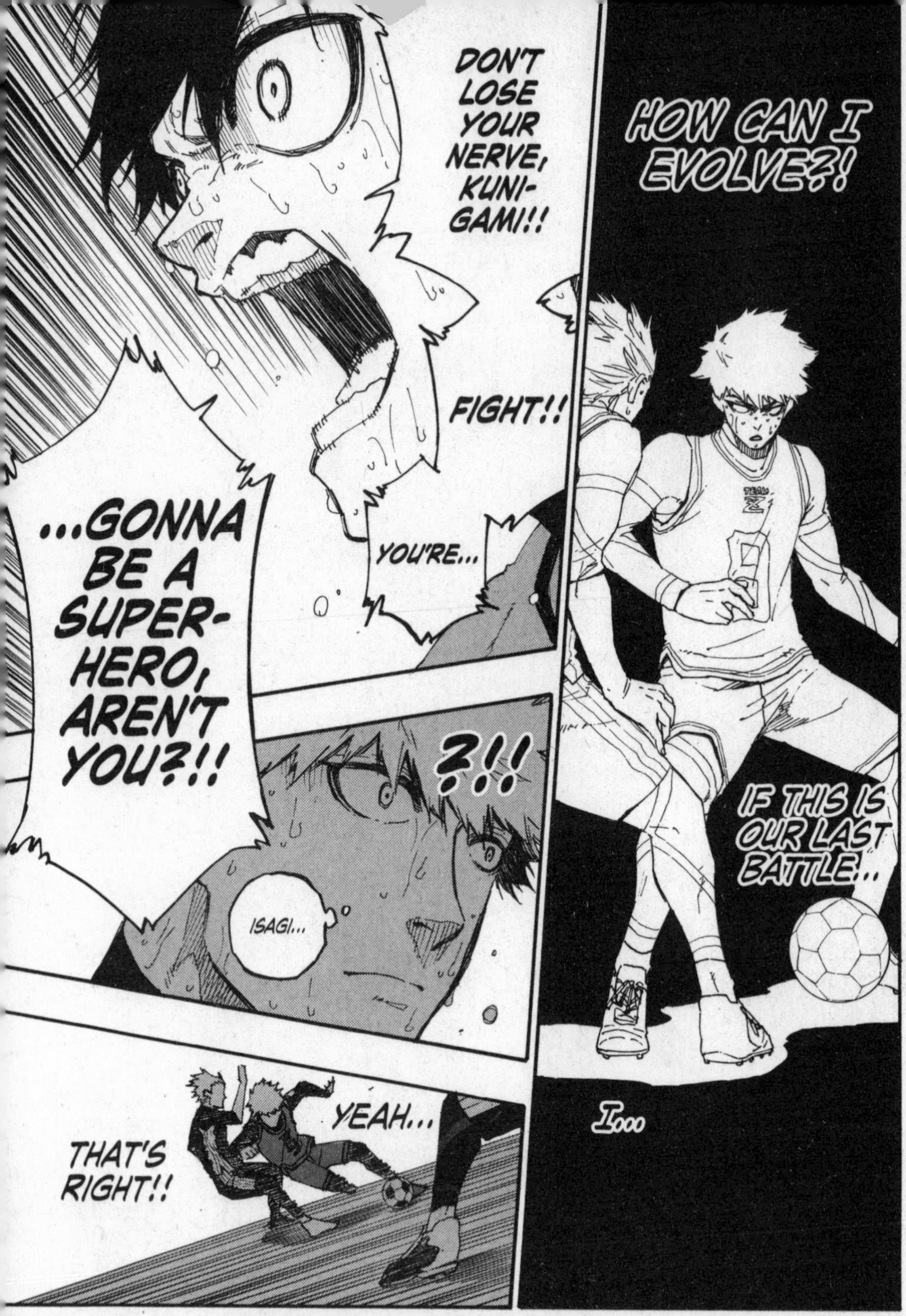
HOW CAN I EVOLVE?!
IF THIS IS OUR LAST BATTLE...
I...
DON'T LOSE YOUR NERVE, KUNI-GAMI!!
FIGHT!!
YOU'RE...
...GONNA BE A SUPER-HERO, AREN'T YOU?!!
?!!
ISAGI...
YEAH...
THAT'S RIGHT!!

IF I WANT TO EVOLVE...
I NEED TO GO BEYOND MY CURRENT LEVEL!!

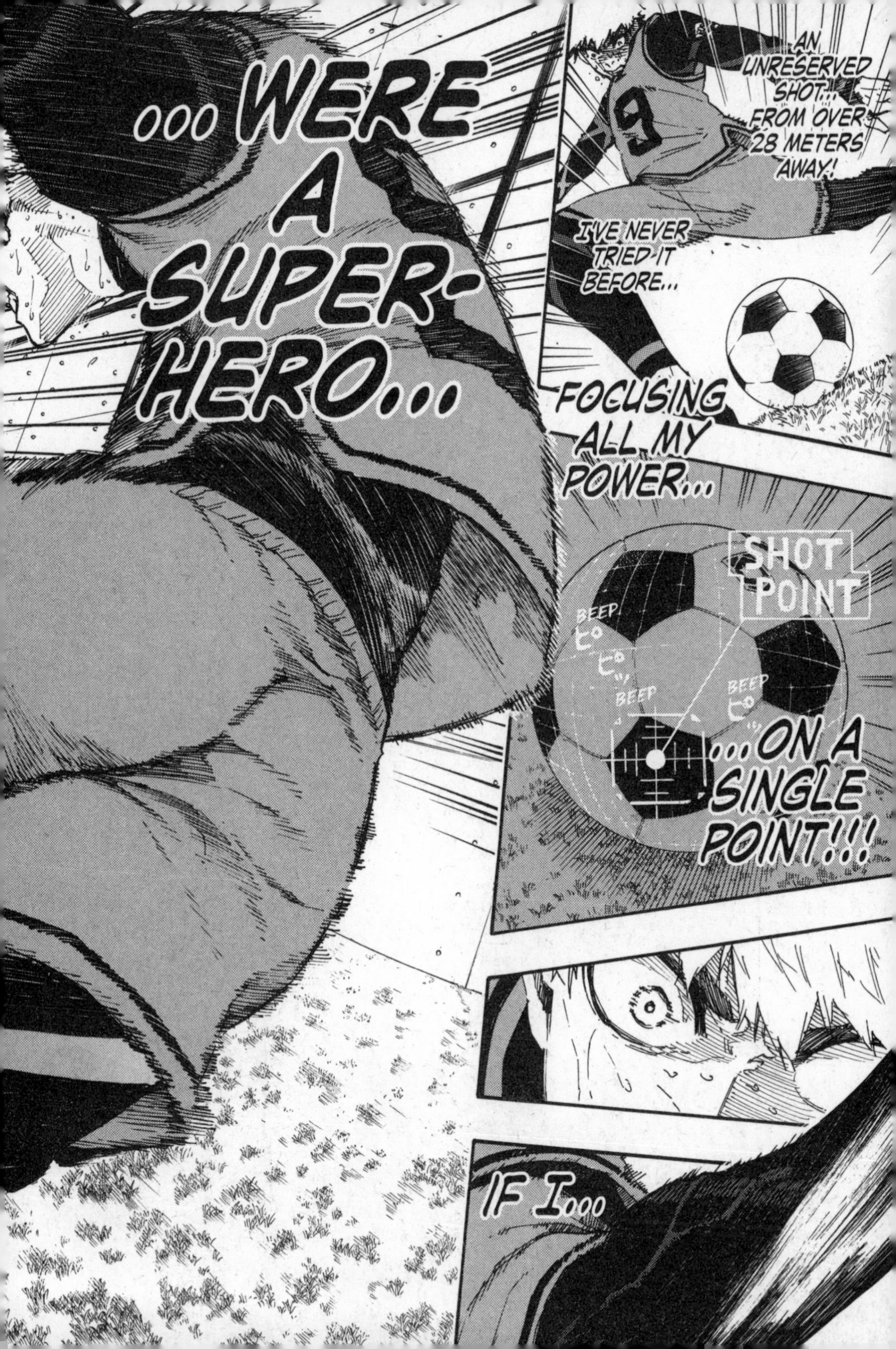

AN UNRESERVED SHOT... FROM OVER 28 METERS AWAY!
I'VE NEVER TRIED IT BEFORE...
FOCUSING ALL MY POWER...
SHOT POINT
BEEP
BEEP
BEEP
...ON A SINGLE POINT!!!
IF I...
...WERE A SUPER-HERO...

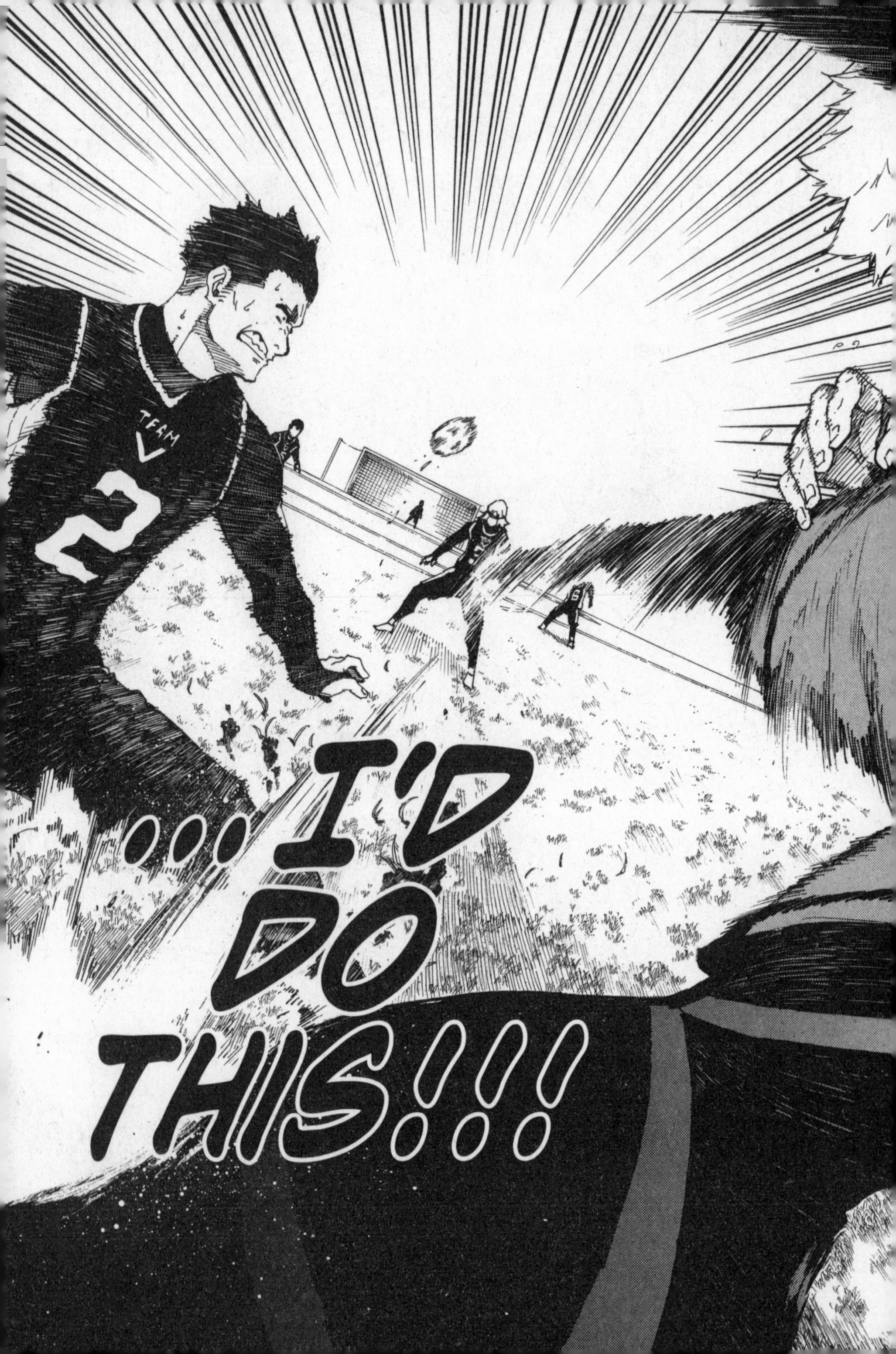
...I'D DO THIS!!!

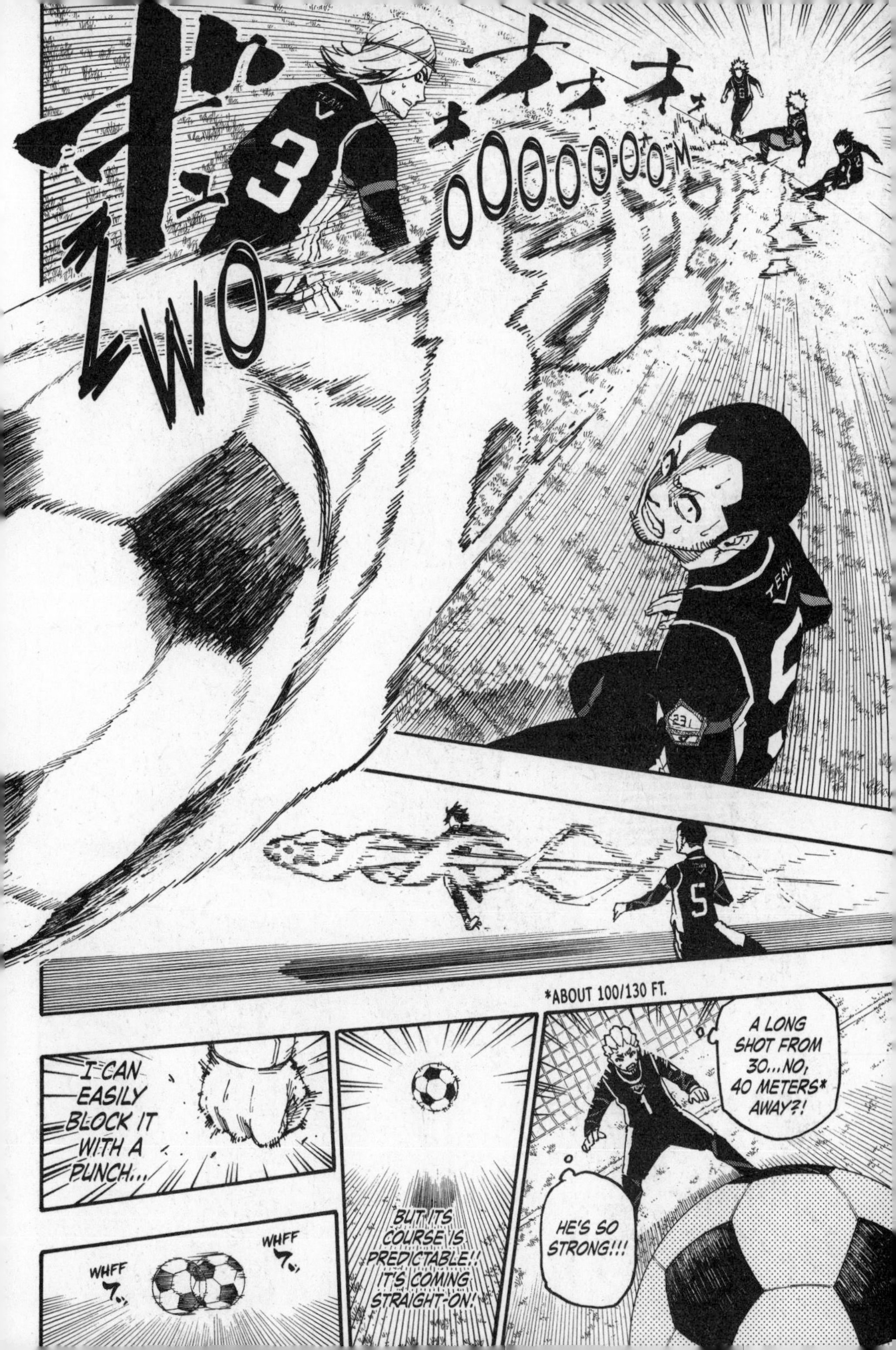
ZWOOOOOOOOOM
*ABOUT 100/130 FT.
A LONG SHOT FROM 30...NO, 40 METERS* AWAY?!
HE'S SO STRONG!!!
BUT ITS COURSE IS PREDICTABLE!! IT'S COMING STRAIGHT-ON!
I CAN EASILY BLOCK IT WITH A PUNCH...
WHFF
WHFF

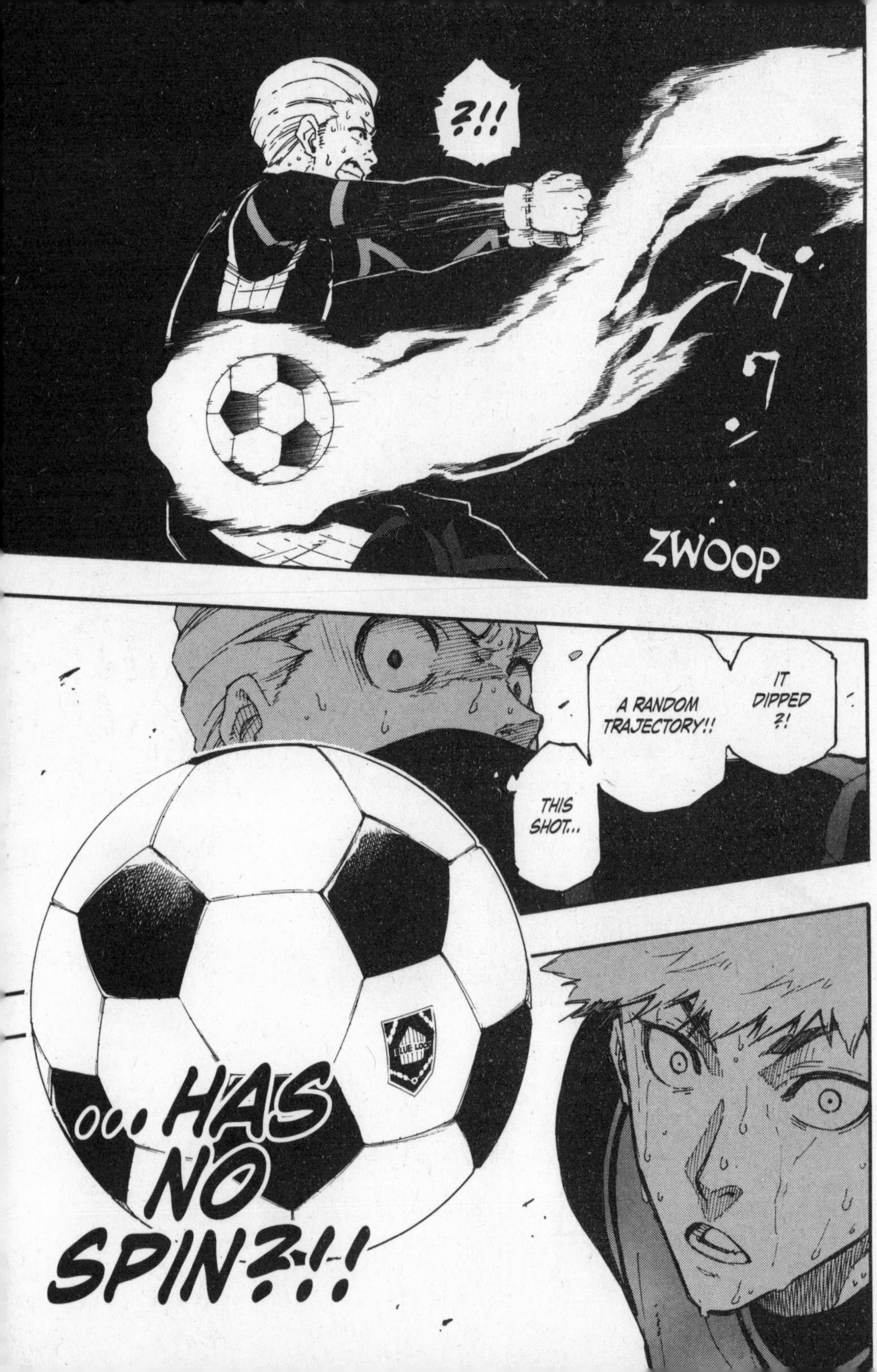
?!!
ZWOOP
IT DIPPED?!
A RANDOM TRAJECTORY!!
THIS SHOT...
...HAS NO SPIN?!!

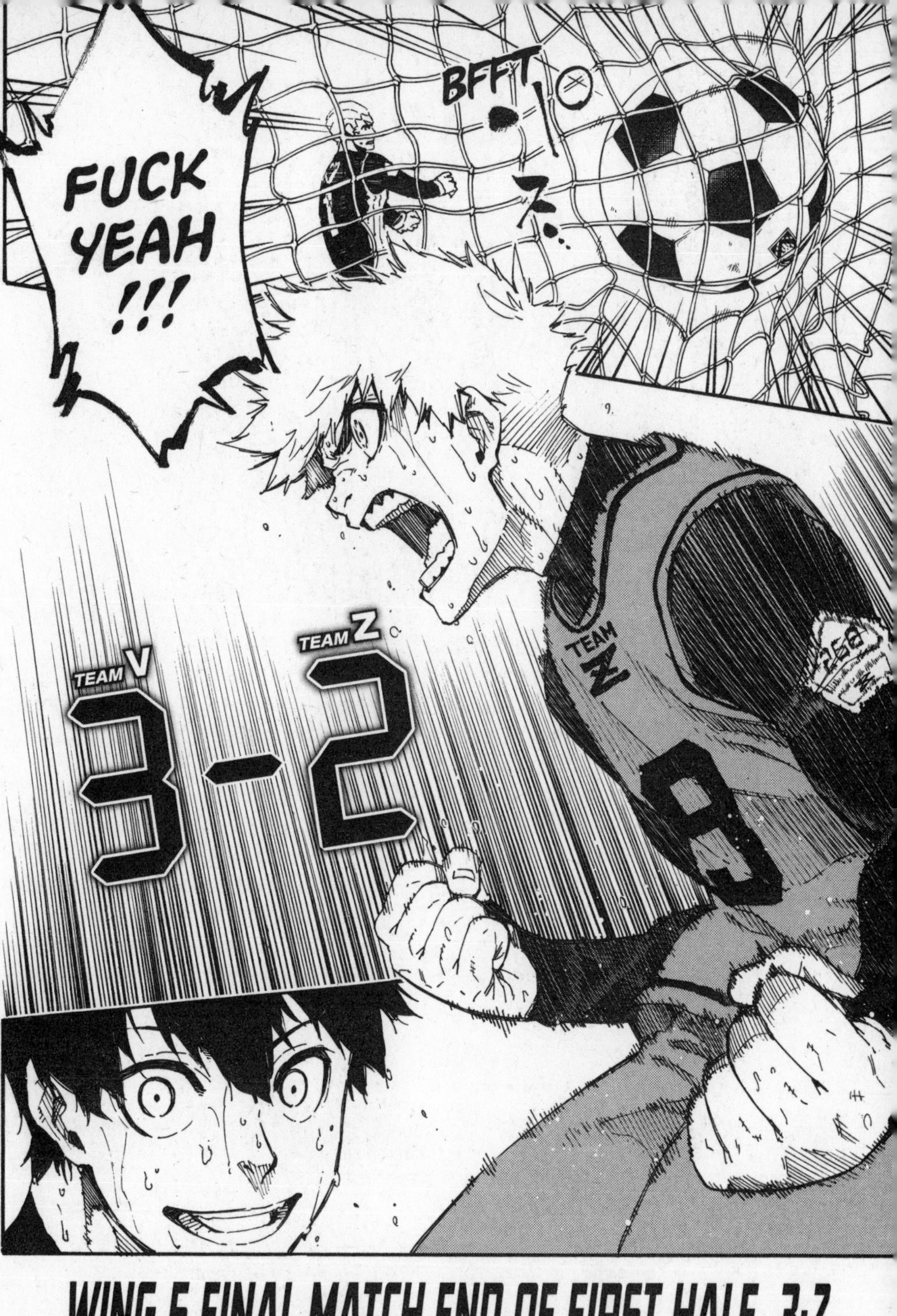
BFFT
FUCK YEAH!!!
TEAM V 3-2 TEAM Z

WING 5 FINAL MATCH END OF FIRST HALF 3-2

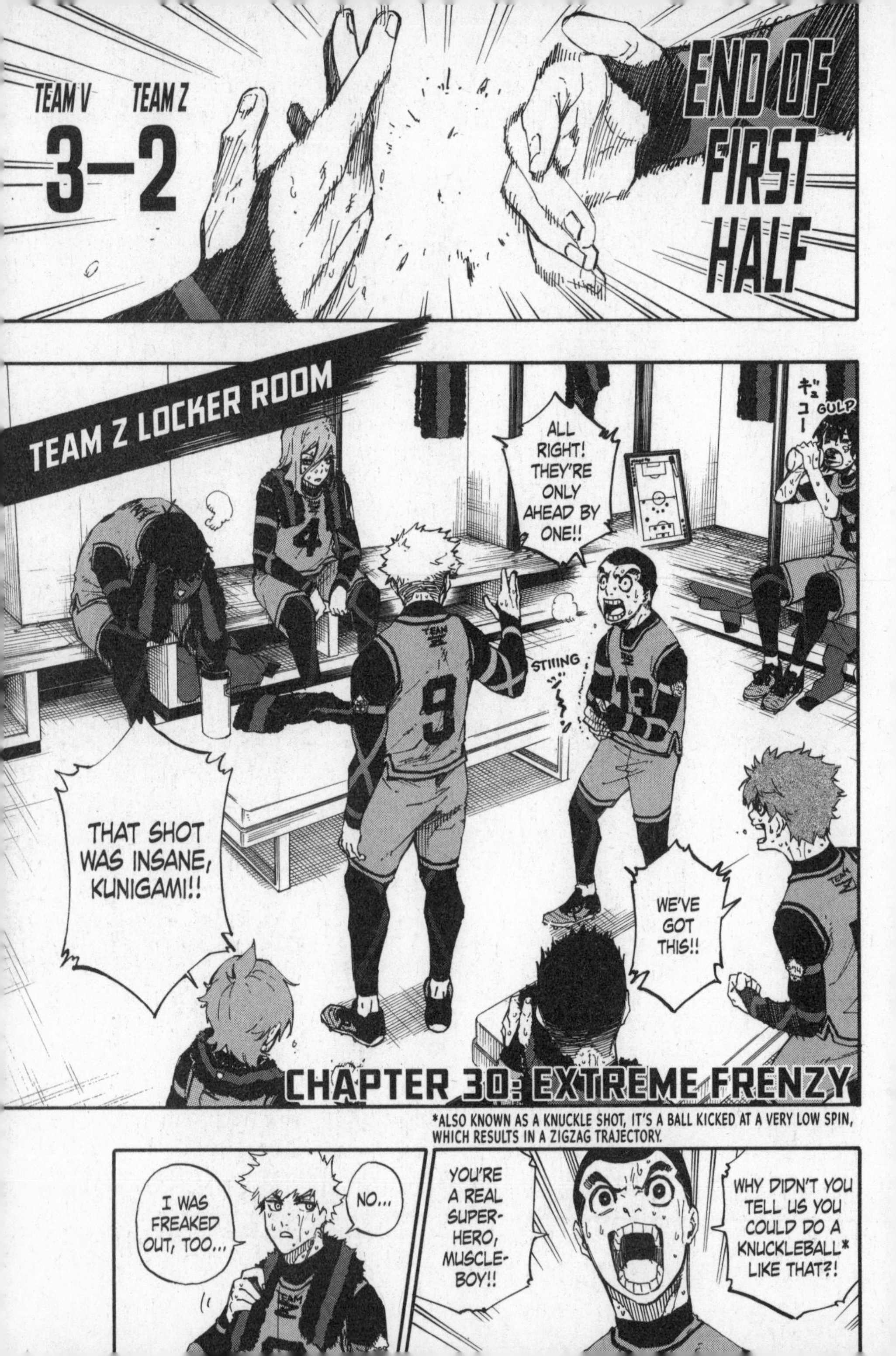
END OF FIRST HALF
TEAM V TEAM Z
3–2
ギュコー GULP
ALL RIGHT! THEY'RE ONLY AHEAD BY ONE!!
TEAM Z LOCKER ROOM
STIIING
WE'VE GOT THIS!!
THAT SHOT WAS INSANE, KUNIGAMI!!
CHAPTER 30: EXTREME FRENZY
WHY DIDN'T YOU TELL US YOU COULD DO A KNUCKLEBALL* LIKE THAT?!
YOU'RE A REAL SUPER-HERO, MUSCLE-BOY!!
NO...
I WAS FREAKED OUT, TOO...

*ALSO KNOWN AS A KNUCKLE SHOT, IT'S A BALL KICKED AT A VERY LOW SPIN, WHICH RESULTS IN A ZIGZAG TRAJECTORY.

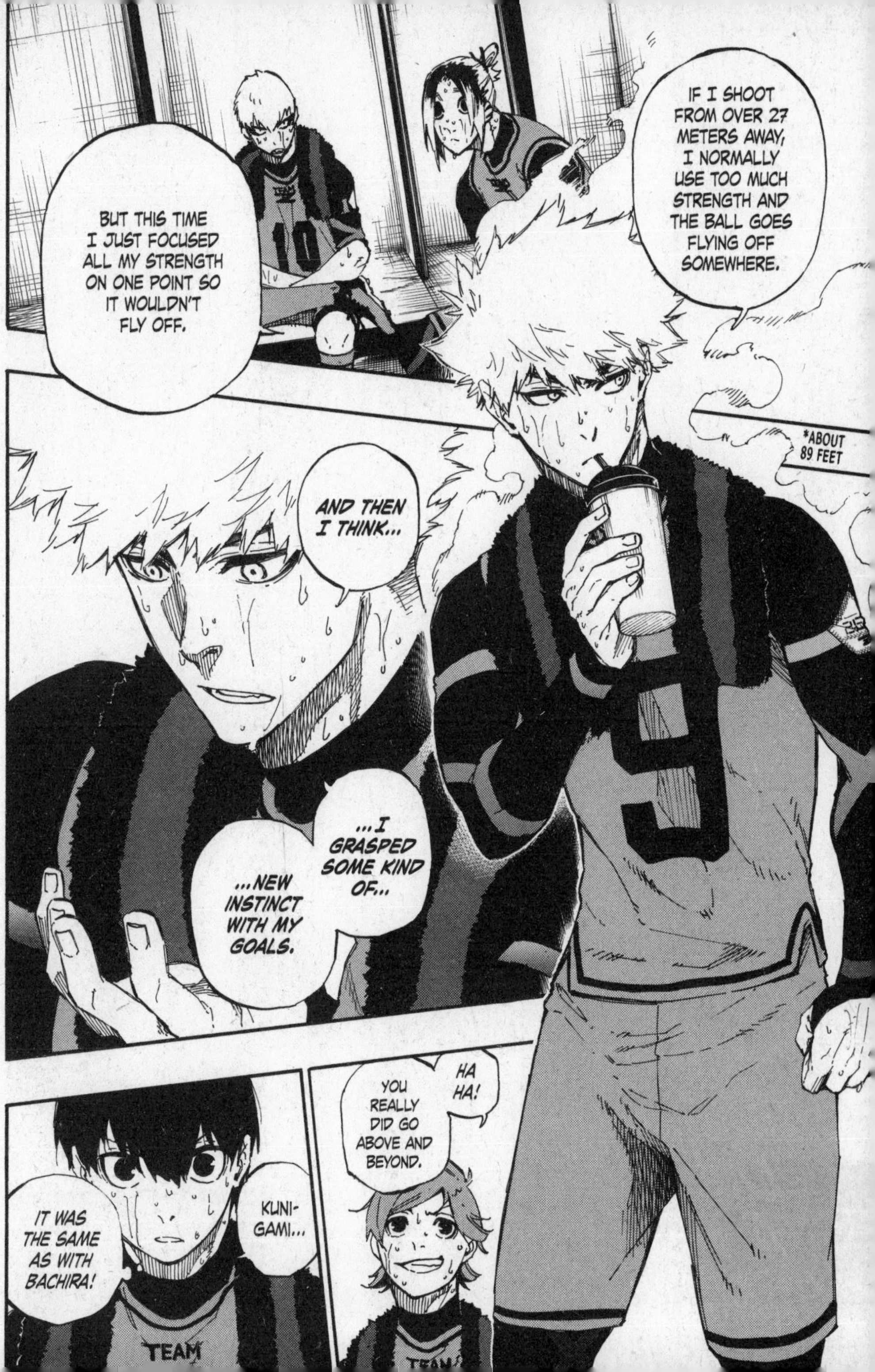
IF I SHOOT FROM OVER 27 METERS AWAY, I NORMALLY USE TOO MUCH STRENGTH AND THE BALL GOES FLYING OFF SOMEWHERE.
*ABOUT 89 FEET
BUT THIS TIME I JUST FOCUSED ALL MY STRENGTH ON ONE POINT SO IT WOULDN'T FLY OFF.
AND THEN I THINK...
...I GRASPED SOME KIND OF...
...NEW INSTINCT WITH MY GOALS.
HA HA!
YOU REALLY DID GO ABOVE AND BEYOND.
KUNI-GAMI...
IT WAS THE SAME AS WITH BACHIRA!

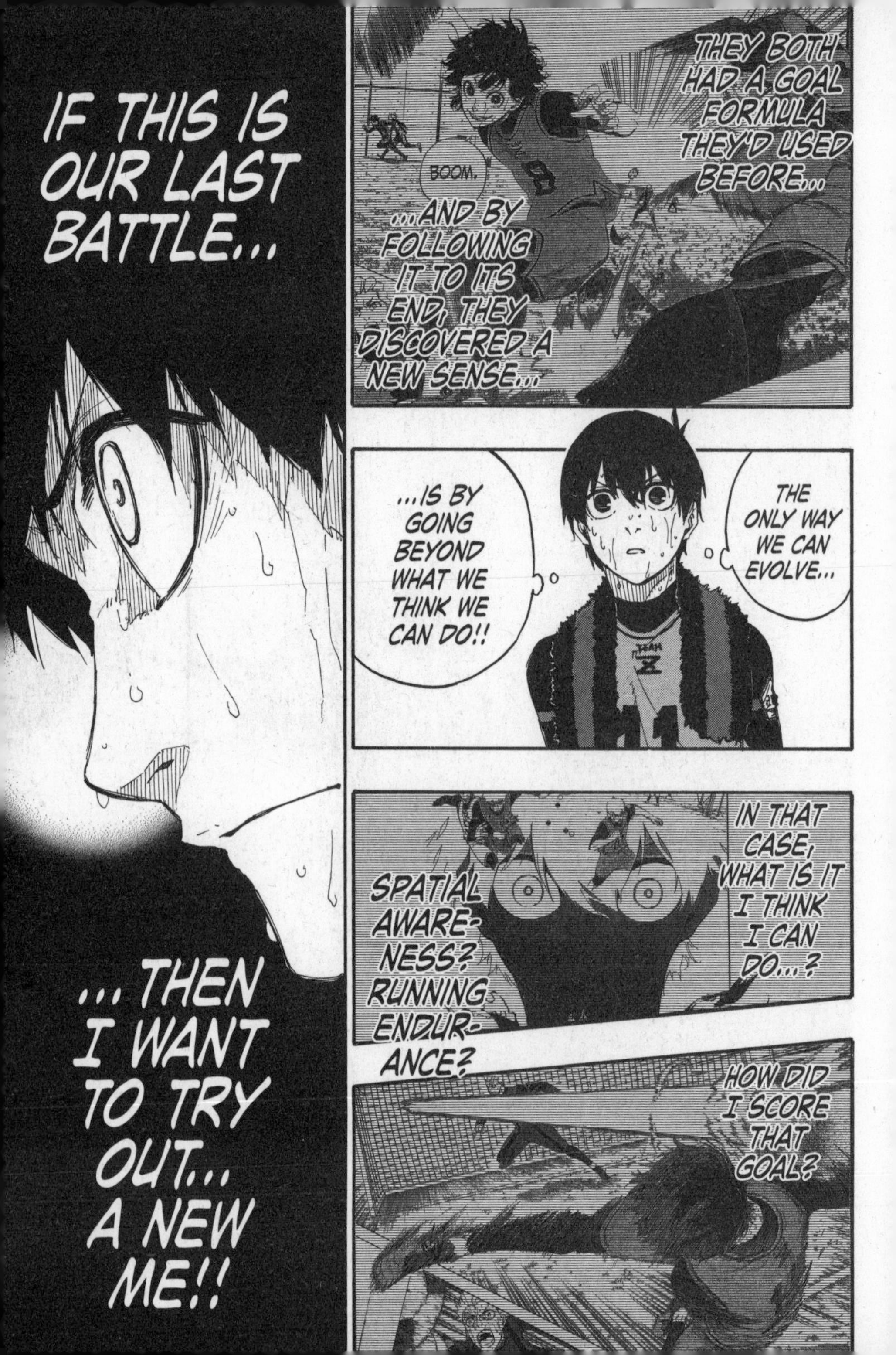

THEY BOTH HAD A GOAL FORMULA THEY'D USED BEFORE...
BOOM.
...AND BY FOLLOWING IT TO ITS END, THEY DISCOVERED A NEW SENSE...
THE ONLY WAY WE CAN EVOLVE...
...IS BY GOING BEYOND WHAT WE THINK WE CAN DO!!
IN THAT CASE, WHAT IS IT I THINK I CAN DO...?
SPATIAL AWARENESS? RUNNING ENDURANCE?
HOW DID I SCORE THAT GOAL?
IF THIS IS OUR LAST BATTLE...
...THEN I WANT TO TRY OUT... A NEW ME!!

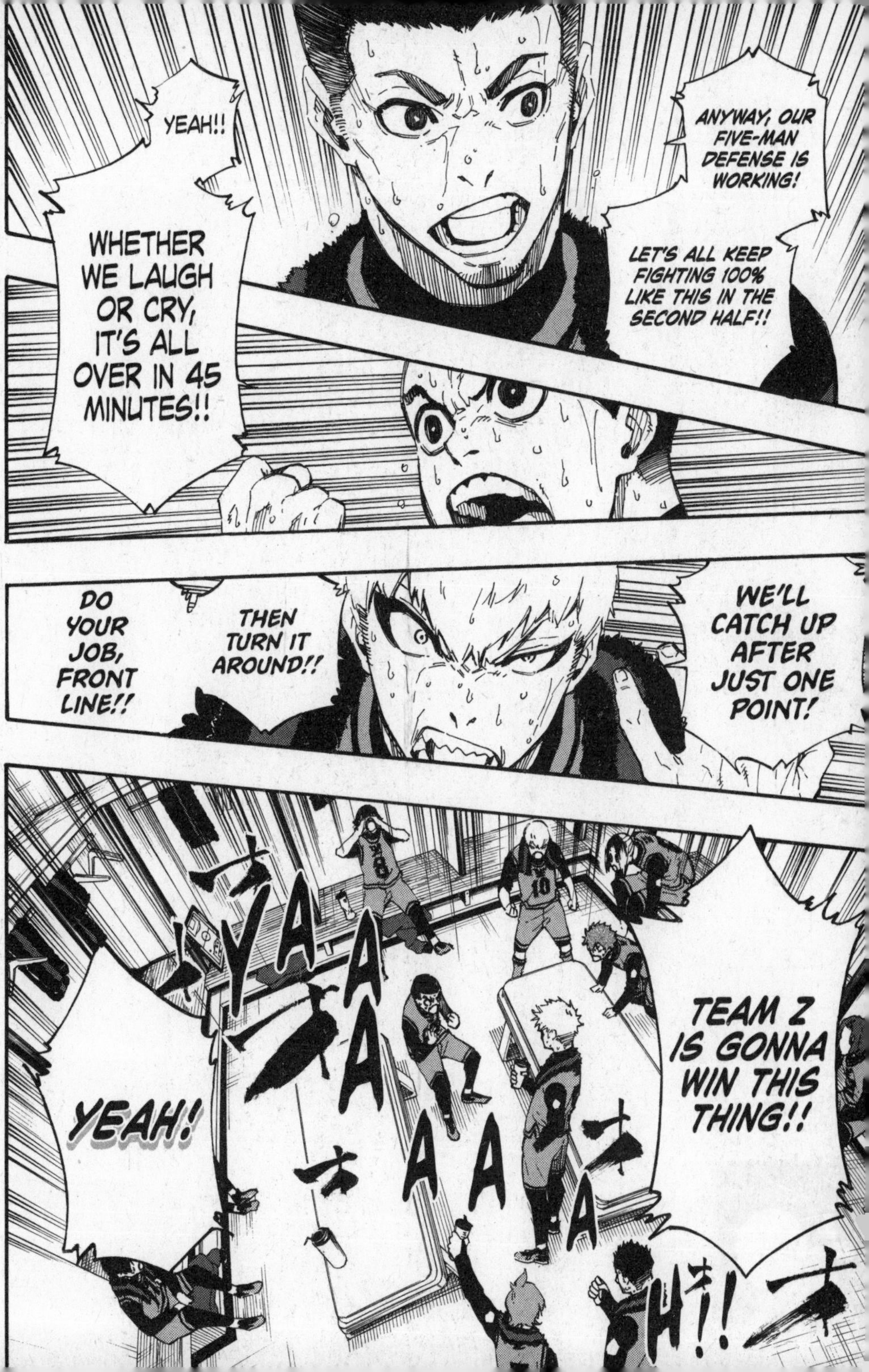

ANYWAY, OUR FIVE-MAN DEFENSE IS WORKING!
LET'S ALL KEEP FIGHTING 100% LIKE THIS IN THE SECOND HALF!!
YEAH!!
WHETHER WE LAUGH OR CRY, IT'S ALL OVER IN 45 MINUTES!!
WE'LL CATCH UP AFTER JUST ONE POINT!
THEN TURN IT AROUND!!
DO YOUR JOB, FRONT LINE!!
TEAM Z IS GONNA WIN THIS THING!!
YEAH!
YAAAAAAAH!!

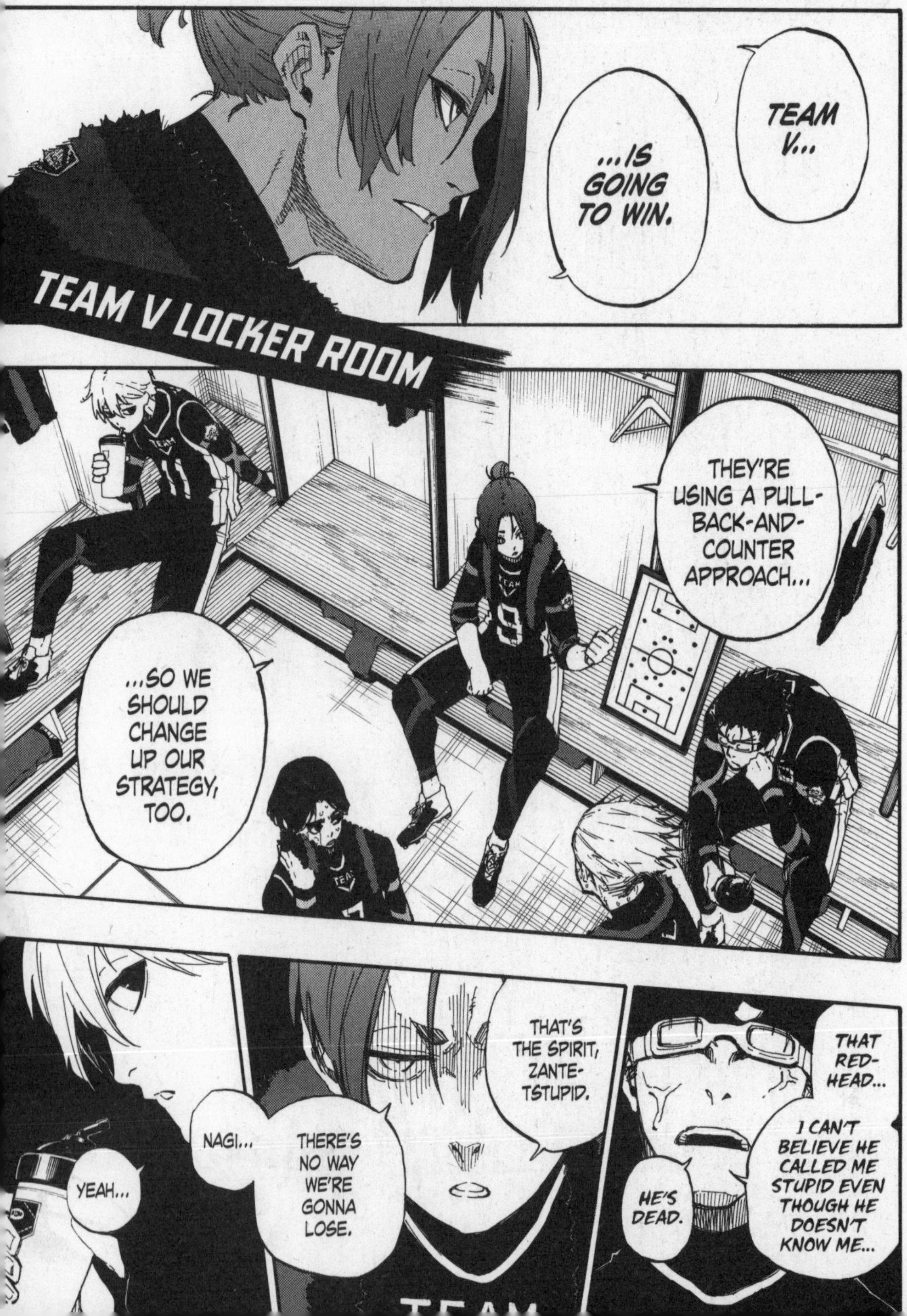
TEAM V...
...IS GOING TO WIN.
TEAM V LOCKER ROOM
THEY'RE USING A PULL-BACK-AND-COUNTER APPROACH...
...SO WE SHOULD CHANGE UP OUR STRATEGY, TOO.
THAT RED-HEAD...
I CAN'T BELIEVE HE CALLED ME STUPID EVEN THOUGH HE DOESN'T KNOW ME...
HE'S DEAD.
THAT'S THE SPIRIT, ZANTE-TSTUPID.
THERE'S NO WAY WE'RE GONNA LOSE.
NAGI...
YEAH...

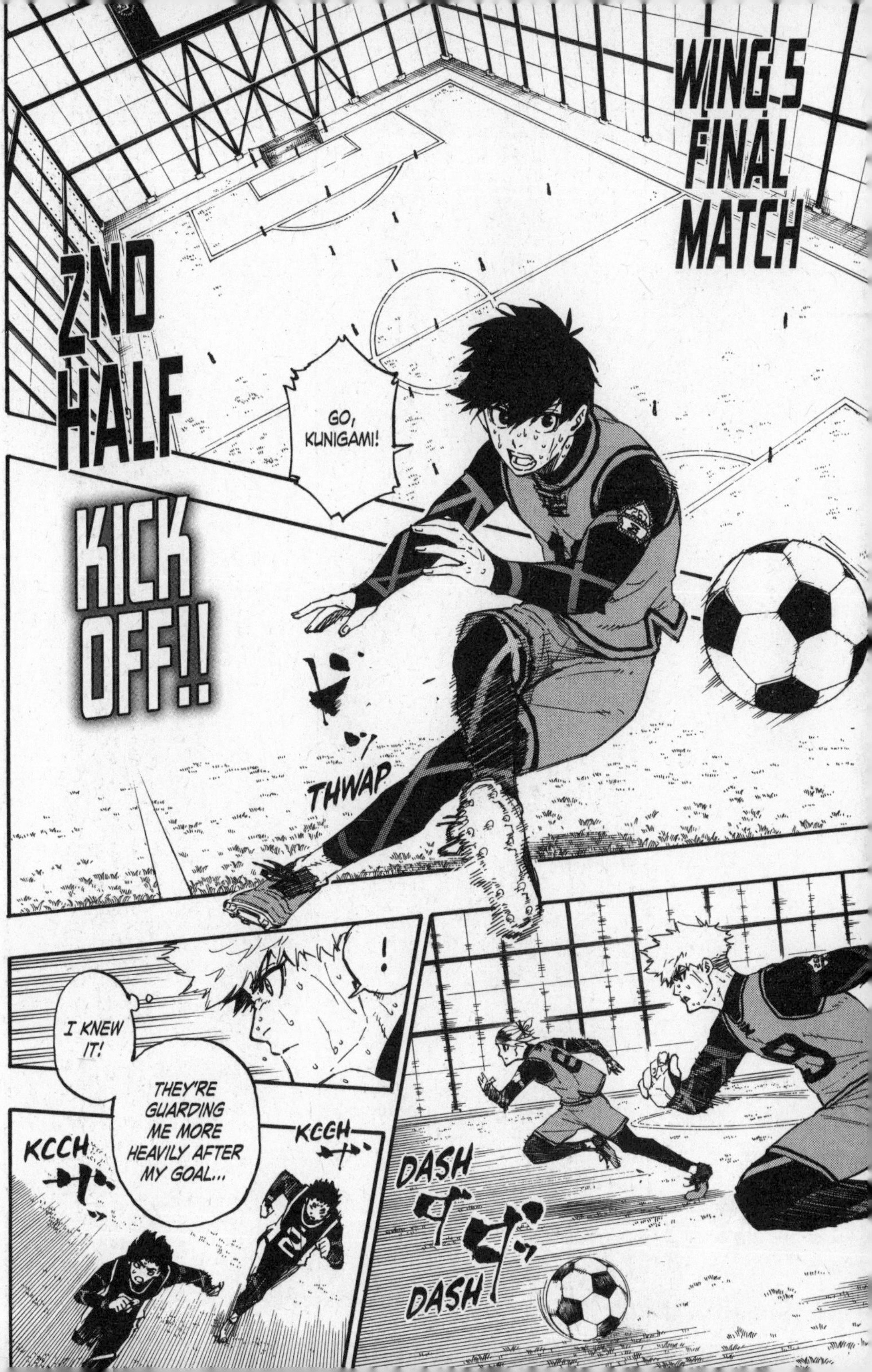
WING 5 FINAL MATCH
2ND HALF
GO, KUNIGAMI!
KICK OFF!!
THWAP
DASH
DASH
!
I KNEW IT!
THEY'RE GUARDING ME MORE HEAVILY AFTER MY GOAL...
KCCH
KCCH

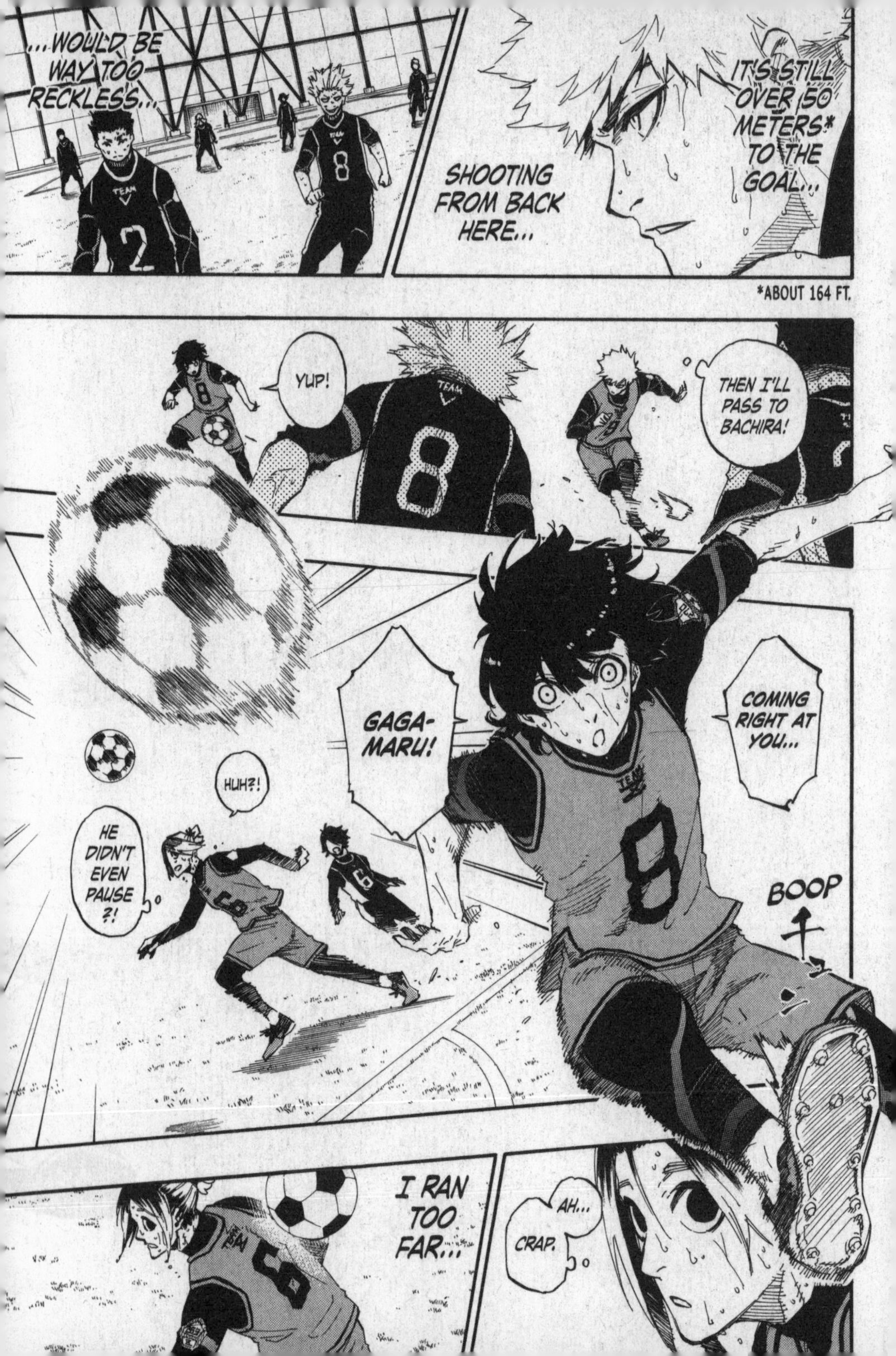
IT'S STILL OVER 50 METERS* TO THE GOAL...
SHOOTING FROM BACK HERE...
...WOULD BE WAY TOO RECKLESS...
THEN I'LL PASS TO BACHIRA!
YUP!
COMING RIGHT AT YOU...
GAGA-MARU!
BOOP
HUH?!
HE DIDN'T EVEN PAUSE?!
AH... CRAP.
I RAN TOO FAR...

*ABOUT 164 FT.

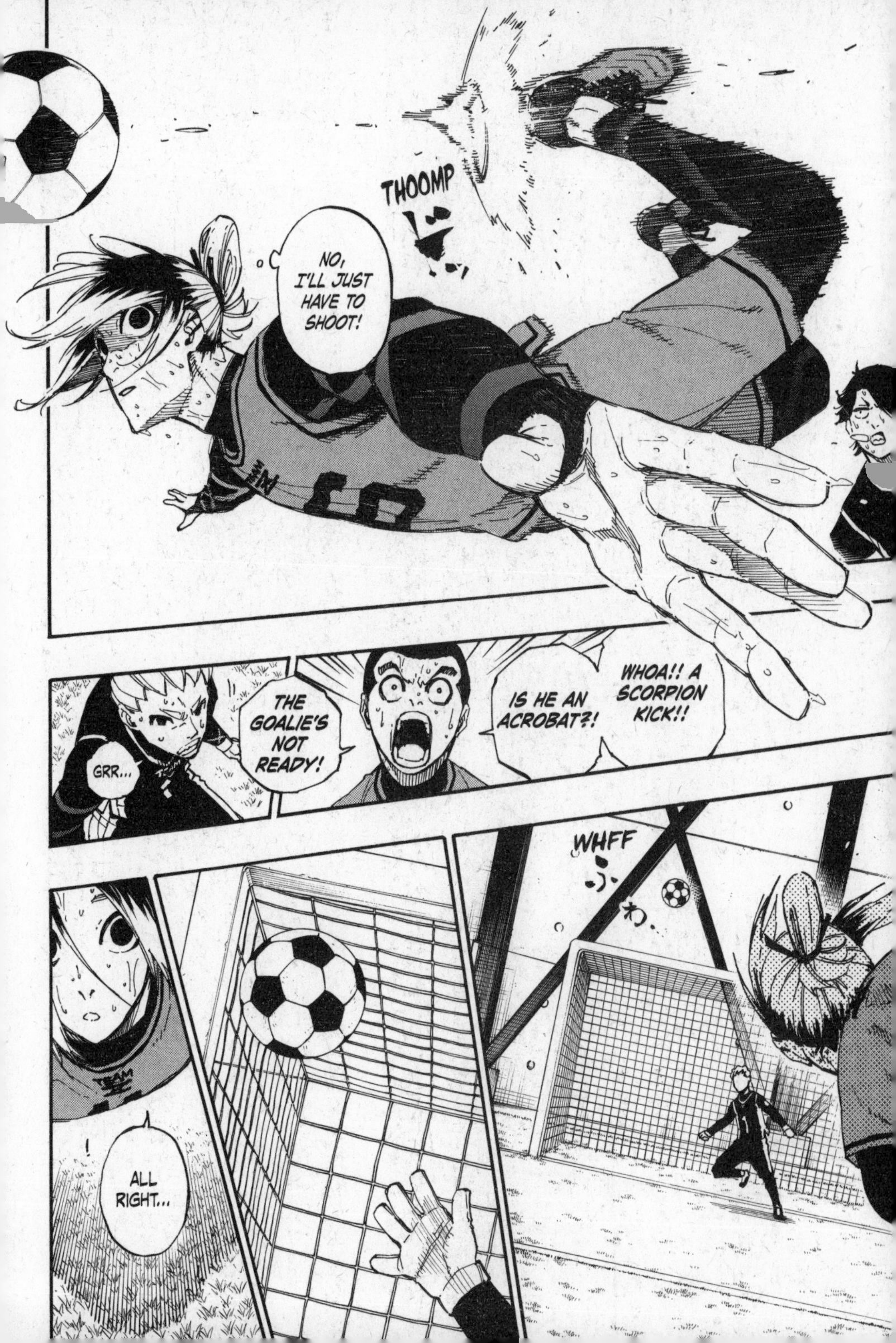
THOOMP
NO, I'LL JUST HAVE TO SHOOT!
WHOA!! A SCORPION KICK!!
IS HE AN ACROBAT?!
THE GOALIE'S NOT READY!
GRR...
WHFF
ふわ...
ALL RIGHT...

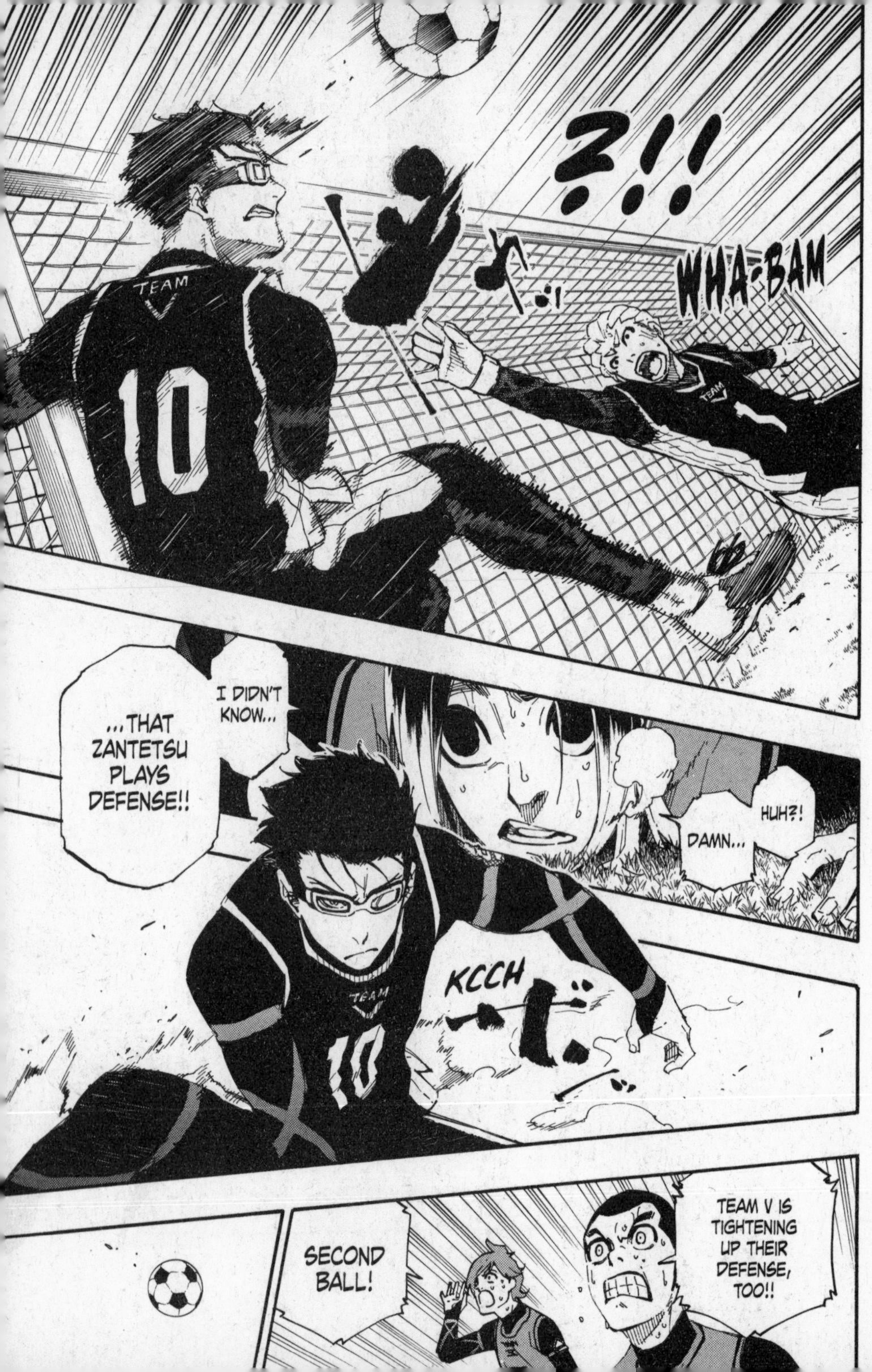
?!!
WHA-BAM
HUH?!
DAMN...
I DIDN'T KNOW...
...THAT ZANTETSU PLAYS DEFENSE!!
KCCH
TEAM V IS TIGHTENING UP THEIR DEFENSE, TOO!!
SECOND BALL!

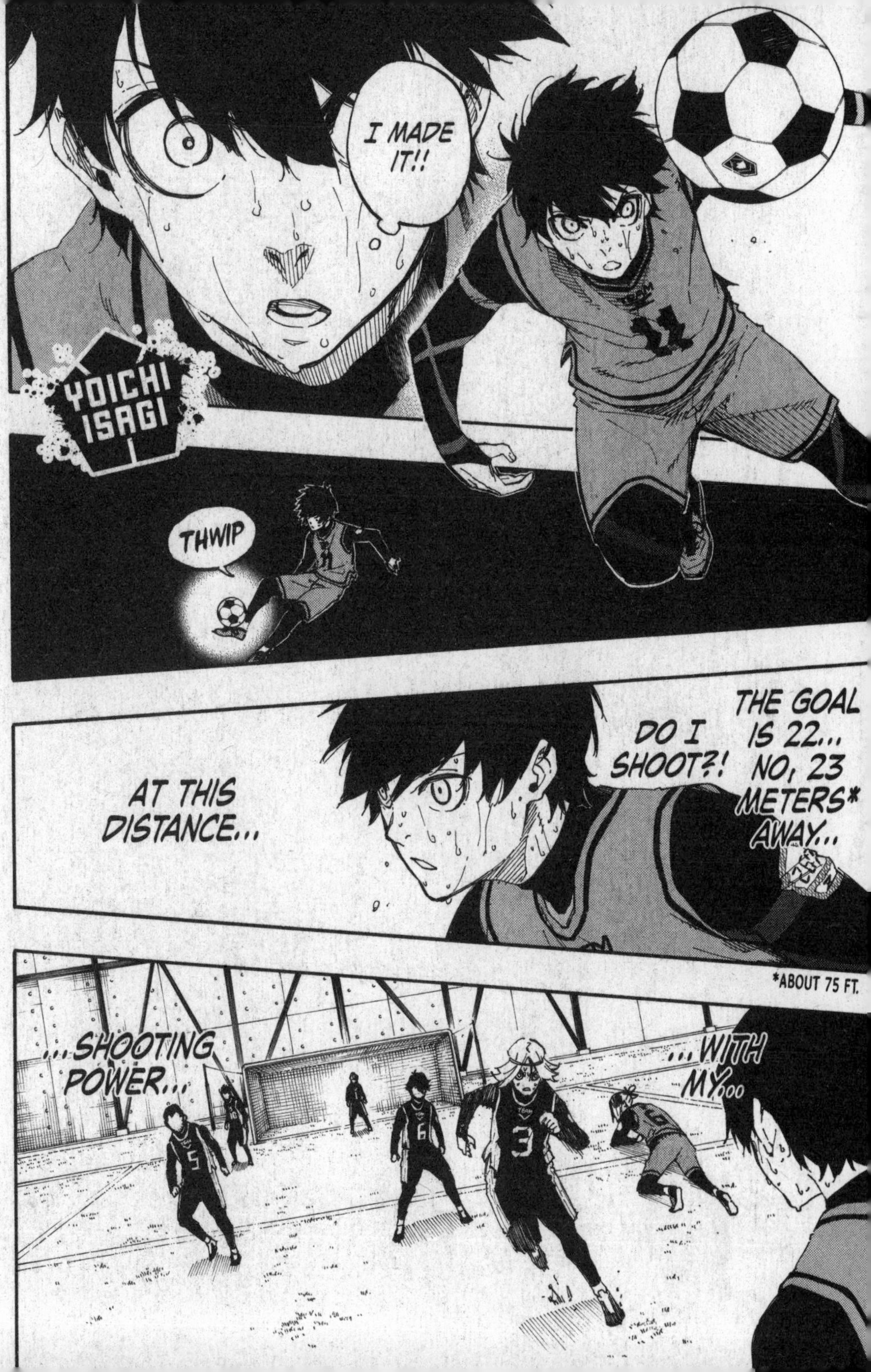
I MADE IT!!
YOICHI ISAGI
THWIP
THE GOAL IS 22... NO, 23 METERS* AWAY...
DO I SHOOT?!
AT THIS DISTANCE...
*ABOUT 75 FT.
...WITH MY...
...SHOOTING POWER...

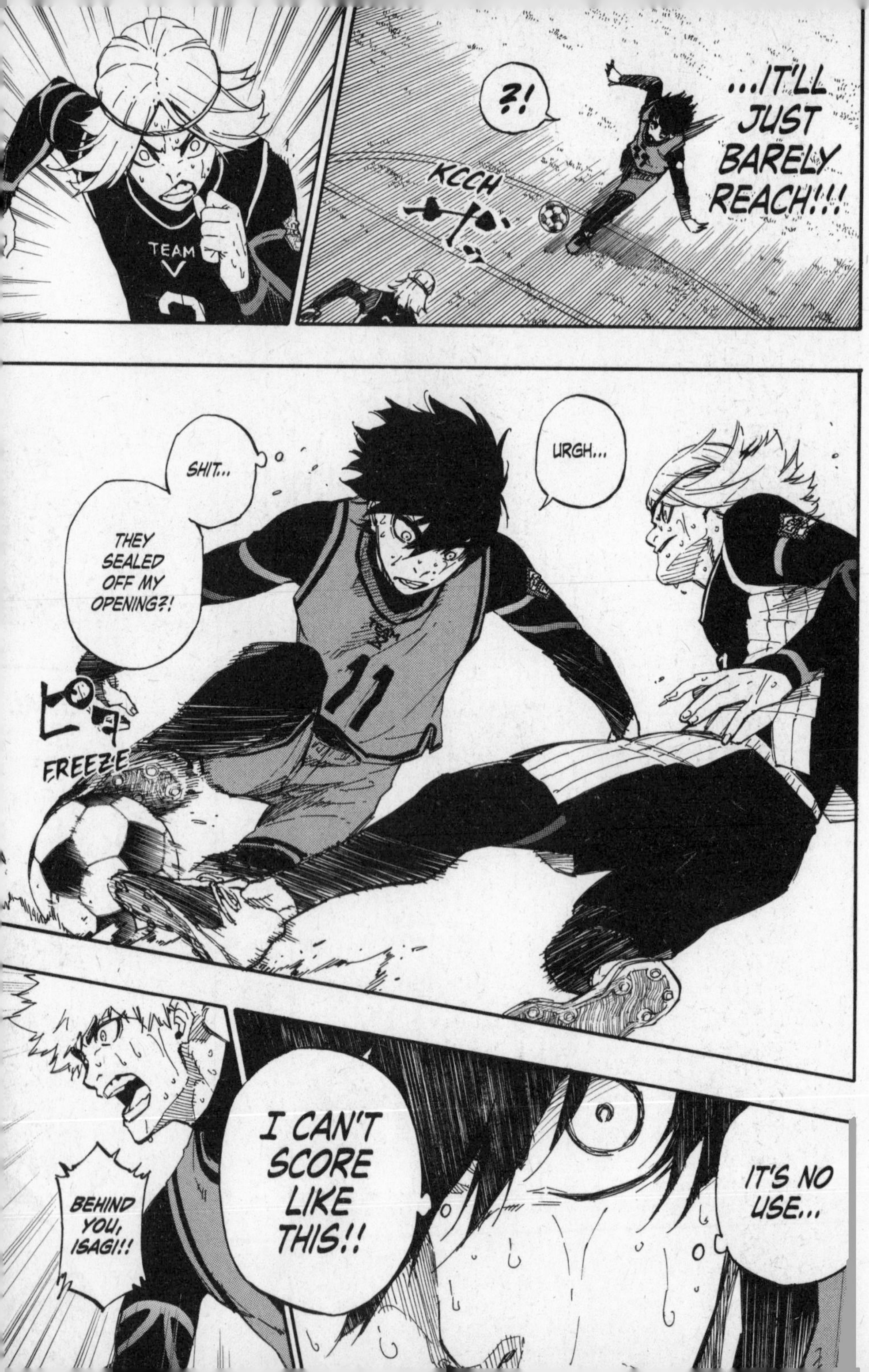
...IT'LL JUST BARELY REACH!!!
?!
KCCH
URGH...
SHIT...
THEY SEALED OFF MY OPENING?!
FREEZE
IT'S NO USE...
I CAN'T SCORE LIKE THIS!!
BEHIND YOU, ISAGI!!

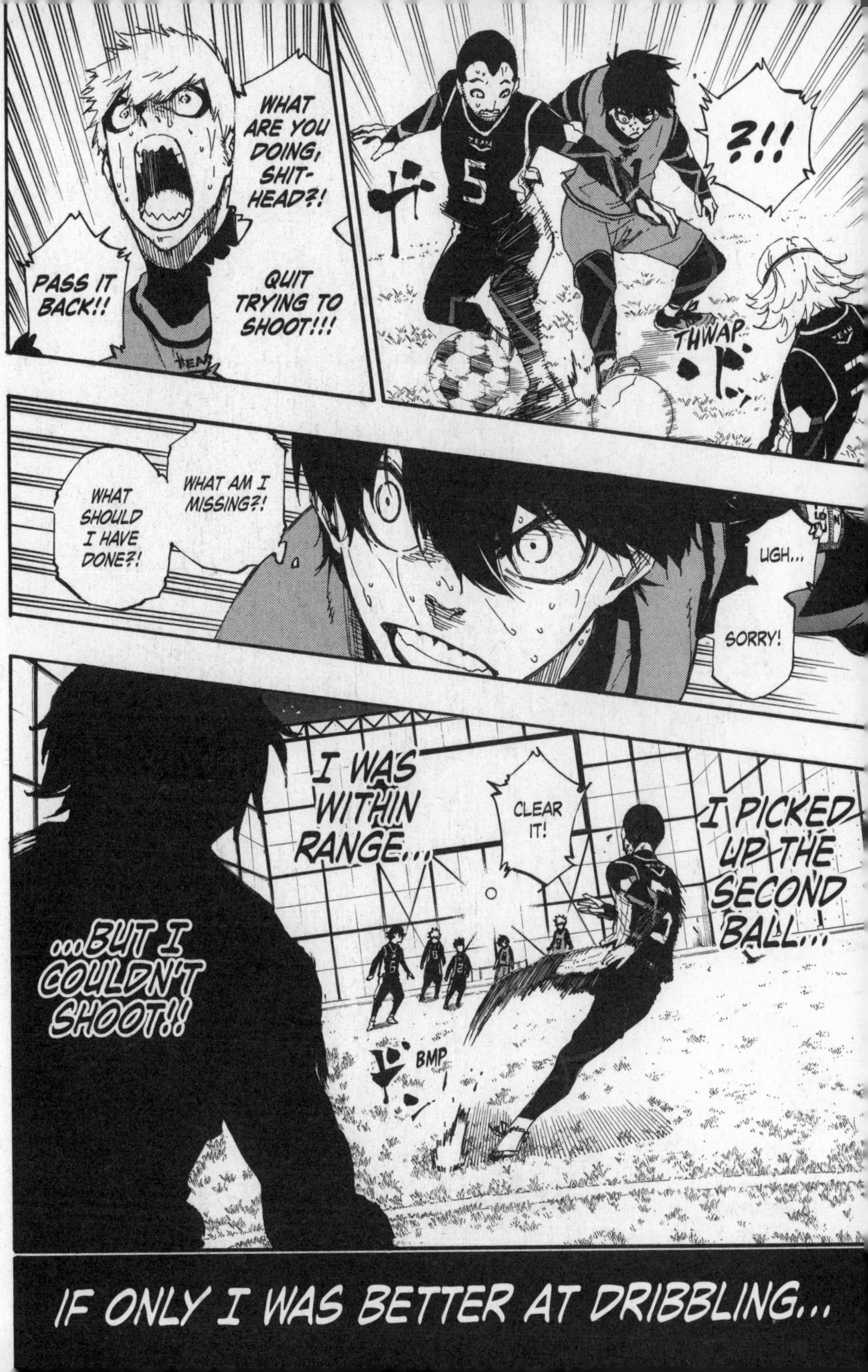
?!!
THWAP
WHAT ARE YOU DOING, SHIT-HEAD?!
QUIT TRYING TO SHOOT!!!
PASS IT BACK!!
UGH...
SORRY!
WHAT AM I MISSING?!
WHAT SHOULD I HAVE DONE?!
I PICKED UP THE SECOND BALL...
CLEAR IT!
I WAS WITHIN RANGE...
...BUT I COULDN'T SHOOT!!
BMP
IF ONLY I WAS BETTER AT DRIBBLING...

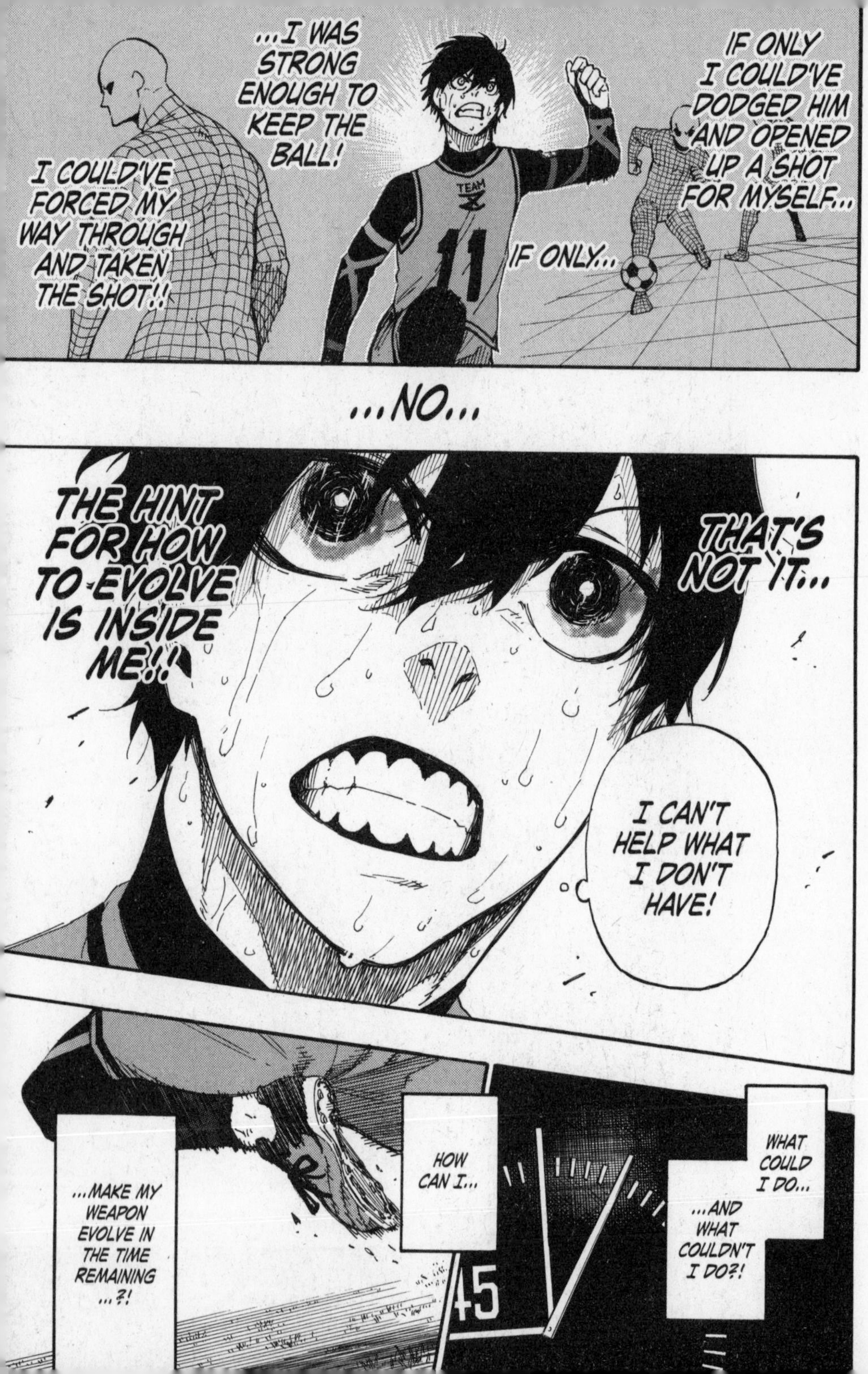
IF ONLY I COULD'VE DODGED HIM AND OPENED UP A SHOT FOR MYSELF...
IF ONLY...
...I WAS STRONG ENOUGH TO KEEP THE BALL!
I COULD'VE FORCED MY WAY THROUGH AND TAKEN THE SHOT!!
TEAM
11
...NO...
THAT'S NOT IT...
I CAN'T HELP WHAT I DON'T HAVE!
THE HINT FOR HOW TO EVOLVE IS INSIDE ME!!
WHAT COULD I DO...
...AND WHAT COULDN'T I DO?!
HOW CAN I...
...MAKE MY WEAPON EVOLVE IN THE TIME REMAINING...?!
45

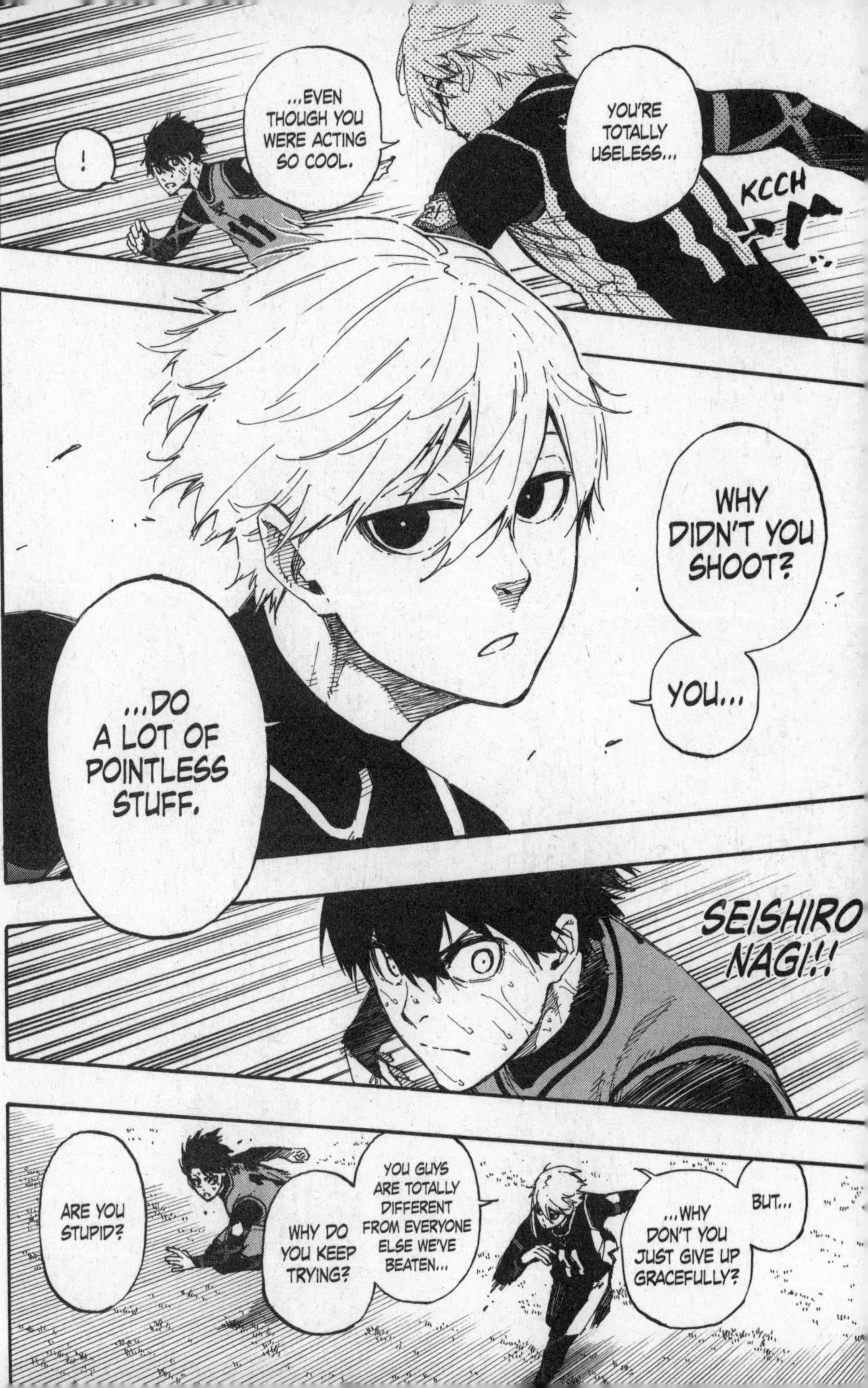
YOU'RE TOTALLY USELESS...
KCCH
...EVEN THOUGH YOU WERE ACTING SO COOL.
!
WHY DIDN'T YOU SHOOT?
YOU...
...DO A LOT OF POINTLESS STUFF.
SEISHIRO NAGI!!
BUT...
...WHY DON'T YOU JUST GIVE UP GRACEFULLY?
YOU GUYS ARE TOTALLY DIFFERENT FROM EVERYONE ELSE WE'VE BEATEN...
WHY DO YOU KEEP TRYING?
ARE YOU STUPID?

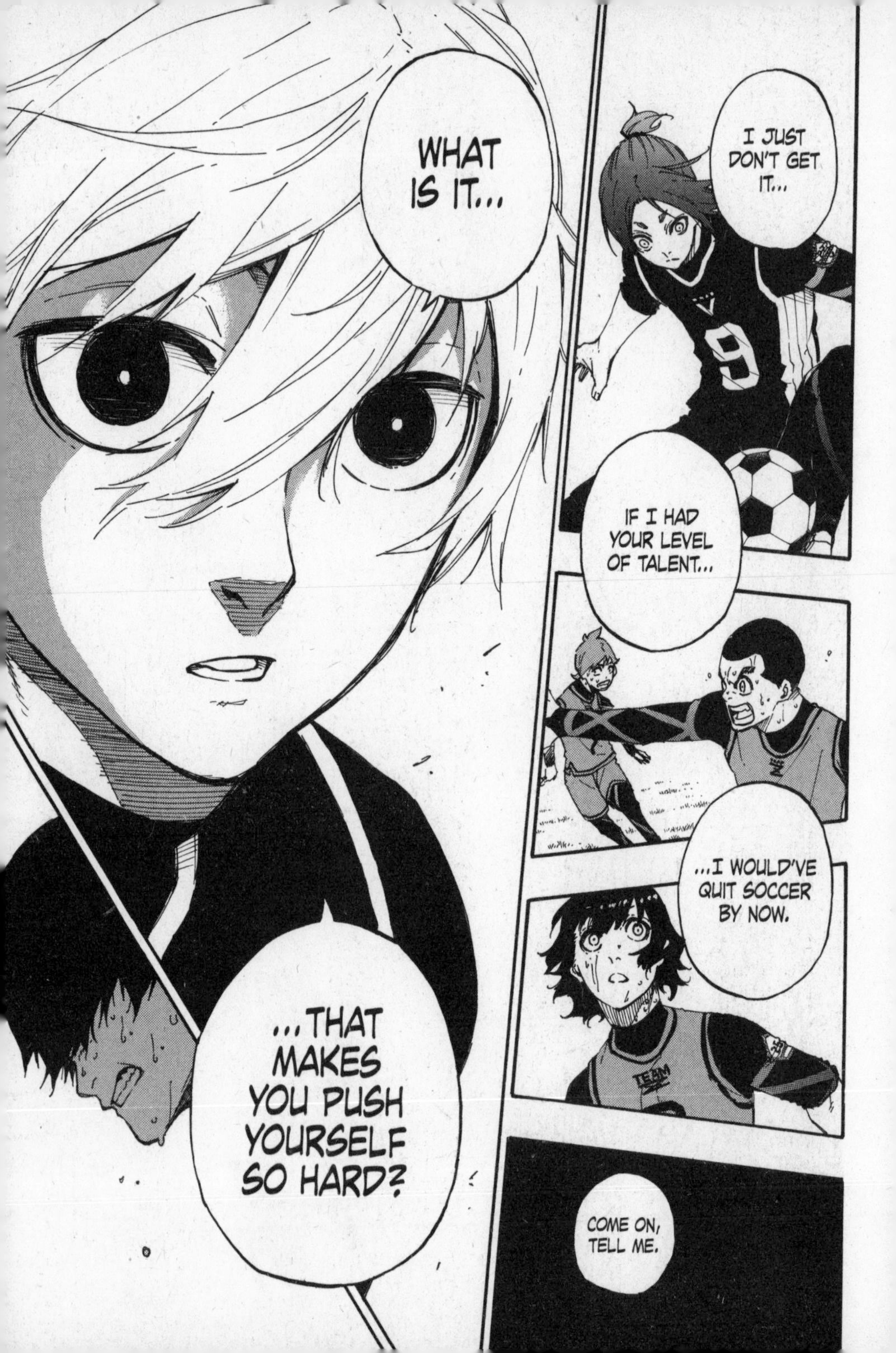
I JUST DON'T GET IT...
IF I HAD YOUR LEVEL OF TALENT...
...I WOULD'VE QUIT SOCCER BY NOW.
COME ON, TELL ME.
WHAT IS IT...
...THAT MAKES YOU PUSH YOURSELF SO HARD?

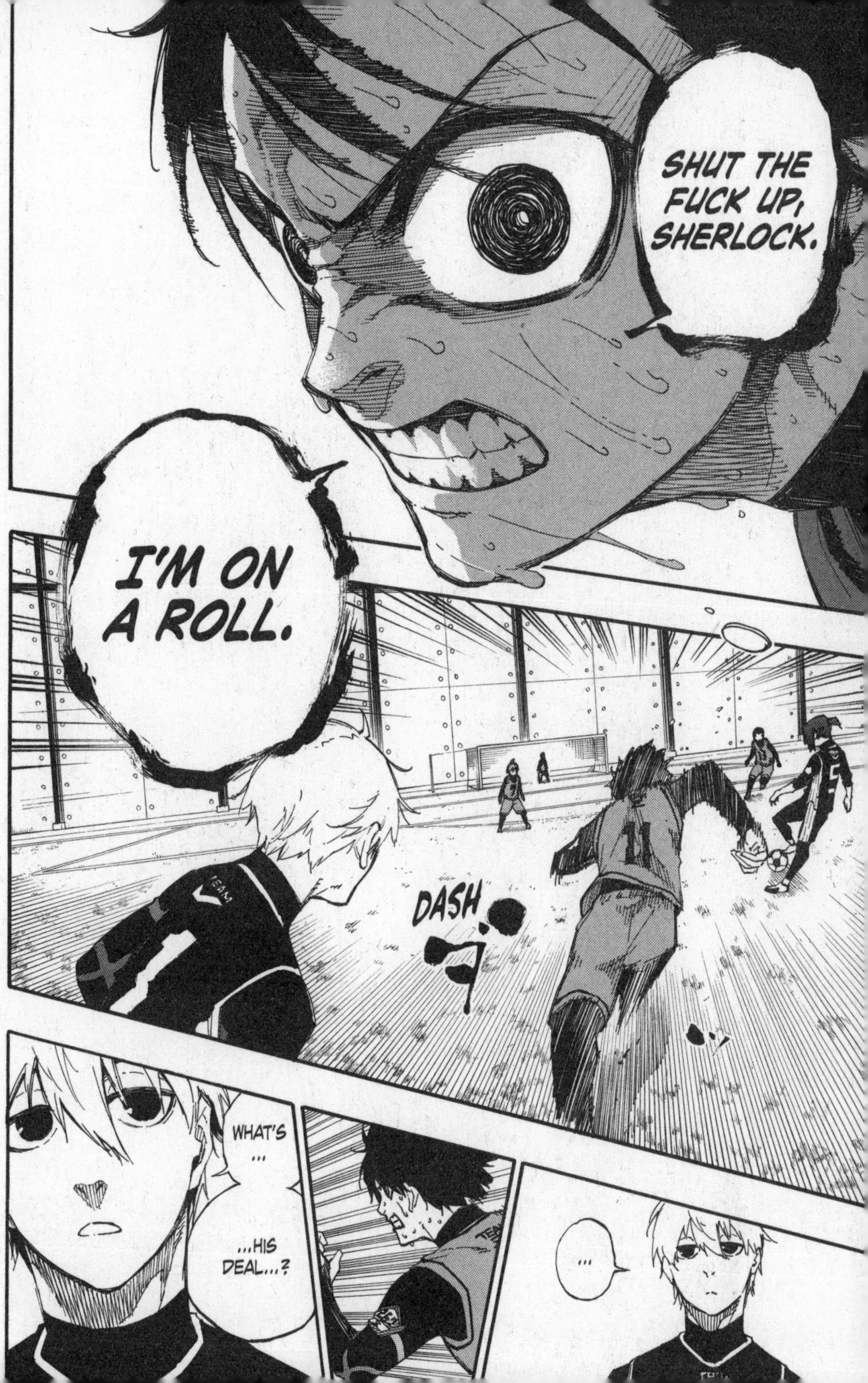
SHUT THE FUCK UP, SHERLOCK.
I'M ON A ROLL.
DASH
...
WHAT'S ...
...HIS DEAL...?

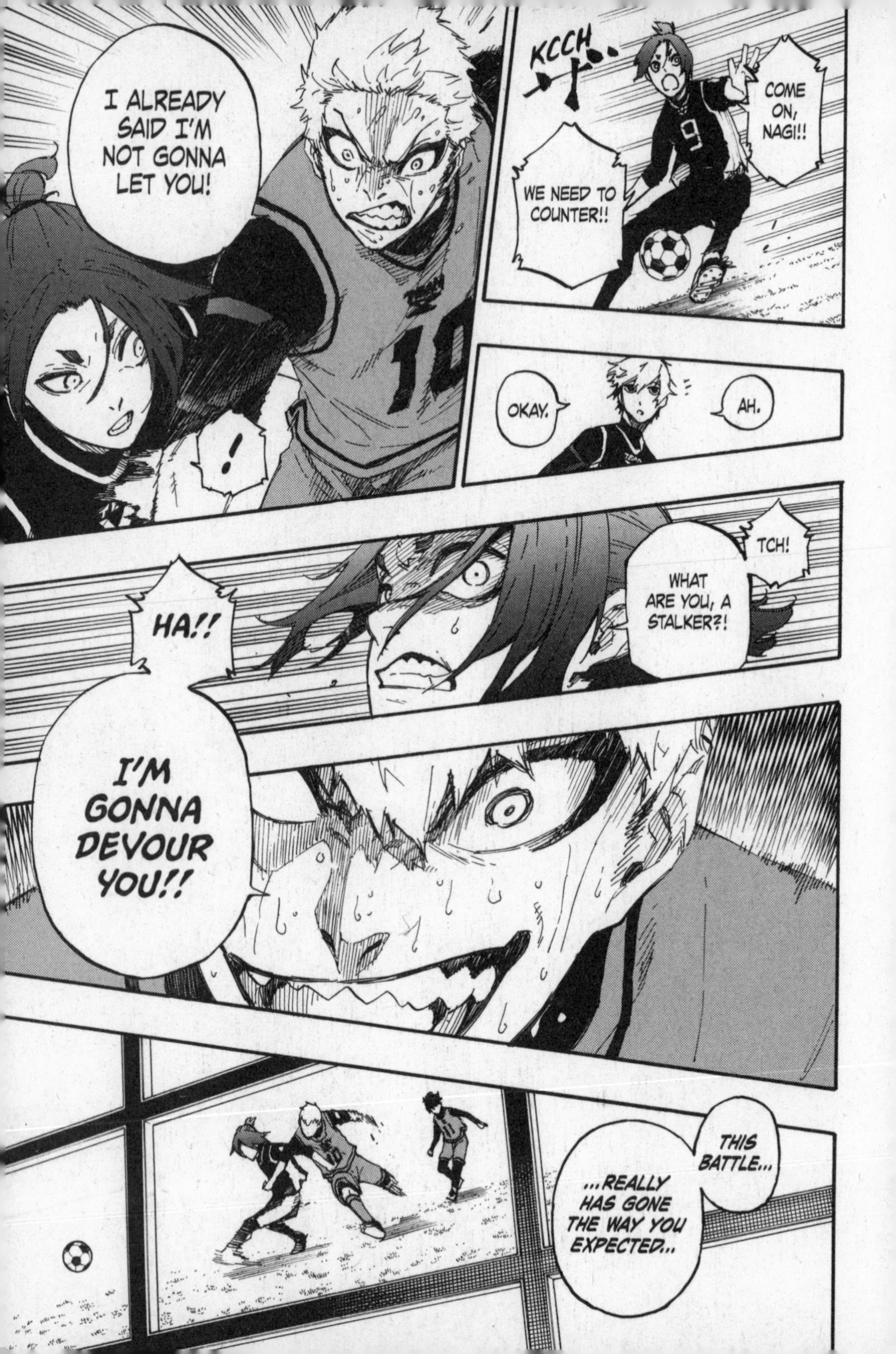
KCCH
COME ON, NAGI!!
WE NEED TO COUNTER!!
AH.
OKAY.
I ALREADY SAID I'M NOT GONNA LET YOU!
!
TCH!
WHAT ARE YOU, A STALKER?!
HA!!
I'M GONNA DEVOUR YOU!!
THIS BATTLE...
...REALLY HAS GONE THE WAY YOU EXPECTED...

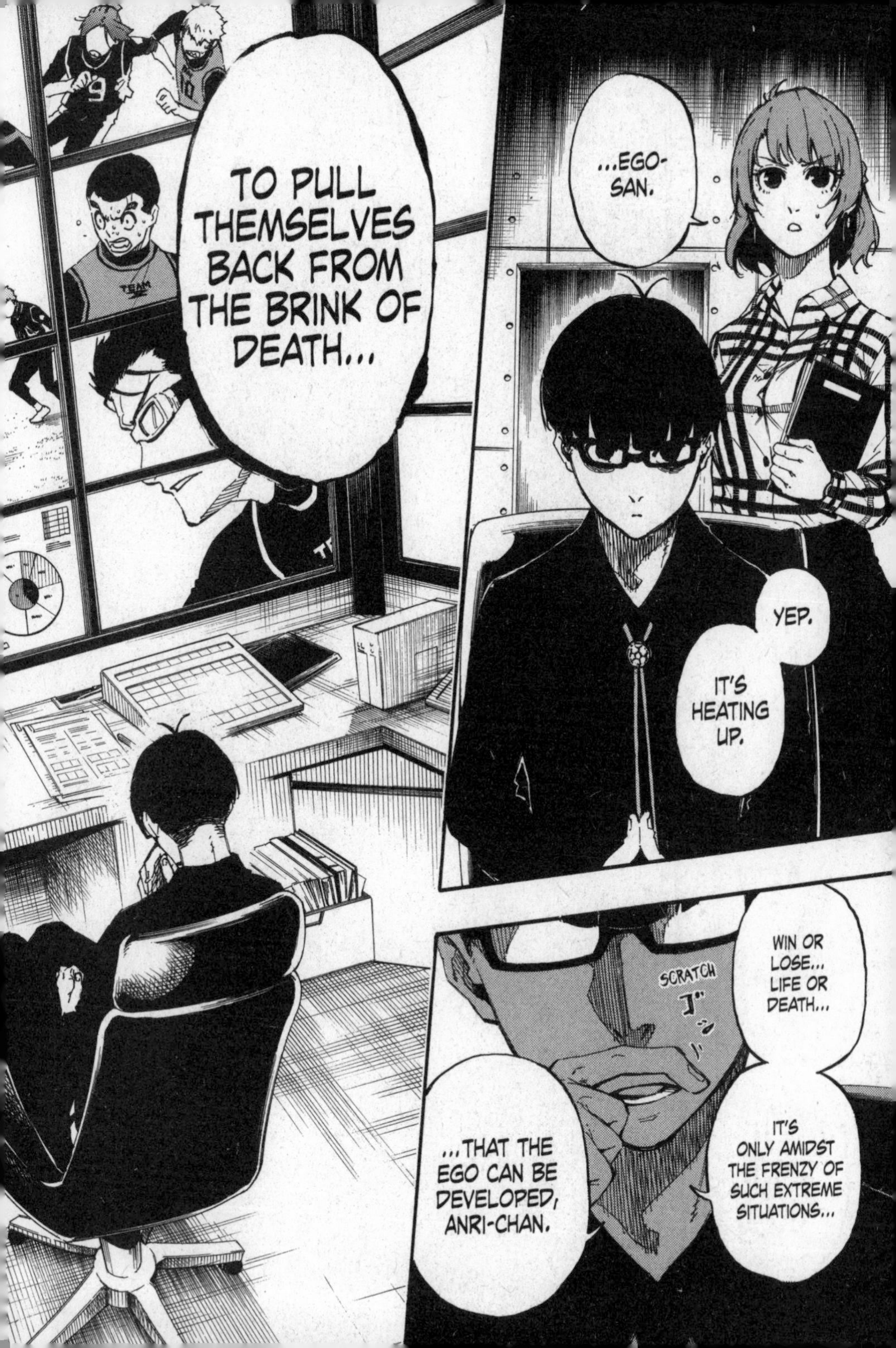
...EGO-SAN.
YEP.
IT'S HEATING UP.
WIN OR LOSE... LIFE OR DEATH...
SCRATCH
IT'S ONLY AMIDST THE FRENZY OF SUCH EXTREME SITUATIONS...
...THAT THE EGO CAN BE DEVELOPED, ANRI-CHAN.
TO PULL THEMSELVES BACK FROM THE BRINK OF DEATH...

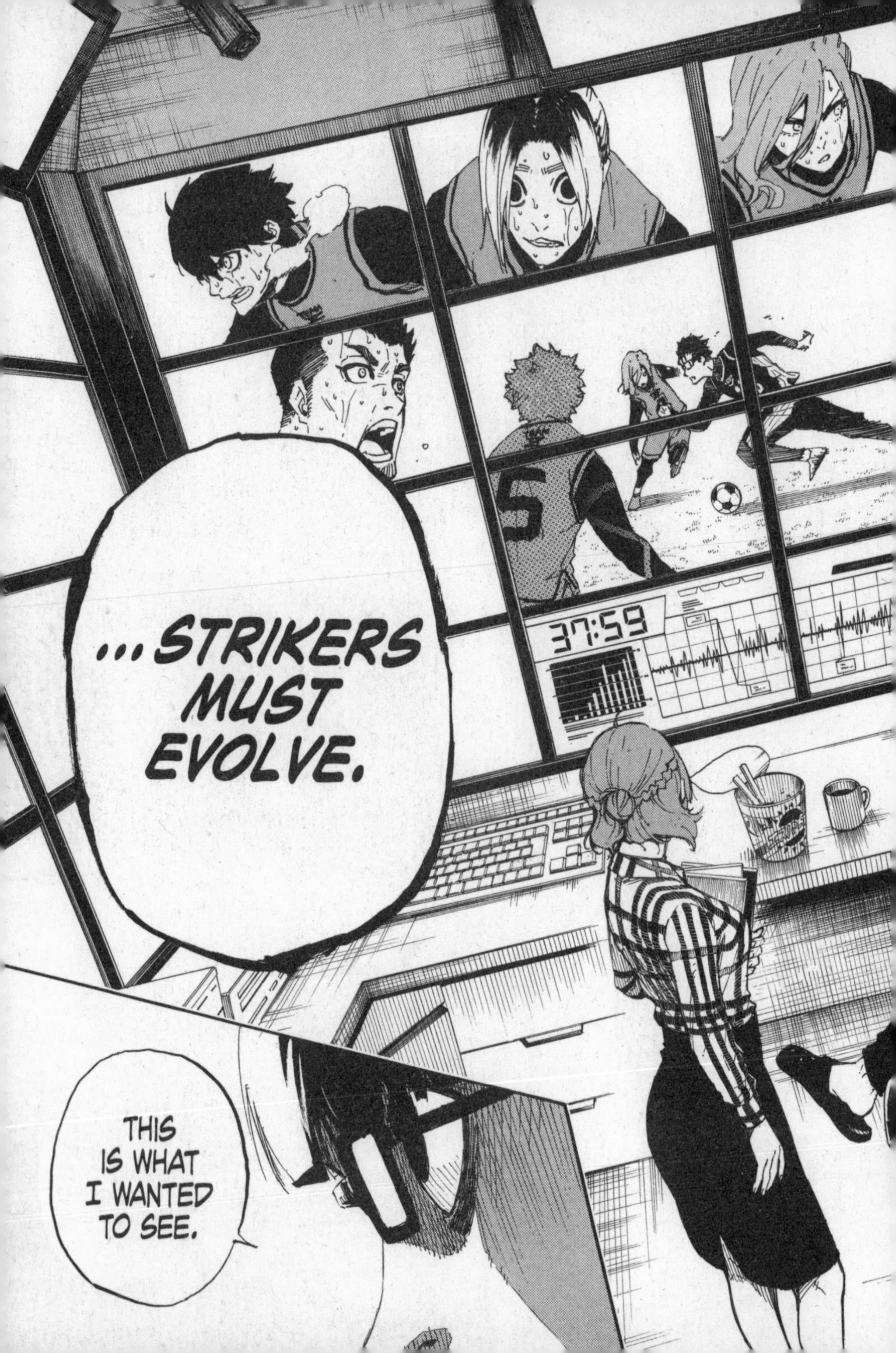
...STRIKERS MUST EVOLVE.
THIS IS WHAT I WANTED TO SEE.
37:59

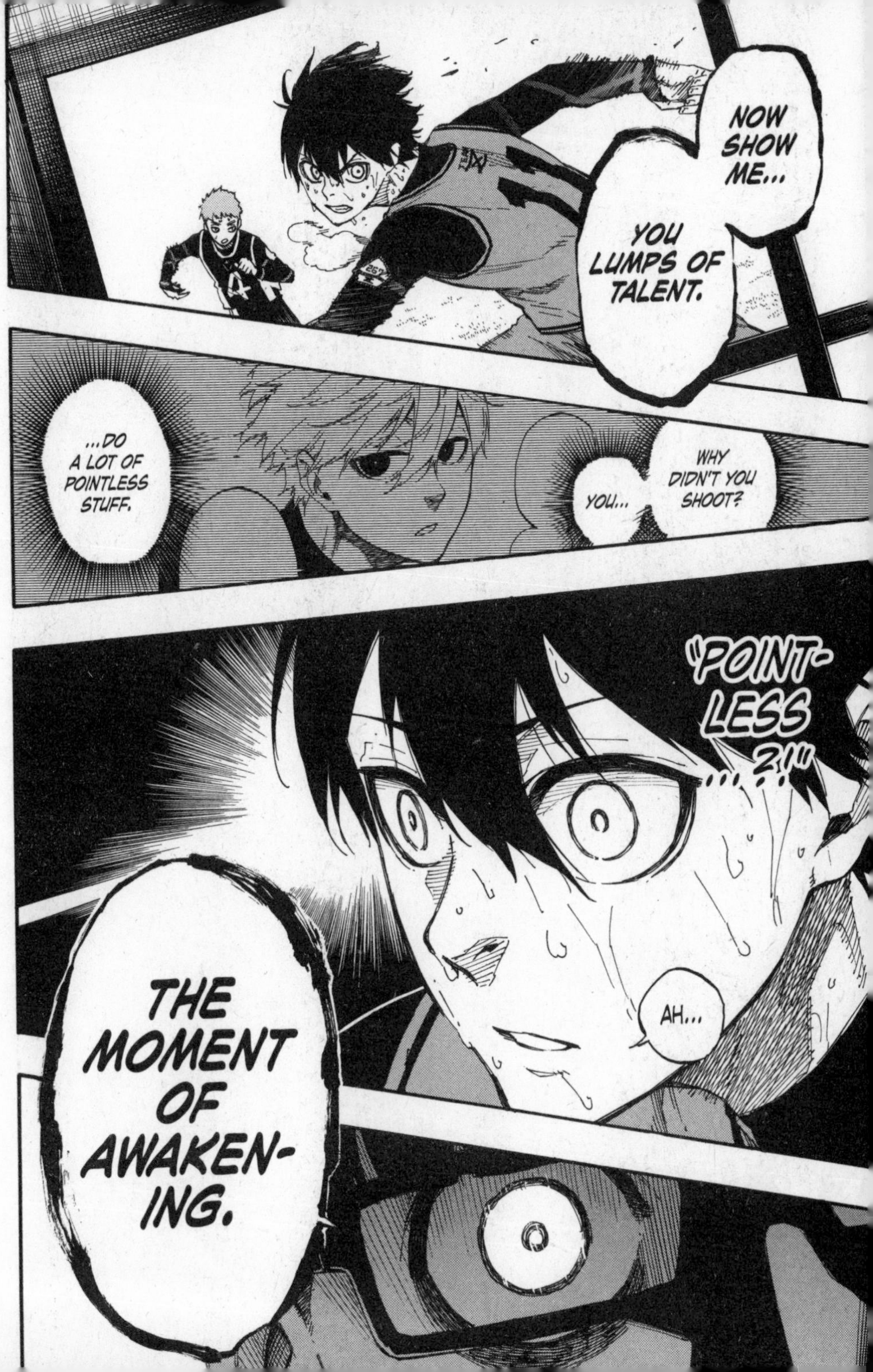
NOW SHOW ME...
YOU LUMPS OF TALENT.
YOU...
WHY DIDN'T YOU SHOOT?
...DO A LOT OF POINTLESS STUFF.
"POINTLESS"...?!
AH...
THE MOMENT OF AWAKENING.

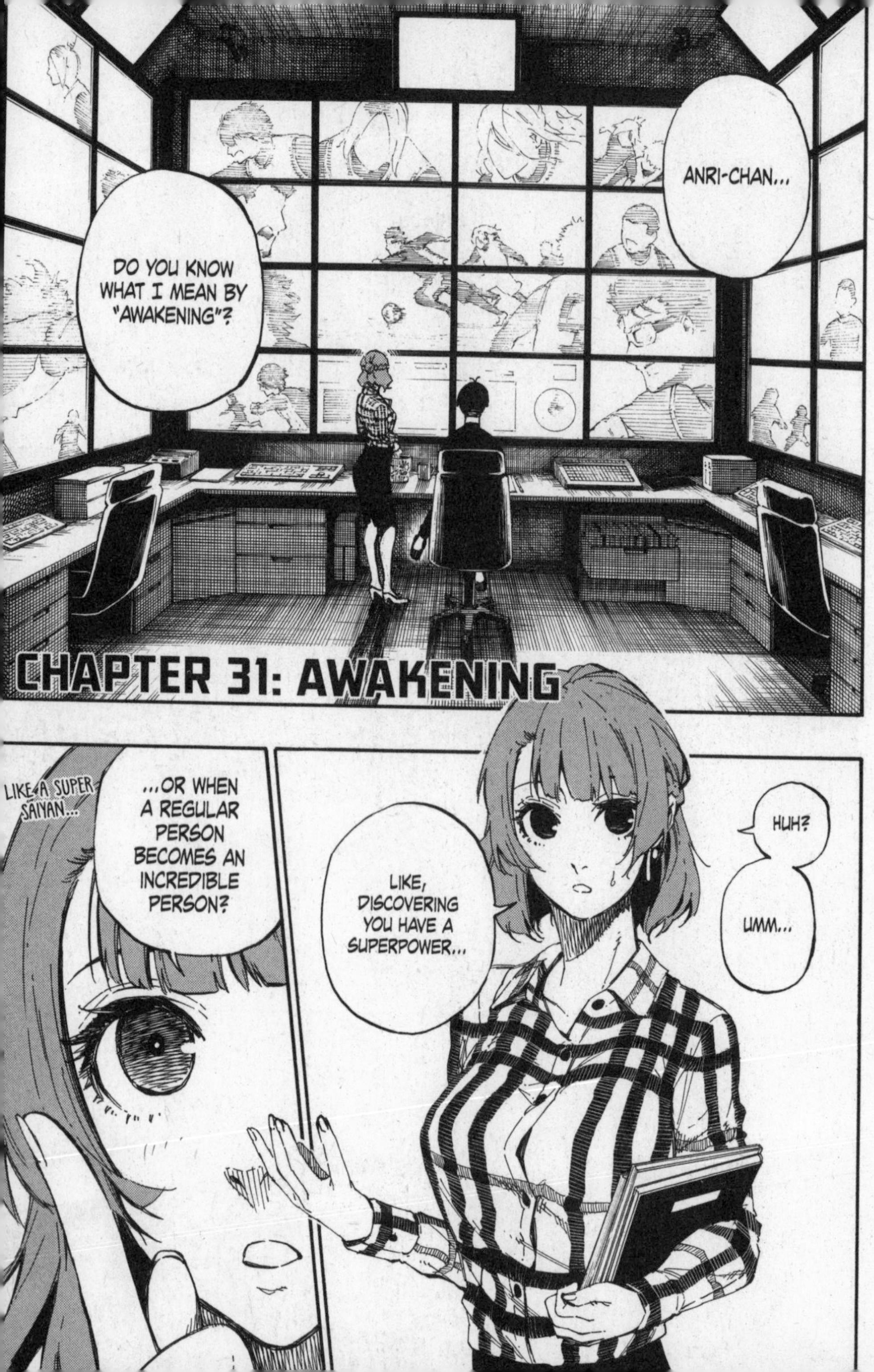
ANRI-CHAN...
DO YOU KNOW WHAT I MEAN BY "AWAKENING"?
CHAPTER 31: AWAKENING
HUH?
UMM...
LIKE, DISCOVERING YOU HAVE A SUPERPOWER...
...OR WHEN A REGULAR PERSON BECOMES AN INCREDIBLE PERSON?
LIKE A SUPER SAIYAN...

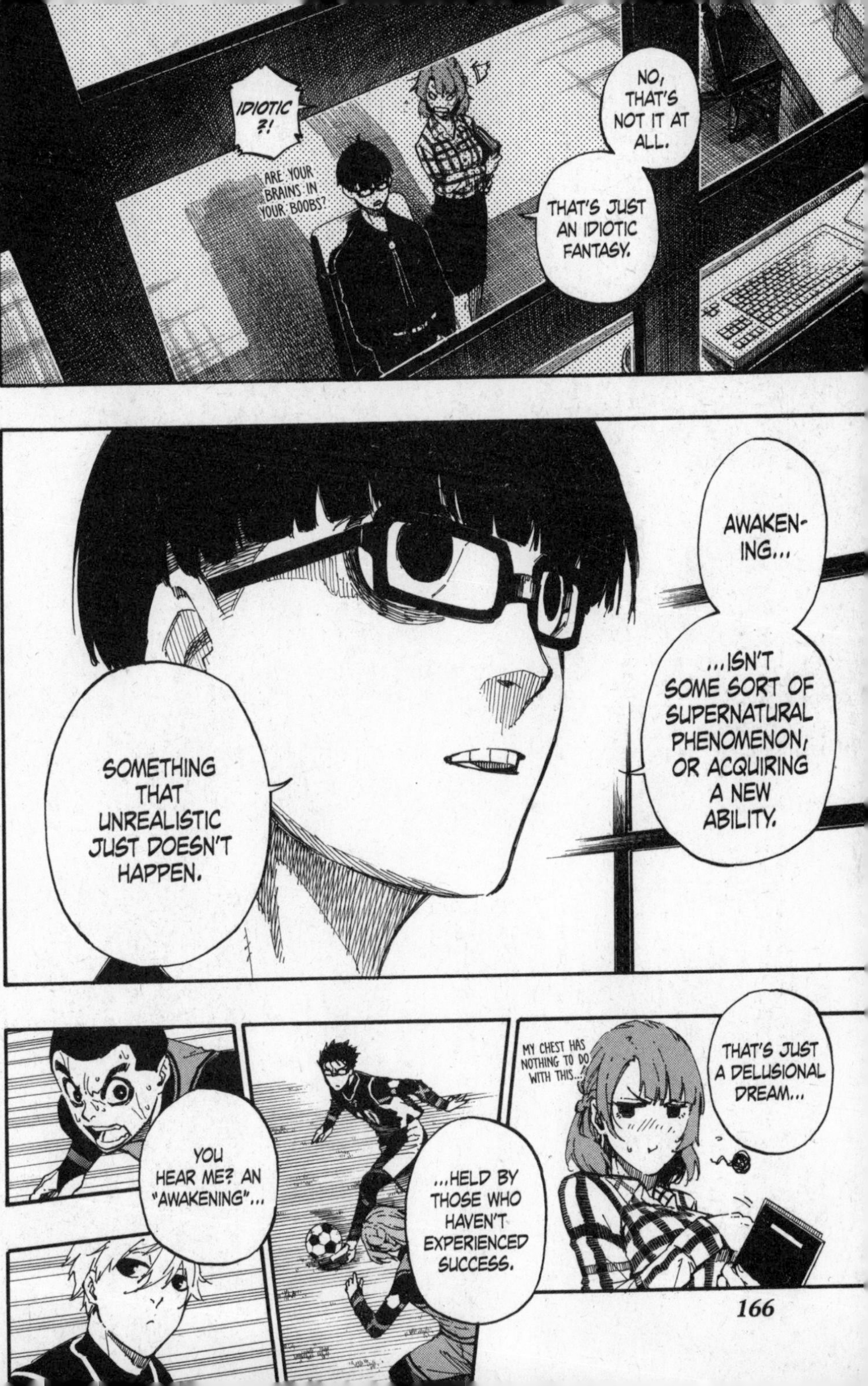
NO, THAT'S NOT IT AT ALL.
THAT'S JUST AN IDIOTIC FANTASY.
IDIOTIC ?!
ARE YOUR BRAINS IN YOUR BOOBS?
AWAKEN-ING...
...ISN'T SOME SORT OF SUPERNATURAL PHENOMENON, OR ACQUIRING A NEW ABILITY.
SOMETHING THAT UNREALISTIC JUST DOESN'T HAPPEN.
THAT'S JUST A DELUSIONAL DREAM...
MY CHEST HAS NOTHING TO DO WITH THIS...
...HELD BY THOSE WHO HAVEN'T EXPERIENCED SUCCESS.
YOU HEAR ME? AN "AWAKENING"...

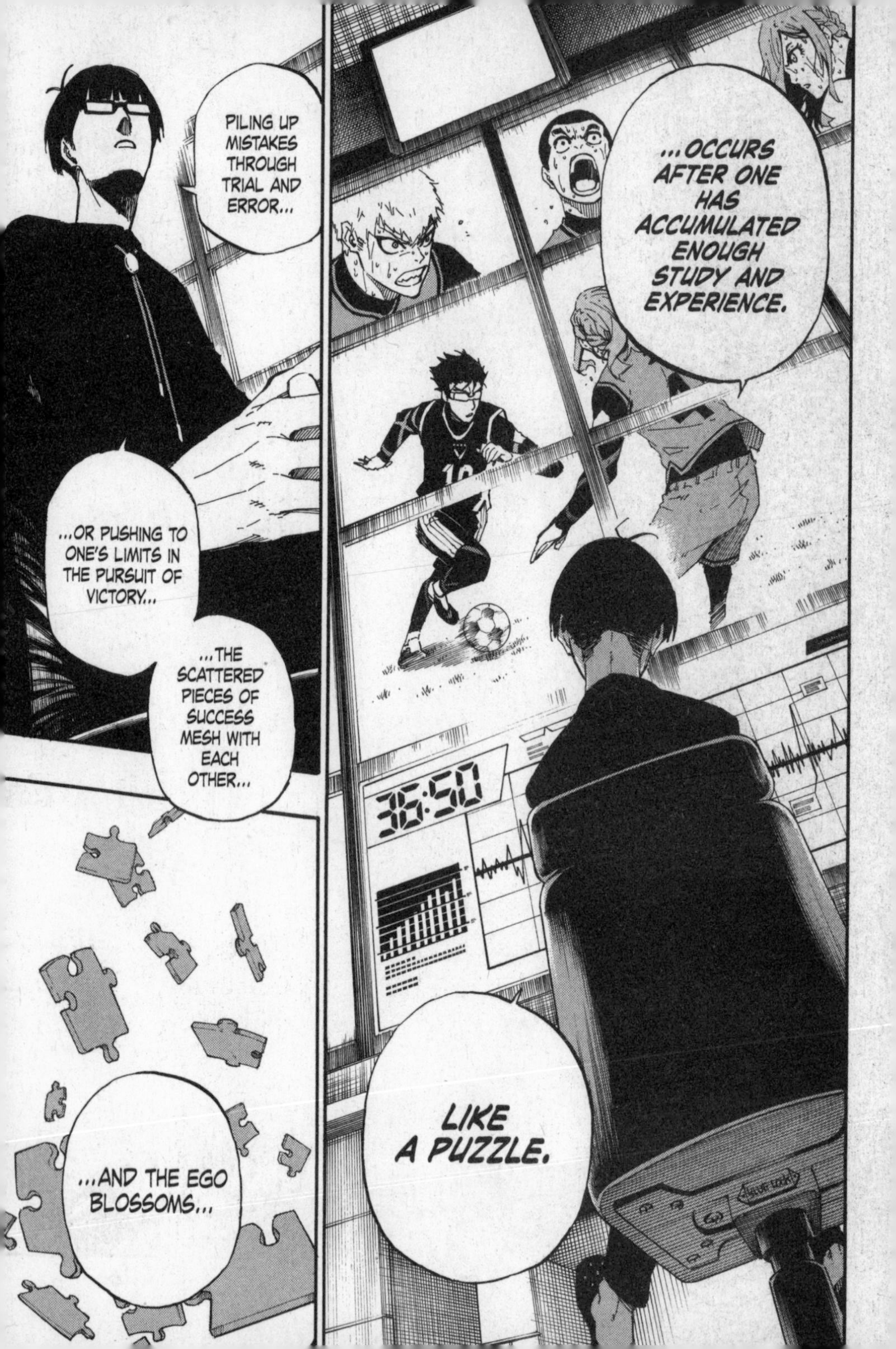
...OCCURS AFTER ONE HAS ACCUMULATED ENOUGH STUDY AND EXPERIENCE.
LIKE A PUZZLE.
PILING UP MISTAKES THROUGH TRIAL AND ERROR...
...OR PUSHING TO ONE'S LIMITS IN THE PURSUIT OF VICTORY...
...THE SCATTERED PIECES OF SUCCESS MESH WITH EACH OTHER...
...AND THE EGO BLOSSOMS...
36:50

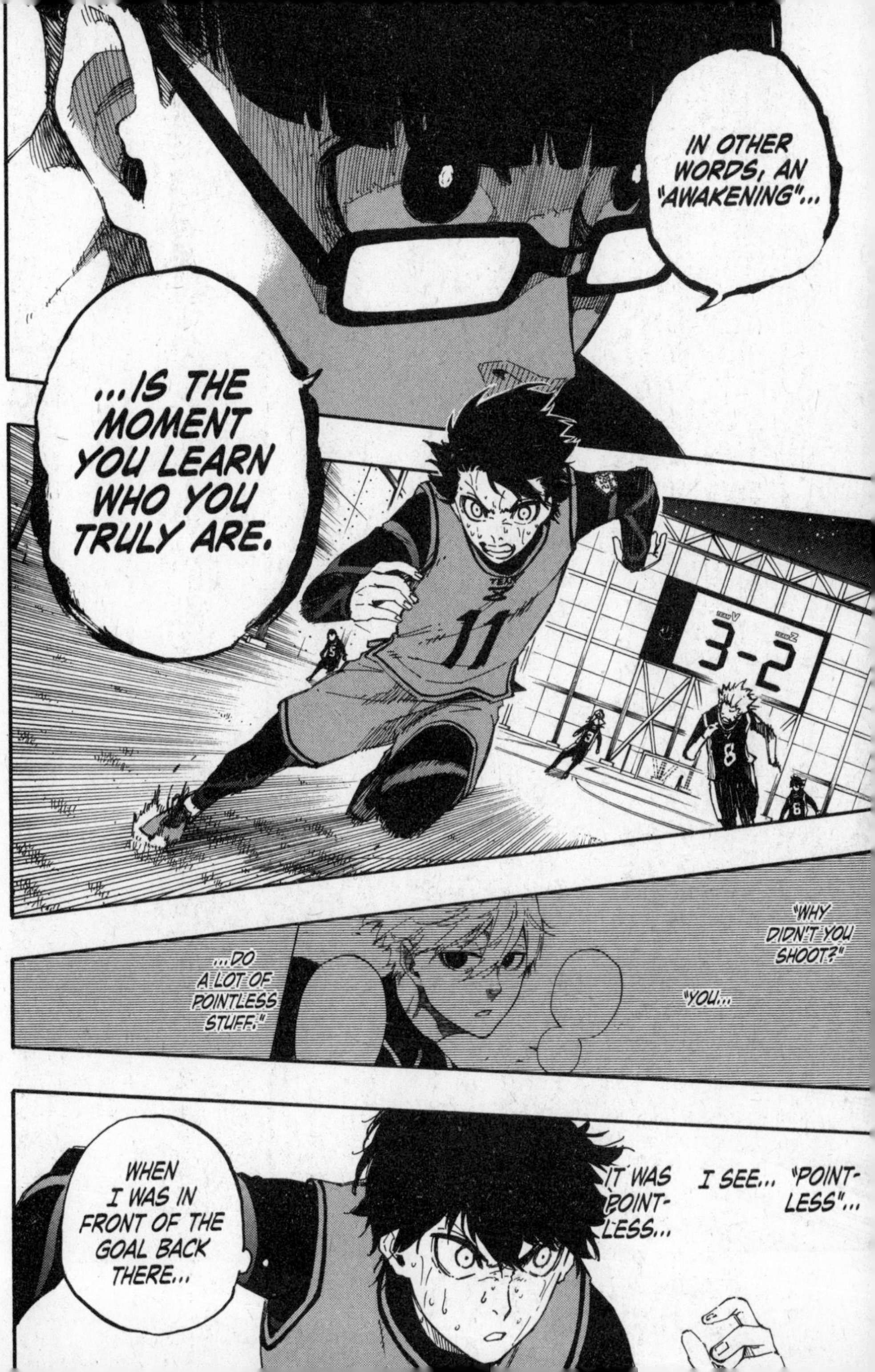
IN OTHER WORDS, AN "AWAKENING"...
...IS THE MOMENT YOU LEARN WHO YOU TRULY ARE.
3-2
"WHY DIDN'T YOU SHOOT?"
"YOU...
...DO A LOT OF POINTLESS STUFF."
"POINT-LESS"...
I SEE...
IT WAS POINT-LESS...
WHEN I WAS IN FRONT OF THE GOAL BACK THERE...

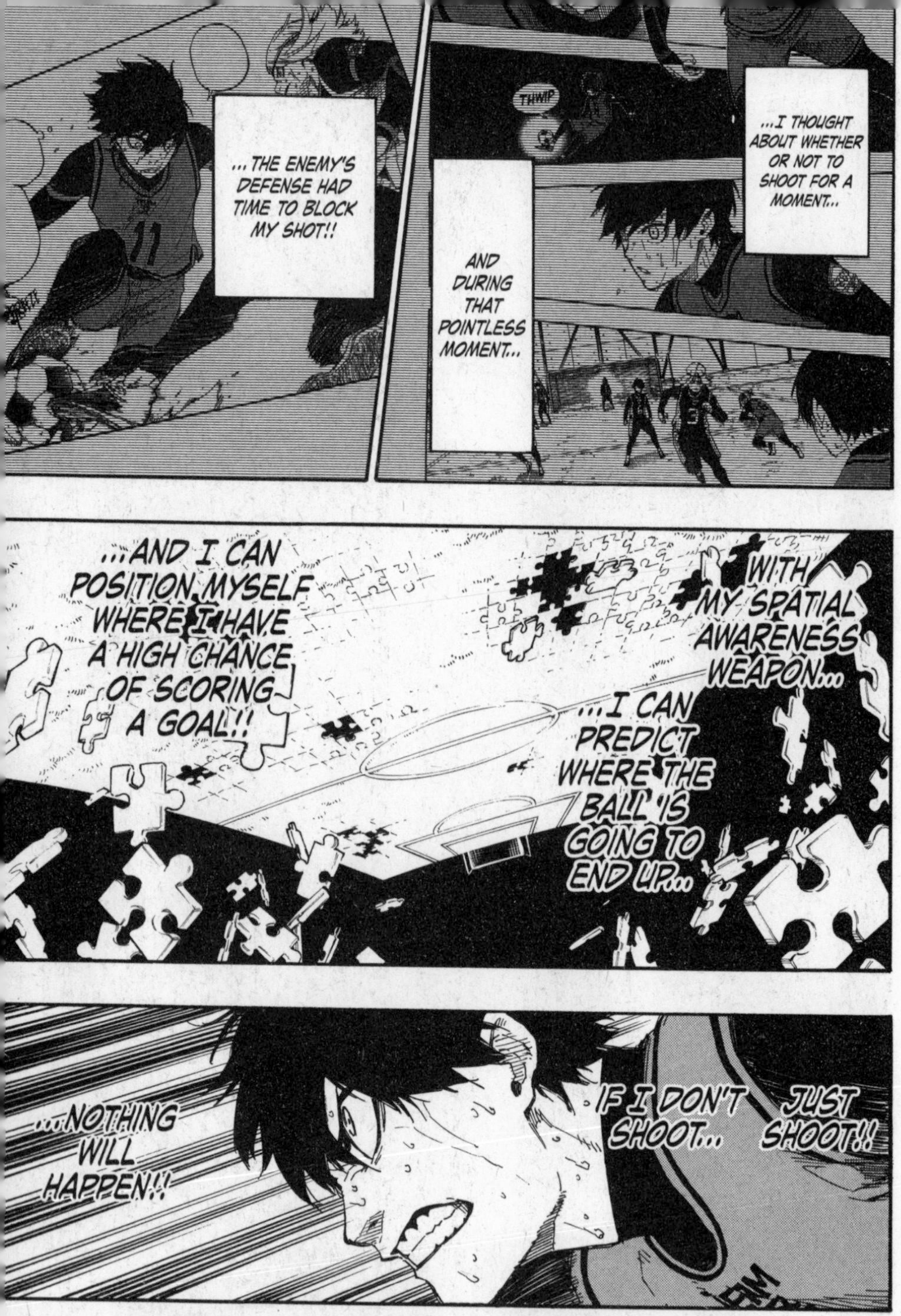
THWIP
...I THOUGHT ABOUT WHETHER OR NOT TO SHOOT FOR A MOMENT...
AND DURING THAT POINTLESS MOMENT...
...THE ENEMY'S DEFENSE HAD TIME TO BLOCK MY SHOT!!
WITH MY SPATIAL AWARENESS WEAPON...
...I CAN PREDICT WHERE THE BALL IS GOING TO END UP...
...AND I CAN POSITION MYSELF WHERE I HAVE A HIGH CHANCE OF SCORING A GOAL!!
JUST SHOOT!!
IF I DON'T SHOOT...
...NOTHING WILL HAPPEN!!

I NEED TO ELIMINATE THE POINTLESS THINGS THAT GET IN THE WAY OF SHOOTING...

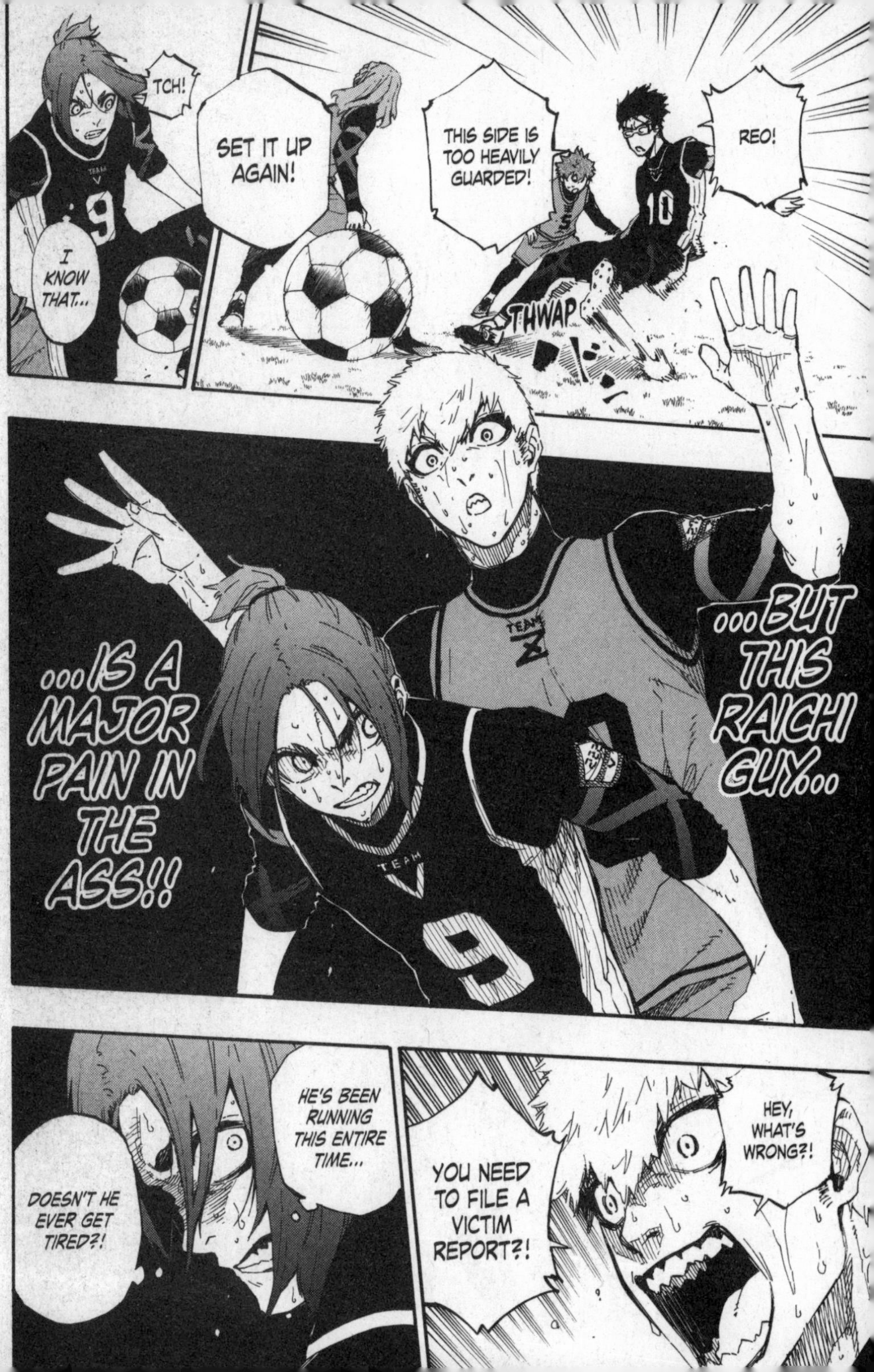
REO!
THIS SIDE IS TOO HEAVILY GUARDED!
THWAP
SET IT UP AGAIN!
TCH!
I KNOW THAT...
...BUT THIS RAICHI GUY...
...IS A MAJOR PAIN IN THE ASS!!
HEY, WHAT'S WRONG?!
YOU NEED TO FILE A VICTIM REPORT?!
HE'S BEEN RUNNING THIS ENTIRE TIME...
DOESN'T HE EVER GET TIRED?!

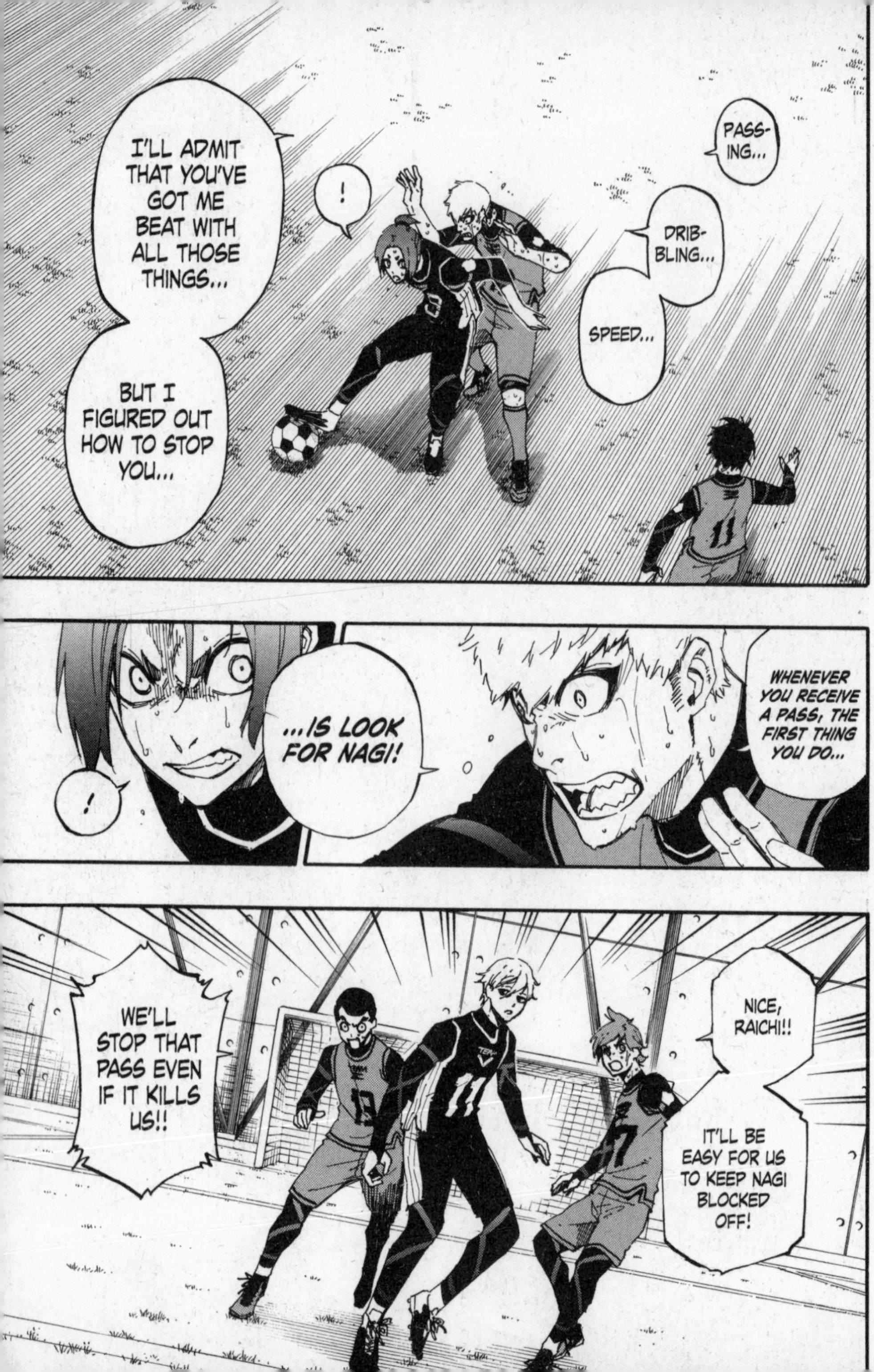
PASS-ING...
DRIB-BLING...
SPEED...
!
I'LL ADMIT THAT YOU'VE GOT ME BEAT WITH ALL THOSE THINGS...
BUT I FIGURED OUT HOW TO STOP YOU...
WHENEVER YOU RECEIVE A PASS, THE FIRST THING YOU DO...
...IS LOOK FOR NAGI!
!
NICE, RAICHI!!
IT'LL BE EASY FOR US TO KEEP NAGI BLOCKED OFF!
WE'LL STOP THAT PASS EVEN IF IT KILLS US!!

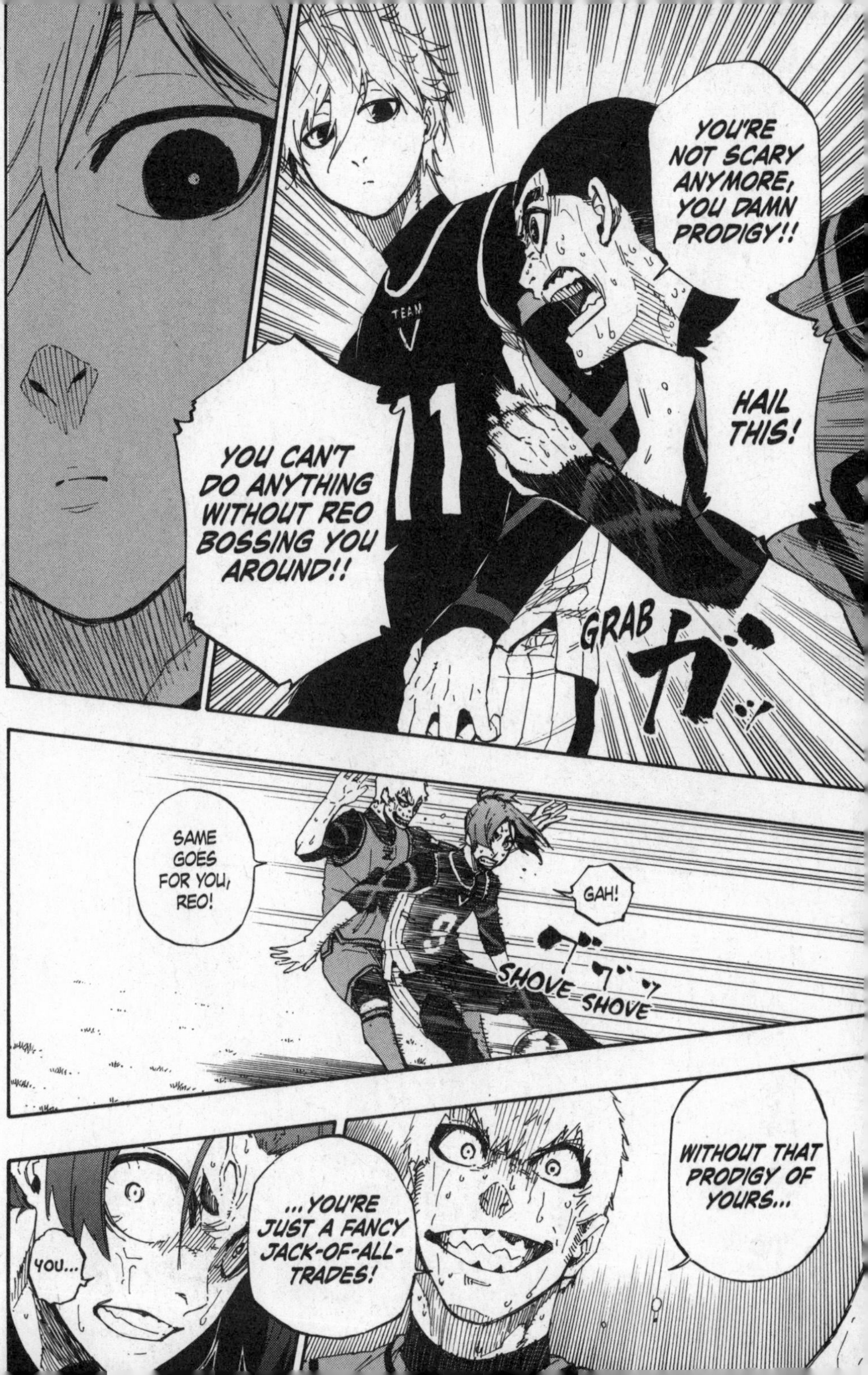
YOU'RE NOT SCARY ANYMORE, YOU DAMN PRODIGY!!
HAIL THIS!
YOU CAN'T DO ANYTHING WITHOUT REO BOSSING YOU AROUND!!
GRAB
GAH!
SHOVE SHOVE
SAME GOES FOR YOU, REO!
WITHOUT THAT PRODIGY OF YOURS...
...YOU'RE JUST A FANCY JACK-OF-ALL-TRADES!
YOU...

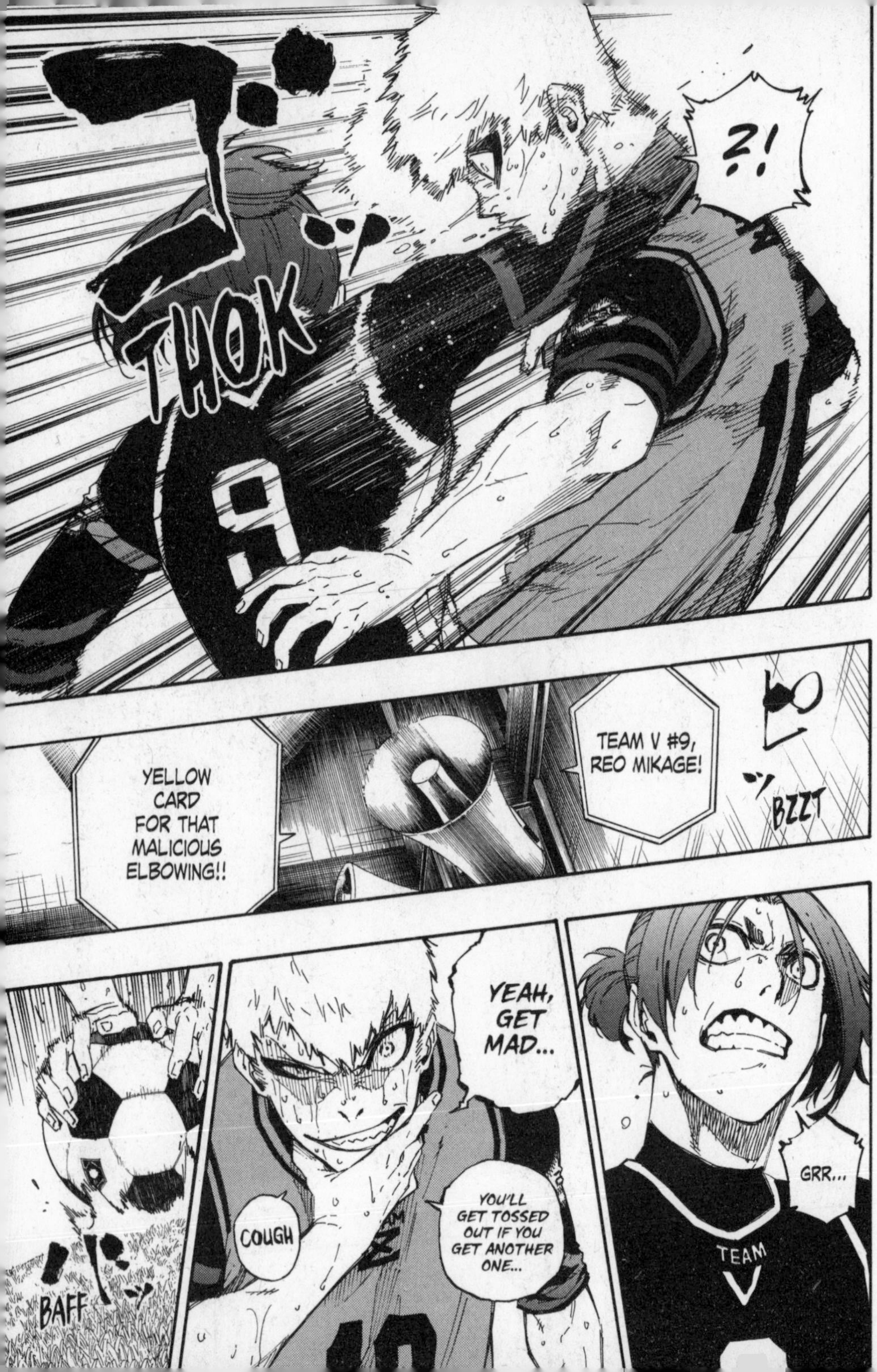
?!
THOK
BZZT
TEAM V #9, REO MIKAGE!
YELLOW CARD FOR THAT MALICIOUS ELBOWING!!
GRR...
TEAM V
YEAH, GET MAD...
YOU'LL GET TOSSED OUT IF YOU GET ANOTHER ONE...
COUGH
BAFF

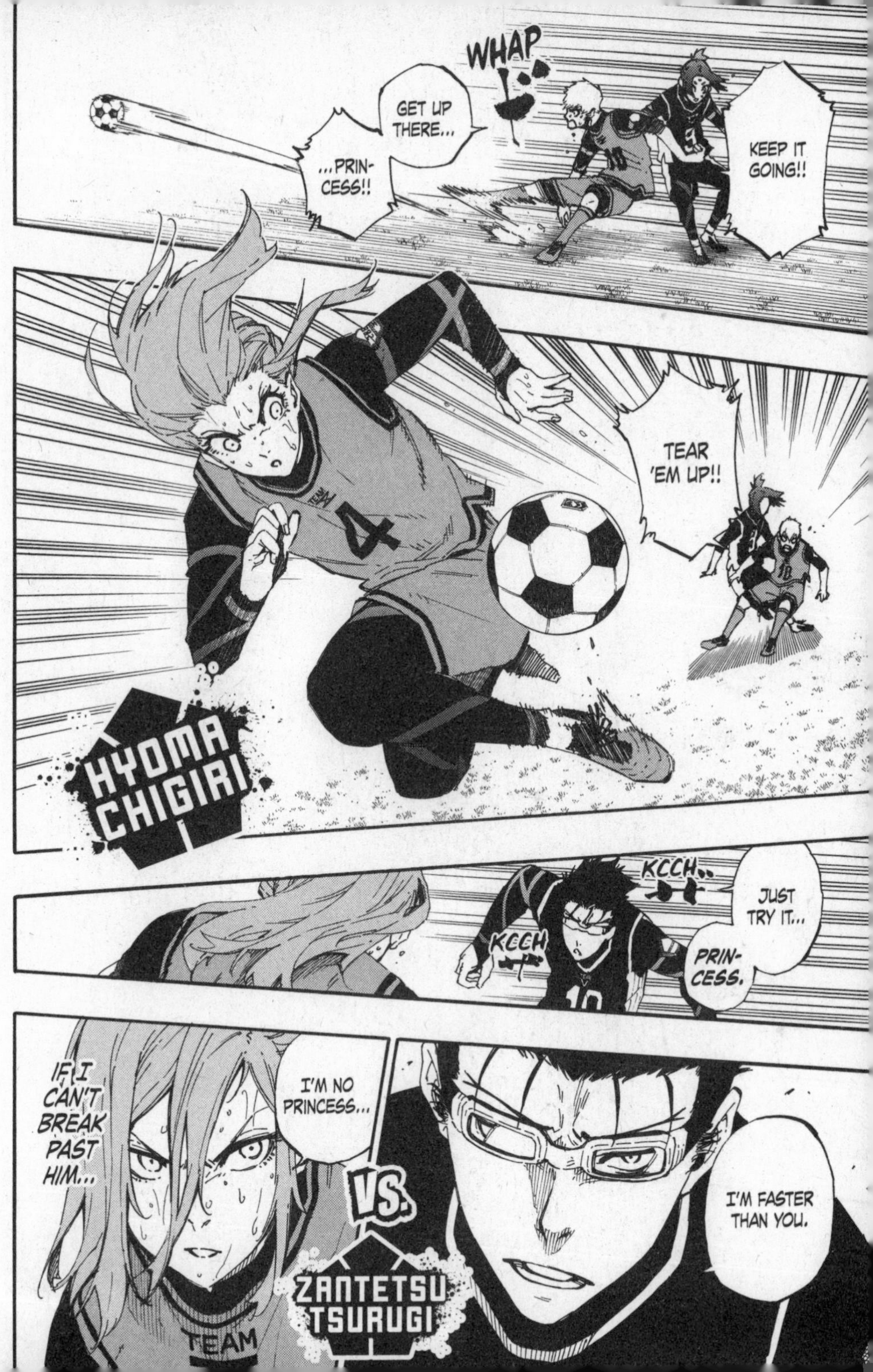
KEEP IT GOING!!
WHAP
GET UP THERE...
...PRIN-CESS!!
TEAR 'EM UP!!
HYOMA CHIGIRI
KCCH..
JUST TRY IT...
PRIN-CESS.
KCCH
I'M FASTER THAN YOU.
ZANTETSU TSURUGI
VS.
I'M NO PRINCESS...
IF I CAN'T BREAK PAST HIM...

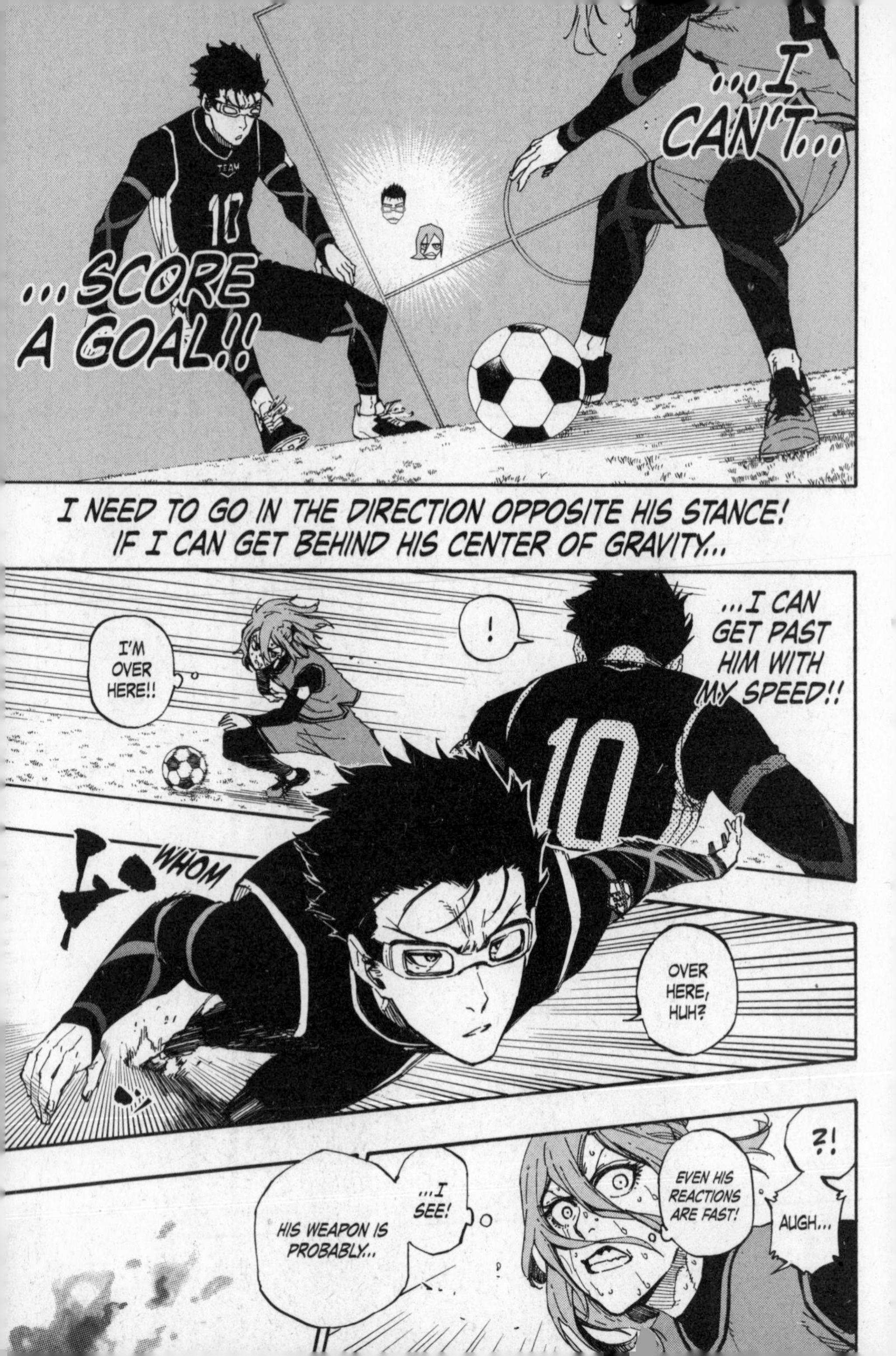
...I CAN'T...
...SCORE A GOAL!!
I NEED TO GO IN THE DIRECTION OPPOSITE HIS STANCE! IF I CAN GET BEHIND HIS CENTER OF GRAVITY...
...I CAN GET PAST HIM WITH MY SPEED!!
!
I'M OVER HERE!!
WHOM
OVER HERE, HUH?
?!
AUGH...
EVEN HIS REACTIONS ARE FAST!
...I SEE!
HIS WEAPON IS PROBABLY...

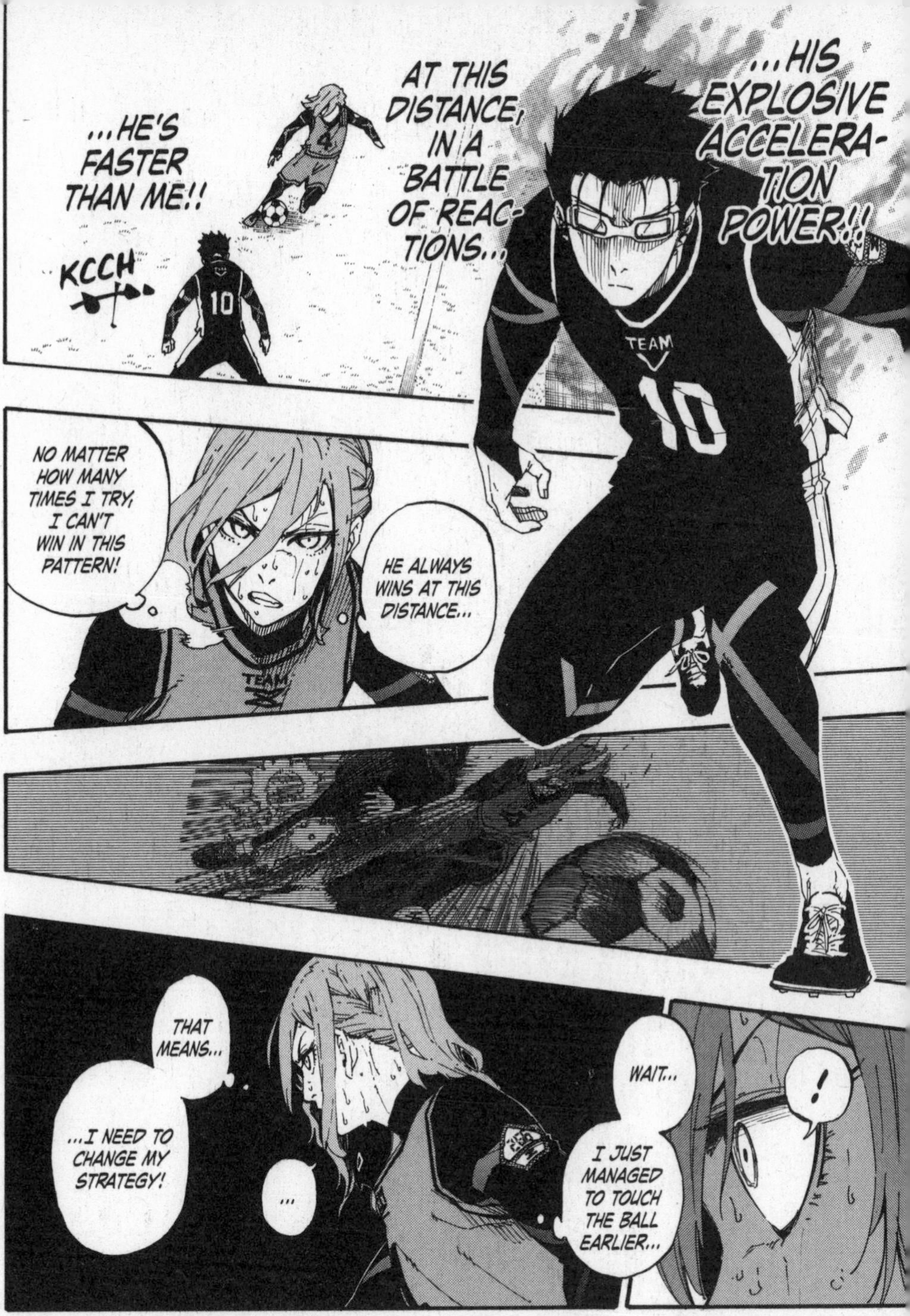
...HIS EXPLOSIVE ACCELERATION POWER!!
AT THIS DISTANCE, IN A BATTLE OF REACTIONS...
...HE'S FASTER THAN ME!!
KCCH
HE ALWAYS WINS AT THIS DISTANCE...
NO MATTER HOW MANY TIMES I TRY, I CAN'T WIN IN THIS PATTERN!
!
WAIT...
I JUST MANAGED TO TOUCH THE BALL EARLIER...
THAT MEANS...
...
...I NEED TO CHANGE MY STRATEGY!

IF I DON'T HAVE IT, I JUST NEED TO CREATE IT...

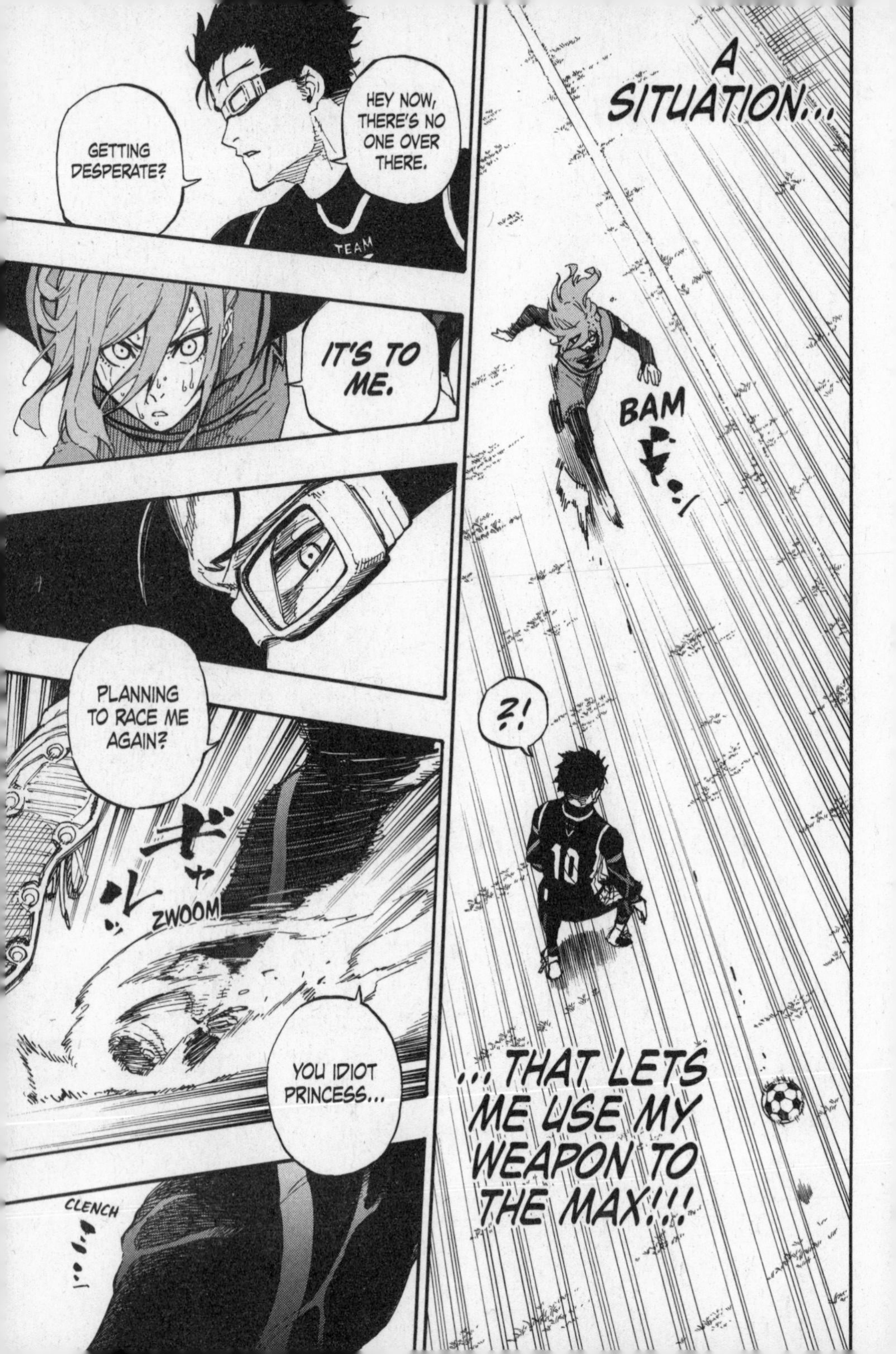
A SITUATION...
BAM
?!
...THAT LETS ME USE MY WEAPON TO THE MAX!!!
HEY NOW, THERE'S NO ONE OVER THERE.
GETTING DESPERATE?
TEAM
IT'S TO ME.
PLANNING TO RACE ME AGAIN?
ZWOOM
YOU IDIOT PRINCESS...
CLENCH

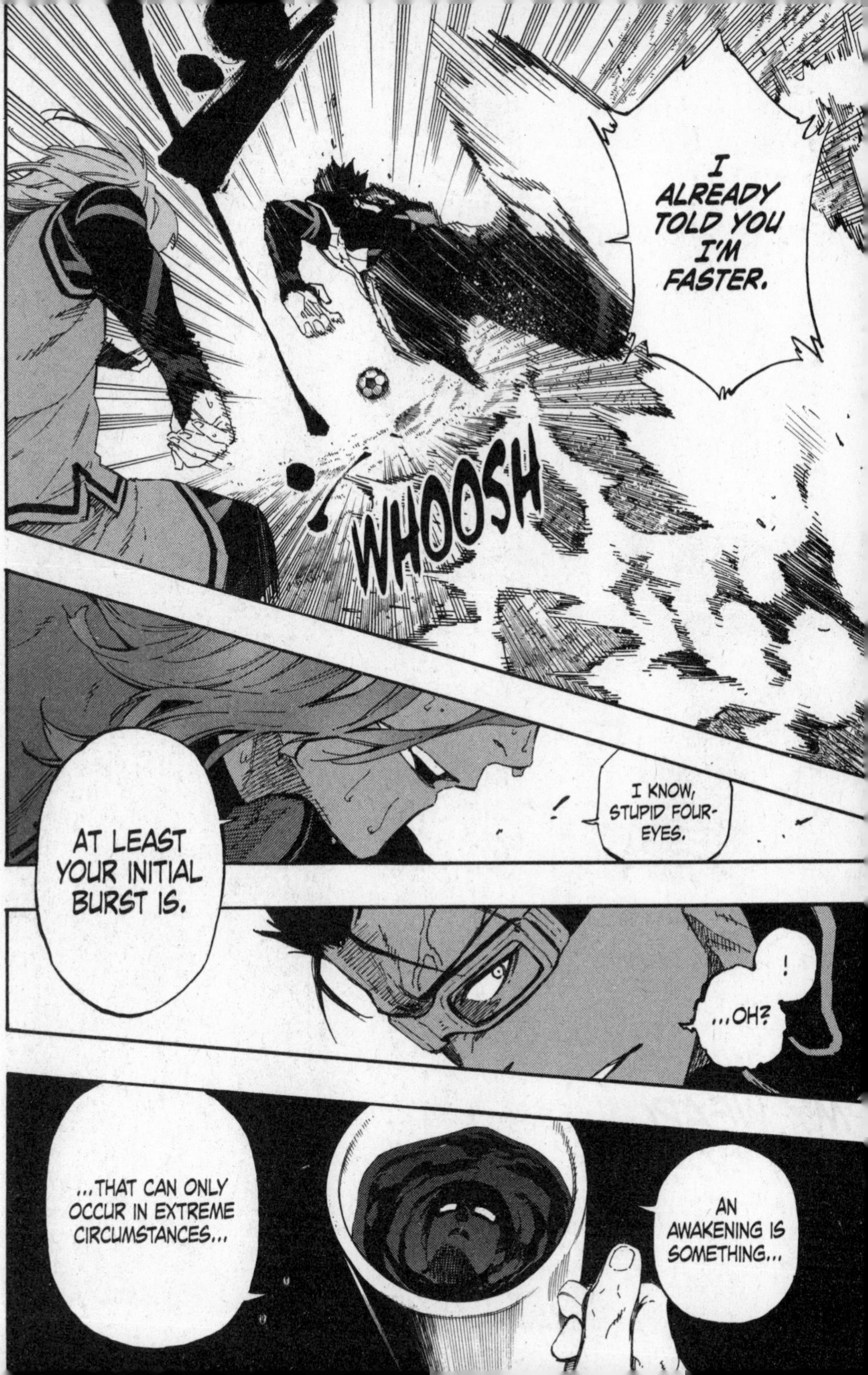
I ALREADY TOLD YOU I'M FASTER.
WHOOSH
I KNOW, STUPID FOUR-EYES.
AT LEAST YOUR INITIAL BURST IS.
!
...OH?
AN AWAKENING IS SOMETHING...
...THAT CAN ONLY OCCUR IN EXTREME CIRCUMSTANCES...

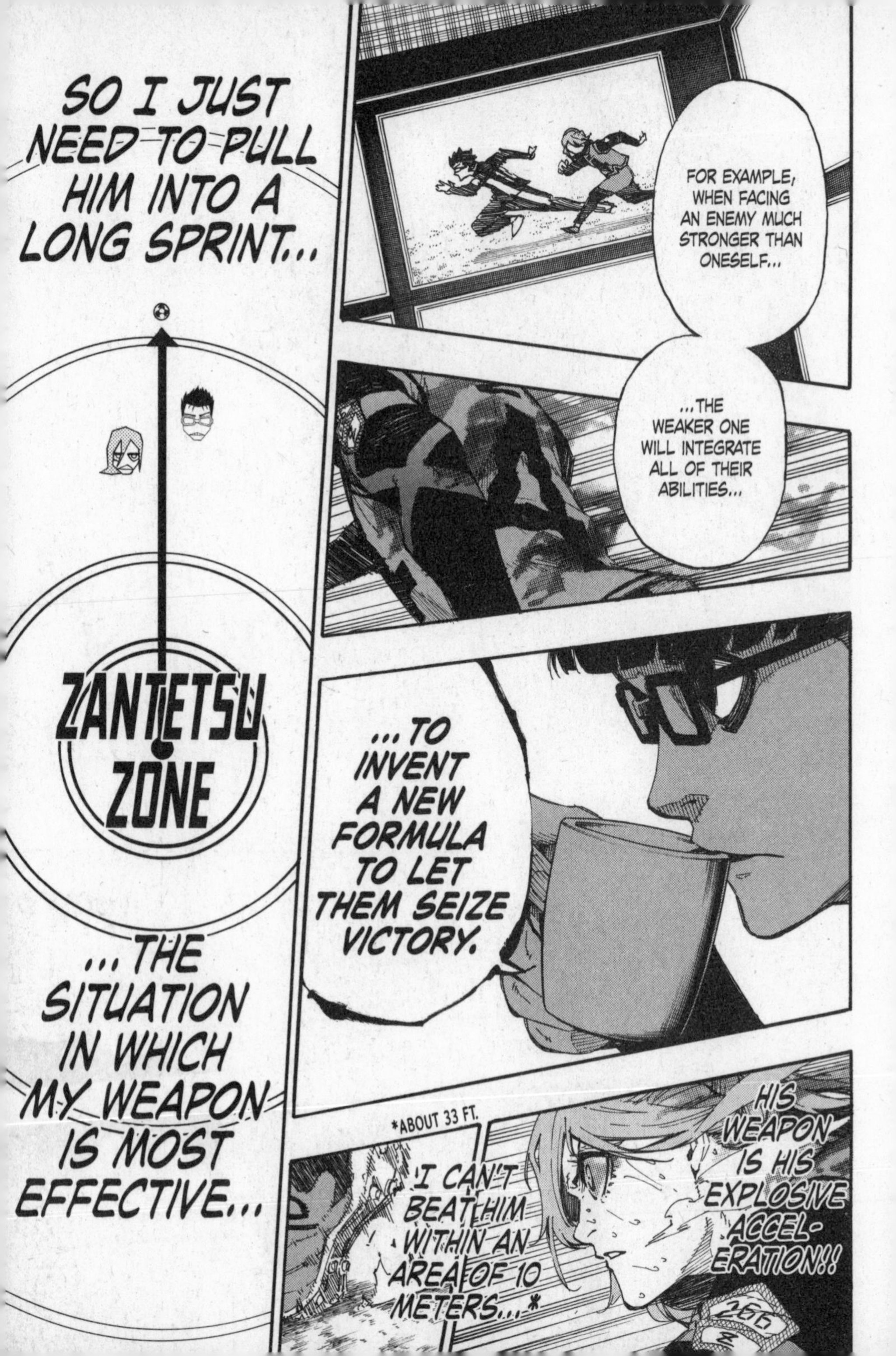

FOR EXAMPLE, WHEN FACING AN ENEMY MUCH STRONGER THAN ONESELF...
...THE WEAKER ONE WILL INTEGRATE ALL OF THEIR ABILITIES...
...TO INVENT A NEW FORMULA TO LET THEM SEIZE VICTORY.
HIS WEAPON IS HIS EXPLOSIVE ACCEL-ERATION!!
I CAN'T BEAT HIM WITHIN AN AREA OF 10 METERS...*
*ABOUT 33 FT.
SO I JUST NEED TO PULL HIM INTO A LONG SPRINT...
ZANTETSU ZONE
...THE SITUATION IN WHICH MY WEAPON IS MOST EFFECTIVE...

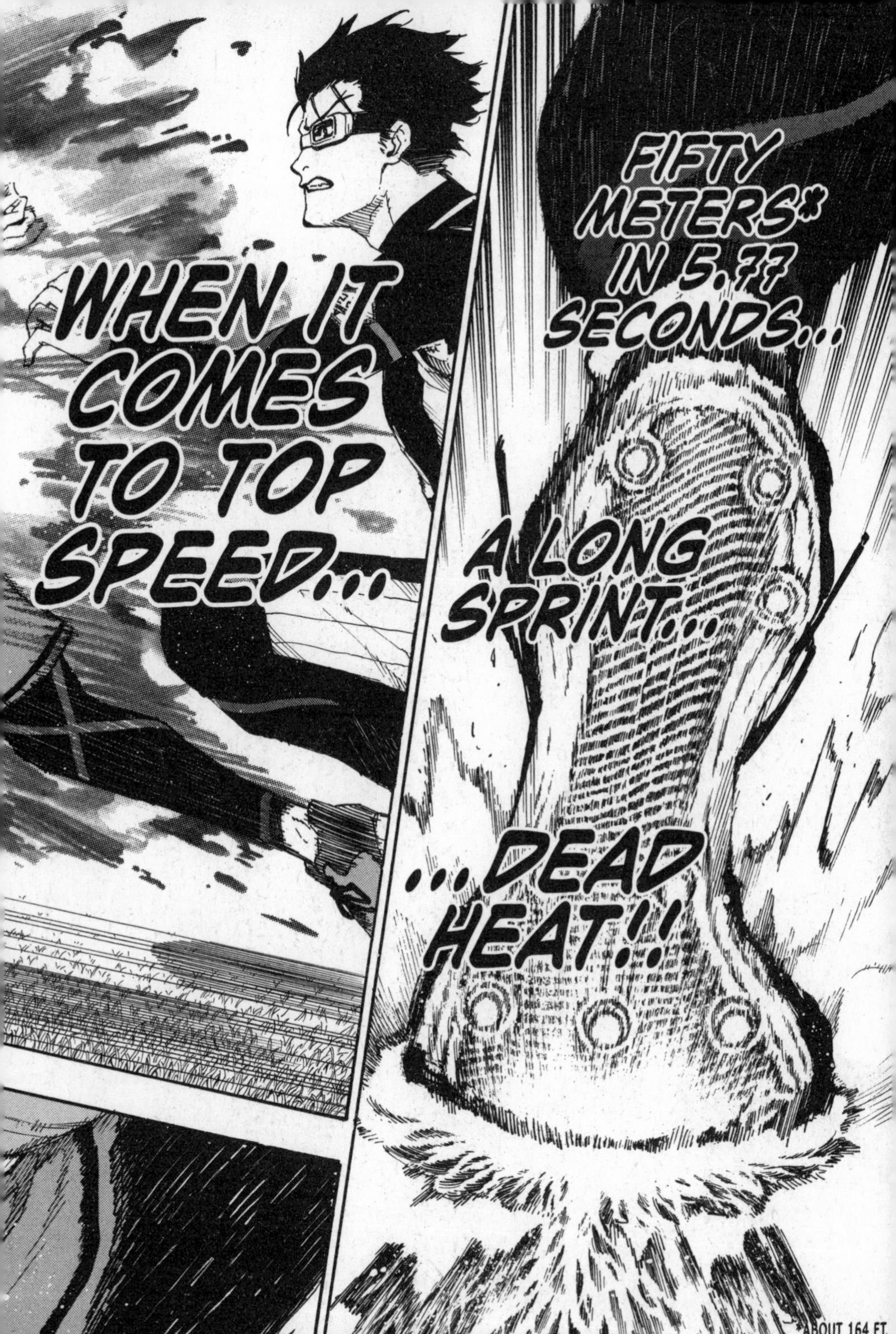
FIFTY METERS* IN 5.77 SECONDS...
A LONG SPRINT...
...DEAD HEAT!!
WHEN IT COMES TO TOP SPEED...

*ABOUT 164 FT.

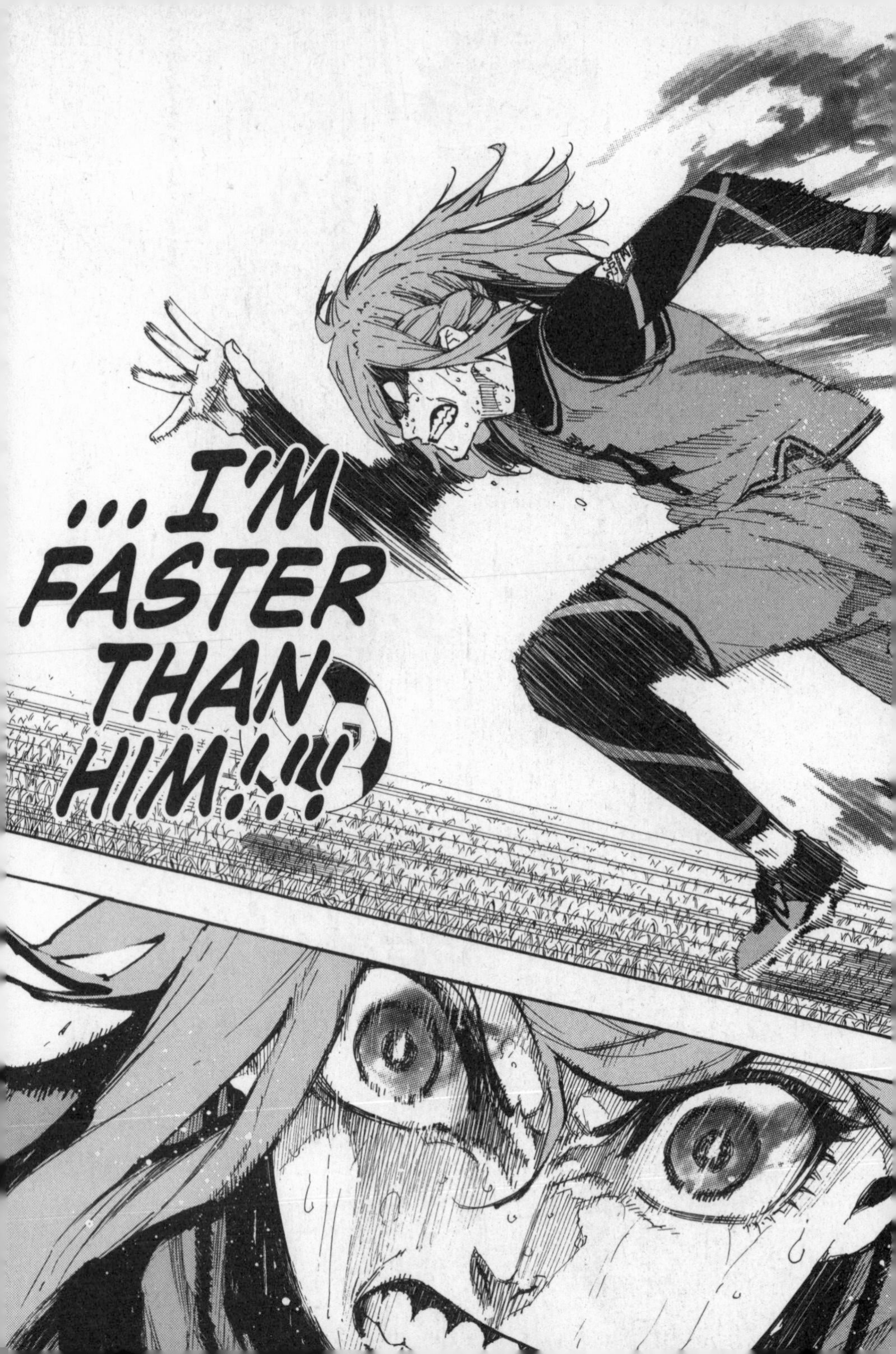
...I'M FASTER THAN HIM!!!

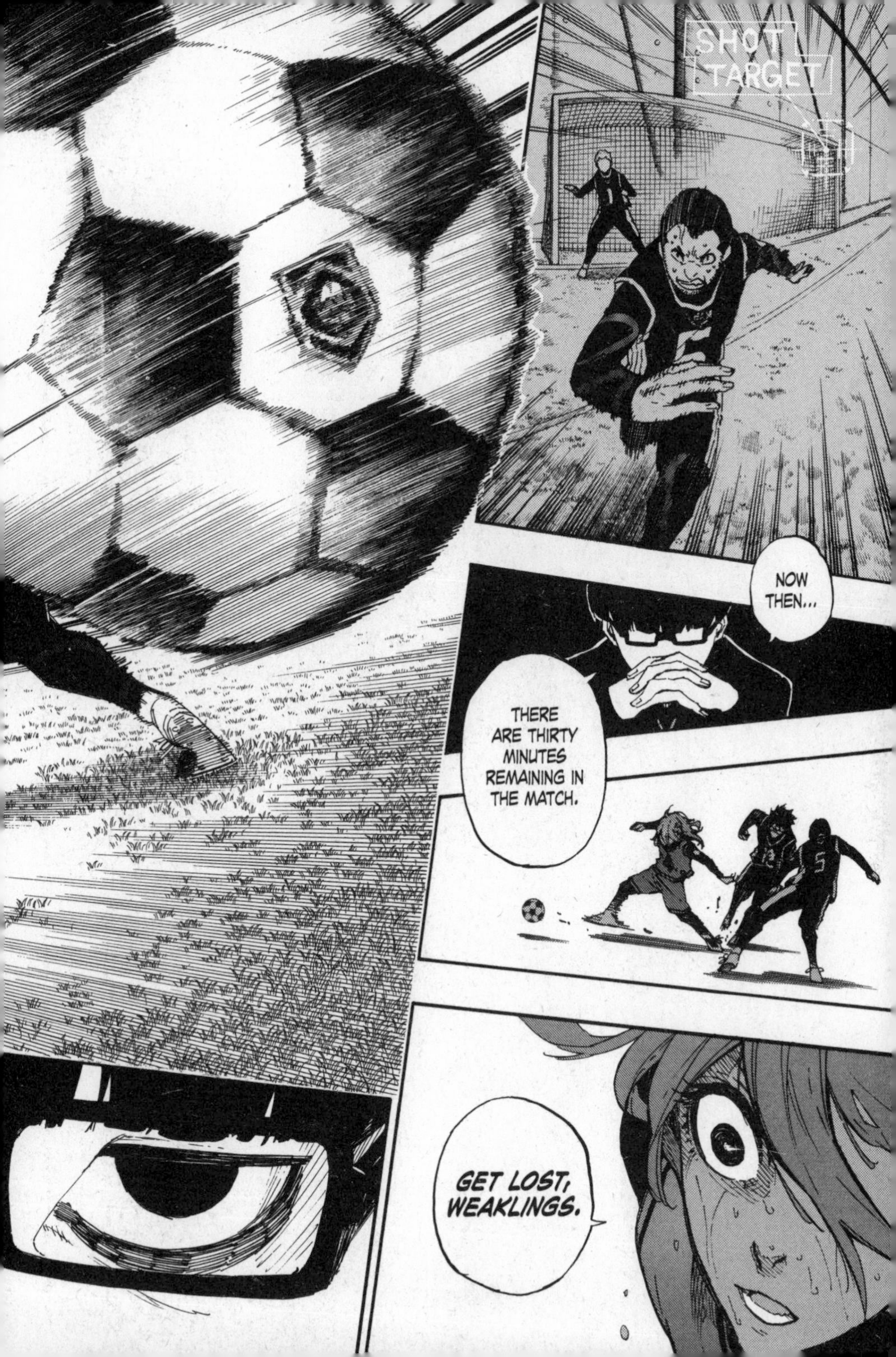
SHOT TARGET
NOW THEN...
THERE ARE THIRTY MINUTES REMAINING IN THE MATCH.
GET LOST, WEAKLINGS.

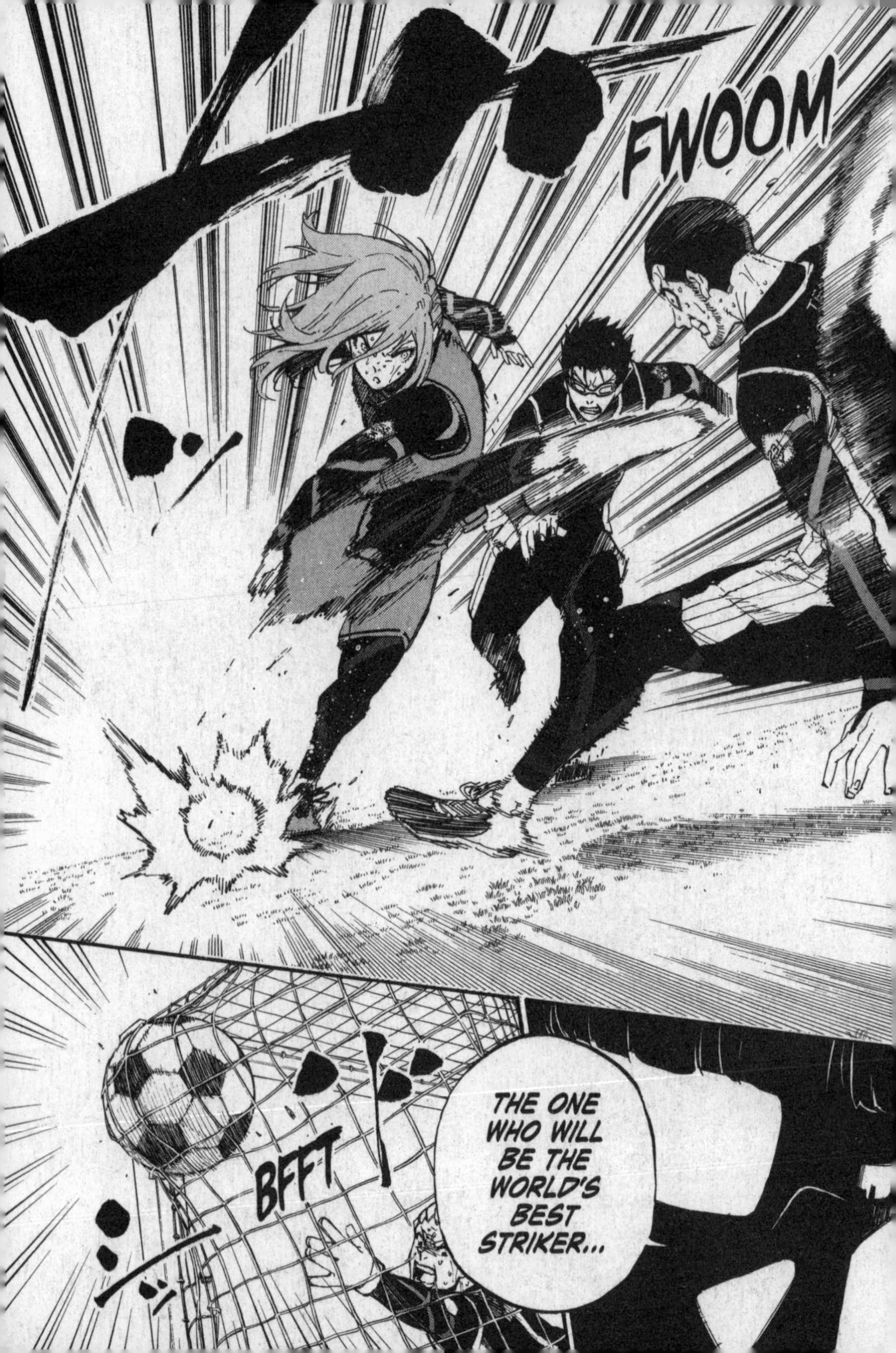
FWOOM
THE ONE WHO WILL BE THE WORLD'S BEST STRIKER...
BFFT

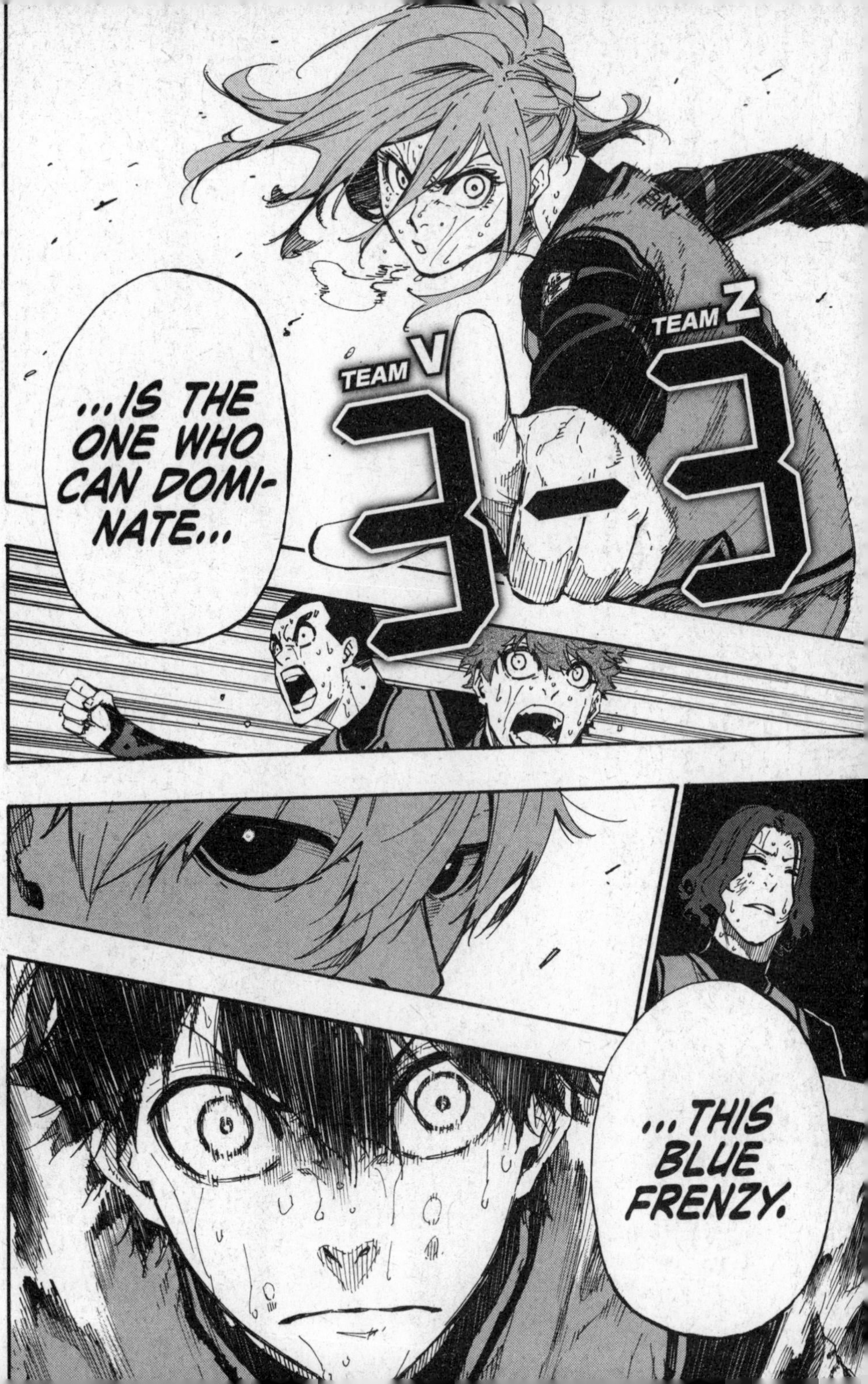
TEAM V 3-3 TEAM Z
...IS THE ONE WHO CAN DOMI-NATE...
...THIS BLUE FRENZY.

BLUE LOCK

CONTINUED IN VOL. 5

VOLUME 4 EXCLUSIVE!

BLUE LOCK SUPPLY LIST! PART 1

BONUS SECTION

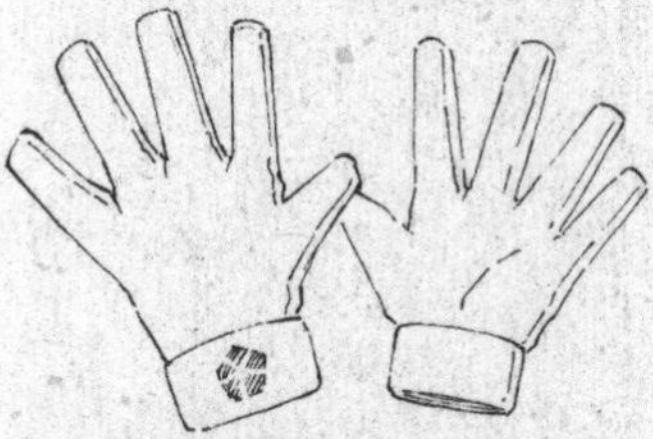

GOALIE GLOVES

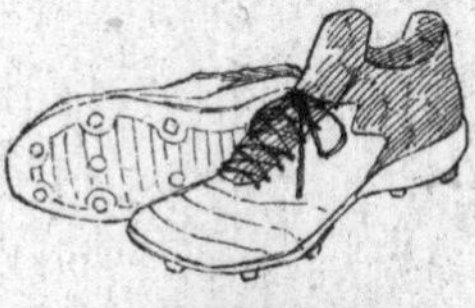

SHOES

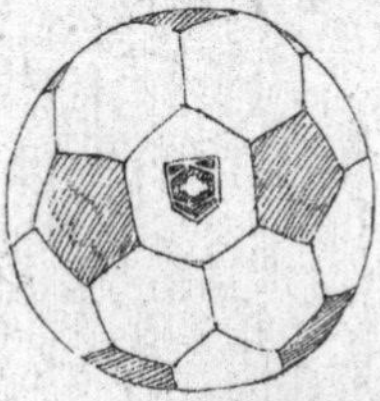

BALL

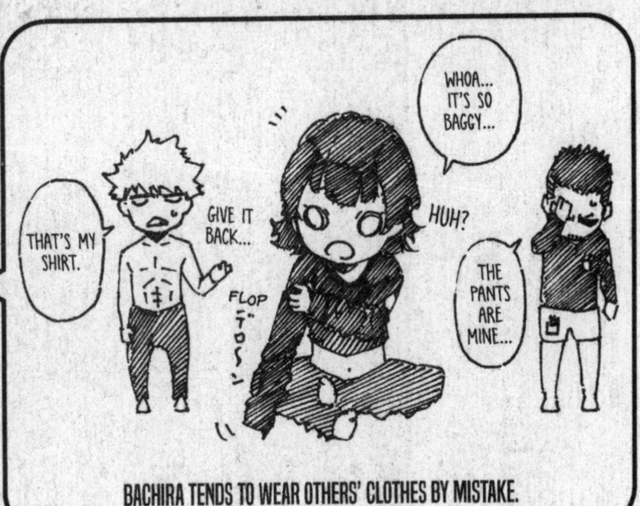
WHOA... IT'S SO BAGGY...
THE PANTS ARE MINE...
HUH?
GIVE IT BACK...
THAT'S MY SHIRT.
FLOP

BACHIRA TENDS TO WEAR OTHERS' CLOTHES BY MISTAKE.

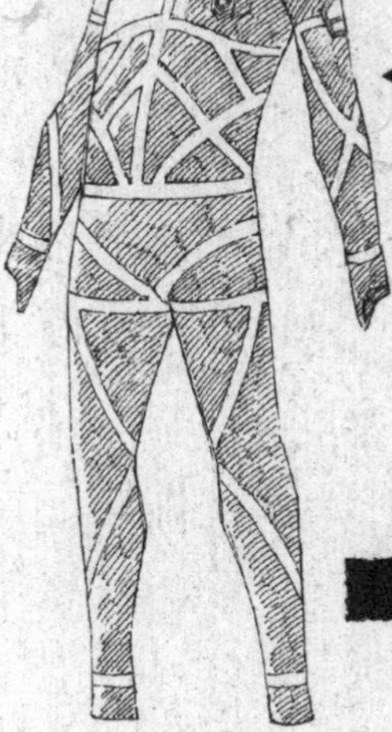

BODYSUIT

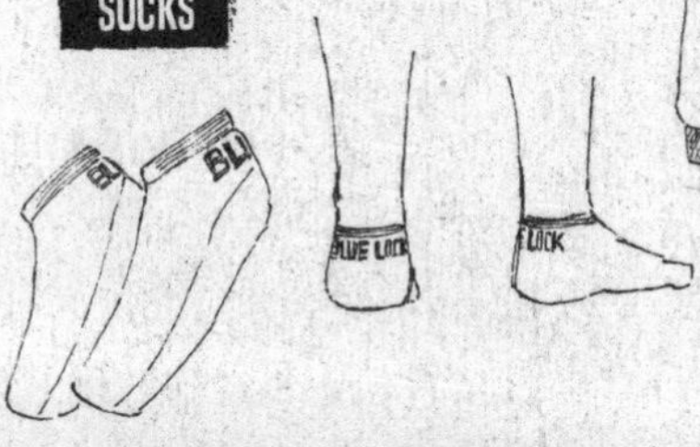

SOCKS

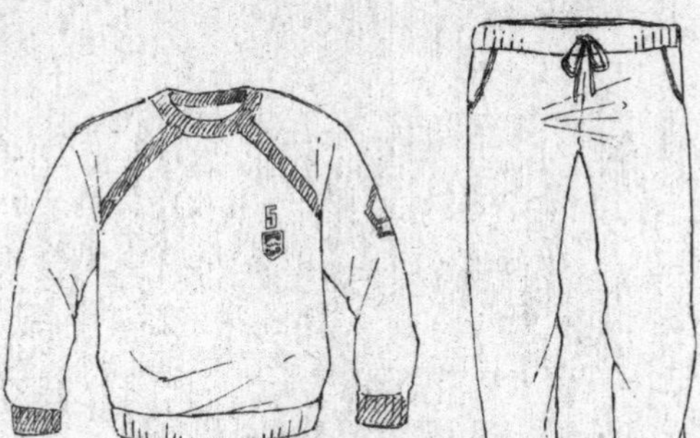

SWEATS

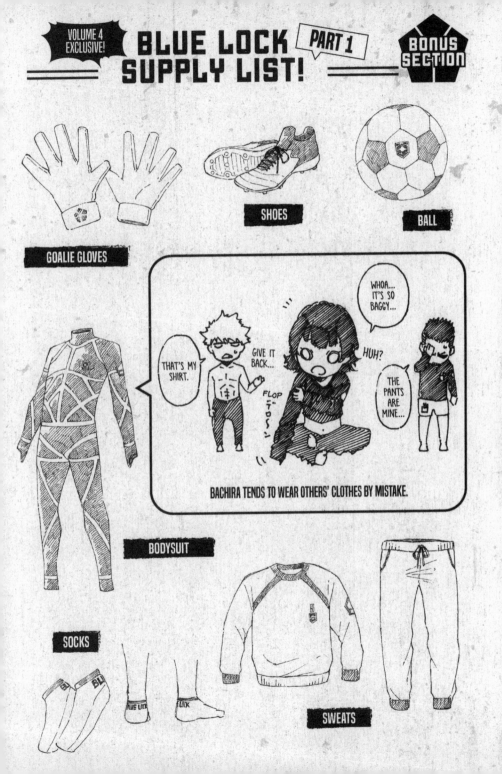

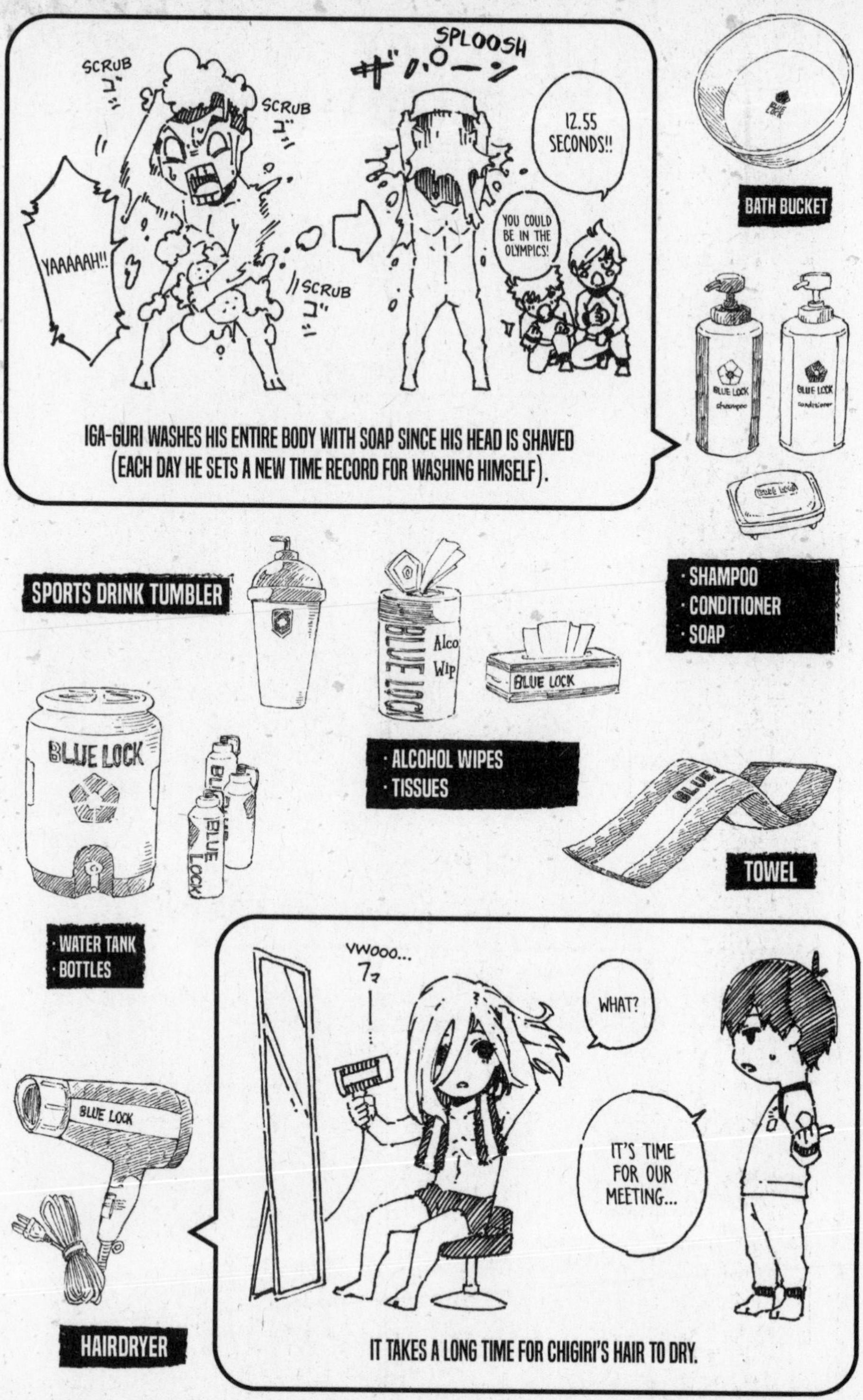

SPLOOSH
ザバーン
12.55 SECONDS!!
YOU COULD BE IN THE OLYMPICS!
SCRUB
ゴッ
SCRUB
ゴッ
YAAAAAH!!
SCRUB
ゴッ
IGA-GURI WASHES HIS ENTIRE BODY WITH SOAP SINCE HIS HEAD IS SHAVED (EACH DAY HE SETS A NEW TIME RECORD FOR WASHING HIMSELF).
BATH BUCKET
BLUE LOCK shampoo
BLUE LOCK conditioner
BLUE LOCK
· SHAMPOO
· CONDITIONER
· SOAP
BLUE LOCK Alco Wip
BLUE LOCK
SPORTS DRINK TUMBLER
· ALCOHOL WIPES
· TISSUES
BLUE
TOWEL
BLUE LOCK
BLUE LOCK
· WATER TANK
· BOTTLES
VWOOO...
ブォ
IT'S TIME FOR OUR MEETING...
WHAT?
IT TAKES A LONG TIME FOR CHIGIRI'S HAIR TO DRY.
BLUE LOCK
HAIRDRYER

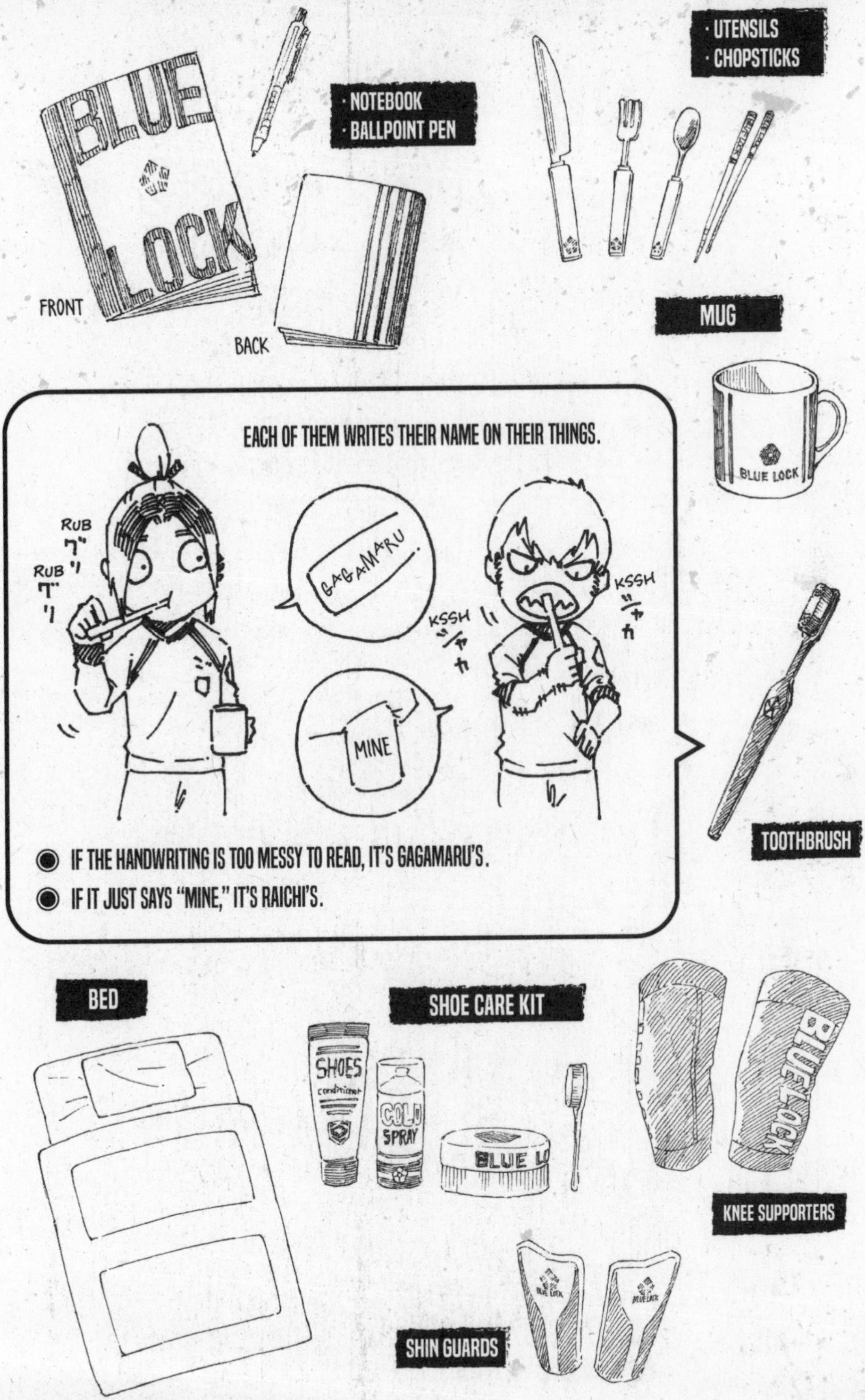

UTENSILS
CHOPSTICKS
NOTEBOOK
BALLPOINT PEN
BLUE LOCK
FRONT
BACK
MUG
BLUE LOCK
EACH OF THEM WRITES THEIR NAME ON THEIR THINGS.
KSSH
KSSH
GAGAMARU
RUB
RUB
MINE
TOOTHBRUSH
IF THE HANDWRITING IS TOO MESSY TO READ, IT'S GAGAMARU'S.
IF IT JUST SAYS "MINE," IT'S RAICHI'S.
BED
SHOE CARE KIT
SHOES conditioner
COLD SPRAY
BLUE LO
BLUE LOCK
KNEE SUPPORTERS
BLUE LOCK
BLUE LOCK
SHIN GUARDS

● STORY | **MUNEYUKI KANESHIRO**

● ART | **YUSUKE NOMURA**

● ART ASSISTANTS

SUEHIRO-SAN	FURUMOTO-SAN
FUJIMAKI-SAN	HARADA-SAN
MAEHATA-SAN	NAKAMURA-SAN
ARATAMA-SAN	KONNO-SAN
TAKANIWA-SAN	SASAKI-SAN
SATOU-SAN	KAWAI-SAN
OTAKE-SAN	(LISTED RANDOMLY)

● DESIGN

KUMOCHI-SAN

OBA-SAN

(HIVE)

EVER SINCE WE STARTED SERIALIZATION,
I JUST HAVEN'T STOPPED STACKING ON THE POUNDS!
THANK YOU SO MUCH FOR BUYING VOLUME 4!!

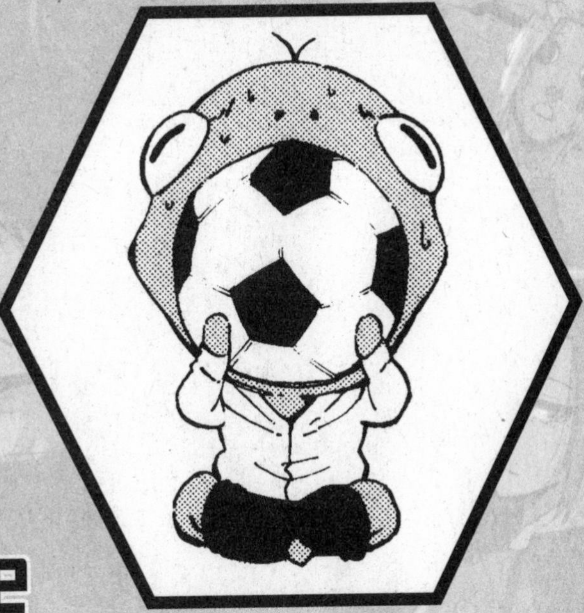

Yusuke Nomura

"Thank you for buying volume four! I couldn't stop visiting the convenience store at night, so now I have grown a happy pouch 'round my stomach."

Yusuke Nomura debuted in 2014 with the grotesquely cute cult hit alien invasion story *Dolly Kill Kill*, which was released digitally in English by Kodansha. Nomura is the illustrator behind *Blue Lock*.

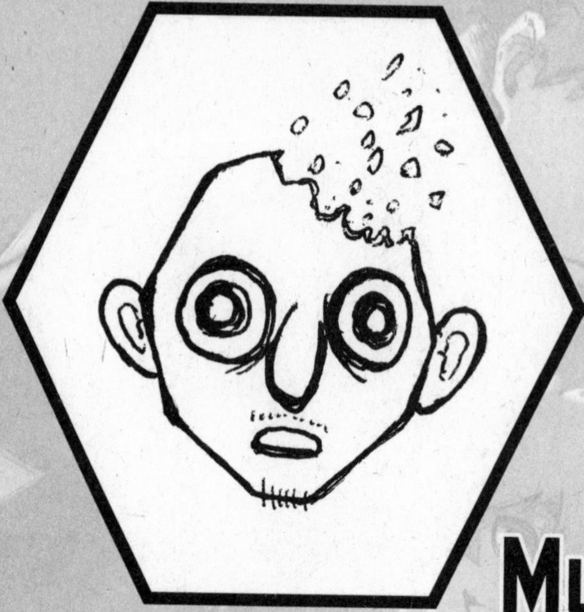

Muneyuki Kaneshiro

"There are probably about twelve chances for the Japan National Team to enter the World Cup, until I die. Only twelve chances...that's so little. I wanna see them win before I die. So much."

Muneyuki Kaneshiro broke out as creator of 2011's *As the Gods Will*, a death game story that spawned two sequels and a film adaptation directed by the legendary Takashi Miike. Kaneshiro writes the story of *Blue Lock*.

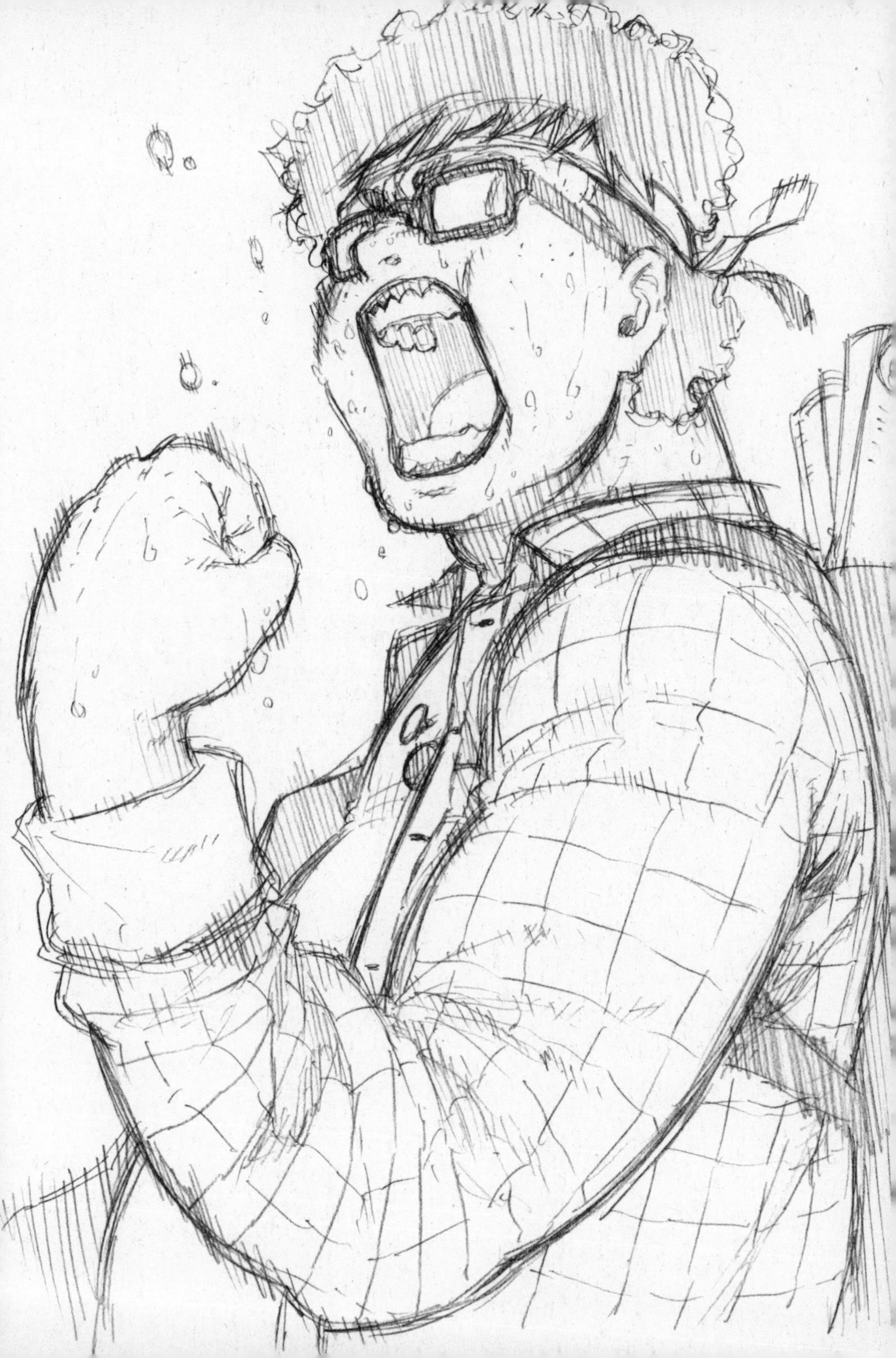

BLUELOCK

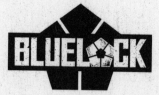

Young characters and steampunk setting, like *Howl's Moving Castle* and *Battle Angel Alita*

Beyond the Clouds © 2018 Nicke / Ki-oon

A boy with a talent for machines and a mysterious girl whose wings he's fixed will take you beyond the clouds! In the tradition of the high-flying, resonant adventure stories of Studio Ghibli comes a gorgeous tale about the longing of young hearts for adventure and friendship!

Knight of the ICE

Knight of the Ice ©Yayoi Ogawa/Kodansha Ltd.

Yayoi Ogawa

SKATING THRILLS AND ICY CHILLS WITH THIS NEW TINGLY ROMANCE SERIES!

A rom-com on ice, perfect for fans of *Princess Jellyfish* and *Wotakoi*. Kokoro is the talk of the figure-skating world, winning trophies and hearts. But little do they know... he's actually a huge nerd! From the beloved creator of *You're My Pet* (*Tramps Like Us*).

Chitose is a serious young woman, working for the health magazine *SASSO*. Or at least, she would be, if she wasn't constantly getting distracted by her childhood friend, international figure skating star Kokoro Kijinami! In the public eye and on the ice, Kokoro is a gallant, flawless knight, but behind his glittery costumes and breathtaking spins lies a secret: He's actually a hopelessly romantic otaku, who can only land his quad jumps when Chitose is on hand to recite a spell from his favorite magical girl anime!

A SMART, NEW ROMANTIC COMEDY FOR FANS OF *SHORTCAKE CAKE* AND *TERRACE HOUSE!*

A romance manga starring high school girl Meeko, who learns to live on her own in a boarding house whose living room is home to the odd (but handsome) Matsunaga-san. She begins to adjust to her new life away from her parents, but Meeko soon learns that no matter how far away from home she is, she's still a young girl at heart — especially when she finds herself falling for Matsunaga-san.

PERFECT WORLD

Rie Aruga

A TOUCHING
NEW SERIES
ABOUT LOVE AND
COPING WITH
DISABILITY

An office party reunites Tsugumi with her high school crush Itsuki. He's realized his dream of becoming an architect, but along the way, he experienced a spinal injury that put him in a wheelchair. Now Tsugumi's rekindled feelings will butt up against prejudices she never considered — and Itsuki will have to decide if he's ready to let someone into his heart...

"Depicts with great delicacy and courage the difficulties some with disabilities experience getting involved in romantic relationships... Rie Aruga refuses to romanticize, pushing her heroine to face the reality of disability. She invites her readers to the same tasks of empathy, knowledge and recognition."
—Slate.fr

"An important entry [in manga romance]... The emotional core of both plot and characters indicates thoughtfulness... [Aruga's] research is readily apparent in the text and artwork, making this feel like a real story."
—Anime News Network

KC
KODANSHA
COMICS

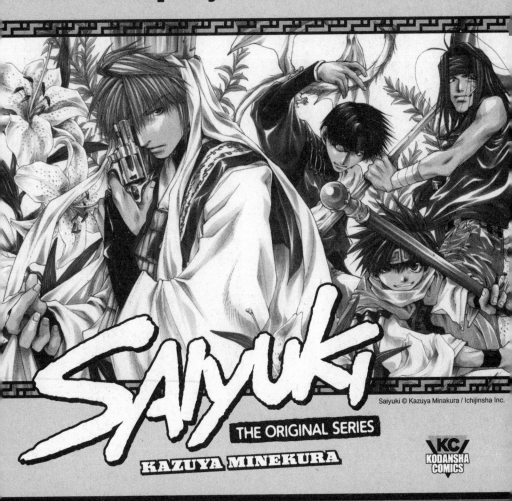